CREATING CONTEXTS

for Learning and Self-Authorship

VANDERBILT ISSUES IN HIGHER EDUCATION is a timely series that focuses on the three core functions of higher education: teaching, research, and service. Interdisciplinary in nature, it concentrates not only on how these core functions are carried out in colleges and universities but also on the contributions they make to larger issues of social and economic development, as well as the various organizational, political, psychological, and social forces that influence their fulfillment and evolution.

CREATING CONTEXTS

for Learning and Self-Authorship

Constructive-Developmental Pedagogy

MARCIA B. BAXTER MAGOLDA

Vanderbilt University Press
Nashville

First Edition 1999

03 02 01 00 99   5 4 3 2 1

Library of Congress Cataloging-in-Publication Data

Baxter Magolda, Marcia B., 1951–
  Creating contexts for learning and self-authorship :
constructive-developmental pedagogy / Baxter Magolda.
    p. cm.
  Includes bibliographical references and index.
  ISBN 0-8265-1343-3 (cloth)
  ISBN 0-8265-1346-8 (pbk.)
  1. Teaching. 2. Learning. 3. Constructivism (Education)
4. Developmental psychology. I. Title.
  LB1025.3 .B39 1999
  371.102—dc21   99-6496

Published by Vanderbilt University Press
Printed in the United States of America

Portions of chapters 2 and 3 appeared in a slightly different version in *Knowing and Reasoning in College: Gender-related Patterns in Students' Intellectual Development* (San Francisco, Calif.: Jossey-Bass, 1992). Chapter 5 appeared in a slightly different version in Marcia B. Baxter Magolda and Jennifer Buckley, "Relational Pedagogy: Investigating Together in a Project Discovery Mathematics Course," *Journal on Excellence in College Teaching*, 7, no. 3: 43–67. Some material in chapter 8 was previously published in M. B. Baxter Magolda, "Facilitating Meaningful Dialogues about Race," *About Campus* 2, no. 5 (1997): 14–18.

To my mother, Marjorie Baxter,
and in memory of my father, R. Woodrow Baxter

For my sister, Ardath Sunderland,
in celebration of her thirty years in teaching

CONTENTS

ACKNOWLEDGMENTS

This book is about bridging the worlds of educators and students. I have had the good fortune to find inhabitants of both worlds who were willing to contribute to connecting the two. The story I tell in this book emerged from the collective stories and experiences of many students and teachers to whom I am grateful for their insights, generosity, and dedication to improving education.

My observation of three college courses, the primary study upon which this book is based, stemmed from an earlier study of college students' intellectual development. These students helped me understand students' worlds and in sharing their stories prompted me to transform my teaching practice. Literature on new ways of teaching written by constructivists, proponents of narrative, feminists, liberatory educators, and critical educators furthered my understanding of the world of educators. These authors are too numerous to thank here; their work is cited throughout the book. Constructive-developmental scholars who linked development to teaching helped me understand how to connect the two worlds. I am indebted to the late William Perry, Mary Belenky, Blythe McVicker Clinchy, Nancy Rule Goldberger, Jill Mattuck Tarule, Robert Kegan, Patricia King, and Karen Kitchener for their conceptualizations of education that both welcome and promote students' intellectual development.

Funding from the Miami University Committee for Faculty Research made it possible for me to observe three semester-length classes in their entirety. Three professors and two doctoral instructors welcomed my research partner and me into their classrooms. Although I cannot name them here in the interest of protecting their anonymity, their masterful teaching inspired me to persist in writing about connecting education and students' development. Observing their classes broadened my vision of ways constructive-developmental pedagogy can be implemented. Students in these classes generously offered their time to share insights about the impact of these courses on their learning. In one course, a group of instructors also welcomed me to their weekly meetings to discuss their teaching. I am indebted to all of these educators and learners for sharing their teaching and learning experiences.

Experimenting with creating contexts for learning and self-authorship in my teaching has been an important dimension of writing this book. I thank my students, whose ongoing feedback and patience with my transformation made it possible. I am also grateful to Judy Rogers, with whom I often team-teach, for her willingness and skill in experimenting with new forms of teaching. Sustained conversations over the years about teaching and learning—in particular with Richard Quantz, Kate Rousmaniere, Peter Magolda, and Nelda Cambron-McCabe—have aided in my quest for understanding contexts for learning and self-authorship. I am also grateful for an atmosphere that welcomes innovative teaching, created in large measure by Nelda Cambron-McCabe and Jan Kettlewell, who served as department chair and dean, respectively, during the time this study took place.

This study and book were enhanced by the contributions of Jennifer Buckley, my research partner in observing the math and science courses and coauthor of those chapters. Jennifer's passion for understanding students' experience, her keen eye for subtle details, and her ability to tell a story effectively contributed substantively to the story told here. In addition, her vibrant personality and dedication made this research effort enjoyable.

The support of numerous colleagues also shaped this book. I am grateful to Vincent Tinto for advocating for this work. John Tryneski, Joan Stark, Robert Rhoads, and Kristy Johnson Schuermann offered feedback that significantly improved my thinking, interpretations, and telling of the story. John Braxton and Charles Backus, coeditors for the series of which this book is a part, both offered valuable guidance and crucial support to produce a quality manuscript. Thanks go also to Jossey-Bass Publishers and the *Journal of Excellence in College Teaching* for their permission to reproduce work they originally published.

My deepest gratitude goes to three people who have created contexts for self-authorship for me. My late father, R. Woodrow Baxter, always encouraged me to think for myself and to trust my own judgment. My mother, Marjorie A. Baxter, is an exemplar of self-authorship and the primary source of my belief in myself. Both helped me to establish the sense of identity that is so essential to self-authorship. My spouse and colleague, Peter Magolda, simultaneously problematizes my thinking, contributes to more adequate interpretations, and affirms my work. His emotional and intellectual support makes my self-authorship possible.

CREATING CONTEXTS

for Learning and Self-Authorship

PART I

WORLDS APART
The Need for
Constructive-Developmental Pedagogy

CHAPTER 1

Seeking Self-Authorship

The World of Educators

I want them [students in winter biology] to appreciate the breadth of zoology and its connections to other disciplines. How do we put together disparate ideas? I'll use my research as examples of how one approaches problems. I want them to understand how information is gained. I want them to appreciate what facts really mean. Tentative facts. That's what all of science is. Subject to change and revision.
    —CHRIS SNOWDEN, PROFESSOR, ZOOLOGY

I take sociology as my minor. It is all opinions, not hard-core facts where you are wrong [like winter biology]. I know he tried to play it off like there is still a lot of research, that it is a really new concept I guess, but still there is some stuff that is [fact]—like freezing cells. I understand what he was trying to do. He was trying to give examples to show what happened. But if he had just said cryoprotectants whatever, just said the point, I would believe him because he is the teacher. I don't need the proof. It's not like I'm going to argue with him about it.
    —ANN, STUDENT, ZOOLOGY

Ann is a college senior taking Chris Snowden's winter biology course, an upper division course offered through the zoology department. It is clear that she and Chris come from different perspectives about the nature of science. Ann views it as "hard-core facts" and interpreted Chris's examples as attempts to prove to her what happened. She did not believe his portrayal of cryobiology (the study of life at cold temperatures) as an evolving field; she preferred for him to just tell her the facts that she is sure exist. Chris, in contrast, views science as tentative facts, subject to revision. As he attempts to get Ann and her peers to appreciate how information is gained, she is busy trying to get the right answers. Most likely, he is unaware of the view Ann holds about science versus sociology and how it affects her learning in his course. Simultaneously, although Ann hears Chris describe cryobiology as an evolving field, her meaning-making system has no room for the idea the way Chris means it. So Ann interprets it within the framework of her current understanding about knowledge and how it is acquired. This gap between instructor and student repeats itself daily across classrooms, disciplines, and institutions, making engaging students effectively in learning a major challenge.

The challenge is complicated by diversity in students' views of knowledge. For example, Erica, who sits two seats away at the same lab table from Ann, offered this perspective on winter biology:

> He has done a very good job at identifying controversial issues and not only with his lectures but also with our experience, with our individual topics. I think that we have all learned that it is an evolving field and there is always more knowledge that is needed to explain exactly what is going on. Overall with the topics he has introduced we got an overall feel for the scientific processes involved. Now writing the grant proposal, I think that is the other part of his goal is to demonstrate that there is a lot more that needs to be known about whatever particular topic that we are doing. To me that is the point of the grant proposal—to get a feel for what else needs to be known.

Erica, also a senior, accepted the uncertainty Chris demonstrated through introducing controversy and focused on learning the scientific processes involved. For reasons probably unbeknown to Chris, Erica was more amenable to his approach than was Ann. One reason is that she holds different assumptions about knowledge from those Ann holds. The comments of a third student in the course illuminate these dynamics.

Lynn, a graduate student in the course, explained having held both sets of assumptions in her experience in science:

> You read it in black and white, and that is just the way it is. That carries over when you start reading scientific literature because you read a scientific paper and you do an experiment. It is in writing and in black and white, and that is the way it is. You see a little bit more of the process in how they came to conclusions, but it is still—it takes a while to start reading literature critically. If somebody did the experiment and they published it, it has to be right, it is true. And then when you pick one part and start reading all of the literature, all the publications on that narrow focus, you start realizing there are a lot of people out there who disagree and then will come up with contradicting results. That is a really strange thing! If this person's right because they got it published and this person is right because they got it published, that doesn't work because they both can't be right all of the time. . . . That is a really neat shift to start reading that literature and realizing that these people, it kind of goes hand in hand that the names on these papers are human beings and reading the literature, and realizing because they are human beings their research is not always perfect either and they can come to

misleading conclusions, or their data could be skewed or whatever, which could lead to different conclusions. To some extent you can become critical of the research and you can also realize that the people are human. So that can make you more critical of the research but it really makes you put it together more. . . . I think it is tough because people always tell you it is just one of those assumptions you have. I am not sure what actually it is that knocks your assumptions off and makes you realize that "big deal, this person published." It is in black and white; that doesn't mean it is put upon a pedestal and it is right and it is truth and that is the end, that is it period. There is always dot, dot, dot at the end. I think that everyone is going to reach that stage at different points. I reached that stage toward the end of undergrad, probably not until my senior year.

The progression Lynn recounts is the shift from viewing knowledge as certain to viewing it as uncertain. Along with the shift, authorities become human and subsequently fallible. As Lynn eloquently points out, this shift is necessary for students to meet Chris's goal for them to appreciate science as tentative facts. If Chris is to reach his goal and prepare his students to function effectively in their future work, he must try to create the conditions for this shift to occur. As a teacher, Chris Snowden faces a substantive challenge as he tries to reach Ann and Erica, as well as the rest of the class, in his course.

Chris Snowden's experience is typical of many college faculty struggling with engaging learners meaningfully. Most believe that contemporary society demands citizens who are lifelong learners. The information age, the fast-changing nature of work, and the increasing diversity of people and cultures mean that simply taking a body of knowledge from college to adult life is insufficient. Productive citizens, no matter what their role in adult life, must know how to learn as conditions change. College faculties want students to think critically, to know how to inquire, to think for themselves, and to be capable of using relevant information to make informed decisions. Educational reformers tell us that our traditional style of teaching—giving students information—does not yield that outcome. Yet when many of us genuinely try to engage students differently, we become the source of their dissatisfaction. Although Parker Palmer wrote that "dissatisfaction may be a sign that real education has happened" (1998, 94), many faculty fear it. Some faculty react by retreating into the "good old ways," despite evidence that those ways are ineffective. Some faculty blame the students: they are not like they used to be, they are not motivated, they care only about themselves, and they are underprepared due to ill-conceived innovations in secondary schools. Nevertheless, many faculty continue to search for new ways to reach students, for new ways to help students construct knowledge effectively for themselves. How people learn, and how to translate that to educational practice, is one of the most important questions in reforming undergraduate education today (George 1996). This book is intended to help college faculty create the conditions in which students learn to construct knowledge.

I advance constructive-developmentalism as the theoretical foundation of creating such conditions. A constructive-developmental view of learning incorporates two major concepts: (1) that students construct knowledge by organizing and making meaning of their experiences, and (2) that this construction takes place in the context of their evolving assumptions about knowledge itself and students' role in creating it. Piaget's (1932) notion that people construct their reality by virtue of organizing their experiences stands at the foundation of this view. Perry (1970) pointed out that human beings organize meaning, and he laid the groundwork for theories of how assumptions about the nature, limits, and certainty of knowledge evolve during adult life. Numerous frameworks are now available to describe evolving assumptions about knowledge and how they mediate learning; they are described in chapter 2. The goal of learning from this view is what Kegan (1994) calls self-authorship, or the ability to reflect upon one's beliefs, organize one's thoughts and feelings in the context of, but separate from, the thoughts and feelings of others, and literally make up one's own mind.

A constructive-developmental view of teaching takes these two major concepts as central to the teaching-learning interaction. Kegan (1994) points out that knowing *what* our students understand is insufficient; rather, we must know the *way* they understand it. By this he means knowing their organizing principles or assumptions for making meaning of their experience. Teaching, then, becomes a matter of understanding and welcoming students' ways of making meaning and simultaneously engaging them in a journey toward more complex ways of making meaning. Numerous authors (summarized later in this chapter) have advanced conceptualizations of constructive-developmental teaching. These conceptualizations revolve around using students' ways of organizing their experience as a foundation for exploring more complex ways of organizing experience.

Three characteristics of this book distinguish it from contemporary books on teaching. First, the book's overarching purpose is to articulate a form of pedagogy that promotes *self-authorship* in addition to subject mastery. Self-authorship extends beyond critical thinking or making informed judgments because it is not a skill; it is, rather, a way of making meaning of the world and oneself. This concept is inextricably linked to the second characteristic of this book—students' epistemological development.

Contemporary literature advocates connecting with students' experience as a foundation for engaging them in meaningful learning. A dimension of students' experience that is often overlooked, however, is their *intellectual or epistemological development*. Ann, Erica, and Lynn respond differently to Chris Snowden's pedagogy because they hold different epistemic assumptions about the nature, limits, and certainty of knowledge. Research shows that college students' epistemic assumptions range from believing that knowledge is certain and possessed by authorities (Ann's view) to knowledge is uncertain and knowledge claims are possible after exploring the relevant information (Lynn's view). Generally, students move from the certain toward the uncertain sets of assumptions during college (Baxter Magolda 1992; Belenky, Clinchy, Goldberger, and Tarule 1986; King and Kitchener 1994; Perry 1970). Self-authorship is possible only from the latter set of assumptions and is often not achieved during college. Students like Ann who expect authorities to give the answers cannot immediately change their assumptions to self-author their own views. After all, these assumptions are the result of years of schooling in which students are socialized to accept authority and memorize knowledge. Thus, they need experiences like the ones Lynn described to help them reorganize their epistemic assumptions. Pedagogy that fails to take students' current epistemic assumptions into account often fails to engage them meaningfully. A central component of this book is articulating a form of pedagogy that hinges on students' epistemic development to help them move toward self-authorship.

The third unique characteristic of this book is its specific purpose: to identify the *structure* and *process* of implementing constructive-developmental pedagogy in the context of students' epistemological development. Many writers have advanced pedagogies based on student experience, self-authorship, or epistemological development; their work is explored further in this chapter. The description of pedagogy in this book is consistent with and indebted to those writers. My intention, however, is to push our understanding of constructive-developmental pedagogy farther. A previous longitudinal study (Baxter Magolda 1992) using extensive interviews with college students identified the underlying structure of such a pedagogy, or the basic principles that make pedagogy constructive-developmental (these are explored in chap. 3). A second study involving extensive course observations (including Chris Snowden's winter biology course) and interviews with instructors and students is the source of my descriptions of various processes through which college faculty used constructive-developmental pedagogy to promote self-authorship. Constructive-developmental pedagogy, as it is described in this book, is more than letting students talk and generate their own ideas. It is a matter of creating the developmental conditions that allow them to generate their own ideas effectively, in essence to develop their minds, their voices, and themselves.

Before proceeding, let me clarify what constructive-developmental pedagogy is *not*. Often educators hear the notion of students developing their own minds as students constructing knowledge without regard to existing knowledge. An example from a recent issue of the *Chronicle of Higher Education* illustrates this reaction. Reacting to calls for students to take a more active role in teaching and learning, Kenneth Stunkel wrote that "the best of all worlds for interactive pedagogy is to eliminate the professor altogether, to let students 'take control of their own learning'" (1998, A52). Stunkel interprets calls for student involvement as calls for student control and what he refers to as "self-instruction." This is not what I mean by constructive-developmental pedagogy. Inherent in developing one's mind is learning complex processes for constructing knowledge in order to become capable of joining knowledge communities in doing so.

Chris Snowden's pedagogy clarifies what students learning to construct knowledge means in constructive-developmental pedagogy. Chris views science as subject to revision through ongoing scholarly research and discussion among scientists. His course objectives, discussed in more detail in chapter 4, included helping students learn the scholarly process through which the scientific community arrives at agreed-upon tentative facts—facts that may be altered by future research and alternate interpretations. Through his teaching, Chris demonstrated the process through which scientific knowledge is socially constructed. He created opportunities for students to learn and practice this process. He did not encourage students to construct knowledge without regard for existing research.

Ira Shor (1992) speaks eloquently to this issue in his discussion of pedagogy that empowers students to think for themselves. He notes that "mutual dialogue is not a know-nothing learning process" (247). Elaborating, he writes,

> [It] does not mean that students have nothing to learn from biology or mathematics or engineering as they now exist. Neither does it mean that students reinvent subject matter each time they study it or that academic expertise of the teacher has no role in the classroom. Formal bodies of knowledge, standard usage, and the teacher's academic background all belong in critical classrooms. As long as existing knowledge is not presented as facts and doctrines to be absorbed without question, as long as existing bodies of knowledge are critiqued and balanced from a multicultural perspective, and as long as the students' own themes and idioms are valued along with standard usage, existing canons are part of critical education. What

> students and teachers reinvent in problem posing is their relation-
> ship to learning and authority. They redefine their relationships to
> each other, to education, and to expertise. They re-perceive knowl-
> edge and power. (35)

Thus, constructive-developmental pedagogy as I describe it in this book is
not a know-nothing process. It requires that teachers model the process of
constructing knowledge in their disciplines, teach that process to students,
and give students opportunities to practice and become proficient at it. As
all educators bring their experience, values, and assumptions to this knowledge construction process, so do students; constructive-developmental pedagogy offers opportunities to examine these as they relate to the subject
matter and knowledge construction process. Throughout the examples in
chapters 3 through 6, you will hear educators invite students into the knowledge construction processes of their disciplines, modeling Shor's reinvented
relationship to learning and authority rather than an abandonment of existing knowledge.

Much of this book stems from students' thoughts and insights about their
learning and the courses that I observed (described later in this chapter).
Despite the attention given to connecting to students' experience, writing
about teaching is often based on teachers' observations rather than those of
students. Understanding students' development and how to promote it requires talking with and listening to students like Ann, Erica, and Lynn.
Their stories become the context through which I invite you to explore using constructive-developmental pedagogy to promote self-authorship.

SELF-AUTHORSHIP

Life in contemporary America is complicated. Because the general purpose
of education in this country has been to prepare students for productive
adult lives, the increasing complexity of adult life in our society requires a
complex kind of education. The capacity for lifelong learning is necessary to
keep pace with changes in technology, science, the economy, and cultural
norms. In every aspect of adult life—both private and public— society demands that people be able to take on responsibility, manage their affairs effectively, and make informed decisions for themselves and their fellow
citizens. Robert Kegan (1994) notes that these demands are not merely demands for particular behaviors or skills; rather, they are demands for the way
we organize our experience. Referring to ways of organizing experience as
"the evolution of consciousness," Kegan describes it as "the personal unfolding of ways of organizing experience that are not simply replaced as we grow
but subsumed into more complex systems of mind" (9). This unfolding of

ways of organizing experience is what Lynn described at the outset of this chapter. The more complex ways of organizing experience, or of making meaning, are necessary to meet the demands of contemporary adult life. In essence, adult life requires the capacity for self-authorship.

For example, Kegan notes that as workers, adults are expected to "invent or own our work . . . to be self-initiating, self-correcting, self-evaluating . . . to be guided by our own visions . . . to take responsibility for what happens to us . . . to be accomplished masters of our particular work roles, jobs, or careers" (153). These expectations require self-authorship because they require the ability to construct our own visions, make informed decisions in conjunction with coworkers, act appropriately, and take responsibility for those actions. Similarly in the private life domains of parenting and partnering, Kegan sketches demands such as "establish rules and roles; institute a vision of family purpose . . . manage boundaries (inside and outside the family) . . . be psychologically independent from, but closely connected to, our spouses . . . set limits on children, in-laws, oneself, and extrafamily involvements" (86). These expectations, like those in public work life, call for understanding these relationships in a complex way that allows adults to assess and contrast individual and family needs, determine a course of action in connection with but not subsumed by other family members, and take responsibility for those actions. These are not simply skills or behaviors; they emerge from the adults' organization of their experiences and their world.

Self-authorship is simultaneously a cognitive (how one makes meaning of knowledge), interpersonal (how one views oneself in relationship to others), and intrapersonal (how one perceives one's sense of identity) matter. Educators often highlight the cognitive dimension of self-authorship. Learned societies participating in the Association of American Colleges' Liberal Learning, Study-in-Depth, and the Arts and Sciences Major project routinely called for cognitive self-authorship in their reports. The authors of the economics report wrote, "In the economics major we share with other disciplines a desire to empower students with a self-sustaining capacity to think and learn. They should know how to pose questions, collect information, identify and use an appropriate framework to analyze that information, and come to some conclusion" (Association of American Colleges 1990b, 27). The mathematics authors noted that "dealing with complex, open-ended problem situations should be one of the highest priorities of undergraduate mathematics" (85). The interdisciplinary studies report advanced this position:

> We prefer to argue that the ideal IDS graduate will demonstrate intellectual facility having depth, breadth, and synthesis. By depth we mean students must have the necessary technical information

about and the methodologies necessary for analysis of a given problem. Students should know how to master the complexities involved in obtaining germane research findings and be aware of the methodologies of the disciplinary contexts in which such information is generated. By breadth we mean students should be exposed to a wide knowledge base and trained to organize information in order to make generalizations from particular cases. By synthesis we mean students should be able to apply integrative skills in order to differentiate and compare different disciplinary perspectives, to clarify how those perspectives relate to the core problem or question, and to devise a resolution based upon the holistic interaction of the various factors and forces involved. (65)

This position articulates the cognitive components of self-authorship advanced by numerous educators and authors of educational reform reports.

Many contemporary educators recognize that the cognitive dimension of self-authorship is intertwined with the interpersonal dimension. Kenneth Bruffee offers an example in the context of the medical profession. He notes that there is a

perception by many in the medical profession itself that although traditional medical education stuffs young physicians full of facts, it leaves their diagnostic judgment rudimentary and does not develop their ability to interact socially, with either colleagues or patients, over complex, demanding, perhaps life-and-death issues. (1993, 2)

Bruffee's observation indicates that one issue is whether physicians exhibit cognitive self-authorship in making a wise diagnosis on the basis of their knowledge. A second issue, however, is their ability to work effectively with others in interpersonal relationships that play a role in making medical decisions. Bruffee believes that this interpersonal dimension is crucial. He writes, "In any college or university today, mature, effective interdependence—that is, social maturity integrated with intellectual maturity—may be the most important lesson college students should be asked to learn" (1993, 2). Many areas of knowledge blur the lines between cognitive and interpersonal. For example, "most of the critical problems society faces have a biological component. These problems also challenge human values and belief systems. Such subjects as world population, abortion, birth control, acid rain, and biodiversity are central to biology but also reach into the family, economics, and religion" (Association of American Colleges 1990b, 19). These issues require a self-authorship that involves both cognitive and interpersonal dimensions, as do other social issues such as poverty, appreciating diversity, and crime.

These social issues also illustrate Kegan's argument that the intrapersonal dimension is centrally interwoven into self-authorship. Students can learn cognitive inquiry skills, yet not be able to use them to decide what to believe because they have no internal sense of identity or belief system. Adults are aware that they are responsible for making decisions that benefit themselves and their families, yet are unable to take a position different from what important others believe because they have no internally generated belief system. This intrapersonal, internally generated belief system allows for "a construction of the self-as author, maker, critiquer, and *re*maker of its experience, the self as a system or complex, regulative of its parts" (Kegan 1994, 133). Kegan argues that this sense of self distinguishes persons who are in control of their issues from persons whose issues are in control of them.

Self-authorship, then, is a complicated phenomenon. It is simultaneously an ability to construct knowledge in a contextual world, an ability to construct an internal identity separate from external influences, and an ability to engage in relationships without losing one's internal identity. And higher education has had difficulty enough achieving even the cognitive dimension of self-authorship. The plethora of reports on educational reform in the last decade have charged that undergraduate education is delivered ineffectively, requires passive rather than active learning, does not meaningfully engage students in learning, and does not produce graduates who exhibit self-authorship. After their review of more than 2,600 books and articles on how college affects students, Patrick Terenzini and Ernest Pascarella (1994) posit that the notion that traditional instructional methods provide effective means to teach undergraduates is a myth. They also note,

> Despite the fact that the research evidence, personal experience, and common sense all suggest these assumptions are untenable, most faculty members persist in teaching (and academic administrators encourage it) as if they were true. Individualized and collaborative approaches to instruction are more effective because they respond better to differences in students' levels of preparation, learning styles, and rates. (30)

The Association of American Colleges report (1990a) offers a similar critique:

> The problem is that it [the major] often delivers too much knowledge with too little attention to how that knowledge is being created, what methods and modes of inquiry are employed in its creation, what presuppositions inform it, and what entailments flow from its particular way of knowing. The problem is further compounded when the major ignores questions about relationships

> between various ways of knowing, and between what students have
> learned and their lives beyond the academy. (6)

These critiques do not stop at recommending pedagogy that acknowledges
the methods and modes of inquiry used in knowledge creation. Connecting
what students have learned with their lives beyond the classroom has also become a central component of educational reform prescriptions. This is more
complex than applying classroom learning to life outside the classroom.
Connecting to students' lived experience means using it as a foundation
from which they can explore knowledge and determine what to believe.
Powerful Partnerships: A Shared Responsibility for Learning (American
Association for Higher Education, American College Personnel Association,
National Association of Student Personnel Administrators 1998) stresses,

> Rich learning experiences and environments require and enable stu-
> dents to make connections . . . through opportunities to relate their
> own experience and knowledge to materials being learned; . . . and
> through pedagogies emphasizing critical analysis of conflicting
> views and demanding that students make defensible judgments
> about and demonstrate linkages among bodies of knowledge. (3)

Self-authorship is impossible unless students are able to connect learning
with their lived experiences; self-authorship requires making meaning of
one's own experience. Parker Palmer asserts that teaching that transforms
people occurs only when it "connects with the inward, living core of our students' lives" (1998, 31)—a core he describes as the inner voice of identity
and integrity.

The National Science Foundation's recent report *Shaping the Future: New
Expectations for Undergraduate Education in Science, Mathematics,
Engineering, and Technology* recommends that science, mathematics, engi-
neering, and technology faculty

> believe and affirm that every student can learn, and model good
> practices that increase learning; start with the student's experience,
> but have high expectations within a supportive climate; and build
> inquiry, a sense of wonder and the excitement of discovery, plus
> communication and teamwork, critical thinking, and life-long
> learning skills into learning experiences. (1996, 4)

Similarly, the Association of American Colleges report captures the integration of student experience in learning:

> Every student should experience the intellectual excitement that
> comes from the capacity to extend the known to the unknown and
> to discern previously unsuspected relationships. Developing these

capacities requires acceptance of specific imperatives. Students must be willing to revise what they have held previously as certain by shifting perspectives and they must engage in the kind of collaborative work in which they become open to criticism. This implies an academic community that sees as an important value of liberal learning bringing private precept into public discourse. It implies equally an academic community that insists that difference be negotiated with civility. Public civil discourse depends, among other conditions, on an ethos of corrigibility. Faculty members must take seriously what students believe about a given subject and engage their prior knowledge so that new learning restructures the old, complicating and correcting it rather than merely living side by side with it. (1990a, 12–13)

This vision of learning recognizes that asking students to shift their epistemic assumptions and reevaluate knowledge claims hinges on acknowledging what they currently believe. Starting with student experience and encouraging reevaluation of how to interpret what one believes lead to restructuring one's views. When faculty ignore student experience, students gather information that lives alongside their own views—a form of education that does not promote self-authorship. Self-authorship requires evaluating one's own views in light of existing evidence and constructing a reasonable perspective as a result.

LEARNING CENTERED EDUCATIONAL PRACTICE

Wide-ranging critiques including those mentioned here have prompted serious reflection on and reconceptualization of education and teaching in the last decade. Among the outcomes are contemporary views of pedagogy that take a learning-centered approach rather than the traditional teaching-centered approach. The teaching-centered approach focused on knowledge acquisition and control whereas the learning-centered approach focuses on student experience as a context for introducing, working with, and constructing knowledge. Robert Barr and John Tagg (1995) offer a detailed account of this paradigm shift and its implications for educational practice. They describe the instruction paradigm's mission as delivering instruction and transferring knowledge from faculty to students; the learning paradigm's mission is instead producing learning and eliciting student discovery and construction of knowledge. Many contemporary visions of pedagogy place student experience in the foreground, and many build on the experience-based learning notions advanced by John Dewey and Jean Piaget. Highlighting a few of these perspectives is useful here to illustrate advances in thinking about pedagogy as well as to show the missing dimensions in developing pedagogy to promote self-authorship. It is not my intention to offer a comprehensive review of this literature, a task that would require numerous volumes, but to identify major strands of thinking that enlighten the learning-centered approach.

The perspectives I have chosen to highlight here are not all in agreement; these writers may not see themselves as endorsing common perspectives about pedagogy. I use them here to note the dimensions of student experience, self-authorship, and student development. Using these dimensions, advocates of basing teaching on student experience can be organized into three broad categories. The first includes proponents of constructivist teaching, collaborative learning, use of narrative, and incorporating care in education who endorse students' experience and support the notion of self-authorship without placing it clearly as the end goal. A second category includes liberatory, empowering, and critical educators who advance self-authorship as a central goal. What distinguishes the third category from these two is the inclusion of student development. This category, comprised primarily of educators with developmental psychology backgrounds, emphasizes student experience as the foundation for learning, directly advocates promoting self-authorship, and incorporates student development as a central component in the process. A brief overview of these perspectives serves as the context for the view of constructive-developmental pedagogy presented in this book. This overview is not intended to be a comprehensive review of these approaches; rather, it gives prominence to work that speaks to the dimensions of interest here.

An Emphasis on Student Experience

A discussion of student experience inevitably begins with educator and philosopher John Dewey's (1916) conceptualization of education as the reorganization and reconstruction of experience. Knowledge, for Dewey, meant "the working capital, the indispensable resources, of further inquiry; of finding out, or learning, more things" (1916, 158). He viewed thinking as discovering connections between actions and their consequences. Dewey argued accordingly that thinking must start with experience, that thinking could not be cultivated separately from experience. This line of thinking led Dewey to remark "the first approach to any subject in school, if thought is to be aroused and not words acquired, should be as unscholastic as possible" (1916, 154). He meant that experience from students' everyday lives should be used as the starting point, and that course work causing reflection in everyday life would arouse thinking. Problems for reflection must be situated in students' experience rather than imposed by teachers for the purpose of teaching a specific school topic. In Dewey's view the latter did not elicit pursuit of the connections between experiences and their consequences. Dewey believed that learning should be an active process in which students relied on their own experiences and available data from others to work through a problem, to generate inferences and tentative explanations or, in his words, "ideas." Students then should be given opportunities to further develop their ideas and test them to determine their value. Thinking requires experience, activity, and reflection, thus requiring joint effort of the teacher and students rather than the teacher providing students with information.

The joint effort of teacher and students also characterizes collaborative approaches. Kenneth Bruffee takes the position that knowledge is socially constructed, noting that "collaborative learning assumes . . . that knowledge is a consensus among the members of a community of knowledgeable peers—something people construct by talking together and reaching agreement" (1993, 3). Teachers are members of a knowledge community that students want to join, but students need to become fluent in the knowledge community's language to do so. The teacher, in order to help them make this transition, needs not only to be knowledgeable in her or his community, but also to be able to converse in the students' community. The skill to converse in both communities helps the teacher facilitate the students' increasing fluency in the new knowledge community. Students' experience is the source of the teacher learning to converse in their community. As students become members of the new knowledge community, their participation in "talking together and reaching agreement" implies the need for self-authorship—constructing their own perspectives in the context of the knowledge community.

The central nature of the students' role in this joint teacher-student work is evident in the current use of constructivism theory in teaching. Constructivism "describes knowledge as temporary, developmental, non-objective, internally constructed, and socially and culturally mediated" (Twomey Fosnot 1996, ix). Piaget's explanation of meaning-making stands at the foundation of this view. His concept of equilibration (1970, 1977) involved encountering discrepancies between one's way of structuring the world and experience that prompted the person to bring the two back into balance. When rebalancing takes the form of altering one's structure to accommodate the new experience, growth and change occur. Thus, learning begins with the students' understanding of their experience and engages them in remaking meaning of their experiences. Applying constructivist theory to educational practice, von Glasersfeld notes, "The teacher must listen to the student, interpret what the student does and says, and try to build up a 'model' of the student's conceptual structures" (1995, 14). Without understanding the student's conceptual structures, Von Glasersfeld argues that changing the student "can be no more than a hit or miss affair" (1995,

15). Linda Lambert and her colleagues (1995) advocate learning activities that help learners access their experiences, knowledge, and beliefs; that allow for sharing ideas with others; and that offer opportunities for reflection and metacognition. Helping students make meaning of their experience and re-shaping conceptual structures is advocating the development of self-author-ship. By virtue of its reliance on Piaget, this literature also acknowledges the role of development in learning, albeit in a relatively abstract way.

Feminist scholarship has contributed substantially to the centrality of stu-dent experience, and to some degree student development, in learning. Nancy Schniedewind's (1987) discussion of feminist values for teaching em-phasizes developing mutual respect, trust, and community in the classroom; shared leadership (or participatory decision making); cooperative structure; integration of cognitive and affective learning; and action to transform val-ues. Schniedewind characterizes feminist education in this way: "We enter into a dialogue with our students, meeting them as human beings, and learn-ing with them in community" (179). The concepts of empowering students to find their own voices, learning from the base of their own experience, and learning in connection with others are central features of feminist pedagogy (Shrewsbury 1987). Yet feminist scholarship moves beyond the role of stu-dent experience to the relational nature of the teaching/learning enterprise.

Becky Ropers-Huilman's study of feminist teachers revealed that they re-sponded to student experience by shifting the content and its expression to respond to students' learning positions, and they also "cared about students' experiences both in and out of the classroom" (1998, 46). bell hooks writes that the learning process comes easiest to those who believe teachers' work "is not merely to share information but to share in the intellectual and spir-itual growth of our students" (1994, 13). She advocates teaching in a way that "respects and cares for the souls of our students" (13). The value of car-ing in the teaching relationship stems from the belief that learning is a rela-tional process in which connections to others and to one's own experience make learning more meaningful (Gilligan 1982; Lyons 1993). Gloria Ladson-Billings (1994) advocates a connectedness with students as a key characteristic of effective social relations in teaching. Nel Noddings (1984), using the terms *receptivity, relatedness,* and *responsiveness* to characterize car-ing, advocates maintenance and enhancement of caring as "the primary aim of every educational institution and of every educational effort" (172). Translating caring to teaching practice, Noddings wrote,

> The teacher receives and accepts the student's feeling toward the subject matter; she looks at it and listens to it through his eyes and ears. How else can she interpret the subject matter for him? As she exercises this inclusion, she accepts *his* motives, reaches toward what

he intends, so long as these motives and intentions do not force an abandonment of her own ethic. (177)

This relationship gives the teacher access to students' perspectives, which she then uses as context to convey her subject matter. Working from the students' motives enhances learning, yet the teacher's motives must be included as well. Self-authorship is implied in helping students pursue their own intentions while learning to understand and interpret the subject matter.

Parker Palmer, acknowledging the value of the feminists' notion of hearing people into speech, advocates a similar stance. He emphasizes "making space for the other, being aware of the other, paying attention to the other, honoring the other" (1998, 46). Palmer notes that teachers who enter empathically into their students' worlds have the potential to be perceived by students as persons able to hear the students' truth. This potential is crucial if student and teacher are to jointly engage in constructing knowledge and if the student is to see herself as a potential author of her own knowledge. bell hooks states that empowering students to author their knowledge also requires teachers committed to their own self-actualization, ones willing to take risks, express vulnerability, and share their own experience in learning settings.

Proponents of narrative in teaching most clearly make the link between student experience and self-authorship. Richard Hopkins (1994) offers narrative as the new root metaphor for education:

> The idea of narrative might provide a cohesive, even protogenic, operating principle for tying lived experience to subject matter in schools. Narrative is a deeply human, linguistic process, a kind of primal developmental impulse. We are storytelling creatures. We do not just tell stories; we live them, create them, define ourselves through them. Our narratives are the expressive, temporal medium through which we construct our functioning personae and give meaning to our experience. (xvi)

Arguing for the primacy of experience in education, Hopkins describes learning as reconstructive query involving "periods of exploration, data gathering, and seeking . . . alternating with periods of reflection, analysis, synthesis, and expressive judgment" (152). When students construct their own stories, incorporating their own lived experience, they are able to open their minds to new challenges and experiences that prompt reconstruction. As a result, narrative education calls for critical thinking and highlights the importance of choice and agency in living one's life.

This reconstruction through narrative is not limited to learning subject matter. Although Hopkins does not use the term *self-authorship*, he links narrative with self-growth and subsequently links education with self-growth, thus using a conceptualization of learning that encompasses multiple dimensions. Other advocates of narrative agree that it is a process through which we envision who we will become (e.g., Bruner 1990; Kerby 1991; Polkinghorne 1988; Witherell and Noddings 1991). The notion of constructing oneself is a part of the process of achieving self-authorship.

An Emphasis on Self-Authorship

A second body of literature on educational reform and pedagogy focuses on liberatory, empowering, and critical education. The primary goal of these visions of education is to empower people to overcome domination. Self-authorship as I have defined it in this chapter is not discussed in these works; however, it is inherent in both the process and the intended outcome of this type of education. Because it teaches students to challenge all authorized knowledge claims, it encourages complex assumptions about knowledge. Paulo Freire's work stands at the core of liberatory education. Freire argued that banking education (or depositing knowledge into students' heads) reproduced culture in its current form, thereby maintaining the oppression of those whose experience was not the basis of the knowledge deposited. Freire's alternative, liberating education, focused instead on a mutual search for knowledge in which learning is jointly owned by students and teachers. The search begins in the students' experience from which teachers and students pose problems for pursuit. Academic subjects become lenses through which they reflect on problems related to their own lives. Freire believed that students became increasingly interested in the problems posed because they could see connections to their own experience and world, and became therefore more critical in their thinking as they reflected on these problems. Freire's goal was to help students recognize their power to reorganize knowledge and society, to think critically to discover meaning in the world and experience, to see and challenge domination in society, and to act to transform society based on that critique (1988; first published in 1970). These achievements necessitate self-authorship, and the joint pursuit of problems relevant to students' lives offers a mechanism for its development.

Ira Shor's account of empowering education adds specificity to Freire's liberatory approach. He suggests that learning starts from the lived experience that students bring to the learning situation, a condition that enhances their participation and their affect toward academic work. It proceeds forward as the teacher and students engage in dialogue or "reflect together on the meaning of their experience and their knowledge" (1992, 86). This democratic process involves shared authority in developing class plans and discussions, selecting themes to address, and summarizing progress. Shor proposed listening to students first, in essence to gain exposure to their language, feelings, and knowledge, in order to establish a base from which to structure the subject matter. Once this foundation is established, the teacher can structure a learning environment in which the students and teacher become coinvestigators of the subject matter. The dialogue that ensues at this point involves students' experience and the teacher's experience, as each explores and exchanges views in learning together. Shor emphasizes that "mutual dialogue is not a know-nothing learning process" (247). The teacher brings her knowledge to the dialogue, but rather than imposing it unilaterally, she introduces it in the context of the students' perspectives and themes. Dewey made the same point regarding the roles of student and teacher:

> This does not mean that the teacher is to stand off and look on; the alternative to furnishing ready-made subject matter and listening to the accuracy with which it is reproduced is not quiescence, but participation, sharing, in an activity. In such shared activity, the teacher is a learner, and the learner is, without knowing it, a teacher—and upon the whole, the less consciousness there is, on either side, of either giving or receiving instruction, the better. (1916, 160)

Shor argues that mutual inquiry involving the teacher's academic talk and the students' everyday talk transforms both. This transformation in students' "talk" undoubtedly involves a transformation in their meaning-making—the dimension I am calling self-authorship. Shor notes, "By sharing authority and assuming teacherly roles, students take greater responsibility for their educations, which can translate into a more intense relationship between them and the learning process" (1996, 199). Shor's extensive stories of shared authority in his own class (1996) illustrate the complexity and possibility of this approach.

Critical theorists adopted Freire's liberation education in addressing the purpose and nature of education in American society, arguing that education should be aimed at democracy and elimination of oppression and marginalization of various groups. Henry Giroux (1988a) called both radical and conservative educators to task for their indifference to "the politics of voice and representation—the forms of narrative and dialogue—around which students make sense of their lives and schools" (114). He argued that educators must pay attention to "the ways in which students, from different class, gender, and ethnic locations, mediate and express their sense of place, time, and history, and their contradictory, uncertain, and incomplete interactions with each other and with the dynamics of schooling" (114).

Giroux argues that student experience, which he defines as "a historical construction and lived practice that is produced and legitimated within particular social forms" (197), should be the object of inquiry in teaching. Starting with students' knowledge offers the opportunity for the teacher to legitimate that knowledge, but Giroux does not argue for unqualified endorsement of that knowledge. Instead he views critical pedagogy as encouraging

> a critique of dominant forms of knowledge and social practices that semantically and emotionally organize meanings and experiences that give students a sense of voice and identity; similarly, it attempts to provide students with the critical knowledge and skills necessary for them to examine their own particular lived experiences and cultural resources. (197)

Giroux argues for using the way students read the world, or their experience, to make school knowledge meaningful for them. Once it is connected, or made meaningful, it is possible to engage students in critical analysis of their experience and intellectual content.

Peter McLaren (1989) also speaks to education for emancipation with students' experience as a centerpiece of learning. McLaren believes that student experience "is intimately related to identity formation" (1989, 226). How students define themselves stems from their experience of culture and society, an understanding of themselves and the world that they bring to the learning setting. He emphasizes the need for teachers to connect with students' experience and self-definitions in order to engage them in critical learning.

Like Dewey and Freire, critical theorists view education as a means to democracy. They believe that empowering students to critically analyze their experience and dominant knowledge will enable them to change social inequities (Giroux 1988b). Critical pedagogy involves respecting and valuing differences among students while simultaneously engaging in dialogue about practices that structure domination; reclaiming histories of marginalized students in an effort to alter social relations; recognizing the role of popular culture in legitimating various versions of history; and attending to identity as an increasingly complex phenomenon (Carlson and Apple 1998). Critical theorists recognize the role of students' unique experience in learning and advocate helping students develop their own voices.

Feminist scholars in the critical tradition also endorse self-authorship in their emphasis on student empowerment, albeit focused on students' "identity and subjective positionality within and among gender, ethnic, class, sexual and other markers of difference" (Carlson and Apple 1998). Feminist pedagogy explores the authority of the teacher, personal experience as a source of knowledge, and different perspectives based on race, class, and culture (Weiler 1998). Many themes of feminist scholarship are inherent in Frances Maher and Mary Kay Tetreault's explorations of feminist classrooms. They identify four central themes in feminist pedagogy: mastery, voice, authority, and positionality.

Mastery takes the form of interpretation rather than definitive conclusions so that students "seek knowledge on their own terms" (17), an idea akin to self-authorship. On the subject of voice, Maher and Tetrault argue that students shape their voices as they "bring their own questions and perspectives to the material, they use relevant personal experiences to shape a narrative of an emerging self" (18). Opening the classroom to students' explorations and voices necessitated new visions of authority on the part of both students and teachers, visions similar to the shared authority Shor advocates. Finally, Maher and Tetrault note that one's position (e.g., gender, race, class), "perhaps more than any other single factor, influences the construction of knowledge, and that positional factors reflect relationships of power both within and outside the classroom itself" (22). Thus, students' position, as women or members of class or racial groups, is a major component of the "experience" from which they make meaning. The notion of position, the same idea Giroux emphasized, is central to Gloria Ladson-Billings's "culturally relevant pedagogy" (1998, 297)— a pedagogy that builds curriculum and learning experiences around students' cultural backgrounds, yet engages them in a critique of social and political systems that marginalize their culture. These perspectives join the centrality of student experience with the intended outcome of self-authorship.

AN EMPHASIS ON STUDENT DEVELOPMENT AND SELF-AUTHORSHIP

The story of Ann, Erica, and Lynn—students in Chris Snowden's winter biology course—at the outset of this chapter illustrated how each woman's assumptions about knowledge mediated her response to the pedagogy used in the course. Proponents of using students' experience (highlighted in the previous sections) emphasize knowing what students understand as a foundation for teaching. Robert Kegan, a leading constructive-developmental theorist and educator, points out, "It is not enough for us to know what our students understand . . . we must also know 'the way he understands it'" (1994, 278). The *way* students understand reflects the organizing principles they use to make meaning of their experience. In the case of Ann, Erica, and Lynn, these are epistemological principles. A body of literature characterized as constructive-developmental illuminates the epistemological, interpersonal, intrapersonal, and moral ways of making meaning evident in adult life. Constructive-developmentalists regard the aim of education as promoting growth in ways of making meaning. Thus, this body of literature emphasizes use of student experience, promotion of self-authorship (an integral component of complex ways of making meaning in all dimensions), and educational practice developed on the basis of students' ways of making meaning of their experience.

Numerous writers who are both developmental psychologists and educators have advocated using the Piagetian foundation of constructive-developmentalism in higher education for the past forty years. Piaget believed that people constructed their reality by virtue of organizing their experiences. Encountering experiences inconsistent with one's current organization (called dissonance) prompted a need for resolving the discrepancy. Piaget advanced that this resolution took place either through incorporating the new experience into the original organization somehow or, if that failed, through reorganizing to accommodate the new experience. The latter process meant growth to a more complex way of making meaning. Constructive-developmentalists believe (and have research evidence to support it) that growth in meaning-making evolves through eras according to regular principles of stability and change (Kegan 1982). These researchers argue for connecting teaching to students' ways of making meaning in order to create the conditions to promote growth to more complex meaning-making. This requires an understanding of ways of making meaning—a topic pursued in depth in chapter 2 of this book.

Several factors affect adults' response to dissonance, and these factors form the basis of constructive-developmental pedagogy. Obviously, adults must experience dissonance and be challenged to determine its relationship to their way of making meaning. This often happens by virtue of a teacher's expectations in higher education, as was the case in Chris Snowden's course. Patricia King and Karen Kitchener advocate specific ways to introduce this challenge, including "create multiple opportunities for students to examine different points of view on a topic reflectively" (1994, 237) and "create opportunities and provide encouragement for students to make judgments and to explain what they believe" (238). They also suggest targeting expectations and goals to the development range within which students operate, and they offer several examples of assignments that target various ways of making meaning (1994). This matching of expectations to ways of making meaning entails both challenge to address dissonance and support to do so.

Support for students' current ways of making meaning is central to promoting complex meaning-making. William Perry, the pioneer of understanding adults' ways of making meaning, emphasized the importance of listening to students and respecting their current perspectives (1970). Using his work, Laurent Daloz articulated how to mentor adult students to promote their meaning-making. He suggested, among other things, offering adults a structure for learning based on listening to their ways of making meaning, sharing ourselves in the learning relationship, and recognizing the difficult nature of changing one's way of viewing the world (1986). Daloz painted the developmental picture as a journey through which adults needed companionship and guidance to move successfully.

Robert Kegan extended the concept of providing challenge and support simultaneously, using a bridge metaphor. Placing students on one side of a bridge and the educational goal on the other, he argued that educators must create conditions that simultaneously respect and welcome students' ways of making meaning on their side of the bridge yet facilitate their journey toward the other end (1994). Similarly, Mary Belenky, Blythe Clinchy, Nancy Goldberger, and Jill Tarule offered a midwife metaphor for what they called "connected teaching" (1986). They described a connected teacher as one who shares the process of knowing and serves as midwife to "assist the students in giving birth to their own ideas, in making their own tacit knowledge explicit and elaborating it" (217). The midwife metaphor communicates helping students bring their own ideas forth, helping to preserve them while they are fragile at the beginning, and helping students to develop and share their thoughts. This metaphor illustrates that students' ways of knowing are at the center of the interaction; the teacher's action hinges on staying with that development. The connected teacher emphasizes that learning and the development of knowledge take place in, and are the property of, the student. Although the teacher is connected to the student in this process, she is also objective. She attempts to view the situation through the students' eyes and does not allow her own perspective to disregard the students' thoughts on the matter. The trust inherent in this connected teaching approach helps students develop positive affect toward developing their own thoughts. Self-authorship is the eventual goal, but the teaching process focuses on the students' current ability (or lack thereof) to think for themselves.

DEVELOPING PEDAGOGY TO PROMOTE SELF-AUTHORSHIP

Collectively, these perspectives provide a rich foundation from which to construct effective pedagogy that promotes self-authorship. They offer compelling arguments for the incorporation of student experience into learning, provide strong evidence for the importance of self-authorship as a goal of education, and emphasize that attention to the ways students make meaning is warranted. Yet they have been used minimally in higher education, even though many of these ideas have existed for years. The lack of their use stems from numerous sources including perceptions of authority, assumptions about knowledge, organizational models in higher education, and the degree of specificity of these conceptualizations.

Our perspectives on our authority as teachers stem from our own experience. Shor (1992) noted that most teachers experienced passive, competitive, and authoritarian methods in school, learning as a result that "to be a teacher means talking a lot and being in charge" (26). Parker Palmer (1993) argued that teachers' diagnosis of students today is one of the major barriers to good teaching. He captures it like this:

> Briefly stated, this diagnosis holds that the classroom behaviors of many students (e.g., their silence, distraction, and embarrassment) reveal them to be essentially brain-dead (due to poor preparation, the dissolution of decent society, MTV, etc.), and that they therefore require pedagogies that function like life-support systems, dripping information into the veins of comatose patients who are unable to feed themselves. If that is a caricature, it is nevertheless instructive: nothing is easier than to slip into a low opinion of students, and that opinion creates teaching practices guaranteed to induce vegetative states even in students who arrive for class alive and well. (11)

Thus, we hesitate to implement new approaches that entail joint teacher-student authority because we are unsure that this amounts to meeting our responsibilities or that students are capable of participating. Palmer warns that "the way we diagnose our students' condition will determine the kind of remedy we offer" (1998, 41).

Views of knowledge are closely intertwined with these notions of authority. Bruffee explains that traditional education operates from a foundational point of view that assumes "knowledge is a kind of substance contained in and given form by the vessel we call the mind. Teachers transfer knowledge from their own fuller vessels to the less full vessels of their students. Teachers impart knowledge that was imparted to them, as it was imparted to them" (1993, 66). This view of knowledge as something to be transferred places the teacher in the position of authority that Shor described. These assumptions about authority and knowledge are inherent in the organizational models prevalent in both secondary and higher education. Hopkins charges that secondary schools display a complete disregard for student experience because they operate from a machine model. He writes, "This model assumes that adults know what children need to know and that the task of teachers is to get what is known somehow into the consciousness and awareness of students and to create conditions in which they take interest and expend effort" (1994, 12). Numerous reports offer evidence that this machine model is alive and well in higher education. Parker Palmer argues that this kind of education has made spectators of students, and he pleads with educators to draw "students into the process, the community, of knowing" (1990, 12). Articulating the link between views of knowledge and classroom practice, he wrote,

> If we regard truth as something handed down from authorities on high, the classroom will look like a dictatorship. If we regard truth

as a fiction determined by personal whim, the classroom will look like anarchy. If we regard truth as emerging from a complex process of mutual inquiry, the classroom will look like a resourceful and interdependent community. (1998, 51)

Finally, the visions of new forms of pedagogy recounted here offer more by way of conceptualization than they do specific processes for implementation. Whereas some of these visions offer foundational principles and examples for implementation, determining how to connect to diverse students' ways of making meaning and how to specifically organize teaching to create conditions conducive to growth of the mind remains illusive. Despite growing dissatisfaction with the perceptions of authority and knowledge noted here, educators often stay with those models because they lack specific alternatives. The current book attempts to move pedagogical reform forward by identifying the structure and process for creating conditions to promote self-authorship as well as evidence to support the effectiveness of such pedagogy.

Structure of constructive-developmental Pedagogy

One of the specific purposes of this book is to describe the structure underlying constructive-developmental pedagogy. Structure differs from a collection of techniques because it remains constant and useful across contexts. Structure here refers to the principles underlying constructive-developmental pedagogy that guide educational practice across disciplines, student populations, and learning contexts. These principles—validating students as knowers, situating learning in students' experience, and defining learning as mutually constructing meaning—by their definition connect with students' experience and meaning-making as educators and students interact. The origin of these principles is detailed later in this chapter and discussed in depth in chapter 3.

Processes of constructive-developmental Pedagogy

Because the structure forms a foundation from which to adapt to diverse students and contexts, multiple possibilities exist for the actual processes for implementing constructive-developmental pedagogy. This book describes specific processes of constructive-developmental pedagogy evident in four higher education courses. Each process is conveyed through accounts of class sessions and analyzed for its relationship to the underlying structure. Students' and faculty's response to these processes are also explored in depth to judge effectiveness of these processes for promoting self-authorship and subject mastery.

ORIGIN OF THE STRUCTURE OF CONSTRUCTIVE-DEVELOPMENTAL PEDAGOGY

The structure I identify for constructive-developmental pedagogy emerged from a previous longitudinal study of students' epistemological development, or their assumptions about the nature, limits, and certainty of knowledge (Baxter Magolda 1992). I initiated that study with 101 students entering college in 1986. Its purpose was to trace epistemological development over the course of college and adulthood with particular attention to the role of gender in that development. In annual interviews I pursued domains that had been shown to illuminate epistemic assumptions. Thus, I invited students to talk freely about their role as learners, the role of instructors and peers in learning, their perception of evaluation of their work, the nature of knowledge, and educational decision making. Qualitative open-ended interviews were used because cognitive development research supported their utility in accessing students' core epistemic assumptions.

The primary outcome of the college phase of the longitudinal study was a description of four ways of knowing, each characterized by a qualitatively different set of epistemic assumptions, and two gender-related patterns within the first three ways of knowing (Baxter Magolda 1992). An overview of these outcomes is presented in chapter 2 to describe students' intellectual development as a foundation for exploring constructive-developmental pedagogy. However, in the course of open discussions of students' learning experiences, they reported experiences that in their view prompted them to alter their epistemic assumptions. Reviewing the transcripts of their audiorecorded interviews surfaced themes that captured the structure of teaching that promoted their epistemological development. I translated those themes to three principles for promoting students' epistemological development (Baxter Magolda 1992). Hearing their stories sparked my interest in pursuing this kind of teaching and led me to the current study of constructive-developmental pedagogy.

The three principles emerging from the longitudinal study are validating students as knowers, situating learning in students' own experience, and defining learning as mutually constructing meaning. *Validating students as knowers* means acknowledging their capacity to hold a point of view, recognizing their current understandings, and supporting them in explaining their current views. Validation as a knower helps students view themselves as capable of learning and knowing, heightening their engagement in learning. *Situating learning in students' own experience* means using students' experience, lives, and current knowledge as a starting point for learning. This places learning in a context students can readily understand. Situating learning in students' experience can draw existing experiences into the learning context or create experiences within the learning context from which students can work. It also means connecting to students' ways of making meaning. *Defining learning as mutually constructing meaning* makes both teacher and student active players in learning. It suggests that the teacher and students put their understandings together by exploring students' experiences and views in the context of knowledge the teacher introduces. Together they construct knowledge that takes experience and evidence into account. Through this mutual construction, misunderstandings in previous knowledge are resolved; thus, validating students as knowers does not mean endorsing misunderstanding. Detailed discussion of these three principles and their integration occurs in chapter 3.

Together these three principles thus form the structure of constructive-developmental pedagogy—a structure that continuously incorporates students' lived experience and the meaning they have made of it into teaching. This structure is crucial in both connecting to the range of students' development and connecting to a wide range of student experience. Because the principles involve listening to students' thinking and dialogue among learners, students' epistemic assumptions can be surfaced in the learning environment. Understanding and connecting to these assumptions help educators assist students in evaluating and altering their assumptions toward increasing complexity. The principles by their very nature encourage the complex epistemic assumptions that are inherent in self-authorship.

This structure also facilitates developing effective learning opportunities for students with diverse backgrounds and experiences. Because constructive-developmental pedagogy hinges on students' own experience, their particular experiences are surfaced in the learning environment. Understanding and connecting to those experiences help educators gain an appreciation for diverse students; welcoming students' experiences simultaneously makes students feel that they have a place in the learning environment. Validating students as knowers and defining learning as mutually constructing meaning let students know that they are an integral part of the learning process and that their experiences count. Given the increasing diversity of student populations, using a structure that accesses and welcomes all students is crucial to effective pedagogy.

IDENTIFYING THE PROCESS OF CONSTRUCTIVE-DEVELOPMENTAL PEDAGOGY

The possibilities of constructive-developmental pedagogy and using the above structure to promote students' epistemological development led to a second study focused on identifying processes through which to implement constructive-developmental pedagogy. Reflections on my teaching during the course of the longitudinal study led to my attempts to promote self-authorship in my courses via constructive-developmental pedagogy. I had only the stories of my longitudinal participants from which to work and hoped to find other instructors who were engaging in promoting self-authorship. I chose to observe courses in hopes of seeing versions of constructive-developmental pedagogy firsthand because my principles had emerged from students reporting to me what they had experienced. My advocacy of constructive-developmental pedagogy resulted in various dialogues with colleagues who viewed the structure as consistent with their values as educators. They were for the most part constructivist and largely unaware of the developmental dimension of constructive-developmental pedagogy. The colleagues who questioned constructive-developmental pedagogy raised issues about its utility in large classes, in content areas such as mathematics and science where subject mastery is vital, and for students with less advanced epistemological development. These issues, in combination with finding colleagues whose values were consistent with constructive-developmental pedagogy, framed my observational study.

I began observing courses in the fall of 1993. I looked particularly for teachers who desired to promote their students' self-authorship, believed that students had something to offer, and were passionate about teaching. My colleague Jo Fischer was coordinating a 200 level educational foundations course that would enroll 286 students. The goal was critical thinking about educational practice. She and another colleague who had conceptualized the course were familiar with my longitudinal study and focused on connecting their course to students' experience. I attended the large weekly course meeting for the semester, attended the instructor seminars (graduate students taught multiple seminar sections), attended the meetings of two seminar sections throughout the semester, and interviewed students in those sections who agreed to participate in the study.

During the 1994 spring semester, a research partner and I gained permission to observe Sam Rivers's Mathematics by Inquiry course taken primarily by juniors and seniors. Sam's course focused on discovery learning, and he was a constructivist teacher at heart who wanted his students to develop their own construction of mathematics. We attended both weekly meetings all semester and interviewed the majority of students in the course.

In the spring semester of 1995, we observed Chris Snowden's winter biology course because Chris thought his values matched the structure of constructive-developmental pedagogy, his course focused on teaching students to think like scientists, and the enrollment was primarily seniors. We attended both weekly meetings of his course and interviewed approximately half of the students enrolled.

All student interviews were conducted at the end of the term to assess students' epistemological development, which was assessed via a written measure at the outset of each course, and to solicit their perceptions of the course and pedagogy. We interviewed instructors at the outset and conclusion of the courses to understand their teaching philosophy and assessment of the course respectively. Further details on the design and methods of the study are included in the appendices.

Context of the Observational Study

Inherent in the social-constructivist approach to knowledge construction is the notion that knowers decide what to believe based on a thorough understanding of the context. Thus, in order for readers to judge whether the picture of constructive-developmental pedagogy painted here is useful for teaching in other contexts, a full description of the context from which this description emerged is necessary. Both my longitudinal study and the observational study took place at Miami University (Ohio). The following description of the institution and the courses I observed serve as the readers' introduction to the context of the observational study. The courses are described in the order in which they appear in the book.

Miami University

Miami University is a state-assisted, liberal arts institution with an enrollment of approximately sixteen thousand. Admission is competitive; most students rank in the top 20 percent of their high school class. The campus is residential, and involvement in cocurricular life is high. Approximately 130 majors are offered in six divisions, including arts and sciences, education and allied professions, business administration, fine arts, applied sciences, and interdisciplinary studies. Nearly nine hundred students participate in the honors program.

All students are required to participate in the Miami Plan for Liberal Education to complement specialized work in their major. The liberal education plan emphasizes four goals: "thinking critically, understanding contexts, engaging with other learners, and reflecting and acting" (Miami University 1994, 20). These goals are carried out in the context of thirty-six semester hours of foundational courses in five areas (English composition; fine arts, humanities; social science, world cultures; natural science; mathematics, formal reasoning, technology), nine semester hours in a thematic sequence of advanced work outside the major, and a three-hour senior capstone experience. EDU 200 and Math by Inquiry both serve as foundations courses for the Miami Plan.

The ratio of students to faculty is twenty-to-one. Twenty-seven percent of the full-time faculty are women. The mission of the institution rests heavily on undergraduate teaching, a focus that is evident in students' reports that faculty are available, friendly, and helpful. The promotion and tenure process seriously considers teaching as the most important function of the faculty. Programs such as the Alumni Teaching Scholars program for both junior and senior faculty are aimed at enhancing faculty teaching, as is the annual Lilly Teaching Conference held at Miami. Graduation rates are 68 percent in four years and 80 percent in five years.

ZOO 400/500: Winter Biology

Chris Snowden's conceptualization of science, as well as the nature of winter biology, was evident on his syllabus (see appendices and chap. 4). He believed that science was an evolving field made up of facts that were subject to revision. He wanted his students to understand how to evaluate scientific knowledge, identify questions, and conduct research that led to such revision. ZOO 400/500 included three juniors, fifteen seniors, and one graduate student who were officially enrolled in the course. Of those students only three were male (a major disappointment to me because the course was also chosen due to its typical high male enrollment). All were zoology majors, and one woman was a double major with zoology and math. Most of the students planned to continue their studies after graduation. Eight were planning to attend medical, dental, optometry, or law school the following year. Others were pursuing physical therapy, environmental science, ecology, or oceanography graduate programs. One planned to work in research and development, and the graduate student planned to pursue her doctorate in the near future. One or two additional people were usually present. One of Chris's graduate assistants audited the course, and others who worked in his lab from graduate students to postdoctoral students sat in routinely. Ten students participated in interviews at the end of the term; all three men enrolled and seven women, including the graduate student and nine seniors.

Chris's love was anything related to the cold. As he said in our first interview, "Some like it hot—in our lab we like it cold!" Thus, the course was his opportunity to engage students with a wide range of subjects, all hinging on life in the cold. His enthusiasm for the topic was ever present in the course, heightened on days when snow was falling outside. Chris's extensive research program, now twenty years in the making, was often used as an example in the course, and he invited students to join him in various endeavors. Some Tuesdays he would share research activities in which he and his lab colleagues had engaged over the weekend. His thirteen years of university teaching made him as comfortable in the classroom as in the lab. He liked his time in the classroom, saying that he could succeed in a purely research environment but preferred the combination of teaching and research, which he viewed as closely linked. His main interest was teaching students "how to do science."

Chris's enthusiasm for teaching was as evident in his classroom as was his interest in insects evident in the ladybug collection that occupied his office.

MATH 400/500: MATH BY INQUIRY

The syllabus (see appendices and chap. 5) for Math by Inquiry outlined the content and format of the course, both emphasizing discovery learning. Sam Rivers wanted his students to leave with a personal construction of how mathematics worked. This course could be used as a requirement in the mathematics area of the liberal education plan. Most students reported taking it because of the instructor's reputation. Of the sixteen students enrolled, all of whom were women, two were graduate students, eleven were seniors, two were juniors, and one was a sophomore. One was a math major; the rest were education majors with concentrations or minors in math. All were preparing to be teachers with the exception of the two graduate students who were already teaching. The undergraduate students ranged in age from 19 to 22, with four age 21 and four age 22. The two graduate students were 24 and 37 years old. One student was African-American. Four of the students reported that their mothers were teachers; one student's father was a teacher. Five of the students' mothers were homemakers. Twelve students participated in our interviews at the end of the term. This group included the two graduate students, the sophomore, one of the juniors, and eight seniors. The African-American student participated in the interviews.

Sam Rivers had been an elementary and secondary teacher early in his career and could use his experience to relate to the students' goals. His longstanding involvement in teacher education, the institution's reform effort in liberal education, and Project Discovery* all culminated in Sam's social-constructivist bent. Sam's personality matched the nature of the course. He had an easy rapport with students, was serious about their learning, and was modest about his extensive expertise. His more than twenty years of teaching at the college level made the college classroom a comfortable place for him. The respect he showed for students as thinkers was a central feature of the course.

EDU 200: SOCIOCULTURAL FOUNDATIONS OF EDUCATION

The nature of EDU 200, as described in the syllabus (see appendices and chap. 6), was to help students think critically about schooling and education in contemporary America. Goals included learning to recognize, evaluate, and defend positions in educational discourse and learning to interpret,

---

*Project Discovery is a statewide initiative, funded by the National Science Foundation and the state of Ohio, to improve science and mathematics education. The project advocates discovery, or inquiry, learning.

critique, and judge educational practices in various contexts. Sophomores made up the majority (54 percent) of the 286 students enrolled. Seventeen percent were first-year students, 22 percent were juniors, and 7 percent were seniors. Women dominated the group, making up 75 percent of the enrollment. All six university divisions were represented, although 74 percent were in education. The next largest group was from arts and sciences (13 percent) followed by fine arts (7 percent), business (4.5 percent), applied science (1 percent), and interdisciplinary studies (one person). Based on research on students' epistemological development, it is likely that most of the students came to EDU 200 expecting the instructor to play a primary role in dispensing knowledge. The thirteen students I interviewed said that they had never had a class like EDU 200 before except first-year English.

EDU 200 was a required course for all undergraduate teacher education majors and also could be used to meet a foundations requirement in the liberal education plan. Jo Fischer, the large group instructor and coordinator of the course, was trained in the social foundations of education and taught in secondary education prior to coming to the university. Her youth and East Coast–upbringing impacted her teaching style. She used her sharp wit regularly, and her command of popular culture helped her resonate with students' experience. She was fearless in trying unusual techniques (such as yelling "sex" at the outset of one session to get their attention) that most instructors would only joke about. Despite her connection to and compassion for students, Jo was also straightforward and confronted students directly about ideas and their academic efforts. She was comfortable with the subject matter and at ease on the stage in front of three hundred students. She preferred to yell instead of using the microphone.

I purposely selected Jan Nichols's and Kim Conlin's sections to observe based on my observations of all the EDU 200 instructors at an all-day retreat before the start of classes. The retreat focused on discussion of the purpose, plan, and implementation of the course. Jan's and Kim's contributions during the discussion led me to believe that they fully understood the conceptualization of the course Elliot Gardner, the faculty member who conceptualized the course, had articulated and that their teaching experience led them to interact relationally with students. Both were doctoral students at the time they taught EDU 200, but both had full-time teaching experience prior to their doctoral programs in educational administration. Jan taught special education at the secondary level for a number of years; her teaching philosophy hinged on honoring students where they are. Kim taught art, music, and humanities previously in a magnet school setting, and she had master's degrees in guidance and counseling and aesthetic education. Her teaching philosophy focused on collaborative work with students. Both women had teenage children of their own as well. Jan is an outgoing, jovial person who seems comfortable with any audience. Kim is a quiet personality, whose flashes of humor are seen regularly when she gets settled in a group. Both women were confident of their teaching skill and excited about the nature of EDU 200.

Kim's section enrolled twenty students, of whom five were first-year, thirteen were sophomores, and two were juniors. Seven students in Kim's section participated in the project. Of the seven, two were juniors, three were sophomores, and two were first-year students. One of the seven was male. The other five males in that section declined participation. Five of the seven students were education majors; one was in communications; and one was in chemistry. Jan's section enrolled nineteen students, including four first-year students, eleven sophomores, three juniors, and one senior. Six of Jan's nineteen students participated in the project. All six were women; the four men in the class declined our invitation to participate. Four were sophomores, one was a first-year student, and one was a junior. Four were education majors, one a math major, and one a business major.

CONTEXT LIMITATIONS

The three courses observed involve different disciplines, a range of class ranks, distinct implementations of constructive-developmental pedagogy, and multiple teaching styles. However, discussion of the processes of constructive-developmental pedagogy stemming from these courses is not intended to be generalized across contexts in line with my social-constructivist views. These processes serve as possibilities through which the structure of constructive-developmental pedagogy can be implemented. As you judge transferability to your teaching context, I caution you to consider limitations of the context described here. First, women greatly outnumbered men in all three courses observed. In addition, men were not interested in participating in our study even after we explained the need for more male participants. Second, students of color were minimally represented in these courses and subsequently in our project. This is largely a function of the small number of students of color at the institution. Third, the institution maintains a strong teaching focus despite its enrollment. Thus, the campus climate may be more supportive than some climates of innovative teaching. These dynamics vary across higher educational institutions and may affect transferability of the processes and outcomes of constructive-developmental pedagogy. I firmly believe, however, that the structure—the three principles—offers sufficient flexibility to make its successful use possible in multiple contexts.

OVERVIEW OF THE BOOK

Because self-authorship is a primary focus of the book, an in-depth exploration of the developmental nature of self-authorship is offered in chapter 2. The epistemological dimension of self-authorship is placed in the foreground; the interpersonal and intrapersonal dimensions are woven around the epistemological to help the reader attain a full understanding of students' development of self-authorship. Chapter 3 pursues the structure of constructive-developmental pedagogy in more detail, illustrating the effects of the three principles on students' development of self-authorship. Chapter 3 also includes my attempts to use this structure in one of my graduate courses. I include these activities and my reflection on them for two reasons. First, I advocate modeling risks that I encourage others to take; thus, sharing my foray into constructive-developmental pedagogy seems appropriate before I ask readers to entertain it in their teaching. My involvement in my graduate course simultaneously allows for an insider perspective and limits my objectivity. Second, sharing excerpts from my graduate course illustrates constructive-developmental pedagogy possibilities with students who hold complex ways of knowing.

Part 2 illustrates three processes for implementing constructive-developmental pedagogy in three different contexts. The variety of processes used in the three courses observed emphasizes the multiple possibilities through which the underlying structure of constructive-developmental pedagogy can be implemented to connect with teacher style, students' development, and disciplinary objectives. Chapter 4 recounts the *interactive lecture* process Chris Snowden used in his senior/graduate biology course. The nature of the interactive lecture is described, illustrated by examples of its use in class sessions. Students' reflections on their learning demonstrate the outcomes of the interactive lecture for helping students learn scientific inquiry. Chapter 5 describes Sam Rivers's *investigating together* approach to teaching and learning mathematics with junior and senior students. Accounts of class sessions show Sam's reliance on constructivist pedagogy and the particular processes he used. His students' reactions demonstrate the effects of learning mathematics in this manner. Chapter 6 illustrates *narrative* processes to teaching social foundations of education to first- and second-year students. Class sessions from two seminar sections as well as the large group session reveal various ways of using storytelling in promoting self-authorship with students whose epistemological development makes self-authorship difficult. Students' reactions highlight how these processes affected their development. The detailed accounts of course sessions in part 2 are intended to offer readers specific details about ways in which constructive-developmental pedagogy can be implemented.

Part 3 explores the issues, challenges, and possibilities inherent in choosing self-authorship as the aim of education and using constructive-developmental pedagogy as a means of accomplishing that aim. Using the courses in part 2 as a foundation, chapter 7 offers a comprehensive theory of learning and teaching. This constructive-developmental theory addresses developing students' minds, the nature of dialogue in and beyond the classroom, instructor expertise, connecting rational and aesthetic knowing, integrating existing knowledge and students' experience, and integrating separate and connected modes of knowing. A detailed analysis of how the underlying structure of the three courses promoted self-authorship closes that chapter. Chapter 8 offers a discussion of both imaginary and real dilemmas inherent in constructive-developmental pedagogy, exploring its implications for teacher construction of knowledge and practice. Beliefs about students, teachers, and the learning process are explored, as well as challenges in connecting to students' diverse epistemological development and promoting self-authorship with students who regard knowledge as the property of authorities. Chapter 9 outlines four possibilities constructive-developmental pedagogy offers for improving education and society, including fostering self-authorship and lifelong learning, enhancing education by linking students' lives—including diverse students— to academic learning in a genuine and substantive way, preparing students to meet the demands inherent in adult roles in contemporary society, and preparing students to take an active role in creating a better society.

I invite you to listen to the students and teachers whose thoughts and experiences are recounted in the following pages. I have taken an inductive approach to sharing their stories based on the belief that you will bring your own experience to them and make meaning of them accordingly. I have offered my interpretations throughout the book, based on my experiences and ways of knowing. The inductive approach will most likely be refreshing to some of you and aggravating to others, which is a reflection of the notion that we all bring our experience and ways of knowing to any learning task. A reader of an early version of this manuscript remarked that the stories and quotes were too long and could be more efficiently replaced with some straightforward analysis. Although that may be true for some readers, it contradicts the process for which I am arguing—allowing people to experience something and make their own sense of it in interaction with how others have made sense of it. From the latter stance, I have shared only the tip of the iceberg of four semester-length courses and participants' reflections on them. For those of you who tire of the stories, overviews and analyses segments are interspersed and clearly marked. I have used the chapters as a forum to advance my interpretations; I hope you will develop your own interpretations and use both to reflect on your educational practice.

CHAPTER 2

The Developmental Nature of Self-Authorship

The World of Students

Self-authorship is an elusive goal for both students and their instructors. A Doonesbury cartoon about teaching captured this state of affairs. The cartoon depicted a teacher at his lectern, speaking on the topic of Jefferson's defense of basic rights to students in rows below him. In the first frame the teacher asks for students' reactions to his views. Hearing only the sound of scribbling and seeing only blank stares, he muses in the second frame that the students are more interested in getting the information down than responding to his query. He makes his next statement more provocative, calling the Bill of Rights "silly," hoping to spark a response. As the students continue to write faster, the teacher offers increasingly bizarre viewpoints to elicit a discussion. In the last frame he gives up, slumping over the podium in frustration, and pronounces teaching dead. Meanwhile the students comment to one another how interesting the course is becoming given the information just presented. Whereas the teacher invites the students to engage in self-authorship, they appear to miss that point entirely. This scenario repeats itself in real classrooms—where good teachers and bright students come together—because educational practice is rarely organized around students' ways of making meaning.

The students in the cartoon, who in this scenario assume that knowledge is certain and possessed by the authority, see the podium and seating arrangements as an indication that they are to listen to the authority, their educational experience has taught them to listen to authority, and they find the bizarre statements of the professor more interesting than the usual fare. Teachers without an understanding of students' epistemological, intrapersonal, and interpersonal development interpret the students' behavior as indicating that students want nothing more than to fill their notebooks, are too disinterested (perhaps even lazy) to engage in discussion, and cannot distinguish between the professor's view and truth.

A teacher who understands the development of students' meaning-making would be far more hopeful than Doonesbury's teacher would. She would muse that the students seem to believe that knowledge is certain because they write down the teacher's words regardless of their quality. She would further speculate that she would have to adjust her approach to get the students to reconsider their assumptions. She would, as a result, contemplate how to reorganize her practice to take into account where the students are starting as well as where she hopes they will go in thinking about the subject matter. This teacher would also understand the complexity of the task ahead.

Accessing students' ways of making meaning of their experience is a complex task. Students are not accustomed to having their experience valued in the learning process, as is evident in the Doonesbury cartoon. Shor (1992) argues that people are born learners and that their natural curiosity is often stifled by educational environments in which they are expected to memorize rules and existing knowledge. Brown and Gilligan (1992) document the silencing of adolescent girls in educational environments that socialize them in ways that inhibit expression of their true feelings and thoughts. Given these insights, it is not sufficient to simply invite students to practice self-authorship. Somehow instructors must convince students that their perspectives are valued and that education is the process of developing one's own perspectives in the context of existing understandings of the world. Teaching students how to self-author their beliefs is a matter of creating conditions to promote their development. The first step in approaching this task effectively is understanding the developmental nature of self-authorship, the topic to which the rest of this chapter is devoted.

DIMENSIONS OF SELF-AUTHORSHIP

Self-authorship, as noted in chapter 1, has cognitive, intrapersonal, and interpersonal dimensions. Constructive-developmental theorists view these dimensions as parts of a single mental activity rather than separate entities (Kegan 1993). The *cognitive* component of how people make meaning is their assumptions about the nature, limits, and certainty of knowledge, or their epistemic assumptions (Kitchener 1983). These generally move from assuming that knowledge is certain and is possessed by authorities to assuming that knowledge is constructed in a context. The shift of knowledge from certain to uncertain is accompanied by a shift from viewing oneself as a receiver to a constructor of knowledge, a shift central to the development of self-authorship. The *intrapersonal* component of meaning-making involves assumptions about oneself. Intrapersonal growth moves from distinguishing one's impulses from oneself and identifying enduring qualities of the self to experiencing and eventually authoring one's inner psychological life. The latter way of making meaning is a central component of self-authorship. The *interpersonal* component hinges on assumptions about the relation of the self to others. Growth in this arena moves from lack of coordination of one's point of view with that of others, through subsuming one's own view to that of significant others, to developing a system that regulates interpersonal relationships. The latter perspective is necessary for self-authorship.

The pressing issues and tasks that students face and resolve as they mature, what theorists often call psychosocial development, stem from these constructive-developmental frameworks about the self and others. These issues include functioning autonomously, developing healthy relationships with others, dealing with one's identity, and defining one's purpose. This type of development is "concerned with those personal, psychologically oriented aspects of self and the relationships that exist between the self and society" (Miller and Winston 1990, 101). Students' views of themselves as knowers are inextricably intertwined with their views of self and relationships with others. The intrapersonal and interpersonal dimensions, which are often perceived as tangential in the study of pedagogy, are also crucial in understanding the development of self-authorship. Self-authorship means believing one can construct knowledge claims, make one's own inner psychological life, and regulate relationships with others to maintain one's own identity. Genuine self-authorship occurs when one reaches self-authorship in all three dimensions.

Constructive-developmental research describes the nature of each of these dimensions, their interrelationships, and the progression of each from simple to more complex forms. An important characteristic of the constructive-developmental approach is the concept of structure. Structure refers to ways people organize their meaning rather than the content of their meaning-making. Kegan describes this as "the organizing principle we bring to our thinking and our feelings and our relating to others and our relating to parts of ourselves" (1994, 29). For example, the epistemological assumption that knowledge is certain is an organizing principle one can bring to deciding what to believe. Two students can adopt different views from this same structure by believing different authorities; their way of deciding what to believe is the same. Two students could also endorse the same knowledge claim but arrive at it from different underlying structures. These structures are believed to be coherent sets of assumptions people use to make meaning until experiences that are discrepant with the structures cause people to alter them to account for new experience. The notion that these structures evolve through eras according to regular principles of stability and change is referred to as developmentalism (Kegan 1982, 8) and brings the possibility of some order to understanding how students make meaning.

I present constructive-developmental theory here as a *possibility* for understanding students' lived experience in a particular context. No theoretical portrait describes all students; rather, each portrait describes a particular group of students. Marilyn Frye's notion of patterns is useful here. Frye states, "Naming patterns is like charting the prevailing winds over a continent, which does not imply that every individual and item in the landscape is identically affected" (1990, 180). I interpret developmental theories to be the naming of patterns that help make sense of students' development but do not affect all students identically. Thus, they represent possible entrees into students' meaning-making processes, the understanding of which must be achieved through interacting with particular students. Perry argued that the student's organization of experience "can often be deduced by others from the forms of his behavior, including, especially, what he himself has to say on the matter" (1970, 42). Developmental theory is presented here as the basis for dialogue with students to access and understand the meaning they make of their lived experience. This chapter places portraits of epistemological development in the foreground so that the reader can "hear" what the cognitive dimension of self-authorship so central to teaching sounds like first. Then portraits of intrapersonal and interpersonal development are described to illustrate how the three dimensions are integrated in students' meaning-making and development of self-authorship.

EPISTEMOLOGICAL DEVELOPMENT

Jean Piaget (1950) established the cognitive-developmental view of intellectual development, describing intelligence in terms of qualitatively different structures through which persons made meaning of their experience. These structures were characterized by particular assumptions about the nature, limits, and certainty of knowledge, assumptions that Kitchener (1983) later labeled epistemic assumptions. In their synthesis of epistemological theories, Barbara Hofer and Paul Pintrich (1997) identify three intersecting lines of research on epistemological development. Identifying epistemological assumptions and their evolution has been the core focus of one line (e.g., Baxter Magolda 1992; Belenky, Clinchy, Goldberger, and Tarule 1986; Perry 1970). Exploring how epistemological assumptions influence thinking and reasoning processes, such as reflective judgment (King and Kitchener 1994), represents a second line. A third line of research explores epistemological ideas as independent rather than reflective of a developmental structure (e.g., Ryan 1984; Schommer 1994). The perspective I advance here is that epistemic assumptions do evolve via developmental structures; I focus primarily on describing epistemic assumptions and their impact on students' approaches to learning.

Four portraits of students' epistemic assumptions identified through longitudinal studies of college students and adults exist. Perry (1970) offered the first comprehensive account of college students' intellectual development on the basis of a predominantly male sample. He described a progression of epistemic assumptions from knowledge as certain to partially uncertain to completely uncertain to relative in context. Dualistic students viewed knowledge as certain, in right-wrong terms, and acquired from authority. Uncertainty of knowledge appeared in multiplicity, replacing the right-wrong dichotomy with a known-unknown dichotomy. As areas in which knowledge was believed to be uncertain expanded, students began to adopt the stance that all knowledge was uncertain, resulting in less reliance on authority. Relativistic thinking emerged with the realization that some knowledge claims are better than others and can be validated by evidence relevant to the context. Perry also described a segment of the developmental scheme called commitment in relativism to reflect the continual reflection and commitment to perspectives that take place in relativistic thinking.

Due to difficulty interpreting women's experience with Perry's portrait, Belenky, Clinchy, Goldberger, and Tarule (1986) constructed a portrait of intellectual development based on a female sample. They found similar epistemic assumptions, yet learned that women in their study used their own subjectivity in the face of uncertainty more so than Perry's men and also identified an approach to knowing through connection to the object to be known. Belenky et al.'s perspectives of silence, in which participants did not perceive their ability to learn from others, and received knowing, in which the primary mode of learning was listening, demonstrated the belief of knowledge as certain similar to Perry's dualists. When the women discovered uncertainty of knowledge in subjective knowing, however, they moved quickly to rely on their own intuition and personal experiences unlike Perry's multiplicity. Increasing uncertainty led to procedural knowing in which two distinct processes for coming to know were evident. Belenky et al. described these as separate—using a logical, detached approach—and connected—using a subjective, empathic approach. The recognition that knowledge can be judged in a context yielded constructed knowing, a stance similar to Perry's relativist. Although Belenky et al. were careful not to essentialize their ways of knowing to all women, their work raised the question of gender-related patterns within ways of knowing. Continued work by these authors further articulated the relationship of separate and connected knowing (Clinchy 1996) and how gender, race, and class relations mediate negotiations about knowledge (Goldberger 1996).

Another model sparked by Perry's original scheme, the Reflective Judgment model (King and Kitchener 1994), offered a more detailed account of the evolution from certainty to uncertainty. King and Kitchener advance a seven-stage model describing assumptions about knowledge and its justification. The first three stages offer finer distinctions than were previously available in the move from certainty to uncertainty. In stage one, knowledge is certain, and authorities' beliefs are accepted. Knowledge remains certain in stage two, although it is not always available. Temporary uncertainty appears in stage three, with the hope that absolute knowledge will become possible. Recognition that some knowledge is permanently uncertain marks stage four, accompanied by the idiosyncratic evaluation of knowledge claims. In the face of growing uncertainty in stage five, rules of inquiry in particular contexts are used to justify beliefs. Generalized rules of inquiry take over as knowledge is viewed as constructed (stage six), and the value of some knowledge claims over others based on critical evaluation of evidence marks stage seven.

The Reflective Judgment model included both women and men but produced mixed results regarding whether gender made a difference in intellectual development (King and Kitchener 1994). My longitudinal study of college students' epistemological development (Baxter Magolda 1992) resulted in a gender-inclusive model in which women and men share similar epistemic assumptions, yet approach them via gender-related reasoning patterns. King and Kitchener (1994) note that differences in reasoning patterns cannot be discerned from the Reflective Judgment data, saying, "Since the RJI was not designed to elicit such information and since the data reported here have not been scored for this purpose, it cannot be said whether such differences might also exist in the context of the Reflective Judgment Model" (177). Subsequently, I use my Epistemological Reflection model in this chapter because it addresses both reasoning patterns and reflects a portrait of epistemological development consistent with those summarized here.

Epistemological Reflection: Four Ways of Knowing

The Epistemological Reflection model emerged from following eighty students through their four years of college.* It is continually refined through the post-college phase, which currently extends eight years after college. Annual open-ended interviews explored students' thoughts on the role of instructors, learners, and peers in learning; how learning should be evaluated; how to make educational decisions; and the nature of knowledge. Glaser and Strauss's (1967) constant comparative method was used to identify themes in their thinking, resulting in four ways of knowing and gender-related patterns within three of these sets of epistemic assumptions. I use the term *gender-related* to convey that the patterns were used more often by one gender than the other but not used exclusively by one gender. (See the appendices for a brief overview of the method for this study; a complete discussion is found in *Knowing and Reasoning in College: Gender-Related Patterns in Students' Intellectual Development.*)

*Portions of this description are reproduced with permission from Baxter Magolda, M. B. (1992). *Knowing and reasoning in college: Gender-related patterns in students' intellectual development.* San Francisco: Jossey Bass.

Absolute Knowing

Discussing his view of learning as a first-year student, Jim offered a perspective that captures the essence of absolute knowing: "The factual information is cut and dried. It is either right or wrong. If you know the information, you can do well. It is easy because you just read or listen to a lecture about the ideas. Then you present it back to the teacher."

The core assumption held by absolute knowers is that knowledge exists in an absolute form, or in Jim's words, it is either right or wrong. They often assume that right and wrong answers exist in all areas of knowledge and that authorities know these answers. Uncertainty does not exist in knowledge per se, although it might exist in the student's lack of knowing the answer. The roles students describe for instructors, peers, and themselves as learners all hinge on knowledge being the purview of the instructor. As learners, absolute knowers focus on obtaining the information—a task Jim describes as reading or listening to lectures. They expect instructors to communicate knowledge clearly to them to aid in their acquiring it. They do not expect peers to have legitimate knowledge, although peers can share what they have learned from authority figures. Notice that Jim does not mention peers in his comment on how to do well. Absolute knowers' views of effective evaluation of students' work reflect the instructor's mastery of knowledge as well as the instructor's ability to determine whether students have acquired knowledge. When Jim presents what he has learned back to the teacher, she will know whether he knows the right answers. Students interpret discrepancies they encounter in the learning process as variations in explanations rather than true differences in knowledge. Finally, they approach educational decisions by looking for the right answers about educational programs, majors, and career directions.

Two reasoning patterns were evident in absolute knowing: receiving and mastery. The *receiving pattern* was used more often by women than men in the study. A central characteristic of the receiving pattern is its internal approach, as shown by Toni's comment: "I like to listen—just sit and take notes from an overhead. The material is right there and if you have a problem you can ask him and he can explain it to you. You hear it, you see it, and then you write it down."

Toni, a sophomore, makes it clear that this approach involves minimal interaction with instructors. Her receiving pattern peers also emphasized the importance of comfort in the learning environment, relationships with peers, and ample opportunities to demonstrate their knowledge. They resolved knowledge discrepancies via personal interpretation.

The *mastery pattern* was used more often by men than by women in the study. Mastery pattern students preferred an active approach to learning, were critical of instructors, and expected interactions with peers and instructors that help them master the material. The active approach to learning permeates most aspects of the learning process. For example, Tim (a first-year student) offered:

> I like getting involved with the class. Just by answering questions, asking questions . . . even if you think you know everything, there's still questions you can ask. When he asks questions you can try to answer them to your best ability. Don't just let the teacher talk, but have him present questions to you.

Tim believes asking and answering questions are necessary to learn; he is not content to listen and take notes as Toni is. Tim and his mastery pattern peers reported engaging one another in debates to further their learning, showing the instructor they were interested, and resolved knowledge discrepancies via research and asking authorities.

Absolute knowers shared the common belief that knowledge is certain and held by authorities. Beyond their shared set of assumptions, receiving and mastery pattern students differed in three areas: voice, identification with authority, and relationships with peers. There was really no student voice per se in absolute knowing. However, mastery pattern students attempted to express themselves while their receiving pattern counterparts remained essentially silent. Mastery pattern students seemed to imitate the voice of authority and worked hard at reproducing it in an effort to join authorities as knowers. Receiving pattern students listened carefully to the voice of authority and repeated it in an effort to show that they had acquired the knowledge.

Although all absolute knowers viewed authorities as holders of truth and knowledge, receiving pattern students exhibited minimal identification with authority figures whereas mastery pattern students exhibited considerable identification with authority. Students in the receiving pattern exhibited a detachment from authority. They described learning as a transaction largely void of interaction with authority unless clarification was needed. Despite their motivation for receiving knowledge, they did not view identification or interaction with authority as a central part of that process. Students in the mastery pattern showed the beginnings of taking their place "next to" authorities in the arena of knowledge. Their learning behaviors resembled those of the active apprentice trying to master the trade.

Relationships with peers were a third point of difference for receiving and mastery pattern students. Receiving pattern students valued peers as providers of comfort in the learning atmosphere. Knowing others in the class made it more intimate, more comfortable, and an easier setting in which to learn and ask questions. For these students peers were a source of assistance in receiving knowledge. Collaboration took the form of support and sharing notes and information. Mastery pattern students valued peers as partners in striving for and testing achievement. They assisted one another in mastering knowledge and took turns testing one another's progress. Collaboration in this form was characterized by individual autonomy.

The path from absolute to transitional knowing involves the realization that not all knowledge is certain, and that authorities are not all-knowing as a result. As the students' stories in transitional knowing reveal, mastery and receiving pattern students encounter this experience differently. Mastery pattern students' identification with authority prompts them to stay with certainty and logic as much as possible in the face of emerging uncertainty. Receiving pattern students' detachment from authority makes it easier to let go of certainty; thus, endorsing uncertainty is preferable. Endorsing uncertainty leads to an increase in activity level over and above listening. Peers are important to students of both patterns, but students endorsing uncertainty more readily assign legitimacy to peers' knowledge.

Transitional Knowing

Uncertainty, upon its discovery, was usually perceived to exist only in particular areas while certainty remained in other knowledge arenas. Fran's statement reflects this perspective:

> Genetics isn't an opinionated kind of subject. Genetics is "These are the experiments; that's what happens. This is what we know now." You wouldn't sit around and have a discussion in calculus . . . or chemistry. In the AIDs class, it's just open discussion, and it makes you really say what you want and think through what you want to think about.

Genetics retained its certainty for Fran, as did calculus and chemistry. On the topic of AIDs, however, uncertainty emerged. This shift in the nature of knowledge sparked changes in the roles students perceived for themselves and others. Students shifted their focus from acquiring knowledge to understanding it. This focus on understanding required that instructors use methods aimed at understanding, many of which included applying knowledge in class and to life in general. Peers took on more active roles, perhaps because understanding was described as requiring more exploration than that required for the acquisition of knowledge. Evaluation was perceived as appropriate to the extent that it measured students' understanding of the material. Uncertainty permeated decision making as well, as students struggled to figure out options for the future. Processes believed to lead to future success replaced direct reliance on authorities for educational decision making. All transitional knowers held these core assumptions.

Within transitional knowing some students, usually women, used an interpersonal approach whereas other students, usually men, used an impersonal approach. *Interpersonal pattern* students were involved in learning through collection of others' ideas, expected interaction with peers to hear their views and provide exposure to new ideas, wanted a rapport with the instructor to enhance self-expression, valued evaluation that takes individual differences into account, and resolved uncertainty by personal judgment. Kris's comments capture the new expectations of peers:

> I get into discussions. Classroom discussions are better for me to learn. You have an opening lecture where you have the professor discuss. Then students can contribute—listening to other students contribute their ideas and putting in my own inputs-that makes learning better for me because it makes me think more and try to come up with more generative ideas as to what I would do in a situation. We react to the material, look at ideas and relate it to ourselves, look at what kinds of action we can take. It's a hands-on type class.

Kris wants to hear the professor but only briefly; then she wants to hear her peers and express her own opinion. Interpersonal pattern knowers tended to focus on areas that were uncertain and viewed this as an opportunity to express their own views for the first time.

Impersonal pattern students wanted to be forced to think, preferred to exchange their views with instructors and peers via debate, expected to be challenged by instructors, valued fair and practical evaluation, and resolved uncertainty by logic and research. Scott described the result of being forced to think:

> The debate and discussion process for me is really interesting; I learn a lot more because I remember questions and I guess I learn the most when I sit and I'm actually forced to raise my hand and then I have to talk. I have to sit there and think on the spot. I learn it better than in a note-taking class that is regurgitation.

Scott has rejected the absolute knowers' approach of presenting information back to the teacher, but he does not endorse Kris's interest in peers' comments. Instead he focuses on his own thinking about the material. Impersonal pattern students also demonstrated a dual focus on certainty and uncertainty, and they wanted to resolve uncertainty when it existed.

Students in both patterns exhibit development of their voice in transitional as compared to absolute knowing. The impersonal pattern voice remains consistent in its closeness to the voice of authority, reflecting now the process of learning rather than the answers. The interpersonal pattern voice diverges more from authority than does the impersonal pattern. The discovery of uncertainty seems to be viewed by interpersonal pattern students as an opportunity to become involved in knowing, resulting in greater activity and exercise of personal judgment. Moreover, a subtle division remains between the interpersonal pattern knower's knowledge and that of authority. Some students remarked that their learning from other students did not necessarily help them learn the material in the book. Yet the interpersonal pattern voice has gained greater distance from authority than has the impersonal pattern voice. Using relationship with authority as a point of departure toward independent knowing, interpersonal pattern students would seem to be more ready to adopt their own voice.

The interpersonal and impersonal difference in the two patterns is clear. Interpersonal pattern students care about their peers' perspectives, want to know their peers, and want instructors to care about them. Relationships are central to the learning process because knowing others promotes sharing perspectives and sharing perspectives promotes adding to one's knowledge. If instructors are uncaring, teaching (and thus learning) is ineffective. For impersonal pattern students these themes did not surface. Although no student wants to be mistreated by instructors, impersonal pattern students prefer challenge to caring. Perhaps this reflects the impersonal pattern students' focus on individual learning whereas the interpersonal pattern students focus on the relationships made possible during learning. Considering peer relationships as a point of departure toward independent knowing, we could expect that interpersonal pattern students would have little difficulty accepting peers' views as valid. For them this will be an extension of knowing in the uncertain arena. For impersonal pattern students a shift will be required to add peers (and themselves) to the ranks of authority.

Independent Knowing

The core assumption of uncertainty in independent knowing changes both the process and the source of knowing substantially. The shift is evident in Laura's description of her discovery of uncertainty:

> Everything's relative; there's no truth in the world, that sort of thing. So I've decided that the only person that you can really depend on is yourself. Each individual has their own truth. No one has the right to decide, "This has to be your truth, too." As long as you feel—it feels right, then it must be right because if everybody is stuck on, "What do the other people think?" then you just waste your whole life. You just do what you feel like you have to do. That's why sometimes I felt that I had to get into business because everybody was going into business. I don't think the world rotates around the business world and

money and materialism. Now I'm relaxed and I'm thinking of what
I want, what's best for me and not for anybody else.

Given this newfound uncertainty, discrepancies among authorities represent the variety of views possible in an uncertain world. Authorities are no
longer the only sources of knowledge but instead become equal with students, who for the first time view their opinions as valid. The emergence of
self-authored knowledge rivets the student's attention on thinking for oneself. Learning how to think independently involves expressing one's own
views as well as hearing others. Instructors are expected to promote this type
of activity in class. They are no longer responsible for providing knowledge;
they are responsible for providing the context in which to explore knowledge. Evaluation, likewise, should reward independent thinking and should
not penalize the student for holding views different from the instructor or
authors of texts. Peers become a legitimate source of knowledge rather than
part of the process of knowing. Independent knowers emphasize being
open-minded and allowing people to believe what they will, as illustrated
by Laura's comment on how she decides what to believe: "I don't know
[how I decide on my opinion]. Something works inside my head and it's
just there."

Gender-related patterns appeared in independent knowing as well. The
interindividual pattern was used more often by women than men in the
study. Interindividual pattern knowers believed that different perspectives resulted from each person bringing her or his own interpretation, or in some
cases bias, to a particular knowledge claim. They simultaneously advocated
listening to other interpretations or biases and espousing their own perspectives, describing how the interaction of the two helped them form their
perspective. Alexus offered an example of this view during her fifth-year interview. Reflecting on her senior year classes, she commented that the senior
year was a time "when you should be most open because you should be able
to listen to what other people say and then come up with your own opinion
on how you feel about a particular thing." Asked how she did that, she
replied,

> I listen to their arguments for it and then I listen to other people's
> arguments against it. And then basically it's just my own personal
> view really, whether I can establish the credibility-so I guess it real-
> ly stems from credibility of the person who's saying it also, as well as
> just the opinion on it. I listen to both sides. Really I usually throw
> some of my own views into it as well. So I'm influenced by other
> people, but in the end I think that each—like each member of the
> group should be influenced by each other. But then when the final
> vote comes in, you should go with what you believe.

Alexus valued hearing others' ideas and felt people should be influenced by one another. She simultaneously held her own view and tried to integrate it with the views of others she perceived as credible.

The *individual pattern* knowers, like their interindividual pattern counterparts, espoused thinking independently and exchanging views with others. However, their primary focus was on their thinking, and they sometimes struggled to listen carefully to other voices. Fully acknowledging that everyone had her or his own beliefs, individual pattern knowers described the role theirs played when differences of opinion took place. Lowell shared an experience in which he and other students had different ideas:

> I'd consider myself conservative. And there was one guy in our group who was quite liberal and acknowledged it. I guess it gave me another viewpoint, another aspect to look at this. Like it or not we're all kind of ingrained one way or another, whether it's to the liberal end or the conservative end. He looked at it in this way and I looked at it in another way. And everybody in the group had their own ways on it. It was a spectrum of—and to try to get your point across without sounding too dominating—I'm searching for words and not finding them. To try to listen to theirs, to really listen, not to just hear it and let it go through. And then to try to take that into account and reach a compromise. There was quite a bit of discussion. But I don't think the attempt was to try to change each other's mind. It was just, "Your point is all right, but you've got to look at this part, too, because this is as relevant."

Lowell's genuine attempt to hear his liberal classmate and his insistence that his conservative perspective also be taken into account stopped short of changing either perspective.

The equality of numerous views in the face of prevailing uncertainty made independent thinking possible. Equality of perspectives also changed the relationship of the knower to her or his peers and to authority. In the case of interindividual pattern knowers this prompted connection to peers and to authority. Connection to peers was evident earlier for interpersonal transitional knowers, but interindividual pattern knowers became more open to peers' views. Their exchanges became interindividual by virtue of the knower including her or his own voice. When the potential hazards to connection posed by criticism were removed by equality of views, interindividual pattern knowers connected more intensely with their peers. This connection freed them to express their voices, which appear to have existed internally prior to this point. For them, the adjustment to independent knowing came in the form of including their own voices as equal to those of peers and of authority. Interindividual pattern knowers reconnected to authority once their own voices were legitimized. Thus, the interindividual pattern represents a union of one's own voice and the voices of others.

In the case of individual pattern knowers the equality of perspectives had a different effect on relationships with peers and authority. Peers' role in knowing created a relationship that bordered on becoming a connection. Individual pattern knowers listened to peers but struggled to hear them clearly and also to keep their own voices in the forefront. The adjustment to independent knowing for individual pattern knowers came in the form of including other voices as equal to one's own. Their voices, expressed routinely in previous ways of knowing, were slightly threatened by the genuine consideration of others' voices. Their interest in and attempt to hold both voices in balance appeared to mark the beginning of genuine connection to others. At the same time, equality of views seemed to free individual pattern knowers from authority to pursue their own independent thinking. The individual pattern includes both self-authored knowledge and the views of others, with the balance of the scale tipped toward self-authored knowledge.

The variation in interindividual and individual knowing can also be cast in the language of communion and agency (Bakan 1966). Communion involves connection and relationship with others whereas agency involves separateness from others. Both patterns moved toward communion: interindividual pattern knowers in terms of intense openness to others' views and individual pattern knowers in terms of genuine consideration of others' views. Both patterns also moved toward agency in the emergence of self-authored knowledge and for individual pattern knowers in separation from authority in the learning process. The degree of movement toward communion or agency is best understood in light of the degree to which either was reflected in earlier ways of knowing. Receiving and interpersonal pattern knowers demonstrated communion in previous ways of knowing, but agency represented a shift for them. Mastery and impersonal pattern knowers demonstrated agency in earlier ways of knowing so that communion represented a shift for them. While interindividual pattern knowers still lean toward communion and individual pattern knowers still lean toward agency, both are moving closer together than in previous ways of knowing.

Contextual Knowing: Relational and Impersonal Modes Intertwined
The fourth set of epistemological assumptions noticeable for a few students toward the end of college emerged more completely during the postcollege interviews. Contextual knowers looked at all aspects of a situation or issue, sought out expert advice in that particular context, and integrated their own and others' views in deciding what to think. Gwen, reflecting on her senior

year, illustrates this perspective in her comment on whether to believe others' viewpoints: "I don't care if people feel this way or that way about it. But if they can support their stance and have some background and backing for that, to my thinking that is valid." The student voice develops to the point of cognitive self-authorship; both peers and authority have valid knowledge if they can support their stance.

Perhaps the most striking characteristic of contextual knowing is the integration of relational and impersonal modes of knowing. Although relational and impersonal patterns emerged as distinct in previous ways of knowing, contextual knowing necessitated both. Contextual knowers felt that rationality in terms of consulting experts and processing evidence was necessary but simultaneously valued working through their perspectives by accessing their own experience and others' perspectives. Contextual knowing involved constructing one's perspective in the context of one's experience, available information, and the experiences of others. Unlike independent knowers, contextual knowers are unwilling to rely solely on their own perspective or rely solely on the perspectives of others. They attempt to integrate constructing their own perspective with remaining open to considering others' thoughts as part of the process. Contextual knowers make judgments about others' perspectives as well as about information related to the issue under consideration. Contextual knowing incorporates the relational pattern evident in earlier forms of knowing through its focus on accessing one's own and others' perspectives and experiences (Baxter Magolda 1995). Once thinking is connected to, or anchored in, the self, standing outside one's experience is viewed as productive. Contextual knowing incorporates the impersonal pattern evident in earlier forms of knowing through its focus on establishing, or constructing, one's own belief system by abstractly processing experience and information.

Reginald's struggle to establish his perspective and simultaneously remain open to new ideas illustrates how the relational and the impersonal patterns came together in his experience. As Reginald introduced important learning experiences he had encountered in seminary, he brought up his struggle to sort out the meaning of intellect and emotion during his second year there:

> I think what I struggle with . . . is to claim it, to claim the experience. . . . I have to have that identity of what I do believe before I can be—well, not before—but along with the open mind and the openness to other views and respecting that. Because if not I'm just sort of wishy-washy, flimsying around, "Oh, okay, okay." And then if anyone asks, "Well, what do you believe?" "Well, I'm just open to

anything." I think that's part of what I was talking about, that self-identity. What is it that makes—that's part of what makes you who you are. That's perhaps the intellect, and then when you live it, that's the emotion or the passion perhaps that you bring to what you do. . . . The belief is sort of a clay that is not hardened, that is always being molded. It can shift; it can take new forms. But it's still the same, still a belief system within your self-identity, within your experience that won't deny your experience. It won't completely just blow away like sand, but it will form and it will be consistent—it has some weight to it.

Reginald chose the word *intellect* to capture the experience he has claimed, the basis of what he believes. Claiming this experience and what he believes forms an identity that helps him balance accessing others' thoughts and acknowledging his experience. He explains this notion further through the idea of boundaries:

In defining that self, identifying that self, is the creation of boundaries in what we do personally and publicly. . . . If I didn't have that boundary I might not bring out what it is that I need, what it is that I do believe if we're talking about—it can be theological, it can be academic, it can be personal. If I disregard the boundary I can be overwhelmed or just I won't be able to present who I am and what it is that I need. . . . I always considered the word *boundary* as a barrier. And so if I created these things I would be . . . a closed-minded person; I would be a person that when it came to—there wasn't a meeting place because there was this wall in the way. The other person would come to one side of the wall; I'd come to the other side of the wall. And we'd look at brick. And there wouldn't be a place where I could meet them. . . . And if I have those barriers I'm not—well, if I created what I thought would be barriers, I wouldn't have that. But also if I don't have anything, if I don't have boundaries, I lose the sense of who I am and I can't learn. And that's another thing: it restricts my learning and restricts other people's learning because I do bring something to that experience.

Reginald's claiming of intellect connects his belief system to himself, resulting in establishing an identity (the intrapersonal dimension of self-authorship). The boundaries of the identity keep him from being consumed as he meets others in dialogue (the interpersonal dimension of self-authorship). His thoughts suggest that effective connection with others does require some separation—in his case maintaining his self-identity. He argues that one cannot effectively "meet" others without having a self-identity. Reginald's perspective illustrates contextual knowers' integration of knowing via communion and agency. It also illustrates the development of self-authorship with regard to considering evidence—in this case his and others' beliefs and experience-in deciding what to believe.

Summary

Students' epistemic assumptions as well as their reasoning patterns affect the learning process. Expectations of instructors, peers, and learners themselves change as assumptions about the nature of knowledge change and vary according to reasoning patterns. Absolute knowers acquire information from authorities, either by listening (receiving) or by actively questioning and responding to authority (mastery). Transitional knowers focus on understanding knowledge; some do so via accessing others' views regarding uncertainty (interpersonal), and others do so via being forced to think (impersonal). Independent knowers feel free to decide their own opinions. Interindividual pattern students focus primarily on their peers' views in this process whereas individual pattern students focus primarily on their own views. The relational and impersonal dimensions merge in contextual knowing in which students construct knowledge by judging the evidence, others' views, and their own beliefs. Following students longitudinally revealed that their epistemic assumptions evolved from absolute to contextual over the course of the study. Absolute knowing was prevalent during the first two years of college and virtually disappeared by the senior year. Transitional knowing was prevalent during college but dissipated after college. Independent knowing emerged late in college and developed further after college. Contextual knowing was rare in college but developed for most participants in the years following college.

Three threads, or story lines, weave through the four ways of knowing and gender-related patterns—developing the student voice, changing relationships with authority, and changing relationships with peers. As epistemic assumptions evolved, the student voice changed from an echo of authority to an expression of the student's own perspective. Relationships with authority changed as the view of them as omnipotent gave way to viewing them as experts in a given context. Relationships with peers also developed as they evolved from simply helping one understand what authority had said to people whose views counted as valid knowledge if they became experts in a context. All three story lines are mediated by students' cognitive, intrapersonal, and interpersonal development. Because epistemological development is intertwined with these other strands of development, exploring their role is necessary to connect to students' experience in the learning process.

SELF-EVOLUTION

The Epistemological Reflection model traces the evolution of student voice in the context of students' assumptions about the nature of knowledge. Students' ability to view themselves as knowers, as persons who can construct valid knowledge, is mediated in part by their self-definition in a broader sense. Kegan's (1982, 1994) constructive-developmental description of the intrapersonal and interpersonal dimensions of self-authorship adds important insights to the epistemological dimension described here. Although numerous theorists describe these dimensions, I use Kegan here because he views these dimensions as an integral part of growth of the mind. Kegan argues that people make meaning from various "orders of the mind," each characterized by a particular organizing principle that affects thinking, feeling, and relating to self and others. These principles are *how* we make meaning of our thinking, feeling, and social relating, not the content of our meaning-making. He describes the core—or structure—of these organizing principles as the subject-object relationship. He defines *object* as "those elements of our knowing or organizing that we can reflect on, handle, look at, be responsible for, relate to each other, take control of, internalize, assimilate, or otherwise operate on" (1994, 32). *Subject,* in contrast, "refers to those elements of our knowing or organizing that we are identified with, tied to, fused with, or embedded in" (1994, 32). The difference, then, is that we cannot operate on what is subject because we cannot stand apart from it. Kegan states, "We *have* object; we *are* subject" (32, italics in original).

Kegan (1994) emphasizes that evolution of the subject-object relationship gives rise to evolution of the organizing principles we use to make meaning. Because what are subject and object for us are not permanent but change as we adjust to account for new experiences, dimensions of our cognitive, intrapersonal, and interpersonal meaning-making that are subject in one organizing principle, or order of the mind, become object in the next. Each new principle subsumes the prior one, resulting in a more complex way of making meaning. Kegan explains, "Liberating ourselves from that in which we were embedded, making what was subject into object so that we can 'have it' rather than be 'had by it'—this is the most powerful way I know to conceptualize the growth of the mind" (1994, 34). Describing the evolution of what are subject and object, Kegan traces five structures through which people make meaning. Two of Kegan's five orders of the mind are most relevant for understanding the meaning-making activity of college-age students and adults.

The Structure of Self-Development

Kegan describes the third order of mind as

> the mental capacity that enables one to think abstractly, identify a complex internal psychological life, orient to the welfare of a human

relationship, construct values and ideals self-consciously known as such, and subordinate one's own interests on behalf of one's greater loyalty to maintaining bonds of friendship, or team or group participation. (1994, 75)

He indicates that this particular balance of what is subject and what is object usually evolves sometime in the teenage years. Its cognitive characteristics—the ability to reason abstractly and to think hypothetically and deductively—are in contrast to the previous order of mind in which these were subject, making the adolescent's thinking concrete. The intrapersonal achievements of the third order are the ability to distinguish between one's needs and oneself (needs were previously subject; now they are object) and to identify enduring qualities of the self. These achievements are made possible by the ability to internalize others' points of view and to coordinate more than one point of view internally, thus the ability to hold values and ideals. This internal coordination also makes possible a change in the interpersonal dimension, that of orienting to shared feelings rather than interacting with others based on getting one's own needs met. This orientation makes subordinating one's own interests on behalf of relationships possible.

The third order of mind is likely to be prevalent among college students, based on Kegan's research (1994). He reports that this order usually evolves sometime between the ages of twelve and twenty, and that half to two-thirds of the adult population have yet to evolve to the fourth order. The third order of mind equips students with some of the cognitive processes to engage in knowledge construction (e.g., ability to think abstractly, hypothetically, deductively). Yet the intrapersonal dimension of the third order embeds the student in making meaning through shared realities with others who are external to the self. Because the system by which meaning is made rests outside the self, the student does not see himself as capable of self-authorship. Being subject to (or "had by" in Kegan's language) shared realities also potentially explains the strong influence of peers in how younger students determine what to believe about themselves, knowledge, values, and their relationships with others. Because their sense of self is coconstructed out of the relation between theirs and others' perspectives, the relationships they participate in heavily influence their sense of self. Kegan notes that "this bringing inside of the other's point of view, this co-construction of the self, . . . is the triumph and limit of the third order" (1994, 126). The triumph is an ability to become a part of society; the limit is the inability to stand apart from this coconstruction to reflect and act upon it. Common campus issues such as abusive dating relationships, alcohol abuse, and even fraternity hazing might be understood more effectively by understanding how the third order of mind makes meaning.

Kegan notes that values, beliefs, convictions, generalizations, ideals, abstractions, interpersonal loyalty, and intrapersonal states of mind are all subject in the third order. The fourth order is more complex because

> it takes all of these as objects or elements of its system, rather than the system itself; it does not identify with them but views them as parts of a new whole. This new whole is an ideology, an internal identity, a *self-authorship* that can coordinate, integrate, act upon, or invent values, beliefs, convictions, generalizations, ideals, abstractions, interpersonal loyalties, and intrapersonal states. It is no longer *authored by* them, it *authors them* and thereby achieves a personal authority. (1994, 185, italics in original)

This system brings the creation of belief "inside" the self, separate from the shared realities and coconstructions of the third order. The existence of this system that generates beliefs makes self-authorship of knowledge possible. It also makes possible identity formation that is more enduring than the earlier coconstructed versions because the internal self is the source of belief rather than the social surround that was the source of belief in the third order. The ability to relate to one's intrapersonal states, rather than being made up by them, makes it possible to see oneself as the maker (rather than experiencer) of one's inner psychological life. The same ability to relate to one's interpersonal relationships, rather than being made up by them, makes it possible to separate self from relationships with others, to in fact have a relationship to those relationships.

These fourth order capacities form the basis for self-authorship in the cognitive, intrapersonal, and interpersonal dimensions of self-evolution. Complex epistemological development, particularly contextual knowing, necessitates fourth order meaning-making because it necessitates self-authorship. Although self-authorship emerges for the first time in independent knowing, the independent knower is unable to articulate the system through which her beliefs have been established. They no longer come from authority, but it is not clear that they were generated from an internal self-system either. It is likely that early independent knowing is consistent with the third order and that the transition from independent to contextual knowing is consistent with the evolution from third to fourth order.

MULTIPLE VOICES WITHIN SELF-EVOLUTION

Just as I described gender-related patterns as qualitatively different but equally complex preferences *within* the structure of ways of knowing, theorists have described gender-related patterns in intrapersonal and interpersonal development that Kegan suggests are stylistic preferences existing *within* the structure of orders of the mind. Carol Gilligan (1982) brought the issue of gender-related voices to the attention of developmental theorists and educators in the context of moral orientations. She argued that women often used a care voice in making moral judgments, focusing on responsibility in moral contexts, in contrast to what she called the justice voice, which focused on rights. Research in this arena resulted in identification of a connected, or relational, preference that was often evident in the study of women and a separate preference often evident in the study of men. These preferences seem to reflect Bakan's (1966) communion and agency notions. These preferences have been the source of exploration in most areas of human development; those most closely related to the intrapersonal and interpersonal dimensions are highlighted here.

Chickering (1969) articulated the psychosocial issues of college students as establishing competence, managing emotions, and developing autonomy as precursors to identity after which developing mature interpersonal relationships, purpose, and integrity was possible. His initial theory, based on males, implied that independence was a precursor to a healthy identity and to mature relationships with others. Josselson's (1987) exploration of college women's identity development revealed the integration of connection with others and developing one's sense of self. She concluded that identity development described as agency (e.g., Chickering's theory), or a process toward a separate self, was less important to women than identity development characterized by communion or connection to others. Relationship to others was also central in Straub's (1987) study of women's autonomy development in college. She reported that 36 percent of the critical events students reported as central to autonomy involved connection to others, leading her to conclude that women work on autonomy from a connected standpoint. Lyons (1983) also confirmed two definitions of self-one connected to others and one separate from others. Chickering and Reisser (1993) reframed Chickering's original picture of identity to reflect the voice of connection. Identity development can take place with either separation or connection as the base.

Taub and McEwen (1991) addressed this same issue in comparing white and African-American undergraduate women's development of autonomy and interpersonal relationships. They report that few differences occurred; the data indicate that both groups were concerned with both tasks simultaneously through college. Branch-Simpson (1984) found that both male and female African-American college students stayed connected to others during autonomy development and identity formation as well as in learning. African-American adolescents apparently value connection as well (Ward 1989). Ward also argues that race plays a role in identity development. Parham (1989) describes the additional dynamics African-American students face as they work through the degree to which they endorse Afrocentric or Eurocentric components in identity and encounter others' perceptions of them as African-Americans. In part their identity formation depends on their preference for and encounter of inclusion or exclusion in the campus environment. Kegan (1994) notes that while individuality and separation are promoted by much of North American culture, connection and maintenance of attachment are promoted by many South American, African, and Asian cultures (as, I would add, Native American cultures). He points out that these different expectations may lead to members of those cultures using preferences that stem from their culture. Collectively, the identity development literature conveys that both inclusion (or connection) and independence (or autonomy) are at the core of defining self for white and African-American adolescents and young adults. The voice adopted by the person indicates the preference in the self-evolution process.

Clarifying the distinction between structure and style, or preference, Kegan describes the connected and separate voices as figure and ground rather than as a polarity or dichotomy. He states,

> Some of us may make the experience of connection the base from which we then move toward experiences of agency that may also be greatly important to us. Others may make the experience of independence the base from which we then move to experiences of connection that may also be precious to us or of paramount importance. (1994, 218)

It is possible for a third order mind to be either "connected . . . relationally embedded in the psychological surround . . . or separate . . . separately embedded in the psychological surround" (Kegan 1994, 220). Likewise, the fourth order mind can be either relationally or separately self-authorizing. Kegan uses the contrast between "deciding for oneself" and "deciding by oneself" to explain. Deciding for oneself, or self-authorship, represents the structure of the fourth order. However, within that structure, one could decide by oneself (separate) or decide with others (connected). Regardless of style, the key element here is deciding for oneself. Similarly, independent knowers who are all moving toward self-authorship in knowledge construction may do so in relation to others (the interindividual pattern) or in separation from others (the individual pattern). Understanding both structure and style helps teachers understand how their students make meaning.

TRANSLATING STUDENT DEVELOPMENT INTO EDUCATIONAL PRACTICE

Portraits of students' cognitive, intrapersonal, and interpersonal development illustrate the complexity of achieving self-authorship as a young adult. Teaching to promote self-authorship requires understanding the evolution of meaning-making structures that bring it about as well as the stylistic preferences students exhibit within structures. Creating the conditions for students to reorganize their meaning-making structures toward those that reflect self-authorship requires connecting with students' experience in two ways. First, instructors must be able to connect to students' current meaning-making structures in order to determine the kind of experiences that might call those structures into question. Recall Doonesbury's teacher at the outset of this chapter; the conditions he created in his classroom did not connect with his students' assumptions that knowledge was certain, and therefore, they misinterpreted his teaching behavior. Had he instead engaged them in an exploration of how the Constitution was created, by whom and for what purposes, he might have enticed them to call the authority of the writers into question. The traditional objectivist approach to education, in which the learner is separate from knowledge, reinforces early epistemic assumptions that are inconsistent with self-authorship.

Second, connecting to students' stylistic preferences within structures also heightens the probability of their meaningful engagement in reorganizing their ways of making meaning. Kegan argues that the institutionalization of one voice (either separation or connection) gives the persons preferring that voice "home court advantage," leaving those preferring the noninstitutionalized voice feeling like "visitors" (1994, 214). The institutionalization of the separate voice in education could make, and probably has made, connected voice persons feel marginalized. Students who are connection oriented tend to identify less with their teachers as authorities (Baxter Magolda 1992; Belenky et al. 1986; Holland and Eisenhart 1990). If a connection does not exist between student and teacher, yet the student is connection oriented, that connection must be found elsewhere. Some evidence suggests that connection-oriented students find these links with the peer group. Because third order students coconstruct themselves with their peer group, this connection can be detrimental to the evolution of self-authorship if the peer group does not value it. This possibility is most evident in Holland and Eisenhart's (1990) ethnography of African-American and white college women. Studying women on two campuses, they found the women caught up in a culture of romance through which they anticipated, interpreted, and evaluated their experience (probably an example of third order coconstruction of self). Gaining prestige through making themselves attractive to men occupied considerable energy whereas less attention was devoted to academic work. Only five of the twenty-two women balanced peer expectations and academic work to their favor; the remaining seventeen downsized their career and academic aspirations.

Fordham and Ogbu (1986) report similar circumstances with African-American adolescents at Capital High who intentionally scaled back or hid their academic prowess to maintain connection with their peer group—a peer group that viewed academic success as acting white. The adolescent girls Brown and Gilligan (1992) followed also chose to stop expressing their true thoughts in order to be perceived as the "perfect girl" and in doing so exchanged authentic relationships for idealized ones. In the process of maintaining these idealized relationships, they lost their voices and self-authorization. Shared realities with peers in all these cases probably reinforced third order meaning-making. Had these third order students been able to join a shared reality with their teachers, they might have had opportunities to coconstruct themselves differently as it relates to learning, as well as receive encouragement to analyze the source of their values and beliefs.

When connection to the learning environment is possible, the evolution of self-authorship is more likely. The five women in Holland and Eisenhart's study who were able to avoid consumption by their peer group held learning as an important component of their identity. The peer culture can also promote knowing as important, as was the case in my longitudinal study. The receiving, interpersonal, and interindividual pattern students found themselves in a peer culture that supported thinking and exploring ideas. Their relationships with peers helped to develop their voices, and through these relationships, they were able to integrate knowing as a central part of their identities. These shared realities, like ones that could be constructed with teachers, included rather than excluded the notion of self-authorship. It is possible that they also set the conditions for evolution into the fourth order (a topic taken up in detail in chap. 3).

Students' development suggests that greater connection in the teaching-learning relationship is useful for creating the conditions that promote self-authorship. Creating these conditions is in effect building a bridge between students' current meaning-making and the structures of meaning-making that reflect self-authorship. Yet it is impossible to build a bridge to something that one does not understand. Most teachers' lived experience is different from that of many of their students, or when similarities do exist, time and growth have a way of diminishing understanding of perspectives previously held. Most teachers have not been exposed to the developmental literature that describes students' meaning-making. It is also impossible to define students as an aggregate in order to provide teachers with a blueprint of students' experience. Connection, given the complexity of student development and learning, can feel like trying to connect to a moving target. Thus, the primary task in connection is the process of accessing and valuing student experience, the dialogue advocated by educational theorists in chapter 1 to get into students' worlds. The next chapter outlines three principles that form a structure for connecting to students' ways of making meaning in learning and teaching. These principles, emerging from the longitudinal participants' stories about how learning connected to their experience, reveal how teachers can access and connect to students' experience, help students connect their experience to knowing, and promote student voice for students who use various ways and styles of making meaning.

CHAPTER 3

Crossing the Border

The student development portraits in chapter 2 suggest that students and educators live in different worlds. Students, like educators, make meaning of their experience from their own frame of reference. Accessing those frames of reference is necessary for educators to help students link their experience with knowledge construction and self-authorship. Bensimon's (1994) understanding of the metaphor of border crossing (Giroux 1992) is useful here. Bensimon argues that to understand others from their frames of reference, we must start with the others, returning to our own frame of reference only after we have captured how to make meaning from the others' point of view. This is not simply a matter of getting enough of an understanding to be able to shout across the border and be heard a little more effectively. It is a complex matter of being able to see the world from students' eyes and our own eyes simultaneously so that we can guide the connection of the two. Guiding the connection is also more complicated than getting students to see it our way. Giroux's (1992) notion of border crossing involves challenging and redefining existing borders that were formed in domination. In the case of teaching and learning, existing borders to challenge and redefine include the teacher-student relationship and students' role in knowledge construction.

Border crossing, however, is more easily articulated than implemented. Constructive-developmental educational practice offers a context for creating the conditions for border crossing. Kegan (1994) uses a bridge metaphor to describe developmental educational practice. Because meaning-making takes place in the context of a person's order of consciousness, understanding that order of consciousness and its effect on meaning-making is essential. Kegan argues that much of what contemporary society (including education) expects of students and young adults is "over their heads"; that is to say, the expectations require ways of making meaning beyond what the students currently hold. To help students develop the ways of making meaning necessary to meet these expectations, Kegan suggests creating

> a holding environment that provides both welcoming acknowledgment to exactly who the person is right now as he or she is, and fosters the person's psychological evolution. As such, a holding environment is a tricky, transitional culture, an evolutionary bridge, a context for crossing over. (43)

This evolutionary bridge must be both *meaningful* to students' current way of making meaning and *facilitative* of a more complex way of making meaning. Kegan notes that "we cannot simply stand on our favored side of the bridge and worry or fume about the many who have not yet passed over. A bridge must be well anchored on both sides, with as much respect for where it begins as for where it ends" (62).

Kegan's notion of welcoming the person as she or he is resonates with Nel Noddings's (1984) notion of engrossment. Noddings describes engrossment as "feeling with" another person, or receiving the other. This requires "apprehending the other's reality, feeling what he feels as nearly as possible" (16), rather than objectifying the other's experience by putting oneself in the other's shoes. For example, encountering a student who hates mathematics might lead a teacher to believe her student would be more successful if he loved mathematics, and she directs her energy toward that goal. Noddings recommends instead, "Begin . . . with the view from his eyes: Mathematics is bleak, jumbled, scary, boring, boring, boring. . . . What in the world could induce me to engage in it? From that point on, we struggle together with it" (15–16). Noddings emphasizes that engrossment is not simply a tool to acquire understanding to facilitate change, but a way of being with the other to welcome him or her into the interaction.

Mary Catherine Bateson (1994) offers a similar perspective on learning, advocating learning as coming home. She writes,

> If teachers were to approach their classes with an appreciation of how much their pupils already knew; helping to bring the structure of that informal knowledge into consciousness, students would have the feeling of being on familiar ground, already knowing much about how to know, how knowledge is organized and integrated. This might be one way for schooling to assume the flavor of learning as homecoming: learning to learn, knowing what you know, cognition recognized, knowledge acknowledged. (205–6)

Kegan, Noddings, and Bateson emphasize the need to respect students' knowledge and welcome them into the learning process.

An example highlights what it means to respect the students' side of Kegan's metaphorical bridge. Kegan (1993) describes two hypothetical teachers, both teaching the concept of irony in junior high school. The first teacher, whom Kegan calls Teacher A, starts by asking for a definition of irony. The first student to respond offers an example rather than a definition of irony. Teacher A notes that although it is a good example, it is not a definition and asks again for a definition. This cycle repeats until the students, able to give examples but not definitions, fall silent. Teacher A then gives the definition, which Kegan speculates students will write in their notebooks. Although Teacher A might perceive that he involved students in coming to an understanding, Kegan's interpretation is that the teacher promoted rote learning because he did not connect to the way the students were making meaning. Teacher A', however, does the lesson differently. She capitalizes on the first student's example, saying that it is a good example and asks for more examples. As the students offer more, she praises each one and circles it after putting it on the board. After collecting numerous examples, Teacher A' circles the whole set and invites the class to figure out what irony is in a way that will encompass all the examples. By going with the students' meaning-making, that is, thinking about examples in this case, Teacher A' engages them where they are, on their side of the bridge, yet maintains her goal of arriving at a reasonable definition. She tries, after meaningfully connecting to their side, to invite them to travel the bridge by stretching beyond examples to a definition. Kegan interprets the approach of Teacher A' as supporting cognitive construction and the exercise of cognitive structures.

Kegan's metaphor implies that both educator and student travel the bridge. The educator, with her ability to reflect on earlier orders of consciousness, listens carefully to students to understand how they make meaning. In doing so she travels to the students' side of the bridge to understand their world. Yet she is also aware of the other end of the bridge and new ways of making meaning that would help students function in modern society. She simultaneously respects students' current meaning-making and creates the transitional culture in which they can entertain more complex ways of making meaning. Her knowledge of both sides of the bridge makes it possible for her to connect the two worlds. If her bridge is well constructed, with genuine respect for the students' end, students will join her in crossing the bridge to new ways of making meaning.

This vision of developmental practice is founded on the notion that students use particular meaning-making structures until they both encounter and receive assistance in resolving discrepancies between experience and those structures. This is not to say that students are incapable of operating beyond their current structure; rather, they use the one they have learned until it no longer works effectively. Because the way students make meaning stems from organizing their experience, they construct structures that make sense of the experiences they encounter. For example, Shor (1992) notes that children's natural curiosity and speculation about the world disappear in exchange for the assumption that authorities know the answers—a structure that "makes sense" of much of traditional schooling experiences. King and Kitchener (1994) point out that students' ability to use more complex structures depends on whether educators expect, ask for, support, and model those structures in their interactions with students. Yet modeling complex structures without linking to students' current structures does not help them reorganize their structures because it "misses" the target of their development. A well-constructed bridge connects to students' current meaning-making but does not leave them there. This bridge, or transitional culture, creates what Giroux calls a borderland—a space "in which diverse cultural resources allow for the fashioning of new identities within existing configurations of power" (1992, 28). The transitional culture offers conditions in which students can challenge and redefine their epistemological, intrapersonal, and interpersonal borders.

Respecting students' ways of making meaning, or their side of the bridge, requires getting over the border to spend time listening to students' stories about their experience. When I started my longitudinal study of college students' epistemological development in 1986, I was unaware that I would be crossing any borders, visiting any other worlds, or learning how to access new worlds. Twelve years of annual interviews, however, have revealed numerous other worlds in which students and young adults live and make meaning of their experience. Discussions with my study participants during their college years yielded stories about how educators had entered their world and in so doing had promoted their epistemological development. From those stories I identified three principles that promote the emergence of student voice (Baxter Magolda 1992). They include validating students as knowers, situating learning in students' own experience, and defining learning as mutually constructing meaning. These principles are not unique to my study; versions of them abound in the educational and human development literature, suggesting that other listeners have heard similar reports. Principles from that literature are woven around those I heard from my participants. I explore the three principles my participants surfaced as ways of accessing students' experience as well as of connecting student and educator experience—in essence they form the underlying structure of constructive-developmental pedagogy. The principles are offered here as guides to creating the transitional cultures Kegan argues are necessary for growth of the mind.

THE THREE PRINCIPLES

In my annual interviews with students during their college years, I routinely asked them to describe teaching environments that they found helpful in promoting their learning.* Students described instructors' attitudes

*Portions of this description are reproduced with permission from Baxter Magolda, M. B. (1992). *Knowing and reasoning in college: Gender-related patterns in students' intellectual development.* San Francisco: Jossey Bass.

toward students, faculty-student interaction, teaching strategies, classroom structure, evaluation methods, and the way knowledge was presented. The themes that resulted from synthesizing their stories revealed three principles that serve as the foundation for the transitional culture Kegan advocates. The three principles include validating the student as a knower, situating learning in students' own experience, and defining learning as mutually constructing meaning (Baxter Magolda 1992). Although the three are inextricably intertwined, I discuss each separately here to highlight its contribution to the transitional context.

Validating the Student as a Knower

Recall that Kegan's evolutionary bridge, or transitional culture, offers "welcoming acknowledgment to exactly who the person is right now as he or she is" (1994, 43). This welcoming acknowledgment was essential for students to realize that they had a voice, a mind, and the permission to express themselves in the learning process. For my longitudinal study participants, this came in the form of a caring attitude toward students. Although caring attitude was described differently by students with different ways of knowing, the bottom line was concern for the student. For example, Fran explained, "My calculus prof knows my name and makes me feel like he cares to go out of his way. He says, 'Come to office hours and call for an appointment if you can't come [during regular] hours.' The teachers this year don't seem against you."

Similarly, Spencer reported that his physics professor "goes the extra mile for you" by handing back the homework and going over it so that students could see their mistakes. Fran's and Spencer's interpretations of these activities (inviting students to office hours and going over homework) as professors going out of their way to help students reveal that it did not take much for them to feel welcomed; perhaps just being *received,* to use Noddings's term, was sufficient for validation.

Sidney and Kelly elaborated on how feeling comfortable with instructors affected their learning. Sidney said,

> I feel more comfortable with professors who can relate to students and enjoy what they are doing. They are not higher than students. They can relate to students on their level, which makes it more interesting. They are accessible out of class to talk with you.

Kelly concurred, offering, "I am very comfortable talking with my professors. They care. They make us know they are there for us. They treat us as future professionals, rather than just students. The level of respect helps me bring in more of my own ideas."

Eileen shared a similar perspective, saying that "they don't talk down to you but meet you in the middle—mutual respect. . . . The teacher is more of a person instead of Dr. So-and-So."

These comments reveal that respect for students is an essential component of their feeling comfortable in working with professors. As Noddings (1991) noted, caring teachers make themselves present to students by starting with respect for the students' interests. The humanness of professors that emerges from their "not being against students" or "not being higher than students" contradicts the notion that educators and their knowledge are beyond the reach of students. Students encounter the frequent and friendly interaction with faculty that promotes intellectual and identity development (Chickering and Reisser 1993).

Students also described teaching strategies that welcomed them as they were, yet also offered the other dimension of Kegan's transitional culture, fostering their psychological evolution. Gwen captured the nature of these strategies, which for her occurred only in later years. She explained,

> As you get toward upper-level classes, there is a lot more one-on-one contact with the instructor and the students. The pedagogical relationship is not the same as it was when you were a freshman and the professor stands at the front of the room and lectures to the class. They try to know you personally; you call them by their first name. It's much more casual, informal, and, I think, more effective: seminars, a lot of active participation in discussion.

This change in the pedagogical relationship from the professor talking *at* the students to talking *with* them validated Gwen as a knower. She elaborated,

> I appreciate instructors who try to get to know you on your level rather than trying to set up the hierarchical structure. The student is less intimidated. And although you know that your experience and your background and your knowledge of the subject are not what your instructor's are, you still feel that your opinions and your ideas are valid.

By connecting to her experience, Gwen's professor validated her opinions and ideas. Gwen is still aware that the professor is more knowledgeable, yet she is less intimidated to share her ideas as a way to learn. She is welcomed as she is, yet her professor encourages her to join in thinking and talking about the subject. Gwen's instructor demonstrated a version of what Patricia King and Karen Kitchener (1994) call "showing respect for students as people regardless of the developmental level(s) they may be exhibiting" (231). Such respect results in greater willingness to entertain the shortcomings of current ways of thinking and try new ones that are less comfortable. Gwen noted that before her junior year, her teachers told her what to think, whereas in her junior year, "They say, 'What do you think?' And you [say to yourself], 'Oh, I'd better think of something.'" The respect Gwen senses from her professor makes it possible for her to enter into the transitional culture of trying to think of something. Gwen's insights also clarify that it is not what she thinks that is necessarily validated, but that she is capable of thinking. Her professor offered her the combination of challenge and support King and Kitchener recommend for promoting reflective thinking—cognitive challenge to entertain her own ideas and emotional support in the form of respect for doing so. Gwen's experience illustrates teaching that involves active learning, encourages faculty-student contact, and respects diverse ways of knowing—the kind of teaching that promotes intellectual, interpersonal, and intrapersonal development (Chickering and Reisser 1993).

Teaching strategies in which instructors rewarded students for taking risks at thinking offered a bridge that facilitated students' growth, made possible by the respect that was inherent in the teaching strategy. For example, Tracy shared:

> The professor encouraged us to critique theory. He made it comfortable to do this because he was down to earth. He gave us real-life examples to relate to. He played devil's advocate—I was initially intimidated because you're conditioned to accept the teacher's view. But he rewarded us for challenging him, and we learned more.

Tracy's side of the bridge was respected—the teacher was down to earth and gave her real-life examples. He also rewarded the students for challenging him. This respect made it possible for Tracy and her peers to express their own voices, thus fostering growth in meaning-making.

Students reported that their validation as knowers even took place in evaluation of their work. Valerie explained that in one class students had input in the multiple choice exam. She said, "If we chose an answer and we thought that another answer might be right also, we got to explain why we thought it was that answer, which I think really helped a lot." Marge liked essays for a similar reason, saying, "I can voice my opinion and see what the teacher thinks about what I'm thinking." Students did not expect every idea they presented to be validated, but appreciated being validated as knowers by having the teacher listen to their thinking. This is an example of what Kegan meant by respecting both sides of the bridge.

When teachers did not offer that respect, students stopped offering their ideas. Deirdre described a journal in which she was working out her thoughts. The professor responded with a query in the margin: "Are you some feminist?" Deirdre took that as a lack of respect for her as a knower and said, "I didn't write any more after that."

Validating students as knowers also occurs through the remaining two principles. However, the educator's concern for the student, respect for the student as a person and a learner, and willingness to engage in a relationship of mutual respect allow students to feel valued as knowers. It is the "welcoming acknowledgment" of who the student is that enables the student to risk traveling to more complex ways of making meaning.

SITUATING LEARNING IN THE STUDENT'S OWN EXPERIENCE

Another aspect of welcoming students as they are is to welcome their experience (both their life experience and their meaning-making) into the learning process. Many students leave their life experience at the classroom door, thinking that it is irrelevant to academic learning. Deirdre expressed this notion in her comment that "in school, you kind of leave your personal life and your personal experience out of what you do academically. And everything's supposed to be kind of detached and formal." Many educators, particularly those in the positivist tradition, reinforce this view by never connecting learning to students' experience. However, the longitudinal study participants reported some educators who did incorporate students' experience in learning, helping students to connect something familiar with new learning. Students began to view themselves as more capable of self-authorship (a new way of making meaning for many) when they were able to use their own experience in learning.

Using their own experience in learning took place in various degrees. The most basic form involved teachers linking the subject to real life. For example, Art reported,

> Our chemistry professor does things that help you relate. Talks about chemicals that curl hair, for example, or nitrates in red meat. He puts it into real life. Sometimes the information is just straight technical. It is hard to understand without ties to the real world.

Art's comments demonstrate that the instructor is relating the material to some experience Art understands. Educators' use of contexts with which students identify can be as simple as language. For example, using *he* as generic aids men in visualizing the idea at hand but causes women to "blank out" because the imagery does not apply to them (Thorne 1990). Students whose experience is not included feel marginalized; they do not feel the welcome acknowledgment necessary for them to participate in the transitional culture. Using language and examples that include students is a basic way of respecting both sides of the bridge.

A more substantial form of situating learning in students' experience is to use students' actual experience, or let them tell their stories. Advocates of using narrative in learning (e.g., McEwan and Egan 1995; Witherell and Noddings 1991) address this principle, as does liberatory pedagogy's focus on generating themes from students' lives (Freire 1970; Shor 1992). Deirdre described how this happened in her college experience and its effect:

> I like writing a journal a lot. I could be a lot more personal and write about things that were really foremost in my mind. I kind of got them out of my head and dealt with. I could look at things a little more objectively and kind of know better where I stood or how I felt about something . . . it's much more of an academic and inter-personal interspersed in the writing. That's what makes it so rele-vant, sort of brings everything together and makes the learning experience that much more powerful. You're finally given an audi-ence to listen to how you feel and kind of legitimize it. I guess, you know, just finding a voice and kind of exploring how you got to where you are.

Deirdre was able to tell her story in her journal. Connecting her experience to the issues dealt with in the class helped her figure out how she felt about the topics at hand. Journals are one mechanism through which teachers can respond individually to students' various epistemic assumptions. These indi-vidualized responses, based on understanding students' particular epistemic assumptions, can be tailored to welcome, yet facilitate movement from, cur-rent assumptions (King and Kitchener 1994).

Other students reported sharing their experience through class discus-sions and gaining perspectives from others in the process. In this way in-structors can help students tell their own stories and expose students to new perspectives simultaneously, a condition Chickering and Reisser (1993) ad-vance for promoting intellectual development. For example, Alice shared how students' experience enhanced a class on rural America:

> One student is from Japan. And when we talk about small towns and culture here, she talks about Japan. It makes you think about stuff a whole new different way. And what's funny is that I figured if you took a class on rural America, there would be more people in there from a small town. But it turns out that I'm the only one. There's a lot of stereotypes that everyone thinks about small towns, and I've been refuting them left and right. But then I have a lot of stereotypes about big cities. It's just interesting to see everyone's point of view.

Alice values sharing her perspective and hearing the perspective of her classmate from Japan. Alice thinks she and her peers have something to offer, and appar-ently, their instructor created a context in which they could share their stories.

Connection between students' experience and a particular area of knowl-edge can also be accomplished by creating real-life learning environments to generate experiences students do not already possess. Class projects offer one way to create experiences from which students can learn the subject matter. For example, Barry described a project in which he and his peers developed a new marketing plan for a company. They worked with an actual company, and after initial guidance from the professor, they assessed the needs of their client and formulated a plan. Barry described how he felt about this type of learning:

> [When] you're actually out there, seeing the results coming back. And, again, it wasn't someone else doing the work, and then you just have a case study on it: "Okay, here's this, this, this. . . . Now what do you recommend?" Well, we had to find out what this, this, and this is. And then we had to make a recommendation. And that was basically the true learning process.

Interacting with a real client, looking at real results, and working through the information were the "true" learning process for Barry because he could relate to the task rather than do it in the abstract. Similarly, many students described Laws, Hall, and Associates, an interdisciplinary course in which students developed promotional advertising campaigns for real corporate clients, as the best learning experience of their college years. These experiences engaged students directly with ill-structured problems characterized by uncertainty and multiple perspectives (as King and Kitchener advise) and provided them with support to tackle making judgments, thereby challenging them to achieve more complex ways of knowing.

Noting real-life examples, sharing stories, and engaging in real-life learning welcomed students as knowers. Using stories promoted self-authorship because students had to analyze their own and others' perspectives. Participating in real-life learning experiences promoted self-authorship because students had to analyze data and take responsibility for decisions that affected real people. This type of learning supported students in relating to the content, investing in learning, and feeling valued as knowers. This support enabled them to participate in the challenge of constructing meaning with their professors.

LEARNING AS MUTUALLY CONSTRUCTING MEANING

Inherent in this principle is the assumption that educational interaction will shape both students and educators—that the meaning made will result from a dialogue in which both voices are considered. Mark described it like this: "To make it clear to the student that the teacher's also a student and that we're all in the classroom engaged in kind of a joint venture. 'I can learn from you, you can learn from me' approach." Mark was describing the dialogue advocated by Shor and Freire (1987): "Dialogue is the sealing together of the teacher and the students in the joint act of knowing and re-knowing the object of study" (100). As noted in chapter 1, Shor clarifies that this does not mean the educator gives up his knowledge; rather, he introduces it in the context of students' perspectives, bringing it to the dialogue but not imposing it unilaterally.

To avoid imposing her knowledge, the educator must move away from the position of omnipotent authority. Longitudinal study participants noted that they saw this take place in two ways. First, they experienced educators who shared their thinking process in class. Belenky, Clinchy, Goldberger, and Tarule (1986) note that instructors usually prepare their thoughts in private and go to class prepared to speak from this previously considered perspective. When this occurs, students see only the final version of the teacher's thoughts, not the process of creating them. Educators who admitted that they did not know and engaged in dialogue with students were perceived as open-minded. Marla explained:

> Our teacher is very open-minded. Someone will bring up something and she'll say, "Oh, I never thought of that" or "that's a good point." Or someone will ask a question and she'll say, "I don't know." Just honest, no pretenses. She also gives you a blank paper with your multiple choice test so if you think a question is ambiguous you can explain yourself. She may give partial or full credit. It makes you feel like she cares what I have to say; she thinks that I have a brain and that I may not put the thing that she wanted me to put, but a least I have my own reason for why I did it.

Marla's teacher not only admitted it when she did not know something, but also praised students for coming up with ideas she had not thought about. When Marla's teacher considered the students' explanations about their choices on tests, she demonstrated that she was willing to allow students' ideas to shape her own, yet she used her own expertise as well. By participating in the dialogue, the teacher communicated to Marla that both their perspectives were important. Marla was more willing to participate because the teacher cared what she had to say. Bruner (1986) describes this as the student "becomes party to the negotiatory process by which facts are created and interpreted. He becomes at once an agent of knowledge making as well as a recipient of knowledge transmission" (127). King and Kitchener advocate bringing students into this negotiatory process by "familiarizing students with ill-structured problems within your own discipline or areas of expertise" (1994, 233). Ill-structured problems are problems that cannot be resolved with a high degree of certainty and about which experts often disagree (King and Kitchener 1994, 11). Offering students the opportunity to struggle with such problems creates situations in which different viewpoints can be examined, and students can be encouraged to make judgments and explain what they believe—two conditions that King and Kitchener believe foster complex thinking.

The second way educators moved away from the position of omnipotent authority was to share leadership with their students. Mark described how a person he called "the best professor of my career" demonstrated this approach:

> There'd be a movie. She'd sit on the side of the classroom—out of the position of asymmetrical relations—the power source being in the front of the room. She'd throw out a question and have us discuss it. If she thought the reactions were getting a little major or whatever, she'd throw in a voice of support. But she'd suggest something to keep it going. Just perfect comments to make sure that the class used the correct critiques or the critique she was teaching them to view the film with. It's hard to describe, but she had a real sense of when to step in and when not to. Very intelligent.

The teacher's physical position in the classroom took her out of the authoritarian role. She reinforced this message by participating in the dialogue when needed, yet shared leadership of the class with the students.

Andrew reported a similar example of shared leadership in one of his graduate classes after college:

> The teacher asks, "When's the best day for the test for you? Let's look at our schedules. Do you want to take it at night so we can have a longer time frame? Do more of an essay test?" There's a lot more of that going on. A lot less, "This is the way it is.". . . When we have [exams] we sat down and discussed, depending on when would be a good break as far as what we're going to be studying and whether we did cases in classes. Do we want to do more than one team project? How do you feel? Do you really want to work on teamwork in this class? So a lot of that was a lot more flexible and it wasn't set for you right away. . . . A lot more of your thinking is put into class.

Sharing leadership and knowledge creation led students to believe that they had a valuable contribution to make in the learning process. Participating in dialogue with students is essential to accessing their world and building bridges between their thinking and the topic at hand. Genuinely mutually constructing meaning achieves the evolutionary bridge or transitional culture Kegan says is necessary for self-evolution.

A Note on Integration of the Principles

Learning as mutually constructing meaning encompasses validating students as knowers and situating learning in students' own experience. By inviting students to join in a genuine dialogue and shared knowledge creation, educators validate students as knowers. Situating learning in students' experience is a necessary part of helping them participate in knowledge creation. The first two principles can be employed, however, without resulting in mutually constructing meaning. These two principles are often mistakenly interpreted as letting students think what they choose without attention to relevant evidence. For example, validating students as knowers validates their capability to think and construct knowledge; it does not validate misunderstanding of concepts under study or interpretations that lack foundation. Mutually constructing meaning requires validating students' capacity as knowers and helping students explore relevant evidence for constructing an informed perspective. Mutually constructing meaning requires situating learning in students' experience and simultaneously introducing the interpretations and knowledge claims experts in the discipline have advanced so that students can link the two. The three principles meet Chickering and Reisser's criteria for an educationally powerful curriculum: they are relevant to students' experiences, recognize individual differences, create encounters with diverse perspectives that challenge current assumptions, and provide opportunities for students to integrate diverse viewpoints. Such a curriculum, according to Chickering and Reisser (1993), "encourages the development of intellectual and interpersonal competence, sense of competence, identity, purpose, and integrity" (270).

Using the three principles as an underlying structure for pedagogy is not a matter of using new techniques; it is, rather, a matter of transforming one's assumptions about teaching and learning. The three principles represent a perspective on knowledge construction, learning, teaching, and human development. I trace my evolving assumptions about teaching and learning next to illustrate the challenges inherent in thinking differently about teaching. I also offer a case example of one of my courses to illustrate using these principles in graduate education with students who are at the threshold of, or are moving into, self-authorship.

PRACTICING SELF-AUTHORSHIP:
STUDENT DEVELOPMENT THEORY II

Had I read about the three principles in someone else's work, I would have initially said that my teaching already incorporated these ideas. I regularly teach a two-course sequence in student development theory. In my original student development theory courses, I asked students to role-play various stages of theories under study after I had presented an overview on transparencies. I regarded this as a way to help them identify with theory. I routinely entertained students' comments on the topic of the day, encouraging them to say what they thought. Our discussion- and activity-oriented class format was intended to offer them a theoretical knowledge base and invite them to adopt it as part of their professional practice. As I taught the course semester after semester, complete with reams of handouts on each theory, the students responded with favorable evaluations. The only doubt in my mind about the course came each year at comprehensive exam time when students wrote about using theory in more absolute ways than I thought we had discussed. Despite that nagging doubt, I continued to refine my detailed weekly course outlines to chart our path toward becoming student development experts. I saw my ability to move a wayward class discussion toward my predetermined end point as one of my greatest strengths as a teacher. Students sometimes commented on my uncanny ability to rephrase what someone said to make it sound better and more relevant.

As the three principles were emerging from the longitudinal stories, I began to reflect on how they played out in my teaching. Much to my dismay, I found that they applied in only a superficial way. Although I asked students to share their experiences as they related to the theories, I did so only after we had read extensively and reviewed handouts and transparencies to fix the main tenets of the theory in our minds. I asked students to participate in discussion and exchange ideas, but I worked diligently to move the discussion in a particular direction, systematically uncovering the issues (and often their resolutions) I had predetermined as important. Thus while it appeared that I was situating learning in students' own experience, I was in fact situating their experience within the theories, tempting them to reinterpret their experience rather than critically examine the theories' ability to describe their experience. It appeared that I was validating students as knowers and mutually constructing meaning with them, yet I subtly controlled the agenda, the direction of conversation, and ultimately the outcomes of the discussion. Perhaps they did not complain because their undergraduate education had to a large extent been dominated by objectivist approaches that rewarded deferring to the instructor's and book authors' knowledge.

For me, hearing firsthand how teachers' behavior affected the development or silencing of student voice brought to the surface a discrepancy I had heretofore not noticed. The approaches I was espousing as empowering students in my classes were new techniques based on old assumptions, what Bensimon (1994) calls strategies of accommodation or what Bruffee (1993) would call techniques based on foundational assumptions. The old assumptions of responsibility to transfer my knowledge to my students, my ability to know what was good for them in learning, and the traditional expectation to maintain control in the classroom and "cover the material" inhibited me from truly living what I espoused. After a sabbatical occupied by intense study of the longitudinal research transcripts and related reading material, I returned to the classroom to announce that I had experienced a major transformation in my thinking about teaching. This transformation, in essence, was realizing that students had to practice self-authorship themselves. Understandably, the first class to hear this announcement regarded me with some trepidation.

And so they should have. My first attempt was disastrous in students' opinions; problematic but hopeful from my perspective. I explained my transformation briefly to them in the opening session and shared my excitement about it. The class seemed somewhat wary but open to going along with my plan. The first sign of trouble came when they acquired the previous year's handouts from previous students after I had explained that I wanted them to create theory first before relying on existing theory. The second sign appeared after a regional conference at which they ascertained that students in similar courses at other institutions knew more of the theorists' names and stages than they did. It took most of the course and the worst teaching evaluations I had ever received for me to determine what went wrong.

In a nutshell, I *told* them that I would now teach in an empowering way. My excitement about this new plan overshadowed its true implications— that is, that it would mean mutually constructing the teaching approach with them! I did not realize that I was imposing a different pedagogy. I also underestimated the amount of support needed for them to participate in a way of learning that was different from what they were accustomed to, different from what they had become good at, and possibly discrepant from their assumptions about the nature of knowledge. In essence, I showed little respect for their world, for their side of the bridge. I did, unknowingly, what Kegan advised against—standing on the other side of the bridge, worrying and fuming about those who had not crossed over.

Since that experience, I continue to learn more about how to mutually construct meaning with students and how to let them self-author reasoned perspectives. I also continually discover assumptions in corners of my mind that represent my traditional socialization as a learner and teacher. Examples include the following: "The professor is responsible for determining grading percentages"; "All students have to do the same assignment for it to be fair"; "Students should not be allowed to rewrite assignments"; and "The professor can usually express an idea more clearly than can a student." With each discovery, I explore the idea with colleagues and students and alter my practice. There are days when the students think I have lost it; there are days when I agree. Most days, however, I feel that I am making progress toward more effective teaching and learning. I continue to be rewarded by more stimulating classes, better work from students, and more complex comprehensive exams. An exploration of one of my theory courses illustrates my use of the three principles as the structure for teaching at the graduate level. I selected this course because the students are generally independent or contextual knowers upon entering the course.

COURSE OVERVIEW

My primary teaching area is student development theory or the intellectual, psychosocial, moral, interpersonal, and self-development of late adolescents and young adults. This area is a standard requirement in College Student Personnel master's programs,* including the program in which I teach, because graduates of such programs use their understanding of traditional age and adult college students to guide educational practice. As my thinking about teaching was in the midst of transformation because of the longitudinal study described in this chapter, student development theorists and educators were also shifting their approach to constructing and using theory. Early theoretical descriptions were assumed to apply to all students, and theories constructed on one population (usually traditional age, white, and male) were commonly generalized to other populations. Increasing awareness of diversity within the college student population led theorists to view students' development as particular to their experience. This shift in my field and the shift in my thinking about teaching and learning resulted in adopting a "theory development" approach in my two-course student development sequence.

The first course in the sequence explores psychosocial and intellectual development from adolescence through adulthood; the second course explores self-evolution, moral development, integration of theoretical perspectives, and their application to educational practice. Using a theory development, or theory building, approach involves class members observing and listening to undergraduate students to collect data, then bringing the data to class for interpretation to generate new theoretical possibilities. This emphasizes the need to construct theory in a particular context with particular students and to regard theory as possible interpretations of student experience. In many ways this amounts to presenting student development theory as an ill-structured problem. Teaching theory as possibility promotes self-authorship as the graduate students are invited to construct their own theoretical understandings in the course of their work with undergraduate students. I share

---

*Such programs prepare students for administrative and student development roles in college and university student divisions.

excerpts from the second course in the sequence here to provide examples of using the three principles with independent and contextual knowers. The specific goals of Student Development Theory II are detailed on the syllabus (included in the appendices). My overarching goal is for students to self-author a reasonable perspective on existing theory and establish their own beliefs about how theory can be used in educational practice.

In any given semester, fifteen to twenty students of the fifty students in the program enroll in Student Development Theory II. Because students have already had the first theory course as a prerequisite, they are minimally in their second semester of graduate work. One of the tasks of the first course is to do a formal assessment (using the Measure of Epistemological Reflection; Baxter Magolda and Porterfield 1988) and reflection on one's intellectual development; this assessment indicates that most students are leaving transitional knowing or already engaged in independent knowing during the first course. Students in the second course are generally independent knowers; a few students, generally those with more work experience prior to graduate school, are contextual knowers. As a result, they are amenable to the format of the course.[*] The format of the course is explained in detail on the syllabus (see appendices) and is the primary topic of conversation during the first class session. Together we discuss what it will take to create a learning environment in which students can practice self-authorship and make plans to work toward such an environment. This usually involves developing a vision for what the class will be like, establishing agreements on ways of interacting that will help students accomplish this vision, and sharing strengths and challenges that various students face in participating effectively in this type of learning environment. These issues are summarized and handed out the following session to promote monitoring of our agreements. Attention to these norms continues throughout the semester. We process issues as they arise during class discussion—these conversations are usually fifteen minutes or less. Often they stem from misunderstandings, and once a student shares her or his reactions, others generate how to resolve the issue. I often introduce brief processing conversations at the end of class to check on our progress and sometimes do so when I feel the dialogue is dragging. Students occasionally introduce these conversations as well. At midsemester I ask the students to write responses to three items: strengths, weaknesses, and strategies for improvement. I share a summary of those comments at the next session, and we decide how to proceed. These process

*Their readiness is also affected by the nature of the overall masters program. The teaching philosophy of the faculty is consistent with my aproach, and numerous programmatic efforts support students who are less familiar with this type of pedagogy. See appendices for additional information on the teaching philosophy and activities of the program.

dynamics are another way to offer mutual construction of meaning about our
learning process.

In the sixth week of the course, our goal was to integrate the self-evolution
theory we had begun to study with theories previously explored in Theory I.
My typical approach is to offer a suggestion for proceeding. In the following
conversation (transcribed verbatim from an audiotape of the class session),
the class concurred with my suggestion, but the dialogue quickly revealed a
need for more exploration of self-evolution theory before most students were
ready for the integration task. This exploration validated students as knowers and brought important distinctions in the theory to the surface. The conversation began like this:

> Marcia: I have an idea of how we could do this; let me see what
> you think about it. What we said last time is that we were going
> to try to put these different dimensions together, not only the
> ones we are talking about in this class, but also string in the orig-
> inal ones from Theory I. So, here is a potential plan. Since we
> have been focusing mainly on Kegan, what do you think about
> us taking Matty, Peter, and Lynn—the three characters in the
> Kegan book—and putting them on a continuum of orders, fig-
> uring out where they are. Then let's go back and see what we
> could guess about them, where they might be on the vectors,
> what we think their intellectual development is, and let's see if
> we can develop a profile of these three people. Does that seem
> like it would work?
>
> Donna: Yeah. [Others nodded.]
>
> Marcia: Anybody have any speculations about where any of those
> people are on the orders continuum? Maybe we can get somebody
> on this end to put a continuum up there?
>
> Jo: I'll do it. I'm not on that end, but . . .
>
> Marcia: That's all right. What do you think? Do you have any
> inkling of where any of those three people are?
>
> Donna: Matty is second.
>
> Marcia: Matty is second Donna says. Anybody want to . . .

William: I agree. I went through this after the last class. I think that—actually I have this kind of worked out. Matty is. . . . What I had was that he is in the principle of durable categories because self is primary; his own perspective takes precedence. He is okay with his parents' perspective as long as it doesn't cost his anything—then I'm like so what does that mean about ways of knowing, maybe like absolute or transitional or second or third stages of reflective judgment, the prereflective stages. That was just my thinking so . . .

Marcia: Hang onto that for a minute and let's get him and his parents on the orders first and kind of settle where they are, then come back and put that layer on with it.

William: Okay.

Although I knew William's thinking—which he had worked out in preparation for this discussion—would be of high quality, I did not want him to offer his full-blown explanation of the integration at this early juncture in the discussion. Instead I wanted the group to work through the possibilities and include more students in the process. William, understanding my motives due to our group agreements about learning, accepted my request and continued to participate in the discussion. Postponing his comprehensive response allowed space for others to explore along with him and surfaced a few other needs for understanding. I tried to draw others into the dialogue, attempting to acquire diverse perspectives.

Marcia: Does anybody else have other perspectives? We have a couple of people who say Matty is second order.

Craig: I think he is pushing into the third order because of his concern with his peers. I don't recall exactly what it says in the chapter. Didn't it say something to the effect that he wanted to stay out with his peers, he is a little bit concerned with his parents, so I think he is definitely pushing into third order. His peers are definitely influencing him . . .

Donna: But I don't know if it said he was concerned with his peers or he chose just to be with them. I didn't get the sense that he was doing it because of his peers; he just wanted to do it.

Karen: Wasn't there a conflict between the two at one time? Or was that just a hypothetical . . .

William: Well, we had talked about how if he stopped somewhere with his friends and sneaked away to call without telling his friends, that would indicate that he was third order but that is a scenario we worked out.

Marcia: So what is the difference then? It sounds like the issue of concern with his peers—could he feel that from both second and third order? Could that be an issue at either one, and if so, then what would be the difference? How would we know that it is a—you used some word, Donna, I forget what it was—you said, "He just wanted to be with them."

I was trying to invite students to make judgments about the characteristics of second and third order, validating their ability to express knowledge about theory as well as the text examples. They were focused on Matty and characteristics of his thinking; my interest was in their attaching their observations about Matty to theoretical insights. Karen responded to my question.

Karen: The difference is if he is really having an internal conflict on who he wants to believe and how much he takes what they're saying to him into his decision making and how much he is trying to . . .

William: Or where the decision comes from. Like is it coming from his peers? For him to be influenced by them. Is it coming from his parents? Or his peers say it is important so therefore it is important to him? Or is it just important to him to be out with his friends? If it is just important to him to be out with his friends and be cool, then I would say he is in second order, but if it is important for him because his peers say it is important, then that would be third order.

Marcia: Didn't it say in the first chapter we read that when he came home that night he had hoped to come in, his parents would be in bed, he could tell them he got home just a few minutes late, and everything would be cool? How does that help us at all in figuring out whether he is second or third?

My emphasis with this comment was on offering evidence to be used in making judgments about Matty's development. I was attempting to balance welcoming students' thoughts and interpretations "as they were" and simultaneously invite a stretch to incorporating the evidence at hand.

Judy: Wasn't he willing to take on and make decisions that concerned others and took in others' viewpoints when he didn't necessarily have to *be* that role? And he wasn't able to do that as I remember it. He could take on those things if it didn't cost him anything. And he could say, "Yeah, I can understand your opinion and that's fine," but he didn't do anything with it? And so when he walked in the house that night, and there were mom and dad, he couldn't deal with that. He didn't know how to deal with that. He couldn't take their perspective into account. It was—I don't know where to go with that . . .

William: I don't want to dominate the conversation, but I'm just thinking, he, um, sneaking into the house and hoping his parents wouldn't be awake, at least to me, indicates that he would be in second order because if he was in third order it wouldn't be so much that he didn't want to deal with his parents, but third order would indicate that he was more defined by his relationship with his parents. So that he would go talk to them and say, "I'm so sorry." But he wasn't sorry. He just . . .

Donna: Didn't want to deal with it.

Marcia: He was sorry that they were up!

William: Right, he wasn't sorry that he was out late with his friends; he was just sorry that they were awake when he got home.

Marcia: Which goes back to Judy's comment about he really wasn't considering their point of view and really didn't know what to do with it.

Rebecca: I think it could be that he—the relationship he had with his parents is important and that is why he didn't want them to know. He went in thinking he could say, "I was just a couple minutes late," and that wouldn't cause any problems within that relationship with his parents. Because he knew his parents would be upset if he was late.

Donna: And I just kind of see it like he was concerned that "I'm gonna get in trouble." That was the bottom line. Not that I'm concerned about my relationship with my parents, but what are they going to do to me because I am late?

William: I see what you are saying. I think with the relationship with his parents being in a good state is important only insofar as it doesn't cost him anything in return, do you know what I mean? It is important to keep that relationship in good standing so he doesn't get yelled at. So he doesn't get lectured at. But if he were third order, it would be important to keep that in good standing because he understands his parents and wants to maintain that relationship with them, you know, genuinely. But in this one, he wants to, only because if he doesn't, it is going to be a hassle for him.

Karen: Do they understand the other point of view in third order?

Ann: They are the . . .

Karen: Or do they just try to take it on? I mean, do they really understand it, or does that start in fourth order?

Donna: That's a good question.

Ann: They can't reflect on it because it is still subject to them. But I think they take it on—that whole line that we talk about, you don't *have* relationships, you *are* your relationships. If you maybe are that point of view but you are acting it out, but you can't reflect on it until you are moving into fourth or are already in fourth.

Marcia: And you could argue along with that, that they do have enough understanding to take it on. They know enough about how the other person feels to be concerned about it. They might be more concerned about it than the other person is actually. So it sounds like he has a lot of two characteristics, maybe some three, but it depends on how we interpret his concern with others. Let's look at his parents and see if where they are helps us distinguish more about where he is or isn't.

The role I adopted in this portion of class is typical of my overall approach: offer a framework for discussion, encourage students to try out their ideas, ask questions that help students clarify their thinking, and synthesize the discussion when it seems to be winding down. In this excerpt, encouraging multiple interpretations about Matty's development set the stage for students offering their opinions, even though they differed from one another. Their disagreements spawned a discussion of the distinction between second and third order in which students were able to clarify aspects of the theory as well as determine how each interpreted it. I intentionally withheld my interpretation that Matty was second order, even when the first two students to participate offered that interpretation. Had

I agreed, the students with different interpretations might not have felt comfortable raising them. The discussion about Matty's third order characteristics, other possible interpretations, and important distinctions to consider in choosing an interpretation might not have occurred. Because my goal was for students themselves to learn to construct theory, the distinctions in interpretation were more important in my mind than where we placed Matty on the developmental continuum. My synthesis was an attempt to acknowledge both the distinction the theorist would make and the students' ability to interpret Matty's behavior in more than one way. Validating students as knowers in this context encouraged them to express themselves, listen to and challenge one another, and develop their understanding together. Keeping my view in the background and asking William to share his as we went instead of all at once kept the floor open for others to express themselves.

Situating Learning in Our Experience: Personal Self-Evolution

The discussion of Matty's parents that took place at the end of the excerpt just cited led to a discussion of the distinction between third and fourth order. This discussion prompted Karen to offer a concrete example for the group to consider. Because personal experiences and stories had been encouraged in the theory sequence, Karen correctly assumed that her story was appropriate.

> Karen: I was just going to say, this might be a concrete example. When I was home over three-day [break], we had a little discussion in my family. My oldest brother has dated the same woman for fifteen years. They have lived together for quite a long time but they never got married. They ran into a lot of problems and she went to counseling and everything else. My brother said to her, they still see each other a lot—it is a long story, but—my brother said to her, "When you went into counseling, you became so me, me, me I was ready to kill you. You couldn't see anything else. You were so out for what was right for you and everything good for you, you couldn't see anything. You could not relate much to the relationship anymore." So I'm thinking if that was her moving into fourth order. It seems to me that they had problems anyway because they were moving out of third order almost—it seemed that that's where they started hitting heads. Then if she works through that counseling, then she might be able to say, "My self is necessary and this is why it is important, but why don't we look and see why we have problems, where were we going wrong," rather than just saying me, me, me, saying, "Here's me and here's what is important to me, and there's you and what is important to

you. Now where is the problem?" Being able to discuss it more—
I don't know if that is a concrete example for anybody, but I was
just thinking through it.

There was no immediate response to Karen's story, and she had offered it
somewhat tentatively. I responded because I wanted to validate its importance and encourage learning from the students' own experiences.

Marcia: It is interesting how many relationship problems might
come from what we would call positive development. Particularly in
the case of third order people coming into their own, as opposed to
doing everything for the relationship, and if that's the way the relationship worked, we've got trouble.

William: I was just thinking, third order to fourth order relationships and the transition stuff probably would be the most difficult.
If Peter is stuck in third and Lynn is moving into fourth, Peter is
thinking, *What about us? What about us? What about us?* And Lynn
is going, "Well, us is important, but so am I." And Peter is interpreting that as she is thinking me, me, me. But really it is just a different way of thinking. I think there would be a lot of problems.
Not only that, then you have a third order person trying to yank
that person back into third order, saying, "No, don't go there, don't
go there." It just seems like there is a lot of resistance all around that
transition.

Jill: But do you think a fourth order person may think in terms of
"we" too? Instead of just me, me, me? They could think that "we"
because they could separate themselves from the relationship so they
can see the relationship and where they are?

Carol: The fourth order person needs to—they can see the "we" but
they need to figure out the "me." [Amid laughter Carol references a
counseling situation.] It is hard for them to figure out somebody
else, like why did he do this? They don't know themselves as to why
they are doing something. It is like, well, why do you think he did
that; instead of focusing on him, why do you think it is important
to focus on him? Then after you figure that out, you can integrate
the two.

Donna: I think, once again, my life is the perfect example of class discussion. [More laughter.] My therapy class here. I just got in this huge
fight with my parents the other night, and I feel kind of ridiculous to

be fighting with my parents at twenty-four about what I'm doing with my life. I feel like I'm in fourth order, I'm trying really hard to be fourth order, but I still have this tendency to go back because the relationship is important and breaking free is very difficult. Even though I know I am trying to get there, there are so many emotions that are tied up in ties with your family or other relationships. To separate—it is very difficult. [After a pause.] How do you do it, Marcia?

Marcia: What makes you think I've done it? [Laughter ensues as students joke about this.]

The joking lightened the tone of Donna's comments somewhat. However, I wanted to acknowledge and take seriously her willingness to share her personal experience and emotions. I shared in the joking briefly, then returned the conversation to a more serious note.

Marcia: Part of this—the whole idea of breaking free—I think that was the phrase you used—we have an idea of what that is going to cost. And what it costs depends on where everybody is in the whole thing. If you operate in the fourth order, going back to what somebody said about Lynn, she is still interested in her and Peter's relationship. That is why she is so aggravated with him for inviting his parents on this trip. It isn't that she doesn't care anymore. She has her own sense of what the trip should look like; and she is a little miffed that he let that get expanded. She is still concerned about it, but in a different way. Just like you are just as concerned about your relationship with your parents, but you want it to look different. [Donna says um-hmm.] And depending on where they are, where you think they are going to be, all that comes into play in your ability to sort that out.

Rebecca: I think my experience with my parents is that struggle between defining myself but including, trying to be fourth order, including them in that. Not completely defining myself by them, but that struggle of being—letting them—that sounds third order though. I don't know. There is something so, genetic, so, you come from those people! [Amid laughter.] I look in the mirror and see my mother!

Marcia: She becomes clearer every day!

Rebecca: She really does! I see myself become more and more like them—and I think, *That's me in twenty-five years*. That's okay with me. There will be those pieces that are either physical, or genetic, or personality wise that will tie us back to our parents; depending on your relationship with your parents—that will influence it too. But for those of us who feel close to our parents, that will always be a consideration even when you are fourth order. You will always consider those people.

Marcia: Something you said is really important—that you can be close. It is not the case that fourth order people aren't close to other people or that they don't have relationships. They are just different kinds of relationships. As opposed to being embedded in them, they have them. They can stand back from them, reflect on them, doesn't make them any less close from a fourth order point of view. The discrepancy between Lynn and Peter is, Peter thinks her definition of close doesn't look like his and it doesn't look as close. Maybe somebody's parents don't think having their son or daughter be independent feels as close—it depends on what their order is. It could be that that relationship turns out to be more close, a more adult-to-adult type of thing. Just because people are beginning to focus on themselves in fourth order doesn't mean they are going to be separate from other people.

Beginning with Karen's story about her brother, this conversation moves back and forth from the reading and theory to students' relatives and themselves. In my initial response to Karen's story, I tried to convey that her story illustrated an important point in thinking about relationship development. William picked up on this point, and others joined in. My encouragement of Karen's story probably encouraged Donna's more personal disclosure. Affirmation by the students and me of Donna's struggle with her parents indicates that it is appropriate to think about theoretical distinctions in the context of our own lives and relationships. I used Donna's example and her phrase "breaking free" to clarify a portion of the text and also offer Donna a way to frame her dilemma. Rebecca extended my idea by sharing her struggle with her own parents. In my synthesizing comments, I emphasized the importance of Rebecca's insights and tried to encourage the personal and text contexts in order to make all students comfortable participating in the discussion.

Allowing students to situate learning in their own experience helped them explore the particulars of theory in their life circumstances. Because their experience is real, they hesitate to discount it and thus see shortcomings or intricacies in theories as Rebecca describes. Using their experience also welcomed independent knowers' interest in expressing their opinions, yet invited them to consider others' experience and theory in deciding what to believe. Thinking about how theory helped interpret events in their lives aided their understanding of theory and helped process some of their personal experiences. The opportunity to share personal experience or use the text as a basis for discussion allowed students to benefit from the discussion without being pressed to disclose personal experience. Because both conversations reported here occurred in the first thirty minutes of the two-and-one-half-hour class session, they reflect these students' familiarity with one another and my endorsement of using one's own experience. Despite that, the excerpt offers examples of how to encourage students to use their experience as a context for learning.

MUTUALLY CONSTRUCTING MEANING: PRACTICING SELF-AUTHORSHIP

Near the end of the semester (week thirteen) the class was working on integration of all the theoretical perspectives covered in both courses. I used my usual approach of offering options, approaching it in a more open-ended way near the end of the term to focus on what students felt was unfinished business. The following excerpt illustrates students trying to work out their own perspectives and trying to convince others of their interpretations. My goal was for them to self-author a perspective on the collective theory studied in the course.

> Marcia: We could do a variety of things. We could talk about the two pieces we read for today, which got at some integrative issues. You could share thoughts you have as a result of just finishing your self-reflection [paper] about how theories go together; you might have thoughts based on having looked at all your handouts about how they go together; you may have questions about how they go together . . . where to begin? Any ideas? [A long pause occurred here. I have learned to wait for a student to break the silence!]

> Craig: A point I made last week was that the basic parts of intellectual theory, psychosocial theory, Kegan's theory seem to mesh very nicely. You can sort of see how it meshes together. But once you start to get into developing within the theories, it becomes increasingly difficult, for me anyway, to see where people fit. I don't know; I kind of lose . . . the more advanced you get within the theories, the more difficult it gets. We are saying how people can be transitional knowers, contextual knowers, absolute knowers. Then we're saying they are third order. But when I think about it, how can that be? How can somebody be in third order and be a contextual knower?

> Jo: Do you think that is really possible?

> Craig: I don't think it is possible.

Jo: And why not?

Craig: If you used the theories absolutely, then no. The whole premise of contextual knowing is different perspectives apply in different circumstances, and the whole idea behind third order of consciousness is that there is the perspective of the relationship and that is the only perspective. So how can—I don't understand—it seems like what people have said so far is that there are people they determined [via their interviews for assignments] are in those places that have those characteristics. So that's my confusion.

Donna: Maybe because of their holding environments or other circumstances, they may not be in the order that it appears they are in. It might seem—I'm still stuck on this. I've talked to people I think are fourth order, but I have a hard time believing that they are in fourth order because they are sophomores. I interviewed four or five people and two of them are in fourth order. It seems kind of strange. So, because their holding environments make them look like they are in fourth order, they have a lot of characteristics that would be similar to someone in fourth order, so I'm putting them in fourth order. But they may not really be there. They really may be in third order, which is why they only have some of the other cognitive or psychosocial dimensions. Does that make . . .

Craig: I don't know. It seems to me that integration is very hard. I like the idea of considering each theory as a perspective; when you start to put them together, that's when you have to take them for what they are worth . . . I don't know.

Cara: I still think it would be possible for someone to be in third order and be contextual to some extent. Because third order is talking about which perspectives have influence on you. It is not saying that you only see one perspective; it is saying you are allowing certain perspectives, which are other people's, to have more influence on you. A contextual knower—you could be a contextual knower to the extent that you could recognize that there are a lot of perspectives out there. You may not be able to make the full step in contextual knowing, which would be to evaluate those for yourself. But you could be somewhere in the middle. Because you would be in third order doesn't mean you are necessarily an independent knower. You could be in third order and start wrestling with whether some of those perspectives are more valuable than others.

Jan: But then wouldn't you be in transition between third and fourth order?

Cara: Possibly . . .

Jan: Or would you still only be in third order?

Cara: I don't know. That's why I said I think it is possible to be in the middle of both of those at the same time.

Karen: 'Cause you could wrestle, but depending on who you were with, you could vocalize that only one perspective was right, but you may still be able to wrestle with thinking and recognizing the different . . . I don't know.

The conversation thus far illustrates encouraging students to struggle to mutually construct meaning and determine their own views. However, intervention is necessary when the dialogue loses direction. Hearing the repeated "I don't know's" prompted me to view the conversation as getting stuck at this point. My next comment was an attempt to capture the complexity of integration, thus validating their struggle, yet challenge the group to continue working with integration across theoretical perspectives. In the exchange between Jo and me that follows, I tried to mutually construct meaning with her by respecting her position, yet offering mine in partial contrast to it.

Marcia: That's where I think the idea of integration is important. I think it is true that it is easier to look at people with only one lens. But then we get too comfortable saying, "They fit here." When you look at the other lenses, that sometimes calls that into question. If a person can think about something in a particular way, but in a particular context we can't see that, so a person can entertain other options but they go along with their peers because they are third order, then by integrating, we are beginning to see another angle. That maybe gets at Donna's question about sometimes somebody looks like they are someplace but we aren't sure they really are. By looking from lots of different angles, we might get a better sense of what combinations are there.

Jo: I'm not very comfortable with the term *integrative* because I think it operates from the premise that there is a similar truth to them all. Or that there is a truth that runs through all of them—there is a match. And I think, when you said, Marcia, understanding people from different perspectives, from different angles, I think that is important. I think rather than integrating, we are overlapping some of the theories. We aren't meshing them together. I think that implies that there is a truth between all of them. They are all just different perspectives, one theorist's or theorists' perspectives on a whole schema or different levels of schema.

Marcia: That's interesting. What I'm thinking about when I think about integration is that different dimensions of people's development mediate each other. Like people's psychosocial development, no matter what theorist we use to define that, is mediated in my mind by their cognitive development. There is some kind of connection back and forth that would be different for different people. But there is some kind of link—that is what I mean by integration. I don't necessarily mean let's draw a chart on the board where we can get all the lines lined up to make sure that if you are fourth order, that tells us where you are on Chickering, Josselson, ninety-two other theories. In my mind it is almost like all of these things keep moving. But somehow the way a person thinks about knowledge, even if we don't yet have the language to detail what that means, that has something to do with how they think about themselves as a person.

Jo: Yeah, I think there can exist between multiple theories of development a symbiotic relationship. I think, yeah, I run into trouble when we try to peg, like you said, a third order could be an independent or transitional knower but not a contextual knower. There are any number of combinations that can be applied. A person could even be in second order and be a contextual knower—I'm sure that person is out there! They are the exception, but . . .

Jan: What would that person look like?

William: I would disagree with that, though. I really have to disagree with that.

Jo: All right, why?

William: Because a second order person is so consumed with themselves.

Jo: That's your value!

William: No, that is what second order is! They are so consumed with themselves that they aren't going to be able to take in the other perspective at all!

I made a choice to intervene at this juncture in the conversation, perhaps a mistake in retrospect. At the time I perceived the upcoming argument between William and Jo (two students who pushed each other's buttons regularly) as a tangent in our mutual construction of how the theories integrated. I tried to remove the conversation one step from their direct disagreement and refocus it on self-authorship with the following comment:

Marcia: Maybe one of the issues behind this is each of us has to make a choice about whether we believe and or endorse the theoretical perspectives that we have been exposed to. If I say I am willing to endorse Kegan's theory, then I am willing to endorse Kegan's definition of what second order is.

Jo: What does that mean, endorse?

Marcia: Believe. It means I buy it, I think it is a reasonable perspective, a reasonable lens from which I could view another person. If I at the same time endorse my own theory about contextual knowing, then I think I could come to the conclusion that I don't think second order and contextual knowing go together. Now someone could say, "Well, the problem with that is that contextual knowing theory has a hole in it; there is something wrong with that. It doesn't have enough options, doesn't convey the different ways you could think about things, and doesn't jibe with ten people we can find who appear to be second order contextual knowers." That is a different kind of issue than saying given what theories convey, if we decide to believe that, there are certain places that do or don't come together. I think those are two different issues. It seems like that is behind the notion of whether—when a person says if you are in this range on theory A, you have to be on this range of theory B. That is an analysis of how those theories go together as opposed to a personal value about those theories. You could say that is how they go together and I don't believe either one of them. Couldn't you?

Jo [laughing]: Yes!

Rebecca: I think for me in trying to think about how to put these together, I am always struck with holding environments. For me, that is what I feel affects me the most. I think in my thinking of

these theories, at least right now this is what I believe, in the different holding environments, the different situations, the different
contexts, depending on who they are with and what is going on,
especially for people who are college age, they will look very different, kind of all the time depending on what they are going through.
It is not that I can't utilize third order, second, fourth, because I
think there are things to utilize. But for me I don't think it will be
that absolute. This will help for me as a practitioner to give me some
guidelines, ideas, ways in which to understand how the students are
thinking. When I was a day camp counselor, I always used to say,
"What were you thinking when you did that?" when they did something really stupid. And I just realized a couple weeks ago, now I
understand what they were thinking! So it will help clarify what
they are thinking and why they are thinking the way they are. But
it may change from holding environment to holding environment.
That's how I am thinking about it.

Craig opened this discussion by sharing what he called his confusion over
what he heard from his classmates' reports of their student interviews for the
application assignment (see syllabus in appendices). The issue he raised was
the complexity of theory when one starts to integrate various aspects of development. In his response to Jo he clarified that his confusion stemmed
from putting the theories together in one way (he used the term *absolutely*)
and hearing his peers put them together in more flexible ways. Donna's interpretation of the dilemma was that students are not where they appear.
Cara played out a possibility that reveals theory and development as a complex matter. My attempt to capitalize on Cara's insight prompted Jo to push
the issue of the truth of theories farther. Jo was willing to disagree with me
to advance her notion that theories are "just different perspectives."

As the excerpt shows, I became more active in the conversation at this
point. I intended to accomplish two goals simultaneously: first, to validate
Jo's notion that theories are not the absolute truth, and second, to challenge
Jo and others to evaluate theories to decide what to believe rather than adopt
the independent knower stance of "just different perspectives." In doing so,
I passed on the opportunity created by William's reaction to Jo. In my interest in getting to the issue of self-authorship and choosing one's beliefs, I
cut off William's and Jo's disagreement about whether William's interpretation of second order was his value or his self-authored perspective. Had I
backed out of the conversation at that point, William and Jo could have
worked this through and accomplished my goal of highlighting the self-
authorship dimension. Rebecca helps get the self-authorship point across by
sharing how she thinks about using theory and her context for doing so.

This excerpt shows students practicing authoring their own views and attempting to mutually construct meaning. The conversation falls short of mutual construction because students do not use one another's insights to alter or refine their own, with the possible exception of the exchange among Cara, Jan, and Karen. In part mutually constructing meaning was difficult because some of the participants were independent knowers. Independent knowers are more interested in advancing their ideas and raising possibilities than evaluating the potential of a possibility and making a judgment about it. Promoting self-authorship in this context means encouraging students to evaluate ideas and make reasoned decisions about what to believe. To accomplish that goal, I needed to focus more on asking students to explain their various perspectives (a closer match to their side of the bridge) before trying to introduce the notion of deciding what to believe.

SELF-AUTHORSHIP BEYOND CLASS DIALOGUE

Although the class dialogue is indeed the primary medium for promoting self-authorship, additional dimensions of my teaching practice for this course offer opportunities for self-authorship. In this course, as in most others in the graduate program, students determine the evaluation percentages for assignments. I ask students to do this individually so that they may use their own learning needs in determining the evaluation process that will be most effective for them. For example, one student may view a difficult assignment as less risky if it carries a lower weight whereas the next student knows that she needs to place a higher weight on the assignment to motivate herself to take the risks involved. Students make these decisions during the first few weeks of class and submit their percentage sheets on a specified date. Some students take advantage of the opportunity to meet with me individually to discuss the advantages of various options. The percentage sheet also contains a space for rationale for the percentages selected. I tell students in advance that I will negotiate with them if I have concerns about their decisions. In the four years I have used this practice, I have negotiated with two students to revise their decisions. Their decisions are usually thoughtful and focused on learning rather than manipulating the grade. I am also open to renegotiating percentages for good cause prior to the completion of assignments.

I encourage students to explore alternative assignments, particularly in the case of the self-reflection assignment (aimed toward situating learning in students' experience), if they feel another assignment would be more helpful to them. Although this happens rarely (perhaps once in every other offering of the course), when a student comes forward with a concern, we determine the objectives of the assignment, brainstorm ways to achieve it, and decide on a plan that both of us agree is workable. I allow students to rewrite papers when we agree that there is a good reason to do so. I discourage rewriting for the sole purpose of obtaining a higher grade. Finally, I encourage students to talk with me if they disagree with my evaluation of their work. These conversations help us clarify what each was thinking and help us connect more effectively. I am willing to alter my evaluation if I misread the paper; students are open to accepting my original evaluation if I can clarify how I constructed it.

These aspects of my pedagogy give students a substantial role in their learning. It validates them as knowers in terms of respecting their judgments about what will help them learn. It situates learning in their own experience by allowing them to frame parts of their learning according to their own world. Mutual construction of meaning is ever-present because I ask for their reasoning while maintaining my input into these decisions. These practices communicate to students that we truly are engaged in a joint effort. It models shared leadership in areas that are usually reserved for faculty authority, namely, evaluation.

Shared leadership permeates the theory courses both in knowledge creation and in learning process. The social construction of knowledge is emphasized in the syllabus, oral introduction to the course, the course format, and controversies in the literature introduced through the readings. Students then experience the social construction of knowledge through gathering data and analyzing it in class. They are validated as knowers when their analyses are given consideration alongside those of experienced theorists. We construct knowledge about student development theory together, integrating their personal developmental experience, the data they collected, my expertise, and the student development literature. Incorporating interviewees from diverse student populations who are underrepresented in the literature also highlights the socially constructed nature of student development theory. Shared leadership in the learning process occurs in establishing group norms, ongoing processing of our adherence to those norms, and making mutual decisions about everything from the direction of a class discussion to evaluation.

Sharing leadership is intended to create a transitional culture in which students can practice self-authorship and knowledge creation. These processes welcome students as they are by valuing their input and invite them to stretch to collaborate with peers and me in evaluating what to believe. The message that I am a teacher-learner and I view them as learners-teachers is clear throughout the course. Opportunities to practice knowledge creation are ever-present. Support for engaging in knowledge creation takes the forms of respecting students' thoughts, praising risk taking and good insights, rewarding students for challenging my ideas, empathizing with the difficulty of facing ambiguity, and providing detailed reading guides and detailed descriptions of assignments.

COURSE EFFECTIVENESS

A primary source of judging course effectiveness is student evaluations. Students complete standard departmental course evaluations for the theory courses each time that they are offered. The second theory course is offered once per year. The evaluation form contains a quantitative portion in which the students use a Likert scale to respond to thirty-two items, which in turn yield ratings on six scales: planning and organization, awareness and sensitivity to human diversity, evaluation techniques consistent with course goals, communicates effectively, effective evaluation system for students, and approachable attitude. The ratings for the Theory II course have ranged from 3.75 to 3.99 on a 4.00 scale, indicating a very positive evaluation of the course on all six scales.

The qualitative portion of the evaluation asks students to comment on the most and least valuable aspects of the course and make recommendations for changes in the readings, examinations, organization of the course, and grading procedures; and it asks for commentary on how the instructor can improve teaching of the course. Themes from these evaluations indicate that students consistently comment that the discussions are most valuable, and many note the paper assignments as valuable. Many indicate that no aspects were least valuable, and a few comment on tangents in discussion and particular readings as least valuable. Recommendations usually involve changes in specific readings or details of an assignment. The overall improvements usually refer to specific recommendations, and often students indicate that no improvements are needed.

Because I use the class discussion and organization as the primary vehicle to implement the three principles, further exploration of students' comments in that area is useful. The most valuable aspects of organization of the course were described as "allowing the class to decide the agenda" and "we molded the course to meet our needs. The flexibility in discussions was appreciated." The discussion format yielded numerous responses. For most valuable aspects one student wrote, "Discussion with peers! Exciting, the interchange of ideas. . . . The readings and organization of the course made it easy to learn and further to apply." Another wrote, "Our in-class discussions have been invaluable. They have clarified the material, aided my own self-reflection, and challenged me. Each class period has been both invigorating and exhausting." Another student wrote, "Class conversations—mutually constructing meaning—building on ideas of peers, synthesizing theories—really felt like a community of scholars." Most students commented favorably on the openness to student leadership and ideas in discussion.

Students also commented on their learning as a result of the course format. The self-reflection assignment was popular as indicated by a comment typical on the forms: "The self-reflection is great—a fantastic learning tool!" Another student was more specific in stating, "The papers were very valuable in making me synthesize what we have discussed in class." Another wrote, "I've loved this course! I feel like I've learned a lot about myself and really made some of these theories my own in the process." This last comment reflects that some self-authorship took place for this student.

The general comments at the close of the evaluation routinely contained comments like this one: "Keep up the great work. I really enjoyed the fact that you were invested and shared your theoretical dilemmas with us. The theory classes are the best I've had yet." A few students wrote, "We want Theory III!" Overall this feedback, despite the specific frustrations students noted about discussion tangents and a few particulars of readings and assignments, suggests that students were highly satisfied with the course. Their subject mastery was evident in final grades, the majority of which were A, A-, and B+. Two students received A+ final grades, a rare occurrence. Fewer grades in the B and C ranges occurred, compared to the grade range in other courses I teach.

Unlike what I did in the courses in the observational study, I did not systematically "observe" my own course or interview students about their reactions. However, a few volunteered thoughts on the impact of the course in their final papers. These thoughts address the issue of practicing self-authorship. One student reported that the course resulted in "an entirely new way of thinking about human growth and development." He wrote,

> Specifically, my study of Kegan in Theory II has literally revolutionized how I view my own and others' personal development. I use the framework so much that sometimes I am not even consciously aware of it. The notion of continuity, confirmation and contradiction stay with me as core guiding principles of my work, and I continually ask myself if I am living by these principles with the students I serve. Kegan's theory of self-evolution elegantly captures my own movement while I have been here, making its application all the more exciting for me to use and share with others. . . . Being a more self-defined person and having developed a clear sense of my own needs is also representative of my own growth a la Kegan. I am amazed at just how much clearer my sense of who I am is, what my needs are and how I am able to maintain my distinctness in relation to others. This growth is freeing.

This passage, and the larger paper from which it is taken, indicates that the student made aspects of a particular theory his own and analyzed his own development accordingly. Using the theory as a framework, he was able to become a more self-defined person—an indication of progress in self-authorship.

The self-reflection component of the course is cited most often as promoting self-authorship in students' own meaning-making. One woman wrote,

> I found this assignment to be a bridge to a new way of making meaning. Naming my feelings is, in Kegan's terms, making them object rather than subject. I find myself in the midst of a transition between third and fourth order meaning-making. If anything, this assignment made me more aware of my worldview and thus caused me to consistently reevaluate.

She gave examples of this reevaluation in her interactions with family and peers. Engaging in self-reflection helped her make conscious decisions about her worldview, herself, and her relationships with others. Reactions like these surface regularly in final papers in Theory II. Although they do not offer a formal assessment of students' progress in self-authorship, they indicate that it is taking place for some students.

TRANSFORMING ASSUMPTIONS

Creating transitional cultures for the growth of the mind is complex work. Promoting self-authorship is a matter of helping students transform their assumptions about knowledge and themselves. Trying to build a bridge to connect to a moving target is hard work because it involves constant and careful listening. The flexibility to adjust to students' experience means discussion is in flux, and it is hard to grab hold of the process or the outcomes. Just as it is hard for students to transform their assumptions in this learning process, it is hard for teachers to transform their assumptions about what the learning process should be. I shared some of my transformation earlier in this chapter. Next I turn to the transformation of readers' assumptions.

Transforming Educators' Assumptions

As I share my enthusiasm for constructive-developmental pedagogy with others at conferences and colloquia, I usually encounter a few colleagues who report that they use some form of constructivist pedagogy and that it works. They are usually not the majority, however, depending of course on the context. From the majority of listeners, I have noticed three themes evident in the questions that follow my explanation:

1. Did you have tenure when you tried this?

2. Doesn't this require a small class?

3. This sounds workable in education, but how could this be effective in disciplines such as math and science in which knowledge does exist that students have to know?

If there are human development theorists in the crowd, someone usually asks, "You can only do this with students who have advanced ways of knowing, right?" These questions have led to the observational study that occupies the remainder of this book. Knowing that my own experience and the stories of my longitudinal study participants were insufficient to answer these questions, I undertook the observational study described in chapter 1.

The courses that I observed illuminate three quite different versions of constructive-developmental pedagogy, both in course structure and in instructor teaching style. Collectively, these stories show that constructive-developmental pedagogy is not an essentialist approach; rather, it is a collection of possibilities for getting over the border or for building a structurally sound bridge. Because instructors, disciplines, and students differ, how all three get put together effectively varies by context. While this may sound disturbing, because truly accessing and valuing students' experience change pedagogy constantly, at the same time it raises hope that pedagogy can be inclusive of diverse students' experience. One way to connect with the increasingly diverse student population is to access their frames of reference. Constructive-developmental pedagogy, specifically the three principles, offers a structure from which to build these connections. It offers a structure through which teachers (and students) can create, enter, and inhabit the borderlands.

LEARNING AS TRANSFORMING STUDENTS' ASSUMPTIONS

Kegan's notion of a holding environment, or transitional culture, is one that accepts students as they currently are, yet invites them to grow. Learning necessitates starting where students are, but seldom involves their remaining unchanged. As they encounter, interpret, and integrate new experiences into their ways of knowing, their assumptions about knowledge change to become more complex. Self-evolution, as Kegan describes it, is the changing of the mind to make meaning in more complex ways. This growth—of one's mind or self—is possible when educators access students' worlds and create transitional cultures in which students can reconstruct how they make meaning. Thus, the next three chapters are organized according to students' worlds and the transitional cultures they encountered in these three courses. Chapter 4 focuses on students who hold independent and contextual ways of knowing. Chapter 5 shares the learning experiences of students who hold primarily transitional and independent ways of knowing. In chapter 6, most students hold absolute and transitional ways of knowing. Each chapter reveals the complex interplay between students' worlds and the transitional cultures they encountered. I invite you to join their experience to see how it affects your assumptions about students, learning, and teaching.

PART 2

BRIDGING MULTIPLE WORLDS

Forms of Constructive-Developmental Pedagogy

CHAPTER 4

Learning Scientific Inquiry

Revising and Creating Science

WITH JENNIFER BUCKLEY

"How can one come to know the nature of the knowledge as something constructed and tentative if one never makes some of it oneself?"
—DYKSTRA 1996, 200 (ITALICS IN ORIGINAL)

Dewey Dykstra, a physicist, raised this question in discussing teaching college physics. He is one of a growing number of scientists and science educators who believe that students must gain experience "making" or constructing scientific knowledge in order to understand its tentativeness. Chris Snowden, the zoology professor quoted at the outset of chapter 1, organizes his winter biology course around helping students learn scientific inquiry. The search for a science course that focused on self-authorship led a colleague[*] and me to Chris Snowden's office. We knew from previous interactions with Chris that he devoted considerable energy to helping students learn and modeled scientific inquiry in his teaching. We approached him to discuss observing winter biology, a course taught in the zoology department for seniors and graduate students. Chris shared that this was a favorite course for him because it drew together many of his interests, all of which centered on cold temperatures. His broad training was evident in the course objective on the syllabus:

> This course provides an introduction to biochemical, physiological and ecological adaptations of plants and animals to not only survive, but remain active during the winter. Emphasis is placed on integrating students' previous knowledge in the physical and biological sciences to understand the cellular, organismal and evolutionary challenges faced by organisms, including humans, living in environments that experience low temperature and related winter stresses. This course requires extensive reading of primary scientific literature, completion of a collaborative small group library assignment, writing a major research paper and grant proposal, and presenting a formal seminar. (Appendix F, 306)

[*]Jennifer Buckley, a graduate student at the time of this observation, observed this course with me and co-authored this chapter.

Chris explained that his goal was to help students think like scientists: learn how to explore the scientific literature, identify useful questions, understand how to determine the next step in a research effort, and learn the communication skills required to function in the scientific community. He wanted them to "appreciate what facts really mean. Tentative facts. That's what all of science is. Subject to change and revision." These goals made it clear that Chris wanted students to think critically and construct knowledge, yet he wanted them to do so within the scientific processes that prevailed in his discipline. He also wanted them to understand how the knowledge creation effort in the discipline took place. His emphasis on students' individual constructions, the scientific processes of the discipline, and knowledge creation in the discipline indicated a focus on self-authorship. He planned to use controversies in the scientific literature and examples of the scientific inquiry process to achieve his goals.

Chris Snowden's approach to teaching reflects aspects of a controversy regarding how to teach science—the debate over covering the subject matter versus promoting critical thinking. Emphasis on subject matter stems from the positivist tradition of transmitting knowledge from instructors to students. Proponents of this approach argue that students need to master particular subjects in order to move successfully into advanced courses. This focus usually results in the traditional lecture format in which instructors tell students what they need to know. Arnold Arons (1989) argued that students emerge from conventional college physical science courses "understanding nothing whatsoever and possessing only strings of memorized technical jargon that help them recognize enough juxtapositions of words on a multiple choice test to get an A or B in the course. The jargon is then quickly forgotten" (15). Arons points out what he calls an unwelcome truth: "Research is showing that didactic exposition of abstract ideas and lines of reasoning (however engaging and lucid we might try to make them) to passive listeners yields pathetically thin results in learning and understanding except in the very small percentage of students who are specially gifted in the field" (1997, vii). Craig Nelson's (1989) story about his own college biology course bears out Arons's argument. Nelson reported that students receiving A's in his course were "unable to analyze ecological controversies effectively and most thought of science as truth" (17). He altered his teaching to focus on critical thinking skills, with the fear that he would have to sacrifice content as a result. However, he found that the steps he used to facilitate critical thinking also facilitated content acquisition, leading him to conclude that the trade-offs between content and thinking skills were imaginary. It appears that the passive transmission of knowledge to students results in their memorization of facts for the short term rather than their acquisition of scientific knowledge, which Dykstra defines as "the nature of beliefs about the essential nature of aspects of the world and how they work" (1996, 182).

Arons (1997) concurs with Nelson's emphasis on critical thinking, advocating use of the thinking and reasoning process underlying analysis and inquiry to enhance students' reasoning capacity, or their ability to develop reasonable beliefs about how things work. He offers ten possibilities, which he says are illustrative rather than exhaustive, of processes teachers could use to enhance students' reasoning capacity. These processes revolve around exploring how we know and choose to believe particular concepts. Helping students consciously explore assumptions, what is known, how we know it, and what evidence is available to support particular beliefs helps them learn how to analyze evidence and form reasonable judgments. Arons argues that the questions of "How do we know?" and "Why do we believe?" are common among preschool children, but formal education teaches them not to ask these questions. He suggests that college students, then, need to be pushed to consciously consider these questions, along with learning how and when to draw inferences, identifying gaps in information, distinguishing between fact and conjecture, and examining their own lines of reasoning.

Arons's processes resonate with the constructivist view of science education in which knowledge "must be constructed by the mental activity of learners" (Driver, Asoko, Leach, Mortimer, and Scott 1994, 5). Driver and her colleagues argue that the nature of scientific knowledge as symbolic and socially negotiated among scientists "means that learning science involves being initiated into scientific ways of knowing" (6). They translate this to the role of the science educator, which they state "is to mediate scientific knowledge for learners, to help them to make personal sense of the ways in which knowledge claims are generated and validated" (6). This view includes students constructing meaning individually by reevaluating their current thinking as well as students participating in the social constructing of knowledge via "becoming socialized . . . into the practices of the scientific community with its particular purposes, ways of seeing, and ways of supporting its knowledge claims" (Driver et al. 1994, 8). Candace Julyan and Eleanor Duckworth also emphasize the importance of students expressing and investigating their own and others' ideas to achieve what they laud as the purpose of the science class—"to achieve a fuller understanding of the workings of the physical world" (1996, 56). Richard Hake reported greater conceptual gains in introductory physics classes in which students interactively engaged as opposed to those in which they experienced passive lectures. He defined interactive engagement as methods "designed at least in part to promote conceptual understanding through interactive engagement of students in heads-on (always) and hands-on (usually) activities which yield immediate feedback to the students through discussion with peers and/or instructors" (1998, 65).

Bereiter (1994) adds a dimension to the constructivist perspective by arguing that scientific knowledge exists as immaterial objects, such as "theories, explanations, historical accounts, problem formulations and solutions, proofs and disproofs" (22) that scholarly disciplines are focused on producing and improving. He believes that this goes beyond students' individual constructions and the cultural practices of particular groups to focus on *improving the knowledge* that is being collectively created" (23). Collectively, these writers emphasize the importance of the individual student engaging in knowledge construction from his own perspective, learning the scientific ways of knowing of the discipline, and participating in the collective effort to create knowledge in the discipline.

The constructivist view of science education is consistent with the three principles of constructive-developmental pedagogy. Helping students make personal sense of the construction of knowledge claims and engaging students in knowledge construction from their own perspectives involve validating the students as knowers and situating learning in the students' own perspectives. Becoming socialized into the ways of knowing of the scientific community and participating in the discipline's collective knowledge creation effort involve mutually constructing meaning. It would seem that constructive-developmental pedagogy would contribute to the goals of science educators as well as human development educators' self-authorship goals.

Chris Snowden's pedagogy emphasized self-authorship and learning the scientific community's methods and existing knowledge simultaneously. In one of our conversations he remarked that some new teaching approaches offer too much inquiry at the expense of understanding. Chris planned to lecture the first half of the course, using his and others' research to model scientific inquiry. Students were required to do short presentations to highlight difficult issues in the textbook chapters since that material was not part of the lecture. The second half of the course consisted of students' twenty-five-minute presentations on their research papers. Sixty percent of the grade hinged on the research paper, the presentation, and a grant proposal based on the research paper. Many of the presentations took place at a half-day symposium that modeled a conference setting.

Our initial reactions to Chris's plan were mixed. Students' experience and self-authorship were clearly a centerpiece of the course via the research paper and corresponding presentation and grant proposal. Students chose topics, and the two-page description on these assignments made it clear that students should pick a topic of interest to them as long as it linked to life in the cold. Because the students were primarily seniors and, as we learned later, independent and contextual knowers, we expected this approach to be well received by the students. The early lectures would model scientific inquiry and synthesize insights from previous courses rather than convey information to be deposited in students' brains. The term *lecture,* however, made us a little uneasy. How would Chris convey the tentative nature of science and the knowledge creation process via lecture? We decided to observe the course, hoping to see whether a lecture format could be consistent with constructive-developmental pedagogy and promotion of self-authorship. What we encountered was very different from what we had come to envision as *lecture.* The story here reveals why.

ZOOLOGY 400/500: WINTER BIOLOGY

We came to call Chris's teaching *interactive lecture.* Readers who prefer to see an overview of this process prior to reading the story are advised to preview figure 4.1. The key characteristics of the interactive lecture are italicized through the story that follows.

It was not unusual for Chris to carry a slide projector into class; he began today (the fourth class session of the term) with a slide. As was his typical practice, Chris placed the slide projector in the middle of the center lab table and moved the podium to the corner of the room so that it did not interfere with his slides or his pacing across the front of the room. The laboratory atmosphere of the room—three lab tables perpendicular to the front of the room, walls lined with creatures in formaldehyde and dissecting trays—was conducive to Chris's sense of the nature of science as well as his walking around during the lecture. Today's topic was the microhabitat under the snow. Chris always began by *introducing a basic phenomenon.*

Chris started by saying, "We talked about maritime effect, the relationship of the earth to the sun. Next effect is the lake effect. We alluded to this with maritime effect—have warmer climates. If you go to the area around Buffalo, they are well known for lots of snow." The slides showed how the snow differed within a short distance. "The wind picks up moisture from the lake; increased water vapor is being carried in the air; it is warmer over large bodies of water. Why?" Kate responded, "The air at warmer temperature can carry more water vapor." Chris agreed, adding, "When it passes over land, the temperature drops, then it can carry less water vapor. It comes out as snow. You find these snow belts on the fringes of large bodies of water." Lisa rephrased this idea to see if she understood, and Chris said, "Exactly right. One of things I'd like to pose to you—would you expect to see different adaptations of organisms in the snow belt versus ones not in it, and what adaptations would you expect? I'll leave you to think about that some."

The slides Chris used to introduce this topic gave *experiential examples* of the issues for the day. He also set them in the context of the previous class discussion. Chris included students in his introduction to the topic by asking a "why" question. This opened the door for Lisa to check her understanding as

Figure 4.1

Interactive Lecture: Practicing Scientific Inquiry

Basic Explanation of Phenomena: an overview of a concept	
Experiential Examples: everyday situations as translations of concept to help put it in students experience; makes concept concrete, creates an experience (slides, description of a story, imagining something), link to experiences students have had.	**Data:** raw data, figures on handouts, transparencies of experiments used to give students a chance to analyze and discuss findings

Oral Interpretation of Knowledge:

they are trying to make sense of phenomena, talking together out loud to understand

- large group: asks questions, entertains their questions, encourages thinking together in large group

- pairs: analyze raw data and share interpretations

| **Synthesis:**

the bottom line (the take home message, the important point here is . . .) pulls information together; incorporates synthesis across disciplines | **Unresolved Exchanges:**

sometimes things are left up in the air; controversial |

he talked. Within a very short period of time, Chris posed a question for the group to think about as they talked. He brought in thinking (or *interpretation of knowledge*) at every opportunity, even in his introduction. He then returned to the *basic phenomenon*.

The next slide was called Chinook wind. Chris started: "Let's talk about the mountain effect." He explained that it is dry on one side of the mountain and asked about the idea of adiabatic cooling. Lynn said, "The pressure decreases on the air as it rises." Chris agreed and elaborated on her statement. Joan asked him to repeat what he had said; he laughed and joked that he might be able to repeat it. He explained how air pressure would be reduced and cooling would take place as a result: "Air has less capacity to carry water vapor, so the precipitation will come out. At the top of the mountain you have dry, cool air; as it continues across the mountain and moves down, the reverse happens—adiabatic warming. Increasing water-vapor-carrying capacity of the air as it moves down the slope. Pick up moisture from this side of the mountain. This is the dry side." He described this as a phenomenon one would see in the mountains out West, going from east to west. Lisa asked for clarification. Chris explained that precipitation would happen at the top, then the air would take the moisture, leaving the mountain dry. He then told a story about experiencing this Chinook wind. He and his colleagues were camping at a project site. Eight inches of snow were on the ground when they went to bed, but there was none in the morning. He explained, "The loss of snow is one inch per hour as a Chinook wind goes by. If you are organism, or animal, and you live in this environment, the conditions you experience on one side of the mountain are different than on the other side. We have to think about the environment organisms are experiencing at different places."

Chris's brief story prompted questions. Lynn asked if Chinook winds were only on the downside of the mountain. Matt asked about the temperature on both sides. Chris explained that it depended on solar insulation, humidity, whether there is a forest—ending with "there are a variety of factors. Think about the temporal component of evolution of organisms. It might very well be critical for organisms to be adaptable to severe events such as flooding as it is for them to adapt under average conditions. Whether organisms are present in an environment may be reflective of rare events. Keep this in mind as we think about this."

This brief segment of the conversation reveals how Chris keeps students active in the conversation and in thinking about the content. He gladly responded to Joan's request to repeat something and Lisa's request for clarification. His willingness for them to chime in made it comfortable for them to do so (thus encouraging *oral interpretation of knowledge*). Chris's story of his own experience (*experiential example*) helped respond to Lisa's question and sparked additional questions. Again, Chris ended that segment with an idea for them to keep in mind as "we think about this."

Chris then put up a transparency dealing with "city effect." He said, "This data was taken within a few miles—from a city, a frost hollow, and a sandy lowland. I want you to compare the number of months the temperatures were at or below thirty-two in the city versus the sandy lowland." Chris pointed them out on screen as he talked through them, highlighting that they revealed habitat variability within a few miles. He used an example of going from the city to the country on a hot day to illustrate as he explained how such variability occurred. Maryann volunteered that pollution would be a factor here, eliciting "a very good point" from Chris. He put up a transparency of a study done in which researchers took temperatures within six-tenths of a mile for a year. The frost-free days ranged from 124 to 276. Chris translated, "The point is, you see more variability in a microhabitat."

These segments on effects and the variability in microhabitats led to the subject of microclimatology. Chris revealed his attitude: "Far too little attention is paid to this." He used a transparency to *overview the topic*. He then asked students to *look at a figure* called snow depth on their handout, making this request: "With a partner write down trends, generalizations you can draw from looking at this diagram. Take three to five minutes to look at this." Students quickly paired, and talking started immediately. Chris moved around the room, answering questions as needed. Six to eight students seated across from one another at the three long stainless steel lab tables that occupied most of the floor space in the room facilitated pairing. The swivel seats on the lab chairs also made it easy for students to turn to those next to them and to turn toward the front of the room when Chris showed slides.

Chris's use of actual *data* for students to *interpret* reinforced his emphasis on thinking. He used the city effect data to have the whole group walk through the meaning of the data. After modeling how to read such data, he asked them to do it on their own in pairs. His request implied that he thought they were capable of drawing conclusions from the chart. The ensuing conversation demonstrated that he was right.

After a few minutes for the pairs to talk, Chris said, "Okay, let's see what you got. Who'll volunteer?" Erica said, "As vegetation decreases, you get a decrease in frost depth." Ann said, "Yes!" and they high-fived across the lab table. Chris repeated the hypothesis, looking at the figure, and agreed. Rich offered another hypothesis, to which Chris responded, "Great, good!" but others apparently did not hear Rich. Jill asked him to repeat his comment. He clarified, "As vegetation gets taller, it can't insulate the ground as well. The snow by itself insulates the ground. There is less frost. The vegetation gets taller and breaks up the snow pack." Lauren said, "If snow is a better insulator, I don't understand." Rich gave her some examples of woods and corn breaking up the level of insulation the snow can provide, using the chart to explain. He asked, "Do you see what I'm saying?" She said, "Yeah, but . . . ," indicating she was not certain. A few other students offered their version of Rich's point.

Then students identified a problem with the chart. Chris looked at it carefully, and his surprised "that is interesting!" indicated that he had not seen the issue before. The conversation continued as Joan said, "In the woods they can reradiate energy—retain it—they would insulate." Melanie offered, "North slopes have more frost than south slopes." Chris worked through the chart and agreed. She added that this did not necessarily mean more snow cover. Chris asked for an explanation. Lynn replied, "Less solar insulation." Kate commented on the woods having more water, the humidity in the air, and the temperature. Chris offered that some farmers do not plow in the fall to retain moisture, noting that the practice seemed consistent with the hypothesis under discussion.

At this point, Chris speculated about wind and the woods absorbing solar insulation. Chris asked, "Why is that important? How does it affect energy?" No one responded. Chris continued: "Try this. When you take a shower, you are all wet; immediately come out and stand in front of a fan. Turn the fan off; think about whether you are warmer or colder." Chris solicited additional ideas about the snow-depth figure: "Other things we could say about this?" Getting no response, he concluded, "You got everything I had—I think that is fascinating. An interesting way to summarize a lot of different factors about snow. Things are getting kind of complex, aren't they? That is the way it is with everything—the deeper you look, the more complex it gets."

This conversation reveals that the students were able to extract the essential information from the snow-depth figure. Chris praised the early contributions, encouraging students to volunteer more ideas. The encouragement to collaborate in pairs sparked students to begin to talk to one another in the large group, helping one another understand the concepts. Chris joined in the learning as well, noting that he had not noticed one of the points students introduced. He also modeled thinking as he worked through the chart to explore students' points. When students were unsure of an issue toward the end of the exchange, Chris offered the concrete example of standing in front of the fan. He validated students' thinking by commenting that they had seen everything he saw in the figure and emphasized that thinking was important by noting the complexity of the subject matter.

THE INTERACTIVE LECTURE PROCESS

After seeing a number of these lectures, we labeled them *interactive lectures* (see fig. 4.1) because they involved students in practicing scientific inquiry. As was the case just described, Chris usually began by using slides of natural phenomena or transparencies containing raw data to introduce the topic. He freely entertained students' questions and comments during these introductions, thus validating them as knowers. To explore the topic, he routinely inserted experiential examples (situating learning in students' experience) such as traveling over the mountains, going from the city to the country on a hot day, and offering his personal experiences to illustrate concepts. These examples usually generated a response from students that prompted exchanges among the group. Exchanges also emerged from data that Chris provided on handouts or transparencies for the group to explore and discuss. Chris often invited students to think about some issue sparked by these exchanges. He left these issues open-ended, demonstrating both the uncertainty of knowledge in science and the component of continual exploration in scientific inquiry. Doing this validated students as knowers and set the stage for the mutual construction of meaning.

In addition to large group discussion, Chris used short activities (again situating in students' experience) to generate thinking and verbal interaction as shown by giving students time to respond in pairs to the snow-depth figure. He then used students' ideas to guide the discussion, generating an opportunity to validate their ideas and give them experience in exploring hypotheses together. His validation of their ideas communicated to them that they were capable of thinking through scientific issues. His often humorous suggestions for things to try to see the concept in action (e.g., standing in front of the fan after a shower) amused students but also translated the concepts to real life. Chris routinely synthesized the day's discussion, distilling it into what he called the "take-home message." Students appreciated this, as Erica described:

> He has a take-home message; he always encourages some kind of result at the end or a conclusion. I think everybody likes to hear a conclusion before you go, "Okay, I kind of forgot." You kind of pull things together, just to maybe constrict things in your head, and you can think about it more later. But I think he does a good job about that.

This form of lecture actively engaged students in thinking, even when they were not verbally participating—perhaps a version of Hake's "heads-on" engagement (1998). Looking at a slide or set of data promoted thinking through the concept, as did Chris's routine "think with me about this" phrase. Commenting on the nature of the course, Jill said, "There are days when I don't say anything, but I'm still involved with the class [because] I am thinking about what he is talking about and what he is saying." She also noted that she appreciated Chris giving students time to think about issues as they arose. Chris often indicated that experts disagreed on issues, that he did not know all the answers, and that the topics were complex. This approach conveyed to students that Chris did not see himself as the omnipotent authority, he acknowledged the importance of reading the scientific literature critically, and he opened the door for their role in mutually constructing meaning.

As the semester continued and the material became increasingly complex, Chris continued to model scientific inquiry by introducing controversies in the scientific literature. The next story illustrates how he used the interactive lecture in exploring such controversies.*

CONTROVERSIES IN FREEZE TOLERANCE

After some preliminary update comments, Chris initiated the lecture with: "Slides, please?" Liz, in her customary place next to the projector, turned it on. The first slide posed the question "What regulates the supercooling point?" Chris joked, "We might as well finish the *Eurosta* [the gallfly] today—you'll be happy to be off the maggots here!"

BASIC EXPLANATION OF PHENOMENON

Chris began with a brief summary of where the class stopped in the previous session:

> The last topic we were considering was what regulates the supercooling point in this particular insect. What we had said was in the wintertime they appear to elevate their supercooling point at the same time they acquire freeze tolerance. Supercooling point, the value at which they spontaneously freeze, is typically around -8 or -10 centigrade when you are working with dry larvae. We also talked about inoculative freezing [this appeared on the next slide]—this can be very important in promoting freeze tolerance. In this case the insect didn't freeze at the highest temperature and couldn't survive as much freezing. Point here as we closed [three graphs appeared on the next slide] was if we only look at fly larvae outside of natural habitat, we may be greatly misled about the

---

*The class lecture described next is reproduced in its entirety to convery the flavor of the experience. Headers throughout the story identify the characteristics of the interactive lecture.

temperature that they will freeze in the field. I must confess that was me for ten years studying this insect. When water content of gall tissue is high, larvae are frozen inoculatively—one or two months earlier than one would expect just based on their super-cooling point. Once again, things are not as simple as they appear on the surface. You have to be careful. Scientists like to have weasel words—in general, it appears—that is the nature of sci-ence. I mentioned before—I spent a considerable amount of time looking for ice-nucleating proteins in the blood of this insect, and they are just not there. We haven't been able to identify them so we need to look somewhere else to explain that.

In this brief review from the previous week, Chris not only highlighted the culminating point of that session; he used his own research as a means to illustrate the role of the scientist in scientific inquiry. By explaining that his focus misled him, he revealed his thinking process and the complexity of scientific inquiry. His suggestion that his research team needs to look else-where for an explanation set the stage for the upcoming lecture and provided the basic explanation of the phenomena to be studied.

Data

As one possible source of explanation, Chris introduced what he called "some work that has been done looking at spheres, some inorganic salts es-sentially that are present in the gallfly." When I saw the slide title—endoge-nous crystalloid spheres—and the larvae pictured in the slide, I suspected the conversation was going to be over my head. Chris set about explaining var-ious characteristics in the slide:

> White masses are called fat body, similar to liver in our cells, so it has a wide variety of important functions. This is where the cry-oprotectants are produced. In other insects this is where the ice-nucleating proteins are produced. You can see this yellowish-brown tissue—these tubes are the Malpighian tubules [part of the excreto-ry system, Chris explained]. If you look closely, however, following some of the clear sections, you can see crystalline structures here. Some larvae have forty or fifty of these crystals. We wondered in looking at these crystals, whether there was ice-nucleating activity—it had been described previously in other studies. But it had not been reported previously in any insect.

Chris showed a slide of one crystal under an electron microscope, ex-plaining a study in which crystals were added to a solution, resulting in an increase in the supercooling point. He continued:

The crystals are found naturally in insects. We've found several of these have sufficient ice-nucleating activity to explain the body supercooling point—they may represent a new class of nucleating agent in insects. We are very excited about this! Find out another mechanism that regulates freezing. Now we will do analysis of proteins in surface membranes to see if we can localize that nucleating activity. Questions?

ORAL INTERPRETATION

Michelle asked, "So they raise supercooling point?" Chris responded, "Right, they are efficient nucleators and explain why some larvae have a higher supercooling point. That was the question: What causes the supercooling point? We went looking for an agent to explain that."

In this segment of the lecture, Chris walked the students through the discovery made by him and his colleagues. The slides served as a means for visualizing the crystals and their placement in the larvae. As Chris talked, he illustrated the questions he and his colleagues had, how they studied those questions, the data they found, and their excitement over the interpretation. Although he did not stop to invite questions until the end of the segment, Chris involved the students mentally in seeing the crystals and data as well as in following his thinking about what was going on in the freezing process. He created an experience in which to situate their learning.

MORE DATA

At this point Chris introduced a controversy related to freezing in the cells. He explained,

> When I talked about freeze tolerance before, one of the things I said was it is generally believed that to survive freezing, ice has to be limited to the extracellular space. You can't have ice forming inside of cells under natural temps and natural cooling rates. Here is the exception. In 1959 and '62, R. W. Salt reported freeze tolerance in fat body cells of this fly larvae from *Eurosta*. The report was ignored for thirty years. It didn't stop cryobiologists from saying if you are going to survive freezing, you have to restrict ice to the extracellular space. What they didn't say was except in fat body cells of this insect. A few years ago, two undergraduates in my lab worked on this. We looked at these fat body cells to see if we could repeat Salt's findings using more sophisticated techniques and tools. We revisited it.

Chris then talked through a number of slides, showing how this work was done. Explaining this controversy gave Chris a chance to reiterate his point about the nature and complexity of science. In addition, he emphasized that two undergraduate students worked with him on this project, making major contributions to his work (another example of validating students as knowers). It also introduced the approach his lab group currently use in furthering their research agenda. Chris turned next to that research:

> Now I'll show you some data we collected using this approach. Keep in mind, I said previously that freeze tolerance occurs within a range. Okay, here is the experiment we did to try to better understand what is happening in respective freezing processes. We had three treatments. [A bar graph on the screen showed the viability of fat body cells after twenty-four hours for each treatment.] We had the fat body cells in Graces' media [a solution] all by themselves with no cryoprotectants. Then we had Graces' media that had 1 M glycerol added to it, and the third treatment froze whole larvae at these temperatures, opened them up and assessed the survival of the fat body cells. So these two, we dissected out fat body cells before we started the experiment, exposing them to temperatures, with the fat body cells in one of these two solutions. In the third, held the whole larvae which had its own cryoprotectants already accumulated. The reason we did this was we are trying to understand why is it an animal can tolerate cooling to -30°C but not to -35°C? Some weak link in system, there is some system, perhaps nervous or other cell type, that is most susceptible to this freezing treatment. And that is why the animal dies. We want to understand the mechanism that determines the lower lethal temperature. Question then is, Can we explain that the lower lethal temperature of the *Eurosta* is somewhere between -25 and -80°C based upon the survival of fat body cells? That is the hypothesis we are testing here.

ORAL INTERPRETATION

Chris paused at this juncture, asking, "Are we all together?" One student asked him to repeat the hypothesis. He said, "Sure. The question is, we want to identify the cell type within the body that is most susceptible to freezing injury. We asked specifically in this case, Can we determine the temperature at which the whole animal dies based on the temperature at which we see lethal injury to fat body cells?" Chris visually perused the room inquisitively, as if to see if there were other questions. Seeing none, he plunged ahead with the outcomes (returning to *data*). As the next slide appeared, he said,

> Here we go. At -5°C, all three treatments had high survival of fat body cells; also at -10°C. Big change at -25°C, where fat body cells

in Graces' media did very poorly. Of course, they have no cryoprotectants. Not too surprising. We add 1 M of glycerol, and
now we get great survival! Makes sense. Not surprised that fat
body cells in whole larvae did better, because whole larvae did better at -25°C. They survived that, formed adults. The last step—
little survival at -80°C. What strikes me as interesting is, we still
have pretty high survival in these two groups. That would lead me
to believe that the fat body cell isn't the most labile tissue in the
insect; some other tissue is the one that is dying and causing the
larvae to die. Because we have seen so much survival in these particular cells.

As Chris described the experiment, the hypothesis it was meant to test, and
the data it produced, he constantly offered a running account of his thoughts.
He interjected why they did particular things, what they wanted to know, and
how particular results were expected, given other data. He ended by speculating on how he was interpreting the outcomes. The data were available, both
on the slides and in handouts, for students to look at while he talked. He
pointed out where he was on each slide so they could follow. This portion of
the interactive lecture wove together experiential examples, data, and oral interpretation of knowledge. It also demonstrated mutually constructing meaning among Chris's research team members.

Synthesis

As was his usual style, Chris wrapped up his lecture with, "What is the take-
home message from all of this?" He summarized as follows:

I don't know whether intracellular freeze tolerance is common or
found in any other freeze tolerant animals. If I was going to make generalizations, I would certainly want to go to other freeze tolerant animals to see if they survive intracellular freezing—rather than going to
something really wimpy like a mammal or a human whose cells never
experience anything less than 37 degrees centigrade. Because that is
where dogma came from that these cells can't survive intracellular
freezing, these cells that never experienced it. It is possible, and we are
doing some things to test this hypothesis, that other animals that are
naturally freeze tolerant—frogs, insects—may tolerate intracellular
freezing in other parts of their body. It may not be that unusual.
Maybe people haven't looked—very little work done in this area. It
may not be unusual that insects have cells that are freeze tolerant.
Come back for the ten-year reunion when we have more data.

ORAL INTERPRETATION OF KNOWLEDGE

The students apparently knew that was the end of Chris's presentation. Joan asked, "Where do the fat cells come from—is it injected?" Chris responded, "No, fat body cell is a tissue in the fly larvae that is comparable in function to the human liver. Fat body is misleading—an unfortunate name. It isn't like, you can't compare to tissue in humans. It is a more metabolically important tissue—like our liver." Rich, attempting to connect parts of the lecture, initiated an exchange with Chris.

> Rich: You were talking about those spherical ice nucleators raising the supercooling point. Is that in conjunction with the fat body cells? Or separate things?
>
> Chris: Separate things; two different studies.
>
> Rich: In the same organism?
>
> Chris: Yes—everything is *Eurosta*. Those crystals are found in lumen of Malpighian tubules. They are blind ending tubes, and the crystals sit inside.
>
> Rich: The fat bodies are also the same way.
>
> Chris: Yes, but outside of Malpighian tubules. They are separate tissues.
>
> Rich: Fat bodies tolerate intracellular ice.
>
> Chris: Yes, but we don't know whether Malpighian tolerates intracellular ice, but the crystals within them . . .
>
> Rich: Raise the supercooling point within the whole animal.
>
> Chris: Yes, ice will nucleate water inside of fat body cells. Looking at different compartments for ice formation. What really helps in this field is to look at different water compartments of the organism you are looking at—think about which ones are going to do. What is control flux across membranes?

At the close of this exchange, Chris turned to the whole group and said, "Questions?"

This class session illustrates the interactive lecture components summarized earlier as well as the three principles of constructive-developmental pedagogy. Although this lecture focused heavily on the existing knowledge and controversies around freeze tolerance, Chris invited students to think along with him about the questions raised and next steps in research, thereby validating their ability to do so. By recounting the various research efforts and his own stories about them, Chris introduced experiential examples to create an experience to which students could relate. His extensive use of data, figures, and charts also offered concrete examples. These efforts helped situate learning in students' experience, even though most of it was created during the lecture. Despite very little verbal participation on the students' part until the end, Chris validated them as knowers when they did participate. He repeated explanations gladly without judging students for not understanding the first time. For example, he did not criticize Joan for asking the question about fat body even though he had earlier explained its similarity to the human liver. His interaction with Rich near the end of the segment validated Rich's thinking and showed Chris's thinking as he joined Rich in speculating and wondering about the topic. Chris set the stage for mutual construction of meaning by checking progress and understanding with comments such as, "Are we all together?" and "Questions?" His interchange with Rich represents mutual construction of knowledge as he and Rich spark each other's thoughts while Rich tries to connect various ideas in the lecture. In his closing synthesis, Chris imparted a take-home message that highlighted the unresolved controversies.

This class session demonstrates that constructive-developmental pedagogy and the exploration of large amounts of information are compatible. Chris was the primary voice during this lecture, yet he did not transmit knowledge to students to passively write in their notebooks. Instead, he re-created each phase of the research under study, engaging students to think about the data, the decisions that were made, and what questions and conclusions were overlooked. He used many of Arons's (1997) processes (highlighted at the outset of this chapter) to involve students in reasoning through the material. He carefully balanced presenting existing knowledge with surfacing the controversies surrounding it as well as emphasizing how scientists make decisions that ultimately result in knowledge creation. Even his synthesis is a statement of what is known, what is not known, and what possible next steps are in answering the questions surrounding freeze tolerance. Chris, in essence, re-created the dialogue on controversies in freeze tolerance and invited students to join it, first mentally, then verbally.

CAN STUDENTS THINK LIKE SCIENTISTS?

Chris's primary goal for this course was for students to think like scientists. For Chris, that meant learning how to explore the scientific literature, identifying useful questions, understanding how to determine the next step in a research effort, and communicating these findings in the scientific community. Chris situated this goal in the context of understanding the cellular, organismal and evolutionary challenges faced by organisms living in environments with low temperatures. Although he wanted students to understand life in the cold, he explained that he was also interested in their ability to understand scientific inquiry: "They [the students] never thought about where these facts that they've been getting stuffed down them come from, and what it takes to do some of that research. Science is done by real people and is influenced by the foibles of real people." It was no surprise to us as observers that students' epistemological assumptions mediated their ability to think like scientists. Consider, for example, Maryann's and Jill's comments on whether this goal was accomplished. Maryann offered:

> Think like a scientist? No, the first part of the class absolutely not. It was just a straight lecture like any other class. The only thinking I did was coming up with questions that were scientific. All the thinking that is coming right now is at the very end. I do find it interesting and think this class is beneficial in the fact that I was able to pick a topic that I was interested in. I guess I am thinking of questions and possible research areas that can be done, and I am starting to critically think about the literature, which is good. But I wish I had more concrete feedback, like am I completely wacko, are my ideas completely invalid? I mean it is good. I really do like the fact that we could pick all the topics that we were interested in because I really do think that I understood my topic better, like he allowed me to come up with my own questions. But he is shooting them all down, so I don't know what to think. I do think that it was good at the very end that he made us think about stuff, but then he is not giving me anything. I have nothing to go by. He is just being very vague. He says you have to think about all the issues of your project; that is a statement he has made. What does he mean all the issues of my project? What are the issues of my project?

Maryann's comments show that she was aware of the goal of thinking critically about the literature and developing her own questions. She appreciated developing her own questions but did not know what to do when Chris "shoots them down." She was stumped by his suggestion that she think about the issues of her project; thus, his suggestion gave her nothing to go on.

In contrast, Jill understood Chris's invitations to think further, as evident in this comment:

> There are some things that are left in the air, but I think that is in a good sense. There are things that we don't quite understand yet, that would lend to grant proposals that would lend to further research. I think that is the key in science; you have to have questions to move further in science. It is the whole idea that science is futuristic; you are coming up with new ideas; you want to invent new things; you need to utilize other research to come up with your own. I think he sparks questions and I think that is what science is about—questioning things, pulling things together from different sources (that is what research is). Everything that has been done in science, you take something that someone else has learned, and you say I have an idea; this work proves this side of my project. I just did a report on cancer and cancer of the kidney. First someone develops an idea that it is in the cortex, and then someone realizes that it is in the tubules that run through the cortex, and even portions outside of the cortex, and then someone takes the ideas of these portions and says I discovered it looks like these type of cells, so that limits it to just the tubules that run in the tubules. I think you have to learn from what other people have done and apply it and ask questions, and that is how you move forward and make discoveries. I think by asking questions constantly you come up with ideas for research and new discoveries.

Why the difference between Maryann and Jill, both of whom are seniors? Our interviews with both women indicated that they held different assumptions about the nature of knowledge and authority. Maryann viewed knowledge as certain and authorities as omnipotent. She tried to follow Chris's advice on her project, but did not understand that he was trying to get her to think beyond what is known. For Maryann, there is not anything beyond what is known. This probably explains her view that the first half of the course was straight lecture because she believed Chris was communicating unquestionable knowledge. She was frustrated that Chris did not give her a concrete response that would help her move forward. Jill, on the other hand, viewed knowledge as uncertain and created by researchers asking questions and gathering data to inform those questions. She sees science as knowledge construction and perceives that she can play a role in that process. Although she attended the same lectures as did Maryann, Jill reported that the lectures raised questions for students to think about.

In chapter 1, I quoted Lynn, a graduate student, who explained having held both sets of assumptions in her own experience in science. Her comments bear repeating here:

> You read it in black and white, and that is just the way it is. That carries over when you start reading scientific literature because you read a scientific paper and you do an experiment. It is in writing and in black and white, and that is the way it is. You see a little bit more of the process in how they came to conclusions, but it is still—it takes a while to start reading literature critically. If somebody did the experiment and they published it, it has to be right, it is true. And then when you pick one part and start reading all of the literature, all the publications on that narrow focus, you start realizing there are a lot of people out there who disagree and then will come up with contradicting results. That is a really strange thing! If this person's right because they got it published and this person is right because they got it published, that doesn't work because they both can't be right all of the time. . . . That is a really neat shift to start reading that literature and realizing that these people, it kind of goes hand in hand that the names on these papers are human beings and reading the literature, and realizing because they are human beings their research is not always perfect either and they can come to misleading conclusions, or their data could be skewed or whatever, which could lead to different conclusions. To some extent you can become critical of the research and you can also realize that the people are human. So that can make you more critical of the research but it really makes you put it together more. . . . I think it is tough because people always tell you it is just one of those assumptions you have. I am not sure what actually it is that knocks your assumptions off and makes you realize that "big deal, this person published." It is in black and white; that doesn't mean it is put upon a pedestal and it is right and it is truth and that is the end, that is it period. There is always dot, dot, dot at the end. I think that everyone is going to reach that stage at different points. I reached that stage toward the end of undergrad, probably not until my senior year.

The progression Lynn recounts is the shift from viewing knowledge as certain to viewing it as uncertain. Along with the shift, authorities become human and subsequently fallible. As Lynn eloquently points out, this shift is necessary for students to meet Chris's goal for them to think like scientists. The majority of students in winter biology, like Jill, had experienced this shift and subsequently viewed the course as a success. The few students who still viewed knowledge as certain, as did Maryann, viewed the course and its outcomes entirely differently.

THE INTERACTIVE LECTURE: ENGAGING STUDENTS IN SCIENTIFIC INQUIRY

The interactive lecture was Chris's primary approach to teaching students to think like scientists. The majority of the students interviewed reported that the interactive lecture promoted learning and retention, encouraged active participation, and fostered a no-risk atmosphere. In contrast, a few students reported feeling pressured to participate and overwhelmed by the format of the course.

LEARNING AND RETENTION

Rich described learning in winter biology as something above and beyond learning the facts. He explained,

> The whole focus of most of my classes in college has been just regurgitating the facts, with the exceptions of a few like winter biology where the base facts were given to you on the ground level and where the actual learning was coming in above and beyond that. The learning was coming in where he would ask, "What do you think about this?" And you couldn't just look on your notes; you couldn't just remember what he said. It is not just blatant memorization; learning comes into it when you are utilizing the ideas toward something new that hasn't been done. That kind of set-up seems to stimulate me more than just being like a computer and storing this information to really do nothing with. This class gave more interest into the applications, what is going on right now, ideas of it, theories on what they don't know. The other classes it was "here is what we know and you have to know it too." There wasn't any fairly mutual exchange between the instructor and the class, no formulations of ideas beyond.

Erica concurred with Rich's view, noting, "We are adding upon our knowledge rather than taking chunks and learning them. I can bring what I have learned and apply that."

Jill linked this gradual learning process to retention:

> I remembered more from that class because of that class format. When he would walk around and look at us, we weren't waiting for him to keep talking; we were thinking about what he had just said. Just an example, I started this thing when I go to dinner with my friends, we have "What did you learn today?" On Tuesdays and Thursdays it was always about his class. It was always something

about his class that I could retain and recall, and I thought, *"That has got to say something."* It forces you to describe it to someone else that knows nothing else about the topic; it forces you to know about the topic well enough. Just that I was able to retain big ideas and be able to pass it on without studying notes per se. I think it made studying time a lot easier because I knew it before I read through the notes. I understood it and the concepts. I don't really think they were easy in the class; I think that it set up for a gradual learning process and that is when you remember. He made it easy to learn, he made it fun, and I knew nothing about winter biology before. It is not like I knew anything about metamorphism.

According to these students, learning occurred because Chris engaged them in thinking beyond the facts and helped them connect knowledge in a gradual way. They became invested in thinking about these topics, even to the point of incorporating them in regular dinner conversation. The thinking process and moving into new territory heightened motivation to learn.

ACTIVE PARTICIPATION

A central component of thinking beyond the facts was active participation. Erica described the effect of active participation on her learning:

We are allowed to express ourselves and encouraged to ask questions. By participating as much as we can, I think that it adds to the learning. I think it is the best part of the class. There is no intimidation. We are allowed, any time we are confused or lost, to ask questions. He gives us the feeling that we are just as knowledgeable, not as knowledgeable as he is, but we have a lot of knowledge under our belts. He gives us opportunities to speak and express our views rather than just sitting there and regurgitating what we have read, so I think that by having more participation in the class we have a lot more ability. In this class I feel like there are many different ways that I can test my knowledge. I feel more secure with what I have learned in this class; I feel like I have had a different approach to what I have learned.

For Erica, an important part of her security came from expressing herself. Chris's message that she was knowledgeable and his encouraging questions increased her ability to participate. These elements of Chris's approach affected Jill too, as is evident from her comments:

As far as I am concerned it is the way he spoke to us and with us and not at us. He wasn't lecturing material in a book form; it was his hands-on experience. It builds a lot of confidence in him when you know he knows exactly what he is talking about. It was his style—I loved him. He is a very intelligent man, but he also has the confidence that we all have something to contribute and I think it makes you feel more intelligent. . . . I think it brings a lot out because you see a lot more openness in that class and people extracting more than I think they normally would in a typical class setting.

Jill had confidence in Chris and felt that he had confidence in her. In addition, Jill noted that Chris modeled the thinking process:

Another thing, which I think is so important, is that he would say something, and then he would think about it himself. When you are learning something new, you have to integrate it and think, *What does that mean? How does that work?* He gives you the time to think about it when you have just heard it. A lot of [classes] when you go home you might think of something, but [here] you can attack your question right then and there.

Chris, in essence, modeled active participation. He was engaging in active participation as he shared his thinking. Making the classroom a place to share thinking and treating students with respect (or validating them as knowers) heightened students' interest in becoming active participants.

Chris also encouraged structured active participation and gave students a chance to engage in thinking when he asked pairs of students to look at graphs or data and draw conclusions about them. Jill shared the importance of these activities:

It is good to work with other people discussing something. It sparks new ideas by doing that with a partner and explaining what you are trying to say. I think more feedback creates more questions. The more discussions you have about something, the more you know about something. I think by having a discussion with another person, their ideas would spark more ideas in us.

Lynn concurred, elaborating on why working with other people might spark ideas:

I like exercises like that because then you are working more with the thought patterns of the students, what is their logical process for looking at information and drawing conclusions because a lot of times that can be very different. Everybody has his or her own methods of logical reasoning. You can start out with the same information, but you might get to this conclusion before you get to that conclusion, depending on how you look at it.

Matt agreed with the notion of learning from others, saying, "There is a student who sees something else in it . . . it shows you a different way of thinking." These students appreciated working together to decipher graphs and charts because their peers' thinking stretched their thinking.

For a few students, though, this activity was perceived as too challenging. For example, Maryann reported:

> I am not sure that we took away all that we could have from that graph because he would just take our comments and say okay, and sometimes I felt that we were missing something and he wouldn't tell us because we had to come up with all of it ourselves. In a way it was good because he made us think about it, but I sometimes think we could have gotten more out of it.

Maryann thought it was good for the students to think, but her focus was on getting everything she was supposed to get out of the graph rather than stretching her thinking. Ann (quoted at the outset of the chapter) was more adamant about wanting Chris to tell the class the points of importance, viewing anything more than that as a waste of time. Both women believed Chris to be omniscient and thought they would learn more by listening to him than thinking through things with other students.

No-Risk Atmosphere

An important factor that encouraged participation for most students was the no-risk atmosphere Chris developed in the course. Students described this atmosphere coming from the way Chris responded to students' questions and ideas. Matt explained his perception of this:

> He is always friendly and open for your questions and opinions. If you say something wrong, he doesn't just ignore you; if you say something, it's not dumb. Every question is a smart question, as long as you ask, because that is why you are here. He gives you the feeling that you are here to learn and experiment with those topics. In his class I don't ever [think I] should not ask something because I may be wrong.

Like Matt, Rich viewed the no-risk atmosphere as important for his learning and reported that it was unusual in science courses he had encountered. He said,

> The amount of participation I put into this class, as a science class, is the most I have in comparison to my overall class work. This is the kind of student I am. I talk a whole lot in class, with the exception of my science classes—I chalk it up to the nature of science. But in this class I was more like the student that I normally am than

in my other science classes. It was because of the openness of discussion, the no fear of being wrong. In other science classes all of
these people are competing; everybody is out for themselves. They
don't want to hear your idea; they just want to get into medical
school. So in my other classes I can sit and communicate about
things, whereas I get into science or zoology and there are primarily pre-med or pre-dent students in there. All I feel is completely stifled. It really is a turnoff to any kind of interest—it stops my learning. But a lot of the people in winter biology are pre-med students,
and Dr. Snowden with his method of teaching at least showed to me
that he could get around the competition factor and could make it
closer to a friendlier environment rather than the cold classes.

Although Rich emphasized that students promote competition, he viewed Dr.
Snowden's teaching method as the factor that made this class different. He described further what Chris Snowden did to promote students taking risks:

[The lecture] has got to have structure because everybody is not on
the same level. And it's got to have a mediator that can guide the
group idea in the right direction and that lets certain instances of
false knowledge kind of seep into the fact and encourage the idea to
come out—but if it is wrong, fine, subtly set it aside so it doesn't get
into the collective. It takes some serious skills dealing with people,
their collective knowledge. It is the best way to utilize other students' knowledge, at least for me. There is a fine line—if I say something that is fundamentally wrong, you have to isolate that response
as an instructor and figure out why that student came to that conclusion instead of being like, "No, that is the wrong answer." Chris
would find out why that came about and steer it over to the rest of
the idea: "Okay, that is not quite right, but how did you get there?
Is this how you got there?" That is what I mean by subtly bringing
it back or saying that I would not be wrong if I came out and said
something.

Rich's explanation, along with the numerous other students who commented on the no-risk atmosphere, illustrated that Chris validated students
as knowers, yet did not validate everything they believed. His structuring of
the learning process and scientific inquiry, coupled with respect for students,
portrayed "being wrong" as an acceptable part of the learning process. As
Rich described, Chris helped students sort out their confusions in ways that
did not make them feel stupid. This is a crucial part of mutually constructing meaning—helping students to share their thoughts so that they can be
connected to ideas in the discipline in reasonable ways.

A few students did not share their peers' enthusiasm for the open discussion atmosphere. Maryann articulated this best:

> I am a different kind of a student. I don't like to participate that much in class if I have nothing to say. But I felt that he was placing such a premium on class participation, so during the lectures I was frantically trying to come up with these types of questions, just so that I can ask them, so he will say that I participate. I felt like he was compelling us to participate a lot. I almost felt that when I asked questions in his class, I had to know the answer. I would feel really uncomfortable asking a stupid or obvious question. I felt that when I asked questions that they had to be some sort of intelligent question, showing some kind of previous knowledge.

Maryann's stress came from feeling that she had nothing acceptable to say. While other students felt they could say anything without fear of being wrong, Maryann was struggling to come up with intelligent questions. Maryann also reported finding the course format overwhelming. She described it like this:

> I thought his lecturing was kind of confusing at some times. It was hard for me when he gave these big handouts for me to follow; it seems like he went very fast. It stresses me when teachers don't write on the board or don't write things down because they always go too fast for me. I always like for teachers to write it out rather than flipping slides because they always go too fast.

Maryann reported having a hard time getting down everything Chris said. For her, the handouts were overwhelming rather than helpful. In contrast, Rich said, "He basically gave us the notes, then lectured so we did not have to have our faces buried in notes." It is clear from Maryann's comments that her way of knowing and the interactive lecture did not connect. Although the handouts could validate her absolute knowing, she did not perceive it that way.

SUMMARY

Lynn's reflections on the course offer insight into how the same course could affect students so differently. She explained,

> I think his class is like reading primary literature. As a student [you can] deal with that in a couple of ways. If you can read critically and think critically and ask questions if you agree with something or don't agree with something, that will work to your benefit and you

will get a lot more out of it. But you can also sit there and just read the articles and say, "It was published; it is right," and you can also just sit in that class and listen to the lecture and take your notes and memorize it and take the test. I am sure there are people in that class who go both ways.

Indeed Lynn was right that there were people who went both ways. For the majority of students who had shifted their assumptions about the certainty of knowledge, the interactive lecture promoted learning. For those who had not shifted assumptions, the interactive nature of the lecture was perceived as a hindrance. These two ways of responding to the course were evident in students' reactions to the assignments as well.

THE PROJECT: STUDENTS PRACTICING SCIENTIFIC INQUIRY

The second major approach Chris used to help students think like scientists was the project assignment of writing a research paper, presenting it in a scientific seminar format, and writing a grant proposal based on the paper. The paper required students to explore the primary literature in science and identify useful questions in the topic area. The paper, presentation, and proposal all addressed communication skills required to function in the scientific community. The grant proposal helped students explore how to determine the next step in a research effort. The paper component of the assignment ran parallel to the interactive lecture portion of the course in which Chris modeled how to explore the literature and identify useful questions. The presentations took place in the latter portion of the course with the grant proposal serving as the final exam.

EXPLORING THE PRIMARY LITERATURE

Although students found the paper, presentation, and proposal challenging, most gave each project their best effort and felt that it was productive. Jill spoke to the fear many students felt in beginning the project:

I went to his office a few times, "I don't know where to begin," and he is really great about [it]. I told him I have gone to the library and I feel worse now than I did before. He handed me this stack of things; they were very specific primary articles. Now how do I take this and not knowing anything about this topic—how do I decide to talk about one specific area? Once you are out there, you realize that it is not so overwhelming; all of these ideas started coming to me about what I could do for my topic. It was almost as if he was saying, "I think you can do this," and we are going, "What?" It makes you think, *Well, all right, we'll try it.* When someone else has that confidence "I think you can do this," and it is not as if he is saying, "I think you can do this and you are being ridiculous." He is saying, "Hey, yeah, it's scary. Just do it." He's realistic about it as much as we think it is a scary thing and to some people unrealistic. He addresses that, and that's what makes you say, "Okay, maybe I can surprise myself," and you do.

Jill's uncertainty about exploring the literature dissipated after Chris gave her some articles to get her started. His confidence in her and her peers encouraged her to try it, and once she got into the literature, ideas emerged about useful questions for her topic.

Matt described a similar experience:

> The research paper we did, it helps to go out and find information and sort information and write something smart about the entire thing. Every time I go to the library to research, I find a better way to find more information. Every time I find more information, you find it better, you know where to look, you have an article in the reference page, and you find there what you can use for your paper and that helps a lot.

Matt and Jill, like the majority of their classmates, learned how to explore the primary literature and begin to identify useful questions. Others like Maryann (quoted earlier in this chapter) were less sure of what they were supposed to be exploring.

LEARNING COMMUNICATION SKILLS OF THE SCIENTIFIC COMMUNITY

Consensus existed among the students we interviewed about the value of learning communication skills to function in the scientific community. Many commented on gaining these skills from the presentations, as was the case with Erica:

> There are a lot of scientific meetings that I will have to attend and speak, not only something formally but also in an informal setting. Maybe someone you just want to talk to about what you are doing, and I think by having the experience of these presentations it becomes easier to talk about what you have been doing in your research. I think it is important for biologists to learn that manner of presentation because it is something that will be an ongoing process. Presentations are basically all you will be doing.

Other students added that the paper and proposal also enhanced their communication skills. James reported that "requiring a strict format for the research paper" was an excellent idea to show students what is required to be published, adding that "getting published is *life* in science." Matt noted that the grant proposal prepared him for an important scientific function, saying, "That is the way you get money for research." Most students reported being nervous about the presentation because they had very little experience in presenting. They agreed, however, that it was a useful way to gain communication skills.

IDENTIFYING THE NEXT STEP IN RESEARCH

Understanding how to determine the next step in research, something students were expected to do in the grant proposal, was intimidating to many students. Michelle reported, "I am scared to death about the proposal. I don't even know what it looks like." Erica, Jan, and Jill also reported being intimidated by this task. Jan reported that Chris helped her once she got a topic, "but until then it was up to us, and very hard to decide. He had a bunch of articles on animals that I looked at—they showed what people are studying. It took a lot to get started." As was the case with the research paper, once students got started, they seemed less intimidated. Jill, who had expressed great consternation over the proposal, shared this reaction retrospectively:

> His point was, he wanted us to learn how to be scientists. I just realized that by making us write this grant proposal, we have to put what we have learned—our topic, our seminar—into a question and be a scientist about it and make a revelation. I have been sitting here talking about how science is moving forward and asking questions, and that is exactly what we are doing by writing the grant proposal. That is why it is so scary. That is what science is about, and if you can't do it and you can't write a proposal, then maybe you shouldn't be in science. But I think the key to really being a scientist is to not just follow what other people are saying about their discoveries but to go out on your own. I think he is doing that.

Jill knew that the proposal was part of extending questions to further understanding in science. She recognized that the entire process was crucial to being a scientist.

FRUSTRATIONS

A few students remained intimidated about the grant proposal at the time of the interviews. Their concerns seemed to focus on what they perceived as Chris's disapproval with their proposals. Erica was worried:

> I was talking to him about my paper, and he said, "I don't know how this individual project will do for the grant proposal." I was a little bit worried about that, which made me a little bit angry when he didn't say anything about that before when that was the topic for my paper, so now I feel like I am kind of locked. Specifically he said

there are a lot of species that have been studied that are like the spider I am studying. . . . Why this particular one? Why would anybody care about this particular species? Why it needs funding? Why we need to learn anything about it?

Erica was not sure what to do with Chris's comments, and apparently did not realize he was giving her the outline for what her proposal needed to accomplish and the specific questions it needed to answer.

Similarly, Maryann felt that Chris was vague in his responses to her request for help:

I just wish he would be a little bit more clear. . . . He's being very vague when he talks. He's saying basically, "You have to convince me that this is interesting." What exactly does that mean, "convince you that it is interesting"? I am not exactly sure how or what to do with this. I think he should know. He knows that I have had absolutely no experience with doing this. I wish he could be a little bit more concrete. He did put one of the student's grant proposals on reserve, which I looked at a bit; I really have to go back and read it.

Like Erica, Maryann did not view this advice as guidance for what the proposal should accomplish; she considered it a vague response she did not know how to handle.

Despite Maryann's confusion, Chris told us in an interview after the course was completed that she received one of the five A's he assigned on grant proposals. He explained his interactions with Maryann near the end of the term and the transformations he saw in her final assignment:

Maryann spent a lot of time talking about a lot of extraneous things rather than focusing in on what is important. I pointed this out to her, and when her research proposal came in later on, it was nice and tight and focused and just what I was looking for. What I had conveyed was not enough for her to operate on because she could surely do it. She is plenty smart.

This is an example of an instructor's advice initially missing the student's way of knowing. As Chris and Maryann continued to interact, Chris realized that his previous feedback to convince him it was interesting was insufficient for Maryann to figure out that focus was the key issue. He then gave her more concrete feedback (i.e., in pointing out her focus issue), thus moving closer to her way of knowing. This concrete feedback connected enough for her that she was able to succeed in focusing her proposal.

Although Chris and Maryann were able to connect, the project portion of the course still missed some students. They were not sure how to explore the literature, identify questions, or determine the next steps in research. This response is most clear in Ann's comments:

> I would have learned more if he had lectured and [we had] gotten tested over it rather than each person talking about polar bears or whatever. He tried to turn it into a research-based class. I didn't really expect that and don't enjoy it. Doing a research paper is monotonous—find ten articles, write it, turn it in, get graded.

Ann apparently took the path Lynn described earlier of reading text that is published as unquestionable truth. Because Chris said the paper had to have a minimum of ten references, she interpreted that as finding just ten articles. Chris had hoped that students would read well above the minimum number of articles required for citation in their research papers. He explained, "What I wanted them to do was read twenty-thirty papers, from that you have a nice set of ten for your paper. As opposed to 'Gosh, I only got six and I need four more and it is due in a week or three days.'" Students who preferred to listen, take notes, and take the test rather than to think critically about the content valued the communication skills portion of the project but did not see the essence of the remaining goals it entailed.

UNEXPECTED BENEFITS

Rich shared one outcome of the grant proposal assignment that was not clearly stated in Chris's goals. He expressed surprise at the interactions he was having with other students about the grant proposal:

> The fact that I am talking with other people in the class and they are asking me questions, and we are communicating without even being in the classroom setting, that is definitely something I have never seen in my other classes. So that whole team goal sort of thing still seems to be going on even without the setting [of class]. The idea was set up and it seems to still be going on even with this assignment, which is great. I helped Michelle with her assignment. I knew it shouldn't be this many words and we condensed it. That was my piece of knowledge. I will write my grant proposal and give it to her, and she will do all my grammar stuff because I can't do that. She'll give it back to me and tell me how I could have said this better. In that mutual exchange of learning between students is just an extension of the class and it seems to be something. I knew Michelle kind of; I never met Ann or Colleen before, any of them around my table.

This mutual exchange of learning was so foreign to Rich that he could not quite explain it, leaving it at "it seems to be something." He clearly saw this collaboration as beneficial.

Overall, Chris believed that the students' grant proposals achieved the purpose he intended for this assignment. In our final interview together, he reflected on what students learned from the experience:

> The purpose of the proposal was accomplished in the sense that they [students] have a better idea now what it means to do primary research and how it is reported. Some of the things one has to think about if you are going to continue work—what it would take to write a proposal, how hard it is to define a question. Maybe a lot of what they got out of this isn't going to show up as a high-quality proposal on a piece of paper and that's okay. Because in some ways they weren't ever in a position to do this, and of course they found it extremely difficult because it is extremely difficult.

Chris recognized that the students had no experience with writing grant proposals, so he created this assignment for students to learn a process of scientific inquiry. The grant proposal became a tangible means for Chris to advance his goal of encouraging students to think like scientists.

FACULTY-STUDENT INTERACTION: RESPECTING STUDENTS AS THINKERS

Chris emphasized throughout the term that he was available to help students with their projects and encouraged them to talk with him about their work. He estimated at the end of the term that about 60 percent had engaged in substantive interactions with him about the projects. Others, he reported, asked brief questions before and after class. The students we interviewed perceived him as available and approachable. Jan said, "He is always there at his computer. Other profs have doors shut, but he doesn't." James, who worked in another lab in the building, said, "I never went during office hours. I just wandered down there and he was there and willing to see me." James added that Chris was a "very sociable, nice guy, easy to interact with. He never lets on if he is not happy to see you." Michelle offered, "He doesn't talk down to us. He dresses like us—wears a T-shirt. He's very—hey, what's up? He is like us." She also appreciated that Chris did not put people on the spot during a conversation. These perceptions helped students approach Chris's office when they needed assistance.

Once in Chris's office, students again reported being comfortable with him. Erica explained,

> He takes the approach that he wants you to do it on your own. He will help you plot through your ideas and he will help you sort out what you are thinking and help direct you and he still encourages you to work independently. He just makes his office setting very comfortable. He'll ask, "What are you confused about?" And he will

ask your opinion on the matter rather than telling you what you should do. He will ask you exactly what is happening and what you need help with and try to direct you from there rather than presenting himself in a way that is kind of intimidating. . . . I think the way I see it is that he wants you to feel that you are at the same level as him, not in as far as the same knowledge. He wants the atmosphere to be such that you feel comfortable asking him or talking to him in any way.

Most students' comments implied that they were generally intimidated by their professors and did not expect to be respected by them. Thus, Chris seemed unusual in their minds. Jill captures this in her trepidation about a visit to his office:

When I lost my voice before my seminar, I was freaking out. I thought he was going to be so angry. I am throwing off his schedule if I can't speak; when am I going to give my seminar? This was the day before the seminar. I thought, *Now I am putting him in a position that he has to fill that extra time if I don't speak,* and I went up to his office. I did not know what to expect. He said, "Hey, how are you doing?" He recognized me right away. And right then and there, I knew it was going be okay. He said, "What's up?" and I said, "I lost my voice," and my voice was just cracking all over at the time. He said, "Well, where is it?" and started bending around his desk looking around. He was not saying, "Oh, my God, this is a problem!" He knew why I was there, [and tried] to relax me a little, and he said all right. It is not that the rules are rigid with him because that is not the way life is and he knows that. He is also a demanding teacher in that he doesn't put up with a lot of fluff and garbage. He sifts those people out of the class, and I appreciate that. He's human.

Jill expected Chris to be angry; she got understanding instead. Her last comment makes it clear that he is still demanding, yet human in his interaction with students. Perhaps this explains why students who were intimidated in their conversations with Chris still felt positively about him. Even though they wanted more concrete advice from him, they did not feel put down or treated unfairly.

SUMMARY

Chris Snowden's course raises the possibility of merging individual meaning-making, social construction of knowledge, and knowledge creation in the

discipline in the teaching process. He invited and helped students to construct knowledge for themselves during his interactive lectures and through
the project. At the same time, he modeled the scientific processes that he and
his fellow scientists use to explore the primary literature, identify useful
questions, determine the next steps in research, and think about controversies. He also introduced them to communication in the scientific community. Chris always mediated his validation of students as knowers with asking
them to think about their ideas in the context of existing scientific knowledge. Perhaps most important, Chris described scientific knowledge simultaneously as it currently exists and as it is evolving. He shared existing
knowledge, encouraged students to learn it, and at the same time encouraged
them to use existing knowledge critically to identify the next useful question
to further knowledge. Chris was able to convey Bereiter's (1994) idea of creating and improving knowledge in the discipline without students' viewing
scientific knowledge as absolute and scientists as omnipotent. Their self-
authorship was informed by the scientific inquiry prevalent in the discipline.
This created a bridge to contextual knowing because it placed self-authorship in the context of relevant scientific practice.

Furthermore, Chris illustrated that content learning and critical thinking
can be addressed through the lecture format. His interactive lecture revealed
that a teacher can engage students in exploring data and primary literature,
finding useful questions, and learning the processes to inform those questions all through the lecture format. That was possible, however, because the
interactive lecture emphasized experiential examples, actual data, and the interpretation (usually oral) of knowledge. The ways Chris presented the nature of science and his role as a scientist, shared his own thinking, and
validated students as knowers were crucial components of his success in getting students to "think with" him.

Another important dynamic of the course was the requirement that students engage in scientific inquiry. Chris offered opportunities to do so during the interactive lectures through group activities and encouragement of
exchanges during the lecture. Their most significant opportunity came in the
project phase of the course. The three project components—paper, presentation, and proposal—required direct experience with the four goals Chris
outlined for scientific inquiry. These opportunities helped those who already
agreed with Chris about the tentative nature of science to participate in developing knowledge further. The concrete nature of the project also helped
some students who had yet to endorse science as uncertain to encounter
some of the controversies directly in an area of their interest.

With regard to the ever-pressing question of content coverage, Chris certainly did not give up teaching content to accomplish his critical thinking
goals. He dealt with many topics during the interactive lectures, and the

student presentations introduced more. He organized the first portion of the course to address topics he felt overviewed the area of adaptation to cold temperatures and allowed the students to select the context for further exploring such adaptations during the second half of the course. His only requirement for their topics was that they must relate to life in the cold. The important dynamic in this course was the manner in which Chris taught content. His ability to integrate individual meaning-making, the scientific process, and knowledge creation in an advanced science course raises hope that constructive-developmental pedagogy can be widely used to achieve both content and self-authorship goals.

CHAPTER 5

Investigating Together

Building One's Own Construction of Mathematics

WITH JENNIFER BUCKLEY

As we approached the mazelike building that housed the mathematics department, we pulled out the directions that Sam Rivers had provided to us to find his classroom.* We found the room for Math 400/500 on the second floor without incident. Sam (the main instructor for the course) was already there, hanging his sport coat on the chair and rolling up his sleeves as he jovially chatted with students arriving early. Sam moved the table at the front of the room to one side. We chose seats on the side of the room toward the back so that we could see the students and the blackboards to record our observations of inquiry mathematics. Although it was the second session of the semester, it was the first class we attended so that Sam could ask the group's permission for our observation before we attended.

Our being here was initially sparked by seeing a flyer advertising Math by Inquiry, a course offered through the Department of Mathematics and Statistics and sponsored by Project Discovery.** We contacted the instructor, Sam Rivers, to talk about our project. Soon after our conversation with Sam, we concluded that the course would be a good place to see constructive-developmental pedagogy in action because Sam's teaching philosophy advocated self-authorship and was consistent with the three principles undergirding the observational project. Sam summarized his teaching philosophy in this early conversation: "*People need to understand that mathematics is human created.*" He continued, "A lot of people believe that math was on the backs of the stone that Moses brought down from Mount Sinai!" Part of his mission, as he saw it, was to help students understand that mathematical ideas and rules were created by humans and that they, as humans, could participate in the creation process. He further explained that students often learned math by

---

*This chapter was coauthored with Jennifer Buckley, who participated in the observations of this course.

**The mission of Project Discovery, funded by the National Science Foundation and the state of Ohio, is to improve the quality of teaching and learning of mathematics and science.

memorizing rules and formulas but had little understanding of the conceptual basis for math rules or the structure of mathematics. Project Discovery, on the other hand, advocated students learning "to seek answers to their own questions and actively building their own knowledge through problem solving and investigations, inside and outside the classroom" (Project Discovery 1993). Sam was affiliated with Project Discovery because he agreed with its mission. He planned to use Project Discovery's emphasis on inquiry learning as his primary approach in this math course. He was a proponent of the constructivist view of teaching being discussed in mathematics education reform. We were interested to see how his approach would work with transitional and independent knowers, the ways of making meaning we expected because juniors and seniors were the majority of Sam's class.

The coverage versus critical thinking debate noted in chapter 4 in science education is also occurring in mathematics education. Taylor and Campbell-Williams (1993) reported attempts in math education "to deconstruct the objectivist myth and develop pedagogies that recast classrooms as communities of mathematicians who engage in purposeful (from the students' perspectives) problem-posing and problem-solving activities that are characterized by social practices of negotiation and consensus-building" (11). They identified two key principles underlying this approach: (1) that individuals construct knowledge via reflection on and making sense of their personal experience, and (2) that knowledge is constructed via negotiation with others. Similarly, Cobb, Yackel, and Wood (1992) portrayed mathematics as both "a collective human activity . . . and an individual constructive activity" (17). Reform efforts in mathematical education support the social-constructivist view. For example, the National Research Council argued that "absent a conscious effort to set mathematics in the context of learners' experiences, mastery of skills (including vocabulary, notation, and procedures) serves no legitimate educational purpose" (1991, 25). The report argued that courses that failed to engage students in their own learning resulted in a "very misleading impression of mathematics—as a collection of skills with no connection to critical reasoning" (24).

This view of mathematics is consistent with constructive-developmental pedagogy because both focus on connecting learning to students' lived experience in order to promote their making sense of their experience. Constructive-developmental pedagogy raises a crucial and often troubling question about the role of the teacher's knowledge. Discussing teaching mathematics from a constructivist view of learning, Simon (1993) stated the question in this form: "How might a balance be developed between the teacher's goals and direction for learning and the teacher's valuing of and responsiveness to the mathematics of his students?" (7). Cobb, Yackel, and Wood (1992) noted the common myth that the constructivist perspective means offering no guidance to students to encourage their independent construction of mathematics. Paul Ernest (1997) argued that accurate mathematical knowledge is essential to a student's personal appropriation of knowledge, yet acknowledged that personal appropriations of mathematical knowledge are unique to the individual due to differences in individual sense-making. Ernest describes this personal appropriation as occurring through conversation:

> Of course the acquisition of mathematical competence by individuals and its use in socially situated performances are irrevocably interwoven. For only through utterance and performance are the individual construals or their consequences made public and confronted with alternative, extensions, corrections, or corroboration. Continual participation in dialogue . . . is necessary for the personal appropriation and internalization of mathematical knowledge, if it is to mesh with the utterances of others, and hence, with their knowledge. Ultimately, such interactions are what allows an individual's personal knowledge of mathematics to be regarded as an interiorization of collective knowledge. (1997, 221)

These writers endorse a combination of existing mathematical knowledge and learners' individual sense-making (or personal constructions, in Sam Rivers's terms)—what Shor and Freire (1987) called the joint act of knowing between teacher and student.

The joint act of knowing inherent in constructive-developmental pedagogy requires more than an awareness of the students' current knowledge in the discipline. It requires an awareness of, and ability to connect with, their epistemology—their way of making sense of experience that underlies their knowledge in a particular arena. Describing this issue in the context of mathematics, Buerk (1985) argued that math is viewed as absolute, as not something created by human beings. Using Perry's (1970) term *dualism* to describe this perception, she explained that students who view math as absolute are unable to construct math knowledge or believe that its construction stems from negotiation among knowers. She also noted that the epistemological orientation of connected knowing, held by some women (Belenky, Clinchy, Goldberger, and Tarule 1986), is inconsistent with the way mathematics is often communicated in classrooms and textbooks. Thus, students' epistemological assumptions and orientation appear to mediate how they know in a particular discipline.

Although Sam Rivers was not aware of the epistemological development dimension of self-authorship, his philosophy, goals, and description of his teaching style led us to conclude that we could learn more about constructive-developmental pedagogy by observing his course. As we waited for the second class session to begin, we read over the syllabus (see Appendix G). Sam's syllabus made it clear that his course was an atypical math class. Sam and his coinstructors* outlined their intentions:

> You will be expected to take a major role in this class, both during class time and out-of-class. Yes, that's correct, in class, too. We want you to be actively engaged in the classroom learning environment, proposing solutions, forming hypotheses, asking questions, even arguing. Your own personal construction of mathematical ideas is our goal. When this is all over, if we have done our job well, you will be much more confident about why mathematics works as it does. We are sure that will make you a much more effective teacher. (Math by Inquiry Syllabus, 1)

This description intrigued us—being actively engaged in the learning experience, struggling to find solutions and create hypotheses, and developing a personal construction of mathematical ideas emphasized self-authorship. The emphasis on problem-solving strategies, listed on the syllabus as things such as making a table (function), looking for a pattern, or trying a different point of view, suggested ways students would be guided in constructing knowledge. The syllabus contained two additional hints at social constructivism. It stated that this method of teaching was new for the instructors, and they would subsequently be learning along with the students. Students would be evaluated by attendance, participation, portfolios, projects and assignments, and a journal. The journal was described as a tool for reflective mathematical thinking and used to demonstrate students' growth and frustrations. These plans conveyed learning as a process in which both students and teachers were engaged. Students' personal construction of mathematics was welcomed alongside existing knowledge regarding "why math works the way it does."

Today, as in days to come, students weighted down with knapsacks and heavy winter coats filed into the room slightly before 4:00 P.M. The classroom was structured with five rows of desks across the room, which spanned six rows deep. At full capacity the room could hold thirty students. Despite the large windows that lined the back of the room and overlooked an interior

---

*Two faculty members from nearby universities assisted Sam with the course to learn how to teach using the inquiry method. They were preparing to offer Project Discovery courses on their own campuses.

courtyard, the sixteen students—all of whom were women—congregated in the front and center portions of the room facing the front blackboard. The room seemed appropriate for math because three walls were lined with blackboards. What transpired here, however, was quite different from what one would expect in a traditional mathematics classroom.

INVESTIGATING TOGETHER

After a few of the initial class sessions, we began to see a cycle inherent in Sam's teaching. The phrase *investigating together* seemed to capture this cycle. The cycle started when Sam provided a topic for the students to pursue before or during class. They then had opportunities individually before class or in small groups during class to work through the topic. Group dialogue ensued when Sam introduced the topic in class and invited them to share their discoveries. During these dialogues, Sam guided the group in connecting their ideas to existing knowledge and eventually synthesized the meaning of the discoveries for the topic at hand. (This cycle is explained in more detail following the class story; aspects of the cycle appear as headers in the story to guide the reader in analyzing the story.)

Early in the semester, investigating together focused on *discovery* of math structure. Later sessions focused on *synthesis* of previous information to come to conclusions about math structure. Toward the end of the semester, sessions emphasized *applying* math structure in practice. The following stories illustrate these emphases.

DISCOVERING MATH STRUCTURE: THE TRANSFORMATION OF A SQUARE

It was typical for Sam to start a class discussion by referring to what he called unfinished business, or areas the students had investigated previously that now could be extended to a new level of understanding. Sometimes these topics had been discussed to some degree in earlier sessions, and other times they were topics students investigated outside class. The following discussion (which occurred in the ninth week of the course) illustrates how Sam used students' investigations as a foundation for discovery of new insights.

Investigation Prior to Class

Sam started this portion of the class by saying, "Do we have any other unfinished business besides proofs? We do have unfinished business—we haven't looked at your transformations of a square." The class pulled papers out of their notebooks. Sam asked Becky for the elements; she responded with a string of letters: "*s, d, t, w, v, p, n, h*." Sam wrote, "The product of two [blank] is a [blank]," on the board. He asked them to look at their tables and figure that out. He made a table on the board with Becky's letters.

Sam asked students for each row and filled in the table as they called out the letters they had put in their tables during their investigations before class. He asked Brenda if she wanted to give a row, and when she said, "No," he responded, "Fair enough." After Denise called out her last row, Sam asked if she could have given the last row if she had not done homework. Becky explained that each row uses a different variable, and Denise could have looked in the h column because it had not been used yet. Sam told them they were demonstrating to him that they were looking, seeing patterns in things.

While Sam constructed the table on the board, I* concentrated on watching the students since our interest was in the teaching-learning interaction. Despite their sitting in rows three deep and five across facing the front board, participation began quickly. Sam's invitation to contribute to the table in essence collected their individual efforts into a framework the group could work from. The topic of the day was clear in Sam's "the product of two [blank] is a [blank]." Sam's cordial acceptance of Brenda's pass on giving a response confirmed the low-risk atmosphere early in the conversation.

Inviting Students to Share Discoveries

Using the table as a foundation, Sam pursued possible patterns:

Sam: Do you see anything in the table?

Donna: There are four different squares.

Sam (highlighting them on the board): What does she mean about that? Karen?

Karen: It is the same pattern repeated in a different order. One was rotations, one flips (or reflections) . . .

Sam: I don't care what language you use. Could use turns or rotations. Language is something you acquire gradually. Anything else to point out? What do you think a subgroup is? You know it is not just a collective noun, right? In math it isn't—it is a proper noun because it means a certain structure. What do you think a subgroup is? Kate?

Kate: A portion of those products. Each quadrant.

---

*The two authors alternated in attending the two weekly course meetings. Marcia observed the session reported here.

Andrea: A group with specific characteristics that are the same for turns as for the whole table—do you know what I'm saying?

Sam: Sorta, pretty good. What about subset—know what that is? Kelly, how many characteristics does a group have? Take a shot.

Kelly: I'm thinking of a field—five.

Sam: Name some.

Kelly: Closure, inverse, identity, associative.

Sam: Let's look at t, v, p subset—does it form a subgroup?

Class: Yes.

Sam: Prove it. Somebody who hasn't talked to me. Can you prove that this set doesn't have closure? [They worked silently at this point; he waited.]

Karen: T followed by p is h.

Sam (after checking her response with the table): I agree. Could you have done it on some basis other than closure?

Stephanie: It doesn't have identity. The subgroup has to have the identity.

Sam: Are we doing okay? Does this thing have closure—can you look at the chart and tell? Monica, can you look at the chart and talk it through a little? [She did and he concurred.] Is identity in this subset? [Many nodded.] Does each element in the subset have an inverse in the subset? Does s have an inverse?

Becky: I thought it would be w; s is identity, isn't it? [Another student said no.] I'm confused.

Sam: No problem. You just made a small mistake.

Becky (after another student clarified): Oh, I knew that.

Sam: I know you knew that.

The group decided that the inverse for *s* was *t*. As Sam asked about other inverses, the class yelled out the answers.

Watching this interchange, I marveled at Sam's ability to connect math language and concepts with students' observations. His opening of "do you see anything" produced ideas about parts of the table that Sam easily translated to subgroups. Although he had a clear agenda in furthering their understanding of the characteristics of subgroups, he used the table to guide the group in exploring the characteristics. Sam kept the exploration going until he was satisfied that most students had discovered how to think through this; when they began to yell out answers, he returned to the main topic of the discussion. I was also taken with Sam's knack for making it comfortable for students to make mistakes.

Connecting Students' Ideas to Existing Knowledge

Sam returned to the statement on the board "the product of two [blank] is a [blank]" and invited reactions, given the conversation thus far.

Sara: Two rotations is a rotation.

Sam: Jackie, do you agree? [In response to her yes.] Are you sure?

Jackie: I'm sure I agree, but I may not be right! [Jackie explained and was correct.]

Sam: Someone give me a different statement.

Kate: The product of two reflections is a rotation.

Sam (writing it on the board): How do you feel? All right? Make sense? How can I see that?

Melissa: In the opposite quadrant, you know, look at the two reflections and you get a rotation. [Laughter followed as Sam mimicked her point with hand motions.]

Sam: If you performed two flips on something, that would be same as what?

Class: Turning it.

Sam: Suppose I put the letter *P,* try to draw this. Draw the image of *P*. If we flip it across that dotted line . . . [He had drawn a large *P* on the board, along with a diagonal dotted line beside it.] Denise is cheating, folding her paper and looking through it. How are you doing, Karen? Robin, how are you doing? [She said guessing and he responded.] That's all right. Try to locate where certain points would go.

They said it had to be perpendicular. He continued to draw on the board, asking them for advice. They did this for each point of the P. He would ask, "Is that about right? Suitable?" They joked about getting a bulge in the P. He then asked them to draw another flip line, parallel and a little lower than the stem of the P, then to flip the image to get another image. Most looked down; Sam reminded them they could talk with one another, collaborate. Liz commented that it was a pain. Sam joked that learning is supposed to be a pain. Kate said, "No pain, no gain," and said several coaches told her that. Sam labeled these images number 1 and number 2, then used the picture to show how two flips produced a rotation. Next Sam asked about the point of rotation.

> Sam: What might be the point of rotation? Don't volunteer if you had a great high school course.

> Becky: It would be . . .

> Sam (joking): Talk it over quietly with Andrea first so you won't be embarrassed.

While Becky and Andrea were conferring, I reflected on what I had just seen. The early responses to Sam's invitation were apparently correct, but he did not seem satisfied that the students understood the dynamics behind them. I interpreted his introducing the drawing of the P as a concrete example through which the students could explain *why* the product of two reflections is a rotation. This also seemed to lead to the issue of the point of rotation, a crucial issue. I was also struck by Sam's encouragement of the group to work together both in drawing the P and in asking Becky and Andrea to confer. Perhaps even more surprising was the fact that the remaining students continued to talk with Sam while the two conferred. The afternoon sun pouring in the large windows across the back of the room and sounds wafting up from the courtyard below did not seem to distract the students from their discussion.

After a moment or two, Sam asked Becky and Andrea, "Have you decided?" At that point Andrea said "because listen" to Becky. Sam picked up on it and commented that they were engaging in reasoning. He continued, "She is trying to convince Becky. She is not appealing to higher authority.

She won't say Mr. Rivers said so, because I haven't said so. I stopped to illustrate this because that's what I want to happen in your classroom." While Becky and Andrea continued to confer, Sam and other students talked about helping students talk through issues during class. Becky interrupted that conversation with her response.

> Becky: Take the point at where two lines of reflection intersect. That will be point of rotation.

> Another Student: Cool.

> Sam: That is cool, isn't it? Fact of the matter is, that is right. Kelly, can you square v and p? Where do flip lines intersect?

> Kelly: At the center.

> Sam: When you rotate your square, the point of rotation is center. What could screw this up? Can two lines intersect more than once?

> Class (after a brief discussion): No.

> Karen: This is just a guess, but what if the angle of the lines was off? If the line wasn't accurate, it would mess up.

> Sam: Well, you couldn't do it exactly in real world. Jackie, what do you think?

> Jackie: What if two lines of reflection didn't intersect?

The class said "Ah!" in unison, and Becky congratulated Jackie. Sam also commented on how nice it was to receive affirmation from the group. Sam said, "By next Monday tell me about this." The class was so excited about Jackie's insight that they started shouting ideas. Sam said, "No! We aren't going to talk about it any more today!"—saying it was important to leave something for them to investigate. Melissa said she had an example, and Sam chided her: "Keep it to yourself!"

At that point they were all talking! Sam reiterated that it was important to leave something unfinished because some students needed to work through it. That explanation seemed to appease those who were anxious to share their insights, and they reluctantly agreed to move on.

As I watched this closing interchange, I marveled at a teacher having to convince a group of students, in math class no less, to stop talking about a math concept. I was surprised that Sam stopped the conversation to engage in another topic. In the rare moments that I encountered such excitement in my courses I usually tried to keep it going as long as possible.

When I shared the story and field notes with Jennifer later that week, she queried, "Isn't that manipulative?" As we reviewed Sam's explanation to the students, it was clear that he believed some students still needed to work through the insight themselves. His pattern was to introduce something, guide the students in exploring it, push the exploration until most students understood, then add a new twist and start the process again. His judgment to stop the conversation reflected a response to the students who had not arrived at the insight yet, a judgment that they were not ready to finish the conversation. Thus, the last part of the cycle—synthesis—was postponed. The more we discussed the issue, the more we viewed Sam's decision as guiding students and allowing students' reactions to mediate his agenda. Discussing our own teaching, we reflected on the difficulty of balancing multiple students' learning readiness. We wondered how Sam was able to create the dynamic class discussions we were observing and maintain that balance.

The Process of Investigating Together

Watching Sam's class for fifteen weeks helped us identify an underlying process in his version of constructive-developmental pedagogy, a process that is evident in the above story (see fig. 5.1).

Learning in Sam's class always started with exploring what students had investigated. In this case the students had explored the transformations of a square as a homework assignment and constructed a table like the one Sam generated with them at the outset of the session. His opening of "Do you see anything in the table?" was today's version of the more general "What did you find out?" question that opened each discussion. This sequence—*assigning a topic to investigate, giving students a chance to investigate, then starting with their work*—situated learning in their own experience and validated them as knowers by encouraging them to contribute their thoughts.

Sam's open invitation and students' advance preparation on the topic usually helped get the discussion started. Sam engaged in three primary approaches to develop understanding. First, he *actively encouraged students to share their ideas and their reasoning*. One of the primary ways he accomplished this was to make not knowing and learning via mistakes acceptable. When Brenda passed on the opportunity to contribute a row to the table, Sam's nonjudgmental response of "fair enough" communicated that it was no problem. When Becky became confused about the identity, Sam noted that it was just a small mistake and confirmed that he knew she understood.

This approach reduced the risk involved in sharing something that was incorrect or in acknowledging one's confusion. As a result, students felt freer to volunteer even when they were unsure of their thinking. Sam's affirmation of the value of students' ideas encouraged risk taking.

Figure 5.1

Investigating Together: Uncovering Math Structure

- **Teacher provides an investigation topic**

  [before class, during class]

- **Students investigate**

  [on their own before class, in small groups in class]

- **Teacher introduces the topic: "What did you find out?"**

  [at the start of class, after group work in class]

- **Students share individual or group discoveries**

  [conjectures, hypotheses, ways to approach, difficulties they had]

- **Teacher draws these ideas out, gets group to expand on them, uses their ideas to connect to existing knowledge [math structure]**

- **Teacher [sometimes students] synthesizes discoveries regarding the course content**

Second, Sam *encouraged the group to expand on ideas* that were introduced by others. He posed questions, asking students whether they agreed with what other students said, and solicited different ways of looking at an issue. Sam asked questions that connected students' ideas to the math concepts he wanted them to understand, such as the questions about subsets, closure, identity, inverses, and the point of rotation in the discussion cited earlier. He gave students opportunities to collaborate informally (in drawing the *P*) and formally (asking Becky and Andrea to confer) in addition to encouraging them to respond to other students' comments and questions. Sam often introduced other ways of looking at issues in order to move the conversation to a deeper level of understanding. For example, when the class determined whether *t, v,* and *p* were a subgroup on the basis of closure, he asked if it could have been done on some other basis, sparking a discussion about identity and inverse. In the process of getting the group to expand on ideas that surfaced, Sam was beginning to connect the knowledge the course was intended to address with their developing understanding, thereby establishing the foundation for mutually constructing meaning.

Sam's third approach to developing understanding was to *connect students' thinking with existing knowledge*. In the transformation of a square discussion, he did this primarily through asking questions and having the students experiment with drawing images to produce a rotation. In this case, he needed only to ask a couple of questions about the point of rotation for Jackie to come to the discovery that the two lines of reflection might not intersect. The group's reaction made it clear that some understood the implication of her insight and some perhaps did not. Rather than synthesizing the discovery at that point, as sometimes took place, Sam used it as a springboard to encourage students to investigate further. It would resurface later for Sam and the group to explore more in class.

Beyond the process of Sam's pedagogy, we observed characteristics that promoted the success of his approach. Sam's easygoing *rapport* with students, often evident in his chiding them or joking with them, set a pleasant tone for the discussion and made him appear more human than the traditional authority figure. He also *modeled thinking as a process,* often encouraging students to take time to think during the discussion rather than call out an immediate response. Sam routinely encouraged students to look at their notes from their investigations as well as talk to other students to gain insight. He openly noted these as processes for learning as opposed to relying on his authority. The process and characteristics of Sam's pedagogy made mutual discovery, and its accompanying excitement, possible. When the discoveries culminated in a particular aspect of math structure, the synthesis was the focus of the classroom work. The next story highlights the use of synthesis in class.

Synthesis: Rational or Irrational Numbers?

The previous week (week nine) Sam had engaged the class in a discussion of two types of decimals: finite or terminating (labeled 1), and infinite or non-terminating (labeled 2). They had also concluded that there were two types within infinite decimals: repeating or cyclic (labeled 2a) and random or non-repeating (labeled 2b). Their task to investigate prior to this session had been to determine whether they could get all three or only 1 and 2a.

Introducing the Topic and Inviting Students to Share Discoveries

Sam wrote W, Z, and Q on the board, and .101101110, square root, and π (pi). At that point he said, "What about the other assignment? We are still interested about these rational numbers. Tell me what you found out."

> Kelly: When you take two prime numbers greater than 7, the remainder is, for instance . . .

> Sam: Wait. I want her to say it again to see if she can communicate it well enough. It's a wonderful idea; we aren't saying it is right or wrong—it all came gushing out!

> Kelly: The number of digits that repeat . . .

> Sam: Suppose it doesn't?

> Kelly: They do. The number of digits it repeats will be less than the denominator.

Sam wrote Kelly's comment on the board. Kelly and Gina said that they were proud of themselves, and Sam concurred. Gina continued, saying, "I am trying to remember if $P1$ had to be greater than 7?" Donna, Stephanie, Gina, and Kelly talked among themselves about this. Sam asked, "If 1 over p repeats, will every n over p repeat?" They said yes, if the denominator is prime. Sam asked if the students understood Kelly's hypothesis, and they said yes. He gave an example, which Liz finished. Karen added, "If it is over 7, it is the same cycle." She explained with an example that Sam wrote on the board as she talked.

> Sam: That means $^6/_7$ will start with what?

> Student: How do you know?

> Donna: Seven, because 7 goes into 60.

Sam: Is there another way?

Gina: Count. [Gina gave an example, but it didn't work.]

Donna: Decimals must be ordered from lowest to highest.

Sam: Third biggest fraction needs to have third biggest digit for starting point. What about $\frac{3}{7}$?

Class, in unison: Four. That's cool!

Sam: I agree, it is cool. Nice hypothesis! Tell me something else you found.

Sam guided the sharing of discoveries during this exchange. He coached Kelly on articulating her ideas in mathematical language. He validated Kelly's achievement and encouraged students talking among themselves in response to Gina's question. He repeatedly asked questions to push the discussion and uncover new ideas. In the next segment Sam pushed the students farther for conclusions and connections to existing knowledge.

Connections to Existing Knowledge

Stephanie: I did it differently. I used repeating decimals to figure out fractions—used Jen's algorithm. There's no way to drop off the repetend.

Sam: What conclusion did you come to?

Stephanie: Wait, I can't think—you can only get 1 and 2a. Can't get 2b.

Sam: Good reasoning. Using Donna's algorithm works because to the right of the decimal you can drop the repetend off. Rational numbers turn out to be repeating or terminating decimals. Somebody else talk now.

Andrea: I used the same number Jen did. I went in determined to find it. I got totally discouraged. I used .1011 whatever, I knew it had to be less than $\frac{1}{9}$; took multiples of $\frac{1}{9}$ and altered the denominator. Like 4 over 36.

Sam (writing Andrea's example on the board): Say something intellectual about these things.

Andrea: Equivalent class. I knew I had to increase my denominator; then took an even larger multiple of $\frac{1}{9}$, used 81 over 729, then increased the denominator.

Sam: One over nine is .111 repeating, and Andrea is saying that is too big and that she is looking for something smaller. [He wrote fractions on the board to show what she meant.] It is remarkable thinking!

Andrea: I can't take all credit. It doesn't matter how big your denominator is; it will just keep going! I never could quite get it.

Sam: The strategy used here is quite bright—intuitive. I have never seen it before—learning something new. Nice! Somebody else give me something.

Kelly: I have one . . .

Sam: You've given one already. Let's share around.

Becky: Others have probably thought of this: take $\frac{2}{7}$, the remainder can only be less than 7.

Sam: And your conclusion is . . .

Becky: Can't have 2b—it will repeat eventually.

Again Sam invited students' discoveries and invited them to connect them to existing mathematical rules. He routinely encouraged students to explain their notions and prodded them to share their conclusions. After these examples, Sam apparently felt it was time for synthesis, as evident in the next segment of the dialogue.

Synthesizing the Discoveries

Sam: Let's take 731, which I expect is prime, a fairly good chance, [Laughter from the class.] and put 13 over it. The fraction can't be simplified. If you start doing division . . .

Becky: There are 730 possible remainders. I would think that if you used all of them, then you didn't divide right! [More laughter from the class.]

Sam: Is it possible to get different remainders?

Class: Only on the 731st time.

Sam: Have you ever put mail in pigeonhole boxes? Twenty boxes and twenty-one pieces of mail. One box has to have two pieces, one might have them all, but at least one has to have two. That is an important principle. It's called the pigeonhole principle.

Class: Really?

Sam: I swear it is true. Is this what this is about? If there are 731 divisions, I have to use one of the remainders at least twice. As soon as you use remainder twice, what happens?

Class: Repeating.

Student: Does it have to?

Sam: Yes. We now have a proof basically. Using pigeonhole principle, if you start with a rational number, you can only get 1 and 2a. If I tell you pi is a 2b, then it's not a rational number. It's an irrational—doesn't mean crazy—we weren't good at picking words in math. What does irrational mean?

Student: It can't be written as quotient of two integers.

Sam: Or written as decimal that is repeating. Number pi is an irrational number—you just have to take my word for it, because I have no idea of a proof to show you. Pi is approximately 3.14, not 3.14.

At that point Sam asked the students to get into their small groups[*] to find out what they could do if the square root of two was a rational number, joking, "Try not to make it your life's work!"

---

[*]Sam often used assigned small groups as a way for students to investigate together during class; he also used informal small groups by asking them to talk to students around them to work through ideas.

This session effectively illustrates the components of students investigating together in class. The conversation began when Kelly offered her hypothesis. Sam wrote it on the board, confirmed its value, and encouraged other students to consider it. This prompted three other students to talk among themselves about it and generated examples from Liz and Karen. Sam put Karen's example on the board as well and encouraged the class to use it. When discussion of a particular hypothesis or idea had reached its natural closure, Sam moved ahead by asking what else students found out. In this session, the cycle of someone volunteering, Sam confirming the idea, the group discussing the idea and its implications, and arriving at some conclusion about the types of decimals occurred repeatedly. At the end of each such cycle, Sam praised their progress and asked someone else to share an idea.

Toward the end of this segment, Sam offered an example that connected to the approach Becky offered. Walking the class through the example of the fraction $^{13}/_{731}$, Sam synthesized the discoveries that had emerged from the class investigation to the notion of a proof. Thus, he arrived at the math structure he intended to teach but did so on the basis of the students' individual and collective investigation. They brought their understanding from their individual out-of-class investigations to the discussion, shared and explored one another's ideas, and accumulated insights that helped them work their way toward the math structure of proofs. Sam also tied in math structure whenever possible, often with the phrase "say something intellectual about this."

The cycle of exploration here is integrally tied to Sam's approach to working with students. His rapport with students contributed to the risk taking that occurred. He chided Kelly at the beginning of this conversation about "suppose digits didn't repeat" and joked about the pigeonhole principle and irrational numbers. His use of humor lightened the tone of the class, allowing class members to make jokes as well. Another dimension of this rapport is Sam's confirmation of students' thinking through expressing pride in their accomplishments and acknowledging that he learns from them. The cycle of investigation and synthesis was intended to enable students to use math structure, the focus of the next story that took place in the eleventh week of the course.

USING MATH STRUCTURE: PROOFS

Sam started this session by announcing that the agenda was to work on proofs. He asked for an update, and various students called out the theorems. Sam wrote theorems 1a through 6 on the board as they talked about them. Upon putting theorem 6 on the board, Sam said, "Mathematicians say it like this—the additive inverse of a sum is the sum of the additive inverses. This is the rule that shows you if you add two negative numbers, you get a negative number. Once you prove this theorem, you finally, after knowing this how many years . . ." The students yelled out "bazillion." Sam continued, "You can finally understand this rule as opposed to someone pronouncing it to you straight from Moses." At that point Sam invited students to put proofs on the board.

Inviting Students to Share Discoveries

> Sam: Let's have a couple of volunteers. I'm counting on your good graces to remember if you have been up here. I'm getting the "look at the book" reaction! I assume you are just not wanting to take more than your share.
>
> Liz: I'll try it.
>
> Sam: This is worth something.
>
> Liz: If I'm wrong . . .
>
> Sam and Andrea: It doesn't matter.

Liz put theorem 5 on the board, joking as she wrote that it had been a long time since student teaching. Sam commented on how left-handers have an advantage (she is left-handed) and confirmed various lines she was putting up. He added a couple of ideas, encouraged her when she hesitated, and assured her that she had enough for the proof. Sam then introduced a short discussion about how to proceed.

> Sam: I want to do two things before we talk about this. How could conversation in class go that would be most helpful to you? One choice is, I could say it is right or wrong—that is the typical way we teach math. What way helps you so you can do the next proof yourself? The other question is, What can I do to make sure you aren't spectators? How should we proceed?
>
> Andrea: We could ask Liz questions. That way we would be actively involved.
>
> Sam: Okay. Other suggestions?
>
> Melissa: We could discuss how you go from one step to the next.
>
> Liz: I could explain, but it might be better for them to discuss.

As things developed, there was no need to be concerned about active involvement. The students had questions as well as ideas ready to share, and Sam's affirmative reply to the next comment set the conversation in motion.

> Andrea: I have a question. Can I ask? [Sam said yes.] In line 3, I multiplied it out and it messed it up.

> Becky: I did that too. [Sam put up what Andrea had done.]

> Donna: You can't just multiply that out; that is what you are trying to prove.

> Sam: I agree. You can't use what you are trying to prove in the proof.

> Becky: In another proof can you use theorem 5 if it's been proved?

> Sam: Yes—look at what she did in line 8. She could do that because it was already proven. Excellent question and excellent response. She could have used it earlier to save herself some writing. [At this point Sara asked a question and another student said she got lost.] Do you want to go through each step?

Rather than respond immediately to Andrea's question, Sam busied himself putting what she had done on the board for others to see. Given that space, Donna responded to Andrea's question. Because Becky had used the same process as Andrea, she was interested in participating in the exchange as well. Sam reinforced their insights, praised both the question and the response, and opened the door for more risk taking.

Connecting to Existing Knowledge

> Jackie: I like what Liz has done—I was frustrated about where to start. Can you explain your logic about where you started?

> Liz: Well, the nature of zero . . .

> Jackie: Oh, the nature of negative one . . .

> Sam: Ooh! Is this about zero? Is the central idea the nature of zero? [Spontaneous conversation erupted around the room. Some students were explaining to each other and pointing at the board.] How did we prove theorem 1? [They offered ideas about

how they proved theorem 1.] Anytime you catch yourself adding something to both sides of an equation to get rid of something, you probably could have used theorem 1 instead. [Sam is at the board, looking at Liz's proof.] Now let's look—wait a second, maybe—in this case maybe it doesn't hold by golly—how could that work?

Karen: You could do theorem 1; it could work.

Sam: Where? [Karen and two other students explained how it could work.] Oh, I think I see where we are. Let's look at this line—what could we do with this? [They gave suggestions so quickly that he couldn't keep up with writing on the board.] Be a little bit patient. Now will one of the theorems help us now?

Liz: Theorem 2a.

Sam: Using her first three steps and these three, we are done. You like Liz's better than the new one, don't you? [They nodded.] You think this is too easy, but I can assure you this is all right. How are we doing? Is this working to go over Liz's proof? [Andrea commented on line 8.] You are doing beautiful. I apologize if I seem to be plodding. I want to make sure you are involved. I want you to be good at this. Thank you for volunteering, Liz—very nice. Somebody want to volunteer for 6?

While Sam waited for a volunteer, it struck me that the students were becoming increasingly proficient at putting their earlier discoveries to use. Despite Liz's hesitation about volunteering, she had produced an effective proof. Sam intentionally asked the group how best to proceed, and they took initiative to process the proof. They used earlier insights, particularly the nature of negative one, to generate ideas among themselves and even explained to Sam how theorem 1 could work. Collectively, Sam and the students connected earlier theorems into their work with Liz's proof. The conversation revealed that the students truly understood the math structures they were using rather than just memorizing them.

After a few moments of prodding, Sam couldn't get anyone to volunteer for theorem 6 and so suggested they all do it together.

Sam: Jackie, what did you say earlier that you got grief about?

Jackie: The nature of negative one.

Sam: Write a true sentence that has additive inverse of $n + k$. [He waited while they wrote a sentence. Sara offered a sentence and gave the reason for it.]

Sam: That gives us a place to start. [He wrote it on the board.] What do we need that we don't have, and what do we have that we don't need? [He pointed out the answers because no one responded.] How can we get them in here?

Melissa: Take out the parentheses. Move to the other side . . .

Sam (joking): We don't have a move to the other side theorem!

Melissa: Drop the parentheses, then add additive inverses of n and k on both sides.

Sam: It might be better off to do one at a time. [He wrote it on the board.] You'd like to use associative law now, wouldn't you? [They nodded. He wrote another statement.]

Melissa: I'm guessing there is a theorem we can use to drop it.

Sam: Not yet.

Andrea: How did she cross over those brackets?

Sam: She used the associative law twice. [He explained.] What happens next?

The conversation continued in this vein as Karen said what was next, and he wrote it down. Monica asked a question about what Sam did, and he explained further. After she agreed that she understood, he added a couple more steps, asking them, "Now what you gonna do?" as he went. He wrote as they responded. After they had eight lines, Sam asked, "Is it clear now how you will finish? Would you like for me to shut up and let you finish?" Sam waited as students wrote in their notebooks and talked to one another. After a few questions and a few minutes, he asked, "What did you do? Robin?" She gave the next two lines and reasons for them. Sam concluded, "Now we are finished—okeydoke? I wasn't going to give you this. It's not my fault; it's Liz's fault. The reason I gave it to you this way was to show you how you could start. You could do it using theorem 5—which is what Liz did. Can you do that for homework for Monday? Can I erase?" They said yes and he erased the proof. In the remaining minutes of the class, they explored what to do for the next session. Sam wrote theorems 6m, 7a, 7m, 8, and 9 on the board as they called out what each one meant in sentence form. As they talked about theorem 9, Sam asked them to get out their Z11 tables (a product from an earlier class session), asking how additive structures behave in a multiplication problem. They tried a couple of multiplication problems in Z11, and Sam connected that to theorem 9. Sam had run a few minutes overtime, and the sound of Velcro backpack fasteners was becoming the predominant sound in the room. As students packed up, Sam reminded them that he did not want them to be spectators.

Despite Sam's active participation in this last proof, the students were thinking along with him and guiding his work on the board. Sam reconnected the proof to Jackie's comments on the nature of negative one, their earlier work with the associative law, and their earlier explorations with Z11. In addition to showing the culmination of many strands of exploration from earlier sessions, this session again reveals the underlying framework Sam and his colleagues used to mutually construct meaning with students. Although Sam set the topic for the day—proofs—he quickly entertained students' perspectives about the best way to go about working on proofs so that they could do them on their own. As students began to discuss Liz's proof, they surfaced areas of confusion, entertained one another's ideas, and hit on discoveries that helped them move along in the proof. Sam helped draw their ideas out and asked them to expand on their thinking. In the last segment he connected their ideas to existing knowledge.

COURSE OUTCOMES: THE VALUE OF INVESTIGATING TOGETHER

Because the goal of Math by Inquiry was students' personal construction of math, assessing the effectiveness of constructive-developmental pedagogy in the course necessitated determining (*a*) whether students were able to see themselves as knowledge constructors and (*b*) how effectively they constructed knowledge. Their ability to think about themselves as knowledge constructors hinged on their epistemological development.

Becoming Knowledge Constructors

Twelve of the sixteen students completed the Measure of Epistemological Reflection (MER) at the start of the semester, sharing their assumptions about the nature of knowledge in six essays. Of that group, more than half probably believed that math, as Sam suggested earlier, did in fact come down on the stone tablets. One student's MER responses indicated that she held an even balance of absolute and transitional ideas. Absolute knowers believe that knowledge is certain and known to authorities. Transitional knowers believe that some knowledge is certain, but that other areas exist in which it is not known at the present time. Five students expressed transitional knowing consistently; three more expressed predominantly transitional knowing with a few examples of independent knowing accompanying their primarily transitional perspectives. For many of the transitional knowers, their responses indicated that math was one area in which they felt knowledge was still certain. Thus, at least nine of the sixteen class members viewed math as certain going into the course. The remaining three study participants held independent assumptions about knowledge; two used these as their primary way of knowing, and one used this in conjunction with transitional knowing. Independent knowers believe that most knowledge is uncertain and subsequently are willing to adopt their own opinion in the face of uncertainty. This range of ways of knowing was similar to that found in a longitudinal study group from the same institution (Baxter Magolda 1992), as well as to seniors at other institutions (King, Wood, and Mines 1990).

ABSOLUTE ASSUMPTIONS IN KNOWLEDGE CONSTRUCTION

Students who assumed math was certain had the greatest challenge to view themselves as knowledge constructors. Melissa, who expressed a balance of absolute and transitional knowing in her MER, explained what it was like for her:

> With math, up until now for me, in my own personal experience, there has always been one answer and how you arrive at it. [Sam's] trying to [help us] see that there is more than one possible answer or one possible solution. It gives you an opportunity to be creative and to try things. Sure you may be discouraged at times, but I think it is very rewarding when you do come up with something and get excited and a lot of times the ideas just start flowing and you don't want to stop or put it down so it's kind of exciting.

Her absolute assumption of one answer was clearly giving way as a result of Sam's teaching. Exploring further how this was affecting her, she explained, "Most of the classes I have had have been a professor or a teacher talking at me rather than with, so I just really like the interaction and the personal relationships between the professors." Having teachers talk with students prompted students to focus on the process of thinking rather than the product of learning they were used to in other courses.

Sam offered guidance when students investigated together by emphasizing that thinking takes time. Melissa noted: "He'll give us an idea and some time to start thinking about it or talk about it with other students before we actually dig into it. . . . Sometimes he'll give us little hints and we have to go from there on our own." Melissa felt that this approach made a big difference in how she thought about the class material. She continued:

> A lot of times, I'll catch myself thinking about it when I am home. It helps me because I think if he just proposed something and sixty seconds later tells me what do you think about it, you would not necessarily come up with as many things as if you had longer time to think about it. A lot of times the things that come off the top of your head aren't always necessarily what you think or feel, but the more you think about it, you may change your point of view. [He says,] "Think about this and tell me what you think and the next class discuss this to show how the ideas have developed or progressed."

Melissa was so sold on allowing students time to think that she was amenable to Sam's chiding her to keep her thoughts to herself. Earlier in this chapter we described a discussion in which the students discovered the possibility that the two lines of reflection might not intersect; Melissa wanted in the worst way to share her ideas. But Sam insisted that she wait. We asked her about this instance in the interview, and she replied,

> I was so excited because I knew what he was talking about and I wanted to share, but at the same time I realized that if I would have been in one of the other students' situations, because I have been there before where I did not exactly know what was going on or what he was looking for. It was kind of good, I guess, that he gave them an opportunity before somebody just blurted out this is what it is or this is how [it works].

Melissa realized that Sam withheld his perspectives at times to help her think. She translated this to withholding her own insights to give other students space to think. Sam's relational dialogue with students and his patience in allowing them time to think were important factors in absolute knowers beginning to see themselves as knowledge constructors.

Using Transitional Assumptions in Constructing Knowledge

Some transitional knowers had an easier journey to becoming knowledge constructors because they already knew math was uncertain. For example, Becky wrote on her MER:

> In factual classes, I memorize. I've learned the routine. I ingest every bit of factual detail and then regurgitate all of it on a test. After the test, 70% of it is gone. I get an A on the tests, an A in the class, a

smile from my parents and a pat on the back. I am suddenly known as "smart." I really didn't learn. That A is not reflective of the knowledge I actually have. I've cheated myself.

Becky reported that memorizing did not net her any long-range learning. As a result, she was excited about Sam's modeling the thinking process by engaging in it along with the class. Becky discussed how Sam combined his objectives with students' discoveries, emphasizing the importance of her instructor practicing the methods he espoused:

> That's really what was different about this class; a lot of what was done was done from our perspective, not his. We came into the classroom, he had a set plan for what was going to happen, but at the same time I think a lot of it was altered because of what was said in class. Like he built off of what we said in class. It was more or less, "Oh yes that's a good . . . conjecture," then he would play off of what we said. It seemed like the learning was more meaningful because it came off of what we said and not his [comments]. A lot of things that get me about some of our education classes is they are speaking about how you should have group work and meaningful learning for the students and hands on, yet you come to school and they are teaching you in a lectured form classroom. It's like they are contradicting everything they are saying. They are saying you should teach this way, yet it doesn't seem like they are looking at themselves and saying, "How am I teaching?" I think that he did that; that's what Dr. Rivers was doing. He was [saying], "Okay, now this is how we are telling our students to teach, and are we teaching that way too?" He was not being hypocritical, like some of the teachers I have had.

Becky realized the importance of working from her own experience and the value of her teachers making her experience central in learning. Her comments highlight the balance between the instructor having a plan and mediating that plan with students' reactions. The fact that learning stemmed from this balance—from the teacher's plan and from what the students said—indicates that shared meaning-making took place. Becky also described the positive impact of teachers validating her as one who is capable of constructing knowledge through shared meaning-making.

Jackie shared a similar perspective in defining the goal of a personal construction of math as "understanding [my]self as a mathematician":

> I have always been good in math. I completed requirements to get an A in math in high school and college. But if you asked me if I was mathematician, or had mathematical thinking, I would say no.

How could you do so well and say this? I know how to produce what the prof wants. In this case it isn't what the prof wants; it is what you want, what are you trying to figure out, how are you going to approach this problem? Math courses helped me, but in this course where it was me, it was not given to me to regurgitate. I'm trying to think of myself as a mathematician. I'm trying; it is a process. [I'm] not afraid to approach it—an eye-opening experience. The knowledge is in there; [it's] just organizing it, figuring out how to tap into it. His goal is for us to understand.

These reactions suggest that both the absolute knowers and the transitional knowers were open to thinking about math another way when given the opportunity. Some were more ready for this alternate conceptualization than others, but most were willing to give it a try.

INDEPENDENT ASSUMPTIONS IN KNOWLEDGE CONSTRUCTION

In contrast, the independent knowers had already let go of certainty in math and readily engaged in knowledge construction. They particularly appreciated having multiple ways to explore math concepts, and although interested in others' ideas, they were also preoccupied with their own. They described hearing others' perspectives as helping them stretch their views. For example, Karen explained how listening to others' ideas caused her to think differently about the subject matter:

I can't think of everything. I have noticed that there are other students who are outstanding with their perceptions; from those I can think of something else. It broadens my way of thinking. I think in a certain set of ways; that set is changeable, expandable. If one is proven wrong, it's out of there. I am always open to learning new ways of doing things, ways of thinking about things. . . . When I hear somebody else say I did it this way, but I did it differently myself, I can ask myself, "Is that right? Does it work? Does it make sense? Is that a better process for this application?" I analyze it; if I think it is, I use it for future reference.

Karen is actively processing what she hears from others and subjecting it to her own analysis.

These reactions show students at varying degrees of ability to construct knowledge. The absolute and transitional knowers who saw math as created by a higher authority had the opportunity to see their instructors create it and to participate with their peers in creating it. Though unsure about the process, they were willing to try, and some were excited about it. Sam introduced sufficient dissonance for them to reevaluate their ways of knowing and sufficient support to work through this difficult transition. The students who already knew math was human created appreciated their instructors recognizing this and used the classroom setting to further develop their own construction of mathematics.

UNDERSTANDING MATH STRUCTURE

The subject matter goals of Math by Inquiry included increasing students' command of mathematical structure, developing one's own personal construction of mathematics, and strengthening students' mathematical confidence. Students and Sam Rivers had perspectives on the degree to which they constructed knowledge effectively. Students reported thinking differently about math and being more confident about their mathematical ability. Sam reported that their work "demonstrated that they knew what they were talking about and they had the intellectual equipment to examine some things that I don't think they had the intellectual equipment to examine earlier."

UNDERSTANDING MATHEMATICAL STRUCTURE

The most prevalent outcome students reported was understanding how and why mathematical concepts worked. For example, Andrea said the class "was for us to understand the math system. I just threw those terms around—*commutative, associative*—I didn't understand them at all. Now I understand them a lot and could explain them to someone else." Monica described one of her major accomplishments as "coming away with [her] own solid background of math ideas," describing it as a "totally different concept for a math class." She viewed this as applicable in other arenas as well, saying, "Because this [course] teaches *how* and *why,* I can be more analytical, interpretive, and critical in other classes. I would always be thinking, *How did that work? Why? How could I do this?* Take this thinking process into other classes. In other classes you don't get the thinking process; you get the math." If Andrea's comments are any indication, in other classes she "got" the math, but she did not "keep" the math. Monica appeared as though she would keep this thinking process and apply it elsewhere.

Sam made it clear that some thoughts were better than others in this investigation process. He worked to balance students' taking risks with constructing knowledge accurately. In one of our interviews he explained:

> You don't want to embarrass a student or do anything to keep them from taking risks. I consciously do this, but it is hard when somebody comes up with something that is really wrong and you just can't say that's right. You have to get it straightened out. It's okay to have an idea that did not turn out right. Everybody does. It is part

of the student's responsibility to get this straightened out, not just me. It is part of the class responsibility.

The safe environment that resulted from focusing on the thinking process and validating students' ability to engage in this process made it possible for students to take risks of thinking "in public." Putting their thoughts into the public dialogue gave Sam the opportunity to facilitate exploration of faulty ideas and help students arrive at more reasonable constructions. Sam noted that students "were forming hypotheses or asking pertinent questions to take it a little bit farther, or defining the problem by asking questions that penned in or kept it from being applied to a new situation."

STRENGTHENING MATHEMATICAL CONFIDENCE

Confidence, another course objective, was a typical outcome for most students. Some students reported the confidence they gained here was related to acquiring the underlying process to use in future mathematical practice. For others, it was a change in their perceptions about themselves as mathematicians. Becky captured the attitude notion most effectively. She traced her progression from her original assessment of her math ability to her thinking at the end of the course:

> I was a little worried about taking this class. I almost didn't. I almost dropped it. I thought, *What am I getting myself into? This is a 400 level math course and I stink in math.* But I don't really believe that anymore! They helped [me] prove to myself that I am not that bad in math. I am not such a terrible problem solver; I can solve things. I am not stupid. I am not the most logical person in the world, but I do have logic and I can apply it. . . . There were times when I was frustrated, especially with theorems. At first I was like, "I don't understand what I am doing." It was very frustrating; it was very hard. Near the end of the theorem unit, I felt a little better. I am not saying that I am the best at theorems now or that give me any theorem and I can solve it. I am sure that's not the case at all, but I am willing now to try. In the beginning of the course I gave up [when I] couldn't get it, thinking I could not do it. But now I'll work a little longer, and I will keep telling myself, "Oh, come on, I can do this; this is not impossible. He would not have given it to us if it was impossible."

Becky trusted her instructors not to give her something impossible, which helped her keep working. Her comments reveal that she must have had some successes in the course that changed her thinking from "I stink in math" to "I am not stupid." She does not judge herself as an expert, but she has a very different perspective about her math ability from what she had when she began the course.

DEVELOPING A PERSONAL CONSTRUCTION OF MATHEMATICS

Students varied in their achievement of developing a personal construction of math. Independent knowers who were ready for this goal moved toward defining their own construction. The remaining students experienced important epistemological growth in moving from acquiring mathematical concepts to realizing they could construct an understanding of them. This understanding of math structure is a necessary foundation for their ongoing work toward a personal construction of mathematics knowledge.

The combination of mastering various mathematical concepts, accessing the underlying structure of math, developing one's own personal construction of math, and gaining increased confidence in one's ability to think provides strong evidence that Math by Inquiry met its objectives. The students appear closer to the goal of understanding that knowledge is constructed by those with sufficient experience in a particular context. This movement from their initial assumptions about mathematical knowledge not only helped them understand mathematics but also introduced them to the mathematical community described at the outset of this chapter. Equally important is the fact that students seemed to view the culmination of Math by Inquiry as more of a beginning—an opening to think differently in math and other areas of their lives. Thus, constructive-developmental pedagogy brought these students into the process of knowing in this course and into the process of knowing in their lives.

CHAPTER 6

Using Narrative to Promote Self-Authorship

Educational Storytelling

As the afternoon sun poured in the south windows, students arriving for the first session of EDU 200 took their places in the circle of chairs in the center of the room. Jan, the instructor, chatted informally with students as they arrived, and she and other students continued to scoot their chairs back to allow newcomers access to the circle. The blackboard and table in the front of the room receded into the background as the circle became the center of activity. I sat just outside the circle near an electrical outlet to power my portable computer. Students arrived in casual attire and many carried backpacks. Four of the five men sported clean-cut looks, and two wore the popular ball caps backward on their heads. The fifth man's appearance was a sharp contrast since he had longer and thicker hair than most of the women in the class. The fourteen women appeared a little less casual in sweaters as opposed to the men's T-shirts.

On the hour Jan introduced herself as a doctoral student, a label that belied her years of experience as a teacher. Her casual and enthusiastic demeanor also made her seem closer in age to the students than her graying hair would imply. She started off by saying, "This will be a neat class!" She laughingly commented to a student who had placed a laptop computer on her desk, "If you think you are going to get a lot of notes, good luck!" The latter comment was the students' first hint that this class would be different from most they had experienced.

I knew how to interpret Jan's comment because I knew how the course was organized. I elected to observe this course because the course architect (Elliot) and coordinator (Jo) had intentionally developed it to promote the social construction of knowledge in a high enrollment course. Their course was aimed at helping future teachers think about the complexities of education. I viewed their conceptualization and implementation plans as creating the transitional culture for absolute and transitional knowers to move toward self-authorship. Because the enrollment was largely first- and second-year students, it seemed likely that absolute and transitional knowing would be prevalent (and in fact it was, a matter discussed in more detail later in this chapter). Jo and her team of instructors (of which Jan was one) were interested in learning about student development and how to promote complex ways of knowing.

Jo had adopted narrative as the primary approach in designing this course. She planned to involve students in some of the most difficult and controversial aspects of education by having them read narratives in texts, experience "live" narratives in the weekly large group session, and share stories about their own education. Witherell (1995) comments on the powerful effect of hearing others' stories:

> Narrative allows us to enter empathically into another's life and being—to join a living conversation. In this sense, it serves as a means of inclusion, inviting the reader, listener, writer, or teller as a companion along on another's journey. In the process we may find ourselves wiser, more receptive, more understanding, nurtured, and sometimes even healed. (40–41)

Getting students into the lives of others, particularly whose experiences differed from theirs, was a key component in getting them to reevaluate their assumptions that knowledge was certain and educational practice had to be a particular (right) way.

The content of EDU 200 would be a challenge to absolute and transitional knowers because it emphasized multiple perspectives and critiques of education's purposes and practices. The first segment of the course focused on how schools have historically been used for national and cultural formation, social practices and norms, and economic goals. The second segment introduced debates and positions in education, "including essentialism and progressivism in education, social and economic reproduction of schooling, the role of cultural capital, exceptionalism and differentiation of students by race, class, gender, sexuality, and physical and mental ability" (Syllabus, 3). The third segment focused on alternative reforms in education. In each session, narrative readings were mixed with readings that explored various issues. The narrative approach was intended to help students access issues raised in the more difficult readings such as those by John Dewey, Paulo Freire, and Thomas Jefferson; it was also intended to help students identify firsthand with issues such as race, class, and gender with which they might have limited experience.

JAN'S INITIAL SEMINAR MEETING

Returning to Jan's first seminar meeting, the first agenda item was introductions. Jan told about herself and her hometown and invited others to do the same. As each person in the circle stated his or her name and hometown, Jan commented on what she knew about the place and encouraged others' comments about who they knew from there. Jim, from Oxford, was designated as the local expert. When Joe named his hometown in Michigan, the woman next to him said, "No way! I just spent three weeks there!" They talked about mutual acquaintances while a student from North Carolina explained to the class where she lived in relation to places they knew. Most students were from Ohio and knew about others' hometowns. I thought to myself that this exercise was not a mere formality but a chance for Jan and the students to begin to connect with one another. Jan was communicating to the students that an aspect of their personal lives was important as the learning process began.

After all nineteen students introduced themselves, Jan commented briefly on the nature of the course. She explained that their two weekly small group sessions were oriented around the Monday evening session that all 286 students from all fourteen sections were expected to attend. Specifically, Jan commented:

> [We will] share a Monday evening experience; the learning we do will be in the small group classes. I use "we" intentionally, [because] knowledge isn't something that I have to pour into your heads and have you regurgitate back—which doesn't mean a whole lot. We'll talk to each other and iron out understanding. The focus is on the small group; themes for the backdrop are on page three of the syllabus.

The content of the syllabus did not appear to be Jan's primary concern today, though. Rather than address the themes, she turned to the subject of participation. She announced that one way to encourage participation was to have students generate questions about the topics listed on the syllabus. She asked them to look over the topics and come prepared to select a topic next week. She made it clear that they would be responsible for generating questions, not for leading a full-blown discussion. She acknowledged that participation was uncomfortable for some, saying some are "more comfortable than others floating thoughts for general consumption." As a result, she asked students to develop a participation goal for the course and offered the option of a learning journal that they could turn in to her, enabling her in turn to "give voice to your ideas, as fodder for general consumption." She emphasized making the most of education, using her own college-age son as an example. When Jan paused to entertain reactions or comments, students inquired about details on the syllabus but not on participation, perhaps revealing their interest in the more concrete details of the course. Jan was offering opportunities for students to take an active role in learning via generating the questions for topics and establishing their own participation goal. They were more focused at that point on what she expected of them.

Commenting that participation can be intimidating if put-downs or discouraging comments become a part of the class, Jan initiated a class activity regarding participation rules. Her instructions were these: "Take a hunk of paper and write down a comment, a put-down, or a behavior that I or anyone else could do that would make you never open your mouth again!" She gave examples. Students wrote their comments, folded them, and passed them around the circle to Jan. Holding up the scraps of paper, Jan said, "What we now have are the rules for the class. Let's see what the rules are and talk about them." She read the first one, which noted sensitivity to negative feedback. Jan interpreted its meaning as risks involved in speaking and commented that they all had something to add to one another's knowledge. She said if she did something that intimidated people, they had permission to call her on it. She opened the second paper, which read "laughing at serious comments." Jan talked about humor and made a joke about whether students watched *Beavis and Butthead,* which produced a laugh.*

The third rule was on defending one's opinion. She asked for reactions, and three students commented on what this meant for them. Jan asked if opinions were right or wrong, and one student said, "No, they are just opinions." The next rule read "puts me down instead of my thoughts." Jan again asked for reactions, clarifying that she was seeking their thoughts because these become the rules. Asking for reactions seemed to be Jan's way of clarifying the rules without putting the people who wrote them on the spot. Another student had written "eye rolling and head shaking when I offer my ideas." Jan asked someone to model that behavior, and a few students did. Jan kept an even facial expression throughout, reinforcing that this was serious business. She asked questions such as, "Can anyone be stupid?" in response to one rule about acting like people are stupid. When all the papers had been read, Jan asked Jim to bury them in the wastebasket, concluding, "They will not be exhumed and therefore will not be a part of what goes on here." This rather dramatic ending to the exercise emphasized to students that she was serious about treating one another with respect.

After a brief discussion in which students shared why they had enrolled in the course (mostly because it was required), the fifty minutes allotted for the session had passed. Jan quickly referred them to the written lecture in the reader and noted that the question at the end of the written lecture would be the focus of the next discussion. That question was, "What *is* the purpose of American schooling, anyway?" Students left their first small group meeting without further details about the course.

---

*Beavis and Butthead is an animated cartoon television program that depicts popular culture.

In the ninety minutes between Jan's seminar and the large group meeting, I thought about how Jan's opening approach connected with these first- and second-year students who probably expected her to function as the authority who would tell them what to do. Jan immediately contradicted the omnipotent authority role by sitting in the circle and joining in the introductions. The introductions were not the routine name, rank, and serial number but a genuine attempt to help students know something about one another. Jan encouraged their reactions to one another, implying that this getting to know one another was important and setting the tone for sharing stories in the class. In introducing the format of the course Jan stated that she and the students would talk together and "iron out understanding." She then modeled that process with the participation rules exercise. In the course of that short exercise, Jan validated the students' perceptions about their learning environment and created an initial example of mutually constructing meaning. In the first hour, Jan had made good on her invitation to talk together and probably created the beginnings of a shared reality for third order minds in the group. This would be crucial to getting absolute and transitional knowers to accept her invitation to learn via talking together.

THE INITIAL MONDAY EVENING MEETING

Details on the course were scant later that evening at the first Monday evening large group meeting as well. Jo, the course coordinator, experimented with the lighting and video equipment as the auditorium slowly filled. The squeak of the wooden seats and the din of nearly three hundred voices made it nearly impossible to hear. Jo's appearance on the stage, her yelling "sit down and be quiet!" and the learned behavior of being quiet when the instructor starts combined to hush the room. Jo was dressed casually, wearing a long, flowing skirt and a blazer. Not using the microphone, she yelled, "Welcome to the first Monday session of 200!" She then offered the only details to be forthcoming that evening: "This will not be a lecture class. We are going to watch a wild film! Anyone needing to see me about adding the course can do so after class in the hallway." With that, the film *All American High* began to roll.[*]

Despite the poor sound and visual quality of the film, the Finnish narrator's comments on her experience as an exchange student at All American High seemed to capture students' attention. Particular portions of the film, such as dissecting frogs in biology class, mock marriages in a sex education class, a beer party, and the election of homecoming queen, produced raucous laughter. Students seated near me often whispered to one another about their

[*]Keva Rosenfeld and Linda Maron (producers), and Keva Rosenfeld (director), *All American High* (Corporate Productions, Inc., 1980)

own experiences as they related to the film. Attentiveness to the film expired, however, at precisely 7:50, the ending time of the session. As the film continued to roll, approximately 75 percent of the nearly three hundred students put on their coats and left under cover of darkness in the auditorium. Since my interest in the film had expired prior to 7:50, I stepped out to the hallway to hear reactions. One student, looking for Jo to add the course, said, "She probably left after she started the movie." It seemed to me that students' traditional understanding of schooling and their epistemological development would clash with the format and intention of EDU 200.

By 8:00 P.M. the auditorium and hallway were empty except for Jo, the section instructors, and me. Jo and the section instructors caucused briefly. Reactions to students' leaving prior to the close of the film ranged from giving them a pop quiz on it at the next session to letting them out five minutes early to compensate for running over this time. The discussion, however, spawned the insight that realizing the goals of the course would necessitate engaging students' current perspectives on their education. The group agreed to use this occurrence to explore the theme for the week, which fortunately was schooling versus education.

Early sessions of EDU 200, as is the case with the two described above, were fraught with signs of student expectations that were in tension with the course goals. Students' laptop computers and open notebooks, their interest in syllabus details, their deferral to their instructors in initial discussions, and their habit of packing up (if not departing) at the assigned time revealed what they had come to expect of classes and the role they were to play. The sound of Velcro backpack fasteners often drowned out the instructors' final words. Since 71 percent of the students in the class were first- and second-year students, it was likely that they had little experience with small, discussion-oriented classes.

As a student I interviewed later noted, she expected the large group meeting to be a lecture. When the film consumed the entire first session, she was unsure what she was to do since she had no notes. Another was surprised that students would be given an opportunity to talk in such a large group. Leanne captured the sentiment of what most students told me in interviews:

> In other classes they don't know who you are. It is so serious and you are out of there. Other classes are lecture, take notes, put it in your head, and put it back on the test. Here she invites you to think about it in your own ways and discuss it. Because you can talk in the small group, it gives you more a way to talk to her. I'm afraid to go to other professors.

Based on research on students' epistemological development, it is likely that most of these students came to EDU 200 expecting the instructor to play a

primary role in dispensing knowledge. Most of the students who participated in my interviews later in the term held these expectations because they
were absolute and transitional knowers. The students I interviewed said that
they had never had a class like this before except first-year English.

A review of the syllabus revealed that students were in for a surprise. All
fourteen sections used a common syllabus, which contained a comprehensive description of the course (see appendices). EDU 200, Sociocultural
Studies in Education, was portrayed as an introduction to the Social
Foundations of Education that applies a cultural studies approach to the investigation of selected educational topics. The theme-based nature of the
course was explained, followed by detailed explanations of the three major
fields upon which the course was drawn: the social foundations of education,
cultural studies, and the humanities. The syllabus defined each of the three
and translated them into the focus of EDU 200. For example, it noted that
"*the social foundations of education* is a field of study that draws upon the disciplines of history, sociology, philosophy, and anthropology to study and debate the foundation of educational practice and ideas. In a social foundations
of education class, students examine, critique, and explain education in light
of its origins, major influences and consequences" (1). Similar explanations
helped students understand the forms that cultural studies and humanities
would take in the course. This explanation served as a preface to the course
objectives:

> 1) Students will learn to think critically about education in con-
> temporary America by learning to recognize, evaluate, and defend
> positions found in educational discourse with an emphasis on cul-
> tural issues such as difference and diversity, subordinated and mar-
> ginalized groups, cultural politics, their own lived experiences, and
> the lived experiences of other students and teachers.

> 2) Students will learn to think critically about schooling in contem-
> porary America by learning to interpret, critique, and judge educa-
> tional practices as they relate to different discourses addressing the
> purposes of schooling.

> 3) Students will come to a better understanding of the context of
> contemporary American education by learning to interpret, cri-
> tique, and judge educational practices as historical and cultural texts
> located in sociocultural contexts. (EDU 200 Syllabus, 1–2)

The introduction to the course made it clear that the instructors believed
that knowledge is something that is socially constructed. The objectives
made it equally clear that students were going to be asked to participate in

that social construction. Words such as *interpret, critique, judge,* and *think critically* emphasized the learner's role in making meaning out of the course material. The syllabus further explained that the large group sessions would consist of narratives to introduce central concepts, which in turn would be the focus of small group discussions. It stated that small group discussions would address "the various readings that students make of the large group narratives and the assigned written texts." This implied that students might have different interpretations of the narratives and texts. The syllabus further noted that central concepts were also introduced in two- to three-page written lectures each week that were contained in the course reader. These written lectures invariably ended with a question about what the student thought about the concept at hand. Reading the syllabus, I noted that

Figure 6.1

Using Narrative: Educational Story Telling

- **Large group [300+] experiences an oral narrative**

    [performance, story]

- **Students individually experience related written narratives**

    [narrative readings for the weekly theme, a written lecture about the

    weekly theme]

- **Seminar groups [25] explore the meaning of the narratives**

    teacher draws out students' reactions to the narratives and students'
    own educational experience in relation to the narratives

    teacher and students interpret the possible meanings of the narratives

    teacher and students analyze the meanings for their implications for
    educational practice

    teacher encourages students to make judgments about effective
    educational practice; critique practice on the basis of the narratives

the instructors faced a major challenge: to build a bridge between students' assumptions about passively receiving knowledge and the course objectives of thinking critically.

Over the course of a semester, I observed the Monday evening large group sessions and two of the fourteen seminar sections (see appendices for details). Although progress faltered at times, the instructors built a reasonable bridge for most students. They did so primarily through using constructive-developmental pedagogy—in particular validating students as knowers, situating learning in students' experience, and mutually constructing meaning with students. The process of constructive-developmental pedagogy that emerged over the course of the semester is portrayed in figure 6.1.

The large group meeting offered an oral narrative on a topic for the week. *All American High* told a story that touched on the theme of education versus schooling. The readings for the week and the written lecture offered related narratives for students to read individually. The seminar was then devoted to exploring the meaning of these narratives. The process inherent in most seminar meetings began with drawing out students' reactions to the narratives and their own educational experiences. Teachers and students then tried to interpret the meanings of the narratives in order to analyze their implications for educational practice. Teachers encouraged students to use this analysis to make judgments about effective practice.

Staying with the narrative theme of EDU 200, I offer next a few narratives about the forms constructive-developmental pedagogy took in the course. First, the seminar sessions that followed the opening narrative are recounted to show how the small groups processed the large group narrative. I then shift the focus to the large group narratives given the question of whether constructive-developmental pedagogy is viable in large courses.

THE SEMINARS: EXPLORING THE MEANING OF NARRATIVES

The two weekly seminar meetings were intended to engage students in discussion of the weekly theme and concepts. Making sense of the narratives, both the Monday evening one and the readings, was the primary vehicle for working with the theme and concepts. Jan and Kim, the two instructors whose seminar meetings I observed, used an array of approaches to accomplish this aim. Both were experienced teachers. Jan had particular expertise in special education and Kim in teaching literature and art. Exploring their seminars on the schooling and education theme (with *All American High* as the Monday evening narrative) demonstrates how they used constructive-developmental pedagogy from the beginning of the course and how their different approaches encompassed the three principles.

Kim started her small group meeting on schooling and education by asking students to form groups of three to discuss Monday night's movie, *All American High*. Then she introduced the task for the day:

> Today is primarily on concepts regarding the film, and next time will be on readings. In groups, introduce yourself, have one person be a recorder, and pursue five questions. If we have time, we will share as a group. If not, I will summarize them and hand that out next week. One paper per group, put names on it. First topic is All American High School—what was it like in the film? Second, what voice told the story? What voices did she use to support it? Also pay attention to voices that were not heard. Were there people who were ignored? Were there ones who would have said the film did not capture their experience at All American High? Third, was it similar to your own high school—your understanding of and experience with high school? Fourth, why did people leave before the film ended? Just jot down a few reasons. Fifth, the message of the film and the experience of seeing the film in a 350-person room—what does this tell us about schooling and education? This is too much to remember, so I will write it on the board. Start with the first one. Go for it!

Discussion started quickly, perhaps because Kim's five questions provided a framework from which to begin for the absolute and transitional knowers. This framework organized their conversation, yet invited them to share their thoughts and experiences.

In the group nearest me the three students immediately started talking about what took place in the film and how it related to their high schools. In another group too far away for me to hear, two women were copying Kim's questions from the board and jotting down notes. Their third group member, Rod (who routinely wore a baseball cap backward), was looking around the room, staring into space. Soon after, the women gave him the sheet and asked him to write down the ideas. Meanwhile Kim proceeded around the room to visit groups. Her interactions with the groups were amiable, and she gave advice when asked. She asked one group questions to get them to think about the issue and then suggested they write those ideas down. When Kim approached Rod and his partners, the women quickly informed her they were talking about why he had left the film early when they did not. Some laughter followed, and I assumed as a result that Kim did not make a judgment about Rod leaving early. When it appeared groups were nearing completion of the task (as evidenced by some groups talking about other things and looking at the assignment explanations handed out earlier),

Kim went group to group asking if they had it together, then called them back to the large group as they said they were ready. Her role as a facilitator during their small group work conveyed that she was willing to help but trusted them to accomplish the task.

Drawing Out Reactions and Experiences

Kim opened the discussion with the first of the five questions: "What was school like in the film?" Hugh noted that it dealt with social life. Leanne offered that it was about education, as opposed to schooling, but not about academic education. Kim asked what academic education meant, and Mandy clarified that it was "subjects, like math, but not life experiences." Ryan added, "It was the girl's point of view from another country—how much fun they had. I'm sure they had good academics there."

Kim seized this opportunity to pick up on the second of the five original questions regarding whose voice told the story, translating Ryan's comment to the story being filtered through the Finnish woman's lens. Theo responded to Ryan also, suggesting that the Finnish student was telling what she saw, so it did reflect the school system: "If academics were so good, she would have talked about them." This prompted Kim to push farther on whether the story was a fair representation of the American high school. The responses immediately shifted to students' personal experience, the substance of question three. After a few students noted similarities to their schools, to public schools, and differences from their schools, Hugh reiterated the point that socializers told the story. Kim, capitalizing on the chance to return to whose voices were left out, added that brains and teachers were not included. She then asked students who could not relate to the high school in the film to comment. A few told stories of academically oriented schools they attended, noting that the social aspects were present but not that important. As this conversation wound down, Kim moved to the fourth question.

Interpreting Possible Meanings

She asked, "What about watching the movie, people staying or leaving before it was over? What would a foreign student have made of that experience?" Susan responded, "They would think that we do not care, are busy, only do what we are required to do. Some might not think that is a true picture of high school, so students got sick of the movie and left." In a nonjudgmental voice, Kim paraphrased, "So some might have left because they felt the film did not accurately portray high school. Other reasons?" Tom added, "It was monotonous, there wasn't a plot, graduation reflected the end, and once people saw a few people leave, they did—peer pressure."

Susan noted, "The obligation issue was important—it is just time—time is up."

Kim brought these ideas together and connected them to the fifth question, saying, "Look at the message of the movie, then the story about college students coming to a required session and leaving. Does that give you any ideas about or make any statement about schooling and education?" Mandy offered, "The individual has a choice—schooling is there if you want an education." Jessica added, "I saw socializing as a major part of the movie, but we left early, showing we don't care that much about education either. We said we don't care about our education. For me it drew a parallel between the movie and our not caring enough to stay." A few more comments returned to why people left, but no one else took Kim's challenge to connect the issue to schooling and education. Kim noted that class time was over, tying the issue of running out of time to the discussion about students' departure from the film.

About 75 percent of the students participated in this discussion. The five questions offered a framework to keep the group focused as they processed the film and generated information to arrive at the concepts of schooling and education. By the close of the session, students began to talk to one another about the concepts. The ability to talk about their own high schools seemed central to getting the small groups and the whole group started on the task. Kim primarily asked questions and clarified responses. She validated the students as knowers by assuming they had insights about the film, their own high school experiences, and their peers' behavior. When they shared their insights, Kim accepted them, asked questions to push their thinking, and refrained from judging their assessment of the film as "not earth-shattering" and "monotonous." Learning was situated in their experience. Using their stories helped them connect to the film and served as a starting point for exploring the concepts of schooling and education. Kim's five-question framework was consistent with their interest in structure, given their epistemological development. Mutual meaning-making about schooling and education was initiated at the very end of the session, even though insufficient time prohibited achieving this goal. Thus, analyzing the implications of the narratives and making judgments about practice did not occur. It is remarkable that the group made this degree of progress toward sharing their thoughts in the second class session.

JAN'S SEMINAR

As I attended Jan's seminar meeting on schooling and education later in the day, I quickly noticed that she took a different approach to the topic; rather than share her framework with the class as Kim did, she kept it to herself, introducing guiding remarks when she judged appropriate. Her opening comments were the following:

You saw a film Monday evening. You read *A Nation at Risk* and a short piece from *The Prophet* (Gibran)—that's a lot to discuss in so little time. Any preferences that struck you more than others? What do you want to talk about, assuming that you are prepared to discuss all three?*

Jan's opening conveyed that students should be ready to discuss all the material but offered them a choice.

Drawing Out Reactions and Experiences

Jean asked, "What we were supposed to get from the film? I don't mean to put it down, but what were we supposed to get?" Jan turned the question to the group, accepting the implied preference to start with the film. Michael responded that it was a party—they did not talk about the teachers. Barb, who had experienced education in Latvia, said, "We have social at school compared to what they have. No social interaction. In terms of school spirit, in Latvia they would have a dance and nobody cared whether anyone went. I think it is hokey in American schools, but it does make school more fun." Jan asked whose point of view the film represented. "Exchange students'" was the simultaneous response of three or four students. Dawn said that Finnish people do not express their emotions (the film narrator was from Finland) and do not have fun, according to a story she had seen on *Sixty Minutes*.** She reported that they do not even make eye contact, and family means more to them than it does here. Jan concurred that the film was a student's perspective and revealed differences in expectations.

Returning to the original question, Jan asked, "What was the topic for this week?" When they responded "schooling and education," Jan feigned an "aha" reaction. Repeating, "What was the film about?" she got a resounding "social experience." Joel (the man with the flowing hair) said this is how American kids bear high school; this is how they get through. Events affected school but really were not school. Jan noticed Sally nodding and asked her if she wanted to comment. She shared a Dutch exchange student's experience that he did not have to try. Barb offered that no one expects exchange students to learn much.

Interpreting Possible Meanings

Jan summarized the film's messages discussed so far, noting that students would not go to school if their friends were not there and the really terrific

---

A Nation at Risk, Report by the National Commission on Excellence in Education (Washington, D.C.: U.S. Government Printing Office, 1983); Kahil Gibran, "On Teaching," from *The Prophet.*

** *Sixty Minutes* is a television news magazine.

classes were auto mechanics, the wedding class, those that were real life. Jan's comment opened a door to a theme in which many students in the room were intensely interested. Dawn introduced empathizing with one of the teacher's viewpoints in the film regarding worrying about keeping students entertained. Hillary, in secondary education, said, "I feel like if I'm not really entertaining them, I'll lose the class. Why do we have to do that? We are there to teach them—yet that's the way American high schools work?" Jan responded, "Great question! What do people think?" Barb said it is because students' attention span is too short. Another said society has gotten people used to this. Kirsten offered an example of her educational psychology class, in which she visited a progressive school. She reported that the students there decided what they wanted to do, students wanted to learn, and it was incredible. She concluded, "You want kids to get excited to learn." Dawn offered, "What is scary is that you could graduate from Miami and be a great teacher, but if you aren't funny, you could not be a good teacher. If you don't have that knack, you could be in trouble."

Analyzing Narratives for Implications

Jan saw this conversation as an opportunity to bring in one of the readings. She responded by asking, "What is a good teacher?" and referring the class to the Gibran reading. After some shuffling through the readers, Michael offered that teachers teach the same thing over and over again, and if you cannot bring it across differently, students are not interested. He added, "You have to apply it to each kid's point of view." Rae commented that "you can't teach someone something they don't already know—they just aren't awakened to it." She added that her friend says people are born to be teachers. Jean said, "I hate to disagree," at which point Jan interrupted to say that it is okay to disagree. Jean said she still hated to do it because she hated it when people did it to her. She offered her disagreement, saying, "One does not have to be born a teacher. My other point was that the teacher has to relate subject to life. I couldn't wait to get out of high school because I couldn't figure out why I was learning cosines—those are my two points." Jan laughed and agreed that she never understood the reason for learning cosines either.

Michael offered that he wants to be a teacher because he thinks he has a lot to say to get others to understand and experience what he has learned. He said he would give people examples they can relate to, like two kegs and two kegs are four kegs for math. Not surprisingly, his comment got a laugh. Joel asked Michael if he was born with that passion. Michael said his dad was an art teacher, but he has always been interested in art. Joel said he talked to a former art teacher who just found a passion for teaching—therefore, you must not be born with it. Kirsten suggested, "Everybody in their own way is a teacher. If you are a baby-sitter, you are teaching kids. You have to learn whether you want to tolerate it for the rest of your life—decide if you want to do it professionally. People are educators."

Jan invited Joe into the conversation, saying, "You're nodding—have at it," and he joined in. Jan referred back to education and schooling and to Gibran, commenting that he is talking about people more than people employed by schools. She asked if a person who knows something could give it to someone else. Michael responded that they have to want to learn. Others agreed, offering that forcing it is bad because it will not stick with them and that it is necessary to enthuse students. This prompted Jan to return to the film, inquiring, "What were students enthusiastic about there?" They chose the wedding, with Jean explaining, "It's something that everyone thinks about—not like going into biology class and asking why you are learning it. Weddings and getting along with others are part of everyday life."

Making Judgments about Effective Educational Practice

Jan, as is her custom, connected this issue to the next reading, *A Nation at Risk:* "What would the writers of that report say about students preferring to learn about everyday life?" Barb, in a response not exactly connected to Jan's question, said she disagreed with the entire thing. In a passionate tone she said, "The problem with Americans is that they have to be the best. We live in a small world and don't need to be better than others." Kirsten replied, "This makes sense, and in a perfect world everyone would strive to be best, but for now everyone groups themselves. So we have to concentrate on the American educational system." Barb insisted that she would work against this. Kirsten maintained that we have to take on our part of the world and make it better. Joel introduced school spirit, noting that you root for yourself. Sally said groups need a goal to reach for, to look forward to; they need an idea to work to be better. It became apparent that some students were helping confirm one another's ideas and working toward ideas.

However, Barb was not to be convinced and told a rather long story about a movie related to the issue. She argued for being proud of being an American but for not being against others. Jan restated the issue: "How do we measure what is best, what is good, what is standard?" Kirsten, not to be deterred from the disagreement with Barb, said she understood comparing educational systems, but schools are so different. She said there is no way we could transform to the Japanese style of education.

Jan continued to try to focus on schooling—reminding them that it was the central question of the week. She asked what schools were for, referring them back to educational platforms they had generated last week and noted themes from those. She noted that the graduation speaker at the end of *All American High* had asked what was next. "Is school for now or for getting ready for later?" Jan asked. Becky said, "For both—skills you use daily and for what is coming next. Things that help you get along in the real world." Dawn asked, "Does that really prepare you for it? What if a kid throws a paper wad at you?" Jean quickly responded, "I would throw it back," amidst laughter from her peers.

In one last attempt Jan asked, "If I were on the commission that wrote the report, what would my judgment be?" The primary response was that they thought the report was too harsh. Jan summarized that the film was a text and only offered a few voices. The group generated who was not heard— teachers, people who did not go to the party, unpopular people, the president of the National Honor Society, parents, or administrators. Jan noted that the perspective was limited and posed the question of whether the authors of *A Nation at Risk* heard all the voices before they made the report. Her question hung in the air as students packed up to leave.

Jan's role in the conversation revealed her striving for the same balance Sam Rivers and Chris Snowden worked to achieve. She had a clear set of themes in mind, yet she introduced them as the students raised them in their conversation. Jan showed particular skill in asking questions to guide the discussion and connect it to ideas in the readings. When students wandered away from the central issues, Jan reminded them of the day's topic. She encouraged students' stories, thus validating students as knowers and situating learning in their experience, but also insisted on linking their ideas to the class topic. Although Jan did not get to the mutually constructing meaning regarding schooling and education she intended, she did convey to students the importance of joining their ideas with those in the education field. She also subtly emphasized that every story, whether the Finnish narrator's or the *Nation at Risk* report, was told from a particular perspective.

VARIATIONS IN THE NARRATIVE PROCESS

Jan's free-flowing approach struck me as being in stark contrast to Kim's more structured one. Upon further reflection and discussion with both instructors, I realized that I had witnessed both an external framework and an internal framework. Kim made her framework external by sharing it with the students; it did not limit their freedom to respond. Jan also had a framework in mind; she introduced it in the context of the discussion. Like Kim, Jan garnered substantial involvement from most members of the class. She situated learning in the students' experience by letting them choose where to begin and offer their personal experiences throughout the conversation. She validated them as knowers by accepting their contributions and turning students' questions to the group for resolution rather than answering them herself. Jan attempted to pursue their questions as means to get at the concepts of schooling and education, encouraging conversation around relevant questions, and reorienting conversation when it strayed from the concepts. Jan introduced opportunities to link students' experience with the material as she elicited connections between the readings and their thoughts. Some mutual construction of meaning was evident, although the group did not come to closure on the schooling versus education theme.

Prior to the session, I would not have believed that Jan's approach would elicit so much meaningful conversation. Whereas Kim's five-question framework organized the conversation in advance, Jan's framework evolved as the students shared their experiences and reactions. Both entailed a balance of structure and student experience that worked even though it seemed to me that Jan's group found a few more opportunities to challenge one another's and their own thoughts. Both approaches welcomed students as they were but invited them to stretch their thinking.

These two sessions were Jan's and Kim's first attempts to explore the meaning of the week's narratives. Even so, they contained the process of constructive-developmental pedagogy that I identified after observing the entire semester. Both instructors were successful in drawing out students' reactions to the narratives and students' own educational experiences. They and the students interpreted possible meanings of the narratives and explored implications for educational practice. Jan's group got a little closer than did Kim's group to critiquing educational practice, perhaps because they worked more with the narratives from the reading. Both groups moved closer to critiquing educational practice in the following session on the same theme because the narrative in the reading assignment told a story about restructuring a school. Over the course of the semester, attention to critiquing educational practice increased, although the students never became very comfortable with that dimension of the course. That discomfort is taken up later in the chapter in the discussion of course outcomes.

THE MONDAY EVENING NARRATIVES:
EXPERIENCING THE STORY

The narrative approach was not limited to the seminar sessions. The purpose of the large all-section meetings on Monday evenings was explained on the syllabus: "The course is organized around narrative presentations in large group sessions. . . . These narratives will consist of visiting speakers, panels, films, and other performances, each of which raise the central concepts to be discussed in small group sessions over the week" (3). Elliot Gardner was the architect of this course, having conceptualized it in broad strokes before Jo Fischer took responsibility for designing it in detail. As Elliot explained in one of the EDU 200 instructors' meetings, the narrative was intended to engage learners with the concepts but did not necessarily require verbal interaction from the students. He said,

> We wanted to move beyond the notion that education takes place in classrooms and things people read. It takes place in other kinds of things like movies, TV, speakers. Most people spend years learning how to figure out what they've read—not always very productive years—recognizing the ways in which things are written to try to influence them. When thinking about a textbook that is authoritative, they have some experience with that. The assumption of this course is that they don't know how to do that very well. But they have even less experience knowing how to approach anything visual or a performance. People in my classes put their pens down when a video comes on—they don't know how to recognize how cameras and lighting work. They miss that the filmmaker has a point of view. What we have are students who have never had to struggle with how to make meaning of texts. We wanted to have a visual and performance session that was like what they are getting in texts. . . . Then the question is, How does it connect? From my perspective it is just like the readings. If you see one visually and read another, the only difference is the way they were done. When students come into small group discussion to engage in dialogue around the concepts—the center, texts are something to play off of—these texts are laid out whether in words, performative, or visual. Getting students to do that is difficult—a goal to work toward, not something to expect walking in.

Elliot's comments reveal that he was aware of the inconsistency between this approach and students' experience in traditional schooling. As I heard his comments, I was reminded of the dissonance this created for absolute and transitional knowers.

The film *All American High* described earlier in this chapter was the first Monday evening narrative. Implementing this concept turned out to be complicated, and the instructors' group talked regularly at their meetings about how to make what they referred to as the "Monday evening session" work more effectively. The formats ranged from no verbal interaction among the students to activity-based sessions. Twice the large group was broken down into groups of approximately forty-five students (two seminar sections) for the Monday evening session.

On one such occasion the instructors felt that interaction was essential due to the concepts for the week: race, racism, institutional racism, and prejudice. These topics, along with social class, gender, sexuality, ethnicity, and exceptionality, were all part of the second theme of the course, society and culture in schools. Instead of presenting a narrative in the large group, instructors assigned students to view an interactive video on multicultural awareness in the campus computer lab prior to the Monday evening session. Then groups of approximately forty-five students met to discuss the video with a peer facilitator associated with the video. The session I observed had a lively discussion, touched on some controversial issues, and got to the issue of whether education should focus on diversity despite the students' lack of familiarity with one another and the peer facilitator's taking a minimal role in moving the discussion toward educational practice. Because of the success of that session, the instructors chose to use the same format for the theme of exceptionality and differentiation (week twelve), this time facilitating the groups themselves.

A LABELING ACTIVITY

I attended Jan's gathering of her two sections, in part because I knew she had worked with exceptional children previously. Her group met down the hall from the auditorium, but the room was not much more conducive to discussion. About twenty lab tables formed two parallel lines through the room, each table accompanied by two tall chairs, all on the same side facing the blackboard. Jan seemed undaunted by the situation and encouraged students to pull the chairs into clusters off to the side of the tables. They, too, seemed undaunted. Students from the seminar I observed regularly clustered on the left side of the room while the other section gathered around the right side.

Jan explained that they were going to do a labeling activity. She told them she would put a label on each person's forehead, and they should treat one another according to that label. She clarified what questions they could ask one another to figure out what label they were wearing and said they would have ten minutes to interact and identify labels. Jan joked with the students as she went around the room putting labels on foreheads. Once the labels were affixed, she asked them to mill around, saying, "Let's get at it and get it figured out!" Jan said she would wear one too. She let the students pick it, and they put it on her. She immediately went to other students and asked questions. Jan's role modeling seemed to get the activity rolling as others followed her lead and questioned their peers. Jan traveled around the whole room, but the students seemed to consult only with others in their seminar section. Jan occasionally went to the board and wrote questions such as "Do others like me?" and "Am I immature?" to give students guidance in determining their label. About ten minutes later Jan asked how many did not know their label yet, and two of the forty students raised their hands. Jan said, "Let's help them," to the group, and others started treating the two according to their labels. They soon guessed their labels. Jan's participation in the activity encouraged students' participation. She set an upbeat tone and modeled the behavior she requested of students.

Jan asked them what questions helped them know what they were, not-ing that the questions on the board were ones she heard people ask. In re-sponse to her question James said he asked if he was slow or a retard. Becky and Hillary described others' behavior toward them as ways of identifying their labels. Another student said that questions others asked her gave it away. Jan wrote questions on the board as students offered them. At that point Jan said, "Take off your labels and confirm your worst fears!" Many said "ouch" as they pulled the mailing labels from their foreheads.

As they looked at the labels, Jan commented, "Some of you may have been flattered by your label. How many were?" A few raised their hands. Jan said, "Am I talking to jocks and gifted? Cheerleader? Were any of you won-dering, 'Why did she put that one on me?'" Some laughter followed. Jan asked the group for other labels of which they were conscious in their school-ing. One woman said, "Upper income." Michelle said, "Popular groups, smart group, everyone was labeled into a group." James added "burnout," and Jan said they called them "hoods" in her school. Jan asked if you could get out of the hood crowd. A woman said you could if you changed your clothes, but you could not get into other groups. Jan shared that one stu-dent's cultural interview assignment revealed that divorce carried a stigma that a person could not leave behind.* Jan asked if vocational education stu-dents hung around with college preparatory students and asked them to think about their yearbooks as a barometer. Many students offered examples of cliques evident in yearbooks.

Jan directed the conversation toward how people get labels. Becky said, "It's from growing up. You are in the same school system your whole life. People know you; new kids never become popular. Intelligence came from your third grade reading group, or when you were put in honors or gen-eral track." Jan asked if anyone tried to ditch a label. Michael said he did; he talked to everyone in his small school because you could change cliques. Rae said cliques at her school interacted. Another woman said, "You would have several labels. The one you felt was more important would be your identity for four years—your leading label." Jan remarked, "Excellent point. We wear multiple labels, and we might be able to choose based on our interests. Is there any other way you would emphasize a particular la-bel?" A woman said students could pick one they thought was the most popular. Jan concurred, offering an example of a woman who was afraid to enter Jan's learning disability classroom; she was also a jock and chose the

---

*The cultural interview assignment required students to interview a peer from a different cultural, ethnic, class, or racial background about experience in schooling. The goal was for students to investigate through personal interaction the linkages between culture and educational experiences.

latter for her identity for that very reason. Jan asked the group to think about how they would introduce themselves at a cocktail party, then quickly changed it to a fraternity party. She used herself as an example, listing the labels white, female, and Christian. A woman pointed out that we do not always tell other people our labels, using how much money someone makes as an example. The group ascertained that people show one another their economic status in other ways. Jan concluded the session, saying, "Now you have something to think about before Wednesday. Wear your labels with pride!" Students put the chairs back in their original positions. As people left, many did wear their labels.

All of the students participated in the label activity, and more than half of them participated in the processing discussion. Despite Jan's expertise in the subject, she offered her experience only when it illustrated a point made by someone in the class. She asked the group to draw on their immediate experience of wearing a label and the questions they used to relate to various labels. Rather than explore the stereotypes inherent in those questions immediately, she transitioned to labels they wore in high school. It was my sense that this transition introduced exceptionality and difference in a context with which they could identify and heightened the meaning of the conversation for students because they could access the feelings associated with being labeled in a real setting. Mutual construction of meaning was evident here as students learned from one another how particular labels were perceived. Jan's processing also resulted in the group's exploration of how labels originate and are maintained. The session gave students a useful foundation for further exploration of these concepts later in the week and offered a nonthreatening atmosphere for discussion of a difficult topic.

To build on this foundation, the readings for the week offered narratives from a man who was labeled mentally retarded, a physically disabled Asian-American woman, and children who wrote about various disabilities. In Jan's first seminar meeting following the Monday evening meeting, a student initiated the conversation by telling a story about a physically disabled student she knew. Jan encouraged students to talk about others they knew. Because most of their stories were about peers they attended school with, the conversation soon turned to how situations with exceptional students played out in schools. One student shared her mother's experience as a principal dealing with whether to mainstream exceptional children; Jan shared her own experience as a teacher in special education. A lively, yet unresolved, discussion took place around balancing the needs of exceptional and so-called normal children in schools. Jan had achieved her goal of linking the narratives regarding exceptionality to school policy. The seminar session gave students an opportunity to further explore exceptionality and difference beyond their larger group labeling activity and to push the conversation toward critique of educational practice. The conversation revealed that students had developed empathy for exceptional children, and this complicated their thinking about effective school policy.

A PERFORMANCE

As the semester progressed, the concepts became more controversial as evidenced by the concepts for week thirteen: sexuality, sexual orientation, and sexual preference. I arrived at the Monday night session with great anticipation because I knew the gay activist who was scheduled to perform. I recognized Rick seated in the back of the auditorium dressed as Androgynous Pat, a character from *Saturday Night Live*.* A single tall stool sat in the center of the stage, with a leather suitcase leaning against it. Jo made her usual approach to the stage, missing three of the five steps as she bounded toward center stage. She yelled "sex" repeatedly until the crowd fell silent. She then said, "We are going to talk about sex and sexuality tonight. We have a guest performer who will raise these issues." With that, Androgynous Pat walked down the center aisle and onto the stage.

Rick used Pat's character to say how uncomfortable it was to talk about sexuality, careful to stay in Pat's androgynous voice. For the next fifteen minutes Rick transformed into three more characters. As he switched from Pat to the next character, he commented that one meets all kinds of people at college, and sometimes it is hard to understand them or to get along. As he talked, he removed the newspaper he had used to give him Pat's stocky build, pulled clothing out of the suitcase, put a baseball cap backward on his head, and rolled up his pants legs. He then introduced Dexter the nerd. Dexter talked about his computer and E-mail, and he used a calculator to figure out the odds of getting a date with a fabulous woman. Rick removed the cap, corduroy pants, and plaid shirt that Dexter wore as he transitioned into a nameless macho man. Underneath the plaid shirt and corduroys were a tie-dyed T-shirt and black pants. Rick added a wig from his suitcase and a few lines of conversation to convey the macho image. Finally, he introduced Charnelle, the gay male. As he removed the T-shirt and black pants to reveal a black tank suit, he talked about how uncomfortable people were around Charnelle. Charnelle then told about his high school guidance counselor telling him he should be a hairdresser. The laughter that accompanied the previous characters disappeared during Charnelle's performance.

Rick stopped his performance and told the group he wanted to share his experience growing up in middle-class suburban neighborhoods. He continued to put all of his layers of clothes back on as he began, then sat down on

---

Saturday Night Live is a comedy in which one of the cast plays Androgynous Pat, a character whose gender is never revealed.

the stool. He told about taking his knitting to show-and-tell in elementary school and being sent to the school psychologist as a result. He told about getting picked last for sports teams on the playground and hearing fag jokes that were not challenged by his teachers. Rick's tone was both serious and witty, and he came across as genuine in inviting the class to understand what being a gay male is like.

Jo dragged an additional stool onto the stage at that point and joined Rick. They opened the floor for discussion, and hands shot up immediately. The first question was whether certain situations made Rick gay or whether he was born that way. Rick's nonjudgmental response led to numerous questions about his personal life, his beliefs about whether schools should teach about sexuality, and what roles teachers should play with gay students. One of the questions prompted Jo to ask the students how sexuality became a part of their school experience. She asked them to think about it for a moment, then talk to the person next to them to tease it out. There was little reflection, and the talking started immediately. After five minutes, she asked them, "Did sex have anything to do with school?" Stories abounded. Some told about their sex education classes, how their teachers taught the technical details instead of about relationships, and personal experiences with gay persons. The final story came from a student whose high school teacher was fired when it was discovered he was gay. At the close of class, Jo asked, "Anyone else have a good experience with sex in school?" Laughter erupted, and she joined in as she realized what she had asked. She encouraged students to carry the discussion to their seminars, and the class applauded Rick's performance. A number of students headed toward the front to talk with Rick after the session.

Rick's performance placed the concepts for the week in a real context. His role-play helped students identify quickly with different personalities with whom they were familiar. The contrast of Charnelle to the other characters helped them access their discomfort with the stereotypical gay male. Rick's return to a more traditional appearance as he talked about growing up gay created dissonance by presenting him simultaneously as a typical student and gay. In addition to experiencing Rick's narrative, the students were given an opportunity to explore its meaning in the same session. His openness to sharing his life story attached emotions to the concepts and invited students to explore them further. Although some of the questions were personal and revealed lack of understanding about sexual orientation, Rick responded to each as though it was valid and useful, thus welcoming students' current meaning-making. In doing so he managed to create a level of openness I did not expect among first- and second-year students in a large class setting. As Rick and Jo moved the discussion to sexuality in schools, the students had an opportunity mutually to construct meaning with them and one another.

The few minutes for students to reflect on their high school experiences and discuss them with peers were a version of what Brightman (1993) calls the nominal group method. This starts with a time for reflection (something that was lost in this session), followed by each person sharing ideas, recording the ideas within the group, and sharing them as the larger group reconvenes. Although Jo used this loosely, it gave all students a chance to share their thoughts briefly in a safe setting. Overall, this session gave students a chance to talk about a sensitive topic in the context of their own experience. Rick's performance also created a positive encounter with a gay male.

The encounter with Rick surfaced repeatedly during the two follow-up seminar sessions. The readings for those sessions included narratives from writers reflecting on the treatment of gay persons; the group also reviewed a collection of comic strips that Jo Fischer saved from the newspaper about a young man who told his mother he was gay. A few students indicated that they had to collect themselves after reading the narratives due to their emotional reaction to the mistreatment of the narrators and noted they felt the same way after hearing Rick. Many students shared stories about gay persons they knew. The discussions quickly reached to the implications of sexuality for schools and beyond to include religious issues and gays in the military. The narratives opened the door for students to explore the controversies around sexuality and the dilemmas they pose in schools. Their investment in these issues appeared heightened by their increased understanding of gay persons.

THE FOXFIRE APPROACH

Theme three of the course, education in the contemporary world, occupied the last few weeks of the term. To raise the concept of democratic education, two teachers from a Foxfire school were guests at the Monday evening session.* Karen, a technology resources teacher, and Judy, a middle school economics teacher, began the session by describing their teaching and courses, "putting themselves in context" as they put it. Karen then asked that the students do the same by answering questions, such as, "How many are education majors?" to which students raised their hands. Karen's high energy and enthusiasm set a quick pace.

Not more than five minutes passed before Karen invited students into the conversation. She said, "You got one minute to turn to five or six people around you to describe buzzwords for public education. You can only use three words or less—no treatise on this. Get with five or six people around you and do it! Any questions? Go!" The noise level immediately escalated.

---

*Foxfire is an innovative, progressive approach to education. See E. Wigginton, *Sometimes a Shining Moment* (New York: Doubleday, 1985), for a detailed description of the Foxfire program.

As students met, Karen walked up and down the aisles, listened in, and helped people. She asked some if they were a group. This encouraged some in the back to group together. She yelled, "Thirty seconds left!" Judy was also walking around helping groups.

Judy asked people to regroup, commenting that going from loudness to quietness is normal in her class. She asked them to yell out ideas, noting that others could yell "ditto" if they had the same word. She said, "The rule in brainstorming is no misspelling. Get ideas out, polish later. Go for it!" One man said "chaotic," "rote," "tracking." Others yelled "underfunded" (others began to yell "ditto"), then "disenchanting," "diverse" (more "dittos"), "choice," "at risk," "normal," "crowded," "archaic," "changing," "secret," "authoritative," "schedule," "mainstreaming," "memorization," "testing," "co-op learning," "discipline problems," and "hormonal." Judy joked with them as they did this. When she asked if there were more ideas, a few more yelled out, "Needs reform," "frustrating," "at a turning point," "illiteracy," "robotic learning." At that point Karen said, "Looking at that list, would you characterize it as positive or negative?" "Negative" rang out in unison. Karen responded, "You are good students, and this is what happens with you. It is what happens with others. We are going to share Foxfire with you, a response to a list like this twenty-five years ago."

Karen and Judy's lively introduction had hooked my attention, and as I looked around the room, it seemed to have hooked most in the group. They pulled us directly into making meaning about the status of education, then posed Foxfire as a potential alternative. As they proceeded to describe the Foxfire philosophy and practice, they gave concrete examples of what took place in their classes. Karen, in particular, interjected humor as she shared her perspective. She mentioned John Dewey in her overview of Foxfire philosophy, saying, "If it works in the classroom, why do we have to have a dead philosopher tell us it is okay?" Both teachers offered opportunities for the EDU 200 students to try out the approaches as they described them. For example, they asked the group to brainstorm for thirty seconds about places in the real world where one would find math. The students generated more examples than Judy could write on the overhead. Judy then explained the role of brainstorming in a Foxfire classroom and its role in getting students involved. Karen summed up Foxfire as "student centered, product centered, tied to the real world, democratic process that tells students that they own learning, teachers are guides, and holds students responsible for learning and evaluating."

After describing their approaches, Karen and Judy asked for students' reactions. A lively conversation ensued, which passed the 7:50 mark with no indication that anyone planned to leave. Shortly thereafter, Karen announced that we were past the time for the class to end, and if people needed to leave, they could. Only a few students left, the rest remaining in their seats asking questions. Finally, Karen invited students to stay informally, and about fifteen did.

The Foxfire approach, as Karen and Judy demonstrated it, endorsed validating students as knowers, situating learning in their experience, and mutually constructing meaning. The practices Karen and Judy illustrated embodied these principles. They used very short brainstorming sessions to pull out students' ideas, then based their discussion on that foundation. The brainstorming sessions in small groups illustrated Brightman's (1993) nominal group method, particularly in bringing the ideas together from the entire group. This process validated students as knowers by encouraging their input. Learning was then situated in their own experience by using the context they generated for discussion, an approach that also contributed to mutual construction of meaning. Presenting their own teaching as open for improvement, Judy and Karen enhanced the mutual construction. The EDU 200 students did not just hear about Foxfire—they experienced it. At Karen and Judy's invitation following the experience, students were invited to share their reactions and explore briefly the implications for educational practice.

In the follow-up seminars Kim's group generated what the EDU 200 course would look like if it were taught according to the Foxfire principles. The group generated many ideas and then concluded that the class already had many of the components they generated. Jan's group focused on generating themes from the reading, George Wood's *Schools That Work: America's Most Innovative Public Education Programs*. The themes that arose sparked discussion about testing, classroom management, administrative policy, and curriculum. The critique of educational practice flowed more easily here, probably due to a combination of the topics, readings, and experience of nearly a semester in EDU 200.

COURSE OUTCOMES

THE VALUE OF NARRATIVES FOR LEARNING

The overarching goal of EDU 200 was for students to think critically about schooling and education in contemporary America. Learning to recognize, evaluate, and defend positions in educational discourse and learning to interpret, critique, and judge educational practices in various contexts were the intended outcomes of this course. Implied in that language was the expectation that students learn to participate in the social construction of knowledge about schooling and education in contemporary America. This world in which instructors wanted students to participate was a very different world from the one that many of the EDU 200 students inhabited. The narrative approach helped instructors hear the many worlds students brought into EDU 200, and the narratives provided throughout the course helped the students begin to access the world of critical thinking.

WELCOMING MULTIPLE WORLDS

Connecting to the students' world in this course meant connecting with multiple worlds. As would be expected with nearly three hundred students, students' ways of making meaning varied from absolute to independent knowing. This range is evident in students' comments on the course evaluation. One student's comments captured the essence of many who complained that they did not know the purpose of the Monday evening narratives and did not get enough concrete information from the course:

> I was somewhat disappointed with this entire class—perhaps because I am just not used to this type of class set-up. I prefer more structure and challenge. I blew off most of the assignments and did not give my best effort at all and still made high grades. At this stage, I feel that I should be learning things that I can take with me as I enter the teaching profession and quite honestly I haven't compiled as much information and ideas from this course as I thought I would.

These comments express the need for practical ideas for teaching as a priority over discussion of issues with no solutions. This student also genuinely expresses the need many felt for structure. This concern for concrete information and structure indicates a way of knowing in which the instructor is seen as the authority responsible for student learning.

Although many shared this student's perceptions, the majority felt differently about the course, as is evident from another student:

> I do want to say that I feel that this was one of the most valuable courses I've taken as far as being informative and enlightening and I would take it again if I could. Perhaps you could make Monday evening available to others who aren't still in the course. I found that I was excited to learn about new approaches and to hear diverse opinions on subjects. I think this course was wonderful because I got the chance to debate and listen to opinions I may not have heard before.

In contrast to the previous student, the latter one makes meaning from hearing others' views rather than hearing concrete information from the instructor. This difference in meaning-making results in an entirely different assessment of the course.

Yet another perspective was evident from a few students, such as this one:

> Some may have complained that they didn't know what the point of
> the course is, but I think they may be just a little too programmed
> for multiple choice tests and lecture-note-taking classes. And they
> missed the point. We learned to think critically about a broad spec-
> trum of philosophies and ideas, and that is valuable.

This student indicates an interest in extending beyond hearing new ideas to
thinking critically about them.

The focus of the majority of the students on hearing others' views suggests that transitional knowing was a common way of making meaning in
this group. Research on college students' epistemological development generally indicates that first- and second-year students hold absolute or transitional epistemic assumptions (King and Kitchener 1994; Kitchener and
King 1990). My research at the same institution a few years earlier indicated
that most college students in my group of 101 were transitional knowers: 32
percent of first-year students, 53 percent of sophomores, 83 percent of juniors, and 80 percent of seniors (Baxter Magolda 1992). It is likely that transitional epistemic assumptions were prevalent among the students enrolled
in EDU 200.

Seven students in Kim's section and six students in Jan's section completed
the Measure of Epistemological Reflection, or MER (Baxter Magolda and
Porterfield 1988; see appendices for details). Although this group is not representative of the larger student population in EDU 200, their comments on
the MER support the assumption that many students in the course used
transitional knowing. The majority of students completing the MER were
transitional knowers (80 percent), meaning that they assumed some knowledge was certain and some was uncertain. Transitional knowers are open to
hear others' views, they are interested in integrating their own experience
with learning, and they believe that there is no certain answer in some areas.
Students using these epistemic assumptions were probably open to the discussion format of EDU 200 but hesitant to judge and critique since right answers are elusive.

Sixty percent of the transitional knowers held transitional assumptions in
all areas assessed by the MER. Another 20 percent of that group held transitional assumptions in two-thirds of the areas and absolute assumptions in
the remaining third. The students in this latter group were probably those
who expressed concern in their interviews that the discussions "did not go
anywhere" and the course purpose was unclear. For example, an excerpt from
Melissa's MER responses shows her expectations regarding learning. After indicating that she preferred that the instructor take a major role in communicating information, Melissa wrote, "I think more along the lines of what

seems to be concrete information to me. I think in an orderly fashion from point A to point B, which is probably why I like math so much." However, Melissa recognized the importance of more nebulous knowledge, although she reported constantly struggling in that type of class. In fact, in her interview she reported that EDU 200 had been a constant struggle for her, and by the end she felt she "had learned nothing." Some of the students who held some absolute expectations, like Melissa, found the course format wanting.

The remaining 20 percent of students completing the MER were independent knowers. They assumed that most knowledge was uncertain and viewed learning as sharing views among peers. One of Jessica's comments on her MER captures this way of knowing: "People see things in different ways. What may seem right to one person may be wrong to another. It's purely up to the individual to decide." As would be expected from this perspective, Jessica said, "I want students to speak their minds—to disagree and argue if necessary." Similarly, Hugh wrote:

> Since everyone has a different background and different experiences, so everyone has a unique point of reference. I believe the sharing of ideas can enable people to get past their own biases and come to a better understanding of certain things. It also teaches students that not everyone thinks the same or believes the same ideas, while teaching at the same time that these differences should be accepted.

These comments reveal openness to hearing others' views and a simultaneous hesitancy to judge different perspectives.

In comparing these ways of making meaning to the course objectives, we see that many of the course objectives were a stretch for these perspectives. Returning to Kegan's bridge analogy (see chap. 3), EDU 200 instructors needed to create a transitional culture that was both meaningful to these ways of knowing and facilitative of more complex ways of knowing. The course objectives accomplished this to a degree. Recognizing positions in educational discourse and interpreting educational practices were a stretch (and therefore facilitative) for absolute knowers; these same objectives were closer to the ways of making meaning held by transitional knowers and therefore welcomed them as they were. Critiquing and evaluating positions and practices were facilitative for transitional knowers but more welcoming to independent knowers. Defending positions and judging educational practices were facilitative for independent knowers. The objectives themselves offered both the meaningful and the facilitative components for transitional and independent knowers, leaving the instructors with the challenge of figuring out how to make these objectives welcoming to those with some absolute assumptions.

The objectives of *recognizing* positions in educational discourse and *interpreting* educational practices as they related to the purpose of schooling required that students value their own perspectives or have a "mind of their own," so to speak. Cheryl described coming to value her perspective in the course:

> I feel more like a part of this class. I feel less than the professor in a lecture where he is telling you his knowledge. I feel equal in this class because it is based on my experience. The students and teacher share experiences. I have something to contribute. I am usually quiet and don't speak in class. I feel like I can in here.

Cheryl also reported that sharing her perspective prompted more internal self-evaluation and questioning. She noted that her family offered what she called a "one-way" background, and the class was introducing her to alternative ways to think.

Mandy reported a similar experience, noting that many of the class sessions, particularly the ones on homosexuality, prompted her to think about things she had never considered. She reported that the readings and talking in class "get you to think on a different level." However, she remained unclear on how to make decisions about these new ideas. Cheryl and Mandy demonstrate that being validated as knowers and being given a chance to use their own thinking and experience in class helped them value their own perspectives.

Students' responses to a question on Jan's final exam about whether the course had changed their views also revealed progress on recognizing positions and interpreting educational practices. Two students who held some absolute assumptions reported that the course forced them to see the importance of other people's point of view. One also said that her frustration of not having a solution made her sit down and think about the problem, resulting in subtle changes in constructing her views. Students who used primarily transitional assumptions commented that the course opened up many new viewpoints and made them less judgmental. One noted that a reading changed something inside her, but she was unable to articulate exactly what had changed. Considering new viewpoints and alternative approaches also arose in students' interviews. Leanne reported that she had learned how to incorporate a variety of students' cultures into her future teaching. She also described a difference in her thinking, saying, "The analysis work—all the hidden stuff, you have to really think. You have to be open to be a teacher, to try to give kids a good idea about the world." Susan reported that she knew how to use the weekly concepts and learned about alternative approaches. These reactions indicate that students with some absolute assumptions and those with primarily transitional ways of knowing came to see the value of others' perspectives as well as their own. This occurred primarily through students being validated as knowers, experiencing others' views firsthand or through powerful narratives, and not having ready-made solutions to educational problems.

Critiquing positions in educational discourse and evaluating educational practices required going beyond an awareness of new perspectives. Elaine, who on her MER expressed interest only in students translating material for one another, said in her interview that she was learning to critique:

> Hearing opinions is important to deciding my own. I read, take my opinions, ideas that have been put forth, look further into it, compare to my ideas, and think about what we should do. I combine different things, get the main idea, compare it to my idea. I become a better person by changing my views as I learn about others' experiences.

Elaine's more recent view assigns greater value to what her peers think, and their views sometimes affect hers in a positive way. Elaine said that she had learned to critically analyze through the text analyses (see syllabus in appendices for description) and felt that the course offered a chance to evaluate her opinions.

Another student concurred in her response to Jan's final exam question. She reported that her peers' interpretations expanded her knowledge and enabled her to create her own opinion. She realized that she could no longer create a definition of effective schools, but would need to develop a set of ideas in which to believe.

Some students felt that although they had learned how to critique and evaluate, the course discussions had stopped short of those activities. Dawn offered, "It doesn't seem like we have judged much. We have our own ideas, what we felt, agreed and disagreed with, but we haven't critiqued much. Critiquing is analyzing, hard-core looking at the readings. I haven't changed my mind on anything I came in with." Denise was hesitant to make judgments because she was unsure whether her classmates had given her good information. Both women were not quite sure what to do with the information they had heard. In contrast, Jessica noted that the class gave her a chance to "think broadly, allows you to think through things critically and hear other viewpoints that will help you in the future." She also felt that she was capable of judging educational practice at the end of the course, although she could not describe to me how she would do this.

Judging educational practice and *defending* positions in educational discourse required taking a stance on what information and beliefs to endorse.
Hugh was confident that he could judge educational practices on the basis
of the course, saying,

> I think I can make judgments about educational practice. I will be
> able to make judgments in the classroom setting. This class has
> helped me by giving me different ways of seeing things and think-
> ing about things. My judgments will be my own; not other people
> who told you, you should think or do this. I appreciate this. I try to
> make decisions that say I've examined this situation and from past
> experience and what I've learned—what is the best way to handle
> this?

These comments are an indication of contextual knowing in which one decides based on appropriate evidence that particular approaches are better
than others, thus representing a shift from Hugh's valuing all opinions
equally at the outset of the course to deciding what he believed at the end
of the course. Hugh thought his classmates had helped him decide on a
viewpoint, and Kim had allowed him to make his own judgments. Mandy
concurred, saying that the course helped her think critically and decide what
kind of teacher she would like to be. Lauren had made a decision on her philosophy about progressivism and thought the textual analysis helped her see
"what is ingrained in society." Becky said, "The discussion helps shape your
perspective on teaching, to build your ideas and values." These students felt
that the course content, discussions, encouragement to make their own decisions, and assignments had helped them process, think through, and make
decisions about educational practice.

Jan provided another source of assessing progress relative to the course
objectives. On the first day of class she asked her students to develop an educational platform that included their description of an educated person,
what they thought the purposes of schools really were, and what they
thought the purposes ought to be. During that first meeting, students paired
up, interviewed each other about these three topics, and recorded their responses on paper. Jan saved the platforms until the end of the course, returning them for students to revise as the final exam. Jan kindly conducted
a theme analysis of the precourse and postcourse platforms for me, which
appears in figure 6.2.

A comparison of the themes for an educated person illustrates that the
notions of open-mindedness and making informed judgments were consistent in both pre- and postcourse platforms. However, there were more details about what these meant and two additions: responsibility toward others

Figure 6.2: Pre- and Post-Course Educational Platforms

Initial Educational Platforms	Final Educational Platforms
Themes re: What is an educated person?	
• possesses a variety of experience, is cultured, well-rounded • makes informed judgments • active learner • respects others, is open-minded	• open-minded, listens to others' points of view • makes own decisions, acts responsibly • life-long learner • accepting of others • self-knowledge • critically analyzes texts/situations • uses knowledge to benefit society
Themes re: The Purpose of Schools (Reality)	
• the three Rs • competition • discipline, proper social interaction, conformity • to sort students • keep children busy • preparation for college/the next level	• teach facts • compliance with government, tradition • discipline • socialization, conditioning, conformity • tracking/separating • baby-sitting • fit into the system • survive in society
Themes re: The Purpose of Schools (Normative)	
• develop critical thinking ability • prepare for the future, application of knowledge • open minds to diversity • social development • awareness of social issues	• critical thinking, questioning • a place where people exchange knowledge • enable students to be aware of and accepting of differences, to respect others' and their own beliefs • learning to learn • student-oriented, meet students needs and interests • provide a safe place for children to be themselves • experiential, cooperative, exploration

and society, and critically analyzing texts/situations. Many also noted the complexity of describing an educated person. The themes for the reality of school purpose remained basically the same, except for some more sophisticated language and recognition that compliance with government and tradition exists. The pre- and postcourse normative purposes of schools are also similar but show the most change in the way students talked about these purposes. The precourse themes were generic, but the postcourse themes contained details about how to develop critical thinking, how to promote openness, and how to help students' develop their own beliefs. Although this theme analysis does not show the positions that individual students took, the difference between the real and the normative purposes of schools shows an *interpretation* and *critique* of school practice and a willingness to *take a position* on what education should be. The theme analysis does not allow for judging individual students' ability to defend their positions on educational practice.

Jan told me in a postcourse interview that she thought the course objectives were achieved to a degree in her section. Specifically, she offered:

> They understood that issues they would be involved in were larger than their building. They understood cultural influences they needed to be aware of and use in their practice. A lot of them in finals said they had these ideas before, but had to think about it again and directly tie these reflective thoughts to classroom practice. I have a feeling that a lot of them will bring it to practice, although perhaps idealistically.

Jan also thought the students gained some exposure to critical thinking through the textual analyses. She noted that most "got it" on the textual analysis of a children's book but had a harder time doing one on popular culture. Here is her interpretation:

> Several did Disney films. They loved the nice message, didn't see the marketing aspects of Disney, and didn't even think about the darker side of questioning the assumptions. The children's stuff is removed from their experience so they can look at it and see the mystification. What they chose for pop culture is still close to their experience. They are enamored with it, can't put the same perspective on it to be critical. Other instructors said this same thing.

Kim concurred that her students made progress on recognizing various positions but were still hesitant to make judgments about educational discourses and practices.

Strengths of the course appeared to be in heightening *recognition* of educational discourses, including cultural issues and the lived experiences of students and their peers (objective one), helping students *interpret* and be-gin to *critique* educational practices related to the purpose of schooling (objective two), and *interpreting* school practices in sociocultural contexts (objective three). Shortcomings appeared primarily in *defending* a posi-tion (objective one) and *judging* educational practices (objectives two and three).

A BRIDGE BETWEEN SCHOOLING AND EDUCATION

Obstacles to constructing the transitional culture needed in EDU 200 abound-ed. Many students came to the course inexperienced in class discussion and critical thinking. Some reported having never spoken in a class before. The format of the course was an experiment in alternative approaches to teach-ing, and one about which the instructors were unsure. Many of the topics, particularly race, gender, and sexual orientation, were topics that most col-lege students find difficult to discuss. Finally, many students expected solu-tions to educational problems and practical knowledge regarding how to teach. The course offered, instead, exploration of the complexities of educa-tional issues and an invitation to form one's own judgment about educa-tional practice.

Yet the two sections of EDU 200 I observed did succeed in promoting their objectives. Students' progress stemmed in large measure from two sources: (1) hearing diverse viewpoints from their peers and the readings, and (2) analyzing their own experience. Hearing the stories of peers and telling their own stories were crucial parts of the transitional culture. Both hearing and telling stories have powerful effects according to the literature on the role of narrative in teaching. Bateson notes, "*Insight*, I believe, refers to the depth of understanding that comes by setting experiences, yours and mine, familiar and exotic, new and old, side by side, learning by letting them speak to one another" (1994, 14, italics in original). The EDU 200 instruc-tors hoped that students would go along on the journeys shared in the Monday evening narratives, the readings, and the class discussions to be-come wiser and more receptive to alternative educational discourse and to gain a depth of understanding about the role of culture in education. They also hoped that the students would find their voices in this process in order to critique educational discourse and practice, leading to their ability to self-author their role as teachers in the future. Cooper (1991) notes that "telling our own stories is a way to impose form upon our often chaotic experiences (Grumet 1988) and, in the process, to develop our own voice" (97). Telling stories in EDU 200 helped students attempt to make sense of an experience that appeared chaotic in light of their expectations. Their voice development was the goal of the course to enable them as prospective teachers to author their own perspectives on education. Richard Hopkins (1994) would approve; he argues that

> narrative might provide a cohesive, even protogenic, operating principle for tying lived experience to subject matter in the schools. Narrative is a deeply human, linguistic process, a kind of primal developmental impulse. We are storytelling creatures. We do not just tell stories; we live them, create them, define ourselves through them. Our narratives are the expressive, temporal medium through which we construct our functioning personae and give meaning to our experience. (1994, xvi)

Hopkins also views narrative as an exercise in critical thinking, writing, "Our narratives are the means through which we imagine ourselves in to the persons we become" (xvii).

The narratives that served as the core of EDU 200 and the learning atmosphere created by the instructors were instrumental in creating the inclusive environment that allowed students to join the conversation and imagine the teachers they would become. The readings and Monday evening narratives offered rich stories about the lives of others that captured students' interest in joining the journey. The validation of students as knowers that both Jan and Kim conveyed helped students begin to think on their own and express themselves. Students' progress in interpreting the meaning of readings and critiquing the utility of educational practice was enhanced by their validation as knowers as well as by discussion situated in their own experience. The latter invited students to add their stories, to share their evolving journeys. Their own experience gave them a comfortable vantage point from which to claim knowledge about educational practice and from which to afford value to others' opinions. My class observations revealed that both Jan and Kim routinely implemented the two principles of validating students as knowers and situating learning in students' experience.

Students' comments confirm that these were important parts of the transitional culture. One student shared, "I enjoyed this class-sitting in a circle, breaking up into groups, discussing, listening, talking, sharing. The class really made me think and share my own experience and ideas." Another said,

> [Kim] sat on the side of the room. She would generate what she wanted to be a discussion, but if she had a point in mind and we went a different direction, that was okay. We felt we had more control over the class. She was a guide. We didn't have to raise our hands and wait for her to call on us.

Likewise, one of Jan's students said, "Jan is a good facilitator. She starts the discussion, keeps it on track, listens to opinions but doesn't judge them. She offers her opinion, usually when we aren't talking." These comments demonstrate that Jan's and Kim's approaches were meaningful to, yet facilitative of, students' ways of making meaning.

Instances of mutual construction of knowledge occurred, but less frequently than Jan, Kim, and the students preferred. In part, students' epistemological development mediated this because transitional knowers are hesitant to make decisions without authority's approval. Independent knowers are not concerned about coming to closure in discussion because they believe everything is a matter of personal opinion. Instructors' hesitations also came into play in these dynamics. Jan reported that the instructors were "so intent on being participative, we lost that we needed to be explicit sometimes." She decided to be more explicit and offer more guidance to help students process the issues in her next semester. Kim also reported hesitations that affected her teaching. She explained,

> What I was hearing instructors saying was this is the students' course, so let them have it, let them construct their own meaning. I thought I should be hands off, but was uncomfortable with that. Now I'm more comfortable with structuring unstructuredness. I think I have a great deal of structure, but it allows for a lot of construction on their part.

Both instructors felt that they had initially pulled back too much in the interest of giving students room to construct meaning. They had fallen into the common misconception noted earlier that letting students construct knowledge means letting them think anything. Both remained committed to the goal of students' self-authorship but realized that they could balance guidance and structure with students' freedom to help students construct meaning in an informed way.

Despite these dilemmas, most students in Jan's and Kim's sections believed they benefited from the course. The outcome data reveal progress on the objectives, particularly in getting students to think critically about difficult issues such as cultural aspects of schooling and the purpose of education in society. The success of some of the Monday evening narratives reveals the potential effectiveness of the large group format. Overall EDU 200 offers evidence that connecting learning to students' lives can promote critical thinking, subject mastery, and student satisfaction. More important, it offers evidence that first- and second-year students can tackle complex objectives and thrive in an environment that gives them responsibility for their learning. Most did not arrive at self-authorship, but they made progress toward it. Jan's and Kim's reflections offer useful adjustments to developing transitional cultures to reach students who are less ready for critical thinking and self-responsibility.

PART 3

THE PROBLEMS AND PROMISE OF CONSTRUCTIVE-DEVELOPMENTAL PEDAGOGY

CHAPTER 7

Rebuilding Educators' and Students' Worlds

In *The Grace of Great Things: Creativity and Innovation,* Robert Grudin writes,

> In the company or with the books of true teachers, I think, we always feel a kind of shock—not the shock of a brilliant exposition but of an unsettling challenge. Whatever their subject matter or style, true teachers always convey the sense that the communication of an art demands of the student not only the effort and attention but cathartic psychological change. To learn is not merely to accumulate data; it is to rebuild one's world. (1990, 152)

The courses described in this book invited students to rebuild their worlds. They created opportunities for students to do more than accumulate data; they offered opportunities for students to reflect and act on data to self-author their own perspectives. They offered the kind of unsettling challenges necessary to spark rebuilding of content knowledge, epistemic assumptions, and self-evolution. All of this rebuilding—of self, epistemology, and knowledge—is, in my mind, what constitutes genuine learning.

The stories of these students, their teachers, and these courses invite educators to rebuild our worlds as well—to rebuild our knowledge of students, learning, pedagogy, and knowledge construction. Exploring the meaning of what transpired in these four courses and its significance for higher education leads to a theory of learning and teaching that extends beyond technique to help educators understand the psychological change inherent in learning. The purpose of this chapter is to articulate a theory of learning and teaching that offers a vision for rebuilding our worlds.

A CONSTRUCTIVE-DEVELOPMENTAL THEORY OF LEARNING AND TEACHING

The theoretical framework I offer here is grounded in numerous sources. First and foremost, it is grounded in the three course observations recounted in part 2; exploring their meaning and significance for learning and teaching is the primary foundation of advancing a theory of learning and teaching.

However, I bring my own experience as an educator in the discipline of human development to this task. My valuing the constructive-developmental approach to human development (see chap. 2) and my foray into new forms of teaching (see chap. 3) strongly influence my thinking, as does my longitudinal work with young adults' epistemological development. The theory of learning and teaching that I advance here is closely aligned to the constructive-developmental approach, so much so that I chose to retain that label to acknowledge that tradition. Yet the course observations from part 2 offer a deeper understanding of learning and teaching that can guide educators in the quest to transform educational practice.

A good theory about learning and teaching ultimately should be about students, learning, teachers, teaching, and knowledge construction. An analysis of the meaning of what transpired in the learning stories told in this book yields insight about all five areas and reveals that all five are inextricably intertwined. Students brought their socialization about the role of students and teachers and their epistemological assumptions about knowledge to each course. These, as well as other dimensions of their personal lived experience, formed their understanding of the learning process. Similarly, teachers brought their socialization about the role of teachers and students and their epistemological assumptions about knowledge to each course, factors that mediated their understanding of the learning process. Effective learning and teaching occurred when both students and teachers were willing to explore new learning/teaching behavior and stretch their epistemological assumptions. Students' and teachers' understandings of knowledge construction differed, and students' ability to join in knowledge construction hinged on teachers' ability to join their students' thinking effectively.

Knowledge construction was the goal in all four courses recounted in this book. The EDU 200 instructors wanted students to establish their own beliefs about educational discourse to inform their future practice. I wanted my students to learn how to construct their own informed theories to guide their work with students. Sam wanted his students to follow their own conjectures and help their future students do the same. Chris wanted his students to learn how to use scientific inquiry to create knowledge in their future science careers. We all wanted our students to learn existing knowledge in our disciplines, yielding different content goals; yet our core goals were the same. This view of knowledge construction implies bringing the limits of knowing to the learning process with the purpose of nourishing the reconstruction of knowledge. This represents a highly complex set of epistemological assumptions, including that knowledge exists in a context, is constructed based on judging relevant evidence, and is to some degree the consensus of a knowledge community about the interpretation of that evidence in a particular context. The student stories told here and research evidence on college students' epistemological development affirm that these goals were exceedingly high expectations for the students in these courses.

Yet despite the chasm between teachers' expectations for knowledge construction and students' interpretations of what the expectations meant, progress toward knowledge construction took place in these four courses. This progress was a result of teachers' attempts to genuinely access and understand how their students understood learning. Although my colleagues were not versed in epistemological development, their interest in connecting with their students created opportunities for them to access their students' thinking. For example, it took Chris Snowden some time to figure out that his feedback to Maryann was not working for her (chap. 4). Once he identified this problem, he shifted his feedback to move closer to her way of understanding. Through most of the course, he was what Kegan (1994) would call good company for the wrong journey. In other words, he was good company for students who were ready to explore the discrepancies in scientific findings and work on the cutting edge of developing new ideas. Maryann, however, like her counterparts in other courses who viewed the world from an absolute frame, was on an entirely different journey—one that involved moving from assuming knowledge was certain to assuming that some of it was yet to be determined. The instances of progress or lack thereof noted in all four courses highlight the crucial component of connecting to students' meaning-making in order to promote learning.

Chris, Sam, and Jo and her colleagues were unaware that their expectation for knowledge construction was simultaneously an expectation for reconstruction of students' epistemological assumptions. Because they developed good relationships with students, expressed genuine interest in students' thoughts, offered help, and adjusted their teaching as they saw the need, they were able to create conditions in which many students were able to reconstruct their epistemological assumptions. Even if they had been aware of the epistemological expectations (as I was in my course), the stories here reveal that teachers do not own a complete vision of learning.

As teachers, we know our disciplinary knowledge base, what students need to learn to be successful in their disciplines of study, and what ways of thinking are needed about this content. We need to interact with students to access *how* they know and the implications of these ways of knowing for achievement of the learning goals. Pedagogy must be an interdependent relationship between teacher and students to engage the students' way of making meaning in the context of the course goals. Connecting to students' experience and using it as the foundation for learning encourage students to rebuild their worlds because the learning experience is meaningful to them. Situating learning in their experience allows for validation of their ability to know, similar to Kegan's (1994) version of respecting the students' side of the bridge. Introducing unsettling challenges via mutually constructing meaning in this context of respect offers students the opportunity to consider rebuilding. This interdependence also calls on the teacher to transform teaching practice to accompany students on their journey rather than on the teacher's journey. Kegan points out that our role as educators is often to help students arrive at ways of making meaning that we have recently rejoiced in leaving.

In the context of these observations, learning becomes a matter of developing one's mind, or developing increasingly complex ways of knowing to meet the challenges of the curriculum. Teaching becomes a matter of intentionally helping students develop their minds. This constructive-developmental theory of learning and teaching also calls for teachers with complex ways of knowing that allow interdependent relationships with learners. I turn now to an exploration of how the three principles from chapter 3 were used in these four courses to develop students' minds. This analysis illustrates the core components of a constructive-developmental theory of learning and teaching. Following that analysis, connections between constructive-developmental theory, social-constructivist, and dialectic views of education are explored.

DEVELOPING STUDENTS' MINDS

Self-authorship is the goal of constructive-developmental pedagogy and was a goal of all the courses explored in this book. Given the ways of knowing of the students in these courses, the goal of self-authorship amounted to developing students' ways of knowing, or their "minds," as Kegan (1993) would say. Using the three principles accesses students' current ways of knowing, problematizes them, and helps students reconstruct them into more complex forms. As such, the three principles of constructive-developmental pedagogy offer a structure through which to accomplish four characteristics of developmental teaching. Developmental teachers (1) support the cognitive, social, affective, and intrapersonal constructions of their students, (2) exercise their students' cognitive, social, affective, and intrapersonal structures, (3) provide opportunities for relativizing those structures, and (4) support the integration of relativized structures into new ones (Kegan 1993, 87). They engage the growing edge of the student mind. The three principles of constructive-developmental pedagogy incorporate these developmental approaches in creating a bridge between the edge of students' minds and the ways of knowing in existing knowledge communities.

Developmental teaching simultaneously engages students where they are and invites them to move beyond where they are, creating the transitional context or bridge for growth. Situating learning in students' own experience sets the stage for all four characteristics because it places learning in a context that is meaningful to students, thereby connecting to their side of the bridge. Validating students as knowers supports their constructions and supports them in exercising their structures. Mutually constructing meaning encourages students to relativize their structures and integrate them into new ones. Continued validation in this mutual construction of meaning supports students in stretching beyond their current structures. An analysis of our four courses from a constructive-developmental framework indicates that they were quite effective in engaging the growing edge of most students' minds. A prominent exception is that of absolute knowers, whose growing edge was not reached effectively in any of the four courses. The stance that knowledge is socially constructed was in direct conflict with these students' constructions and structures; therefore, they probably perceived very little support for their current way of thinking. Chapter 8 addresses creating support to assist such students.

Transitional Knowing and Third Order Meaning-Making

Transitional knowing was prevalent in EDU 200 (80 percent of the students who participated in interviews) and Math by Inquiry (75 percent of the students participating in interviews). Some students in my theory courses and in Chris's science course also used transitional knowing, but it was less prevalent in those courses. Although students' orders of consciousness were less evident than their epistemological structures from the class observations and interviews, third order meaning-making would be consistent with transitional assumptions about knowing (refer to chap. 2 for further discussion of the integration of epistemological development and self-development). The acceptance of uncertainty in some areas of knowledge leads transitional knowers to focus on exploring and understanding those areas. Students in the third order coconstruct their ideas with others. These students were open to exploring together—with the instructor included to match their assumption that instructors still know more than students—to understand the content of their respective courses.

Situating learning in their experience gave students a meaningful starting point for exploring uncertainty in math, science, education, and human development. Validation of students as knowers encouraged expression of their ideas, provided access to others' views, and supported the mutual nature of meaning-making. Students' cognitive constructions were supported in a variety of ways. Accessing others' views, an activity central to interpersonal (connected) transitional knowers, was encouraged in all four courses. The EDU 200 narratives and seminar discussions gave students in-depth opportunities to get inside others' perspectives and feelings. The theory interviews and class discussions also actively involved students in seeking out, listening to, and making sense of others' views. Coinvestigation in math and hearing one another's projects in science accomplished this same goal. For impersonal (separate) transitional knowers, thinking through ideas as a process for dealing with uncertainty is the preferred construction. The textual analysis, cultural interview, and pedagogical project supported this construction in asking students to analyze what they had encountered. Identifying themes and analyzing their meaning for student development offered this process in the theory course. Using math principles and rules to explain one's thinking and using the process of scientific inquiry in projects supported these constructions as well. All of these dynamics gave students the opportunity to exercise their transitional cognitive structure, that is, to engage in a process to understand uncertainty.

At the same time, these dynamics supported students' social, affective, and intrapersonal constructions and offered opportunities for students to exercise them. Group activities in all four classes and various forms of team work supported coconstruction of ideas. Students worked in teams to conduct their theory interviews and analyses, their EDU 200 assignments, and the library assignment in winter biology. Sam Rivers assigned groups in math for in-class group investigations, and students often paired informally to investigate together as well. Mutual constructions about class process were also prevalent in math, Jan's EDU 200 seminar, and my theory course. All of these activities validated coconstruction with others and gave students opportunities to practice it.

Kegan's notion of giving students opportunities to relativize their structures means helping those structures move from subject to object to enable the student to reflect upon them. For transitional knowers it means becoming aware of the assumption that some knowledge is certain and some is uncertain. In the case of third order meaning-making this means students becoming aware that they coconstruct themselves and their ideas with others. Awareness of both these assumptions releases the student from embeddedness in them, making reflection, judgment, and action on them possible. Support for integrating relativized structures into new ones, Kegan's fourth developmental characteristic, means facilitating students' rebuilding their world to take their increasing awareness into account.

Mutually constructing meaning was the primary principle that contributed to students' relativizing structures and integrating relativized structures into new ones. All these instructors' emphasis on the social construction of knowledge conveyed the idea that human beings make decisions about what to believe, that they often disagree, and that no solid answer exists outside humans' activity of making these decisions. Sam insisted that mathematicians "made up" math structure. Chris contended, and illustrated, that scientists make decisions that are fallible. I demonstrated that different experts made different decisions regarding how to portray student development theory. The EDU 200 instructors introduced students to numerous disagreements about educational purposes and practices. These approaches provided unsettling challenges to students' transitional cognitive structure and offered the opportunity to reconsider it. By modeling the knowledge construction process in each of our disciplines, all of us provided support for students to consider reshaping their transitional cognitive structure into a new one that endorsed uncertainty more readily.

Mutually constructing meaning also supported relativizing and integrating social, affective, and intrapersonal structures. Although we validated and encouraged mutual coconstructions, we simultaneously endorsed disagreement and conflicting opinions as inherently good for knowledge construction. For example, I demonstrated how conflicting opinions led to further research about student development theory that enhanced our understanding of students. Chris emphasized how arguments in science helped identify useful questions to further scientific research. In this context of differing opinions, students were encouraged to decide what they believed. Sam's students were asked to explain why they took a particular approach to working on a math concept. The EDU 200 students were asked to take a stance on the educational purposes and practices they would endorse as professionals. My students were encouraged to decide what they believed about student development theory. Chris's students were asked to identify a research question and choose a reasonable path for pursuing it. All of these expectations challenged students to construct themselves and their ideas outside mutual relationships with others. Collectively, the dynamics described here welcomed transitional, third order meaning-makers as they were but also welcomed them to become something more.

INDEPENDENT KNOWING AND FOURTH ORDER MEANING-MAKING

A few students in EDU 200 and Math by Inquiry were independent knowers. Independent knowing was common in my theory courses and Chris Snowden's course. Independent knowers believe that most knowledge is uncertain, ushering in self-authorship for the first time. However, independent knowers are subject to the system through which their beliefs are generated, focusing instead on the fact that they *are* their beliefs rather than coconstructions with others. The ways of thinking and beliefs they used to codefine with others now come inside the self, and the person can describe how those beliefs are a part of him and owned by him. These students can describe how their self-belief system is arranged, but they are not yet able to reflect on the system that arranged it or recognize that it is only one possible system through which to arrange one's beliefs. This fourth order meaning-making is consistent with independent epistemological assumptions.

The activities described in the previous section to encourage relativizing and integrating structures for transitional knowers simultaneously supported independent knowers' individual constructions and exercised their independent cognitive structure. Validating their expression of their own ideas occurred in ways that matched both the interindividual (connected) and the individual (separate) patterns. In EDU 200 and my theory course students were asked to take stances in group conversation (meaningful to interindividual pattern students) and in individual papers (meaningful to individual pattern students). Sam Rivers focused primarily on students making and supporting conjectures together, a better match for interindividual pattern students, but he did validate students who operated independently from the group as well. In contrast, Chris Snowden relied more heavily on students taking a stance individually in their research project. All four courses provided a welcoming context for students' self-authored cognitive constructions. Being encouraged to view themselves as knowledge constructors as teachers, student development theorists, scientists, and mathematicians also welcomed their fourth order independent self systems.

Helping independent knowers relativize and reintegrate their structures came in the form of engaging students in the ways of knowing in their respective knowledge communities. These ways of knowing emphasized the need for evidence to adopt a particular knowledge claim. Chris routinely highlighted the evidence supporting scientific claims as he modeled scientific inquiry, and he expected students to do the same as they pursued their research project. Sam routinely asked students to use math structure to support various contentions they advanced. I expected students to produce data from their interviews or own experience to support theoretical stances they advanced. Inviting students into mutually constructing meaning in these contexts offered two unsettling challenges. First, their notion that one could decide independent of evidence (an independent knowing assumption) was challenged by advocating decision making by using relevant evidence (a contextual knowing assumption). Second, their notion of working out their perspectives through their independent self systems was challenged by asking them to practice the systems used in their knowledge communities to work out their beliefs. This latter challenge provided the opportunity to relativize social, affective, and intrapersonal fourth order structures and supported reintegrating them into fifth order structures.

The approaches that challenged fourth order independent knowers were not prevalent in EDU 200, probably appropriately so. Because most of the students there were probably transitional and third order meaning-makers, the dynamics of EDU 200 were consistent with their growing edge. This, however, probably also explains why the goals of critiquing and judging were accomplished only by the few independent knowers in that course. Students would not be able to engage in genuine critique and judgment until they had constructed a self-system to generate beliefs.

The few students in these courses who used contextual knowing already believed in using evidence for making decisions in a context. The opportunity to engage in mutually constructing meaning within the ways of knowing of a discipline supported and exercised their cognitive structures. Because their structures were consistent with the philosophy of their courses, they needed only to work on integrating their use of both modes of knowing and continue the transition from fourth to fifth order meaning-making. The use of both modes described earlier offered them this opportunity. Continued involvement in various ways of knowing in the disciplines also encouraged relativizing fourth order structures to become increasingly aware of the multiple systems used for knowing. Internalizing these multiple systems as one's own would complete the rebuilding of fourth order structures into fifth order ones. These fifth order structures, characterized by the ability to understand and access multiple systems of knowing, would truly enable the knowledge construction expected of college graduates.

SOCIALIZING STUDENTS INTO KNOWLEDGE COMMUNITIES

The social-constructivist view of education advocates bringing students into knowledge communities and teaching them how to join their colleagues in knowledge construction within the community. As is evident from the preceding discussion of developing students' minds, epistemological assumptions are a key component in socializing students into joint construction of knowledge. The courses observed here reveal that the three principles of constructive-developmental pedagogy were centrally involved in engaging students in dialogue in their knowledge communities.

DIALOGUE IN AND BEYOND THE CLASSROOM

The notion of dialogue stands at the center of the social-constructivist view of education. Shor (1992) described dialogue as "a capacity and inclination of human beings to reflect together on the meaning of their experience and their knowledge" (86). In describing this dialogue, social-constructivist writers such as Shor (1992) and Shor and Freire (1987) distinguish it from the traditional hierarchical discourse by emphasizing that it is mutual, democratic discourse among students and their teachers. The word *discourse* has led many educators to think of dialogue in terms of verbal exchange. The four courses described in this book reveal that dialogue is not limited to verbal exchange but is in fact a broader concept—an overall approach to a course of study. The three principles can be seen in both the verbal form of dialogue and the broader notion of dialogue.

Sam Rivers's class resonated with my early conception of dialogue as a verbal exchange. All of his class sessions, such as the ones recounted in chapter 5, consisted of verbal exchanges among him and the students. These exchanges stemmed from situating learning in students' experience, in Sam's case their investigations of various mathematical ideas prior to or during class. Sam's validation of students as knowers created the mutual nature of the discourse and the teacher-student camaraderie characteristic of social-constructivist dialogue. Sam downplayed his role as authority, yet never denied his knowledge and expertise in the mutual construction of meaning. His openness to learning through the dialogue in essence matched one of Shor's (1992) qualities of classroom dialogue: "frontloads student expression and backloads teacher expertise and bodies of knowledge" (88). Sam's pedagogy reflected the idea of learners and teachers knowing and reknowing their object of study, in this case math structure.

I also used the three principles in my graduate classroom to create this verbal, mutual dialogue. I placed students' interpretations of the material and their own development in the forefront of the class discussion, working my expertise into the process as warranted. I was always careful not to take up too much space in the conversation, hoping to create a dialogue in which student expression flowed freely. I saw this same process while observing Kim and Jan teach EDU 200. Watching Chris Snowden, however, made me stop to reflect on this notion of dialogue as verbal discourse. Many times in his class, a prime example being the story in chapter 4 on controversies in freeze tolerance, verbal dialogue was limited. As I reflected on this, I realized that verbal dialogue was also limited in the large meeting of EDU 200. Elliot Gardner (who conceptualized that course) explained that mental engagement was the goal of the large meeting narrative rather than verbal dialogue.

A closer look at Chris Snowden's class and EDU 200 broadens the definition of dialogue. There were instances in Chris's course in which students and he reflected together and talked together about an object of study, for example, exploring charts of data together. There were more instances, however, when the dialogue took place beyond the confines of classroom talk. In the first half of the course, Chris introduced bodies of knowledge upon which he invited the students to reflect as they explored the nature of scientific inquiry. Students introduced their own themes and interests in response to Chris's openness to their thoughts and questions in class. He acknowledged his expertise in cryopreservation yet simultaneously presented expertise as judgment that is never infallible. By emphasizing the vulnerable nature of expertise, Chris put the concept within reach of the students, thereby validating them as knowers. Students could put this notion to use outside class, where they were exploring a research topic of their choice, reading the discourse about that topic in the scientific community, and reflecting on how to enter that dialogue via their research paper. When those research projects became the focus of the second half of the course, student expression came to the forefront as students took the role of expert during their presentations. Students contributed to the content of the course by selection of their research topic. Collectively, the students and Chris reflected on their knowledge and experience.

Numerous components of EDU 200 also represented dialogue beyond verbal exchange. In interviews students often commented on talking with friends in EDU 200 or others who were not taking the course about the Monday evening narratives and the readings. Narratives in both forms invited students to reflect on the meaning of their own experiences and those recounted in the narratives. Because many of these produced unsettling challenges for students, students reflected on them individually and collectively with others. Their cultural interview assignment offered an opportunity for mutual reflection with their interviewee as well as with their instructor via feedback on the paper. The same was true of their textual analysis assignments. The pedagogical project was an opportunity for students to reflect together on the meaning of a topic of their choice and engage the class in further dialogue on the topic.

The courses recounted here illustrate dialogue about the process of learning as well as about student development theory, educational practice, math structure, or scientific inquiry. Shared decision making with students, one of Shor's qualities of classroom dialogue, occurred in my course through mutually developing the discussion each week, the final exam, evaluation practices, and our learning community practices. Sam Rivers shared his authority with students as he routinely checked with them on the pace of the discussion, asked what they wanted to pursue, and codeveloped assignments with them. Both Kim and Jan included students in making seminar session plans, in particular by having students volunteer for guiding conversations about the readings. They not only were given responsibility for developing important questions for the group to pursue but also were given latitude for facilitating the class discussion. Chris Snowden's midterm evaluation entitled "Is there a better way?" allowed students to critique and reshape the learning environment in the course. Jan's introductory session on group norms and my shared authority in creating the learning environment are further examples of shared decision making about the process of learning.

Reflecting together, then, on our experience and knowledge is the key element of dialogue. Some exchange is necessary to mutually construct meaning, but that exchange is not limited to verbal discussion. Assignments, readings, projects, presentations, and evaluations are possible means of creating dialogue in which teachers and students reflect together on what they know. Truly reflecting together, that is, the mutual reflection in which teacher authority does not overwhelm student experience, can be achieved by using the three principles of constructive-developmental pedagogy. Situating learning in students' experience, whether by connecting content to their existing knowledge or by connecting learning processes to their meaning-making, gives students a meaningful opportunity to join the dialogue. Validating students as knowers, whether by encouraging their voices in verbal discussion, welcoming their thoughts on the learning process, or providing an audience for their thoughts in writing, encourages their participation in the dialogue despite the unsettling challenges it raises. Mutually constructing meaning, whether about knowledge or learning process, helps students actively participate in the dialogue. In the process, they are able to assess the world they inhabit, determine whether they want to make changes, and rebuild as they see fit. In this type of dialogue, as in constructive-developmental pedagogy overall, the student is in charge of the decision to rebuild. That notion brings us to the issue of the teacher's role in dialogue.

INSTRUCTOR EXPERTISE IN DIALOGUE

From the framework of traditional pedagogy in which I, like most educators, have been socialized, giving the students responsibility for their own decisions in learning seems to be a radical shift. Often educators hear Shor's advice to "backload" instructor expertise as a recommendation to "unload" instructor expertise altogether. For example, as Kim Conlin shared in chapter 6, her initial interpretation of letting students construct their own meaning was for her to "be hands off" and to let the students have the course. Her discomfort with that approach prompted her to find a balance between her expertise and the students' opportunity to construct meaning. My own comfort with this balance increased when I discovered a significant passage in Shor's *Empowering Education,* in which he wrote, "Mutual dialogue is not a know-nothing learning process. It is not permissive, undirected, unstructured. It is interested in skills development and in systematic knowledge. The teacher must know a lot and must actively use that knowledge in a dialogic way" (1992, 247).

Shor describes the teacher's role in dialogue as both being directive and sharing authority. The teacher uses her authority to direct the dialogue yet shares authority with students. Similarly, Haroutunian-Gordon (1991) wrote, "Teaching, Plato says, is *turning the soul,* which I take to mean directing the students toward objects that draw out the vision or understanding they already possess, thanks to their experience in the world" (6, italics in original). Gitlin (1990) pointed out that "dialogue does not assume equality of perception or judgment between actors, but rather enables participants to work together to understand the topic under discussion" (541). These writers make it clear that teachers play a significant role in dialogue. What does this role, this combination of direction with shared authority, look like? The stories in this book reveal a few possibilities.

Returning to the notion of dialogue as an overall approach to a course, teacher participation emerges in many taken-for-granted activities including developing the syllabus that outlines the flow of topics for the course, identifying the readings, creating the assignments, and stating the system to evaluate students' work. These activities are directive and reflect the instructor's knowledge about the course content. They can also be mutually decided to varying degrees. At first glance Chris Snowden's course appears to be directive. He handed out the syllabus, chose the textbook, and specified the assignments and the percentages used in evaluation. These items were not up for debate in the course. By virtue of his design, he included students in decision making more than the other instructors described here in terms of course content. The design specified that student research topics, selected by students based on their interests, would constitute the second half of the course. A portion of their reading during the first half was articles for their project, again their choice. Also during the first half of the course, students did short presentations to review chapters in the textbook and turned in possible questions for the midterm. Students completed peer feedback forms for the research paper presentations, which became part of the evaluation process. Although his design was not placed on the table for mutual reflection, Chris's course offered students opportunities to share in decision making in the overall dialogue.

Sam Rivers initially appeared to offer the most shared leadership in the context of these activities. He had a general syllabus that outlined topics, such as number systems, but said little about what they meant. There was no textbook or readings, in order to focus on the students' discoveries according to the syllabus. Evaluation was explained in a general paragraph that said it would be based on attendance/participation, projects, a journal that would contain the student's reflective thinking about math, and a portfolio, all of which was to be discussed later. The syllabus placed more emphasis on discovery learning and learning together than it did on the content of the course. And indeed Sam did share authority in the course, but he was still appropriately directive. As questions about the journals arose, Sam and the students talked about what was useful to put in them. Students' responses prompted Sam to make some changes in the course as they went along. Students' investigations were the focus, but they stemmed from Sam's giving them a problem to work on for each session. Sam determined what pieces of homework he wanted to collect. He also outlined the portfolio contents but adjusted his expectations based on students' input. Sam's structure of the course was not as obvious as was Chris's structure, but it was clearly present.

EDU 200 also revealed a mix of direction and shared authority. Jo prepared the syllabus and the themes for the course; she and Elliot wrote the lectures for the reader and selected the readings. As the course proceeded, section instructors had input into the plans for Monday evening narratives. Section instructors also elaborated on how to approach the assignments Jo had specified. Built into the calendar of topics, however, were seminar conversations about the textual analysis assignments in which students chose texts of interest to them and sessions to work on the pedagogical projects selected by students. Presenting their projects at the end of the semester allowed students to shape some of the class content. Jan and Kim offered students the opportunity to rewrite assignments to improve their learning, thus giving students some shared decision making in the evaluation process.

My student development theory course offers more directiveness in content and more shared leadership in how we work with the content. I develop the syllabus and course topics, and I specify the readings. I also write detailed descriptions of assignments, but offer options for students to work with me on alternative assignments that might suit their learning needs more effectively. We develop the final exam (when there is one) together. Students are given authority to specify the percentages used to evaluate their work; I participate in that process upon request or negotiate if we disagree. Students are free to rewrite their papers to improve their learning, and I also encourage discussion when they disagree with my feedback. Students develop the content of the sessions based on their interests and interpretations of the readings. In another course that serves as a capstone for the curriculum, I am able to meet with students in advance of the semester to coconstruct the syllabus, readings, and assignments. In such cases, when students have more knowledge about what the course should address, greater opportunities for shared decision making are more meaningful for students.

Just as variation is apparent in the overall dialogue of these courses, it is apparent in the verbal discourse. Kim's statement (chap. 6) that she was "more comfortable structuring unstructuredness" speaks to the dimension of structure in the verbal component of the dialogue. As Kim demonstrated in her seminar discussion of the film *All American High,* she provided students with a framework (five questions) through which to explore the meaning of the film. That structure, however, did not restrict the meaning they could make of the film. Her participation as various groups shared their thinking about the questions focused on raising questions to further their thinking rather than expressing her own opinion about the film. Kim directed the conversation with the goal of having students translate ideas in the film to the distinction between schooling and education, yet they were free to construct their own translations. When Kim heard something she thought was problematic, she asked a new question to open that area for exploration.

Jan Nichols also provided structure in her EDU 200 seminar, although as I advanced in chapter 6, hers was subtler than was Kim's. Jan often opened a discussion by asking students what they noticed or reacted to in a narrative. She then listened carefully to the ideas and issues that students raised and inserted questions or comments that connected other narratives from the readings or Monday evening to the conversation. At first glance, Jan's approach did not appear to be structured. Watching it repeatedly revealed that she had a variety of ways to approach the topic of the day and she wove the readings and crucial questions around the stories students shared. On occasion she used a more overt framework, such as the labeling activity for understanding exceptionality and difference.

My approach to framing the verbal dialogue hinges on a few core objectives for the class session, which I share with students at the outset of the meeting. I then engage them in a brief discussion of how to proceed to meet those objectives, resulting in our coconstructing the structure for the session. That structure gets the dialogue started but may change as we weave in and around students' ideas. Similarly, Sam Rivers told his class the topic for the day and asked what they had discovered about it. He kept his objectives in mind and sometimes turned or stopped the conversation in light of them, but as long as the dialogue was relevant to the objectives, he allowed it to take its course.

Chris Snowden used a variety of approaches to verbal dialogue. He sometimes structured it through asking students to meet in pairs to analyze data. He introduced questions for exploration in the midst of his presentation. Chris also used an unstructured approach periodically throughout the interactive lectures when he would stop and say, "Questions?" It was a time not only for questions but also for student comments and ideas about relating the topic to others of interest to them. These interludes in the interactive lecture were free-flowing, and Chris took the students' lead in determining both the content and the length of these segments. He rarely resumed the interactive lecture until these dialogues fell silent.

The principle of defining learning as mutually constructing meaning is the essence of the conceptualization of dialogue I have been describing in this chapter. Mutually constructing meaning requires giving up omnipotent authority to place teacher authority alongside that of students to, as Gitlin said, "work together to understand the topic under discussion" (1990, 541). In order for students to view sharing authority as appropriate, they must see themselves as capable of self-authorship. Validating them as knowers is a crucial part of welcoming them into the dialogue and the knowledge construction process. Situating learning in their experience is equally important to give them a foundation from which to learn and construct knowledge and to entertain new ways of making meaning of their experience. Defining learning as mutually constructing meaning is a challenge in and of itself (a topic taken up in chap. 8). Drawing students into this mutual process is equally challenging.

CONNECTING THE RADICAL AND THE AESTHETIC:
A DIALECTIC VIEW

Parker Palmer's (1990) plea for "drawing students into the process, the community, of knowing" (12) has been difficult because of education's traditional focus on objective knowledge. It is difficult to draw students into knowing when the primary mode of knowing involves maintaining a distance from knowing to minimize subjectivity. Using the three principles of constructive-developmental pedagogy requires adopting a broader view of knowledge in which rational and aesthetic modes of knowing[*] are intertwined. Jerome Bruner advocates this view of knowledge. Calling the rational mode of knowing "paradigmatic" and the aesthetic mode "narrative," he stated, "Efforts to reduce one mode to the other or to ignore one at the expense of the other inevitably fail to capture the rich diversity of thought" (1986, 11). Bruner said the paradigmatic "deals in general causes, and in their establishment, and makes use of procedures to assure verifiable reference and to test for empirical truth" (13). In contrast, he described the narrative mode as dealing "in human or human-like intention and action and the vicissitudes and consequences that mark their course. It strives to put its timeless miracles into the particulars of experience, and to locate the experience in time and place" (13). Bruner argued that we cannot know independently of what goes on in the minds of people, that the two modes of knowing must live side by side. Elliot Eisner (1985) made a similar argument for using both modes of knowing. Labouvie-Vief (1990) calls this perspective a mutually enriching dialogue between the two modes of knowing. Her term to capture this mutually enriching dialogue is *dialectic;* I use that term here to refer to this view of knowledge. Engaging students in this dialectic, of course, is connected to developing their minds. Early epistemological assumptions do not recognize the intertwining of both modes of knowing that characterizes more complex forms of meaning-making. The courses I observed illustrate how the three principles of constructive-developmental pedagogy enabled integration of both modes of knowing.

INTEGRATING EXISTING KNOWLEDGE AND STUDENTS' EXPERIENCE

As is evident in the preceding discussion of dialogue, constructive-developmental pedagogy aims to connect students' experience with existing knowledge to enable students to self-author reasonable knowledge claims. Teachers

---

*Various labels exist for the two modes of knowing. The objectivist mode is often called rational, paradigmatic, or foundational. The relational mode is referred to as aesthetic, narrative, or nonfoundational. These terms are used interchangeably here.

and students reflecting together and making meaning of their knowledge and experience involve both the rational and the aesthetic modes of knowing. Situating learning in students' experience in my student development course meant introducing and valuing the narrative mode of knowing. I asked students to gather stories about development—from other students as well as their own development—so that we could explore theory in the context of their experience. Immersion into the stories and students' interpretations of them appealed to the interindividual pattern independent knowers. Connecting their experience then to existing student development theory introduced the paradigmatic mode of knowing since many of the theories deal with the general causes and their establishment that Bruner (1986) highlights as the nature of the paradigmatic mode. This more separate, analytic stance appealed to the individual pattern independent knowers. As we analyzed existing theory in light of our experience, students were validated as both rational and narrative knowers. We explored the richness and the particulars of the stories as well as the precision and the procedures of the theories. Advocating a mutually enriching dialogue between the two ways of knowing, Labouvie-Vief writes:

> One mode provides precision, the other richness. One performs analysis, the other gives direction and significance. Without one, the dialogue would be without rule and form; without the other, it would not matter to anybody—it would not stir our fancy, capture our interest, incite our feelings. (1990, 50)

Our mutual construction of meaning about student development theory was enhanced by combining the richness of the particulars of students' stories with the form of theoretical analysis. Emphasis on merging the two also encouraged students to integrate the individual and interindividual patterns within independent knowing, an integration that is characteristic of contextual knowing.

Despite its focus on narrative, the sociocultural studies of education course used both modes of knowing. Situating learning in students' experience meant using students' own experiences in schooling as a foundation for exploring current educational discourse and practice. The narratives (both oral and textual) augmented students' personal experience with the experience of diverse others and validated narrative as a useful way of knowing. Jan and Kim welcomed student stories about schooling into their seminar discussions. As students worked toward recognizing and interpreting various educational discourses and practices from their experience base, their functioning as narrative knowers was validated. Jan and Kim routinely interjected opportunities to translate ideas to judgments about educational practice. As students worked on critiquing and judging educational discourse and practice, they were validated for using the rational mode. Mutual construction of meaning via judgment required that students use both modes effectively. The assignments also required students to get into the particulars of an issue (another culture, a text, a pedagogical issue) and then stand back from it to analyze its meaning. The former validated the interpersonal pattern transitional knowers; the latter validated the impersonal pattern transitional knowers. Elliot Gardner's (the architect of EDU 200) goal of students being able to "read the word and the world" incorporated both modes of knowing.

In Sam Rivers's course, the connection was between math structure and students' thinking about it. Sam elicited students' thinking about math structure by asking them to investigate various math topics. Classroom dialogue about their explorations placed learning in their experience, in this case their own thoughts about mathematics. Sam validated all kinds of responses during these dialogues, ranging from students' guesses and intuitions (the narrative mode) to their use of mathematical rules (the paradigmatic mode). When students offered narrative knowing, Sam often invited them to explore how they might decide on why they believed a particular notion. When they offered rules, Sam routinely asked them to explore what the rules really meant and how they worked in the context of the investigation. Thus while Sam validated both modes of knowing, he continually asked for their integration. He welcomed interpersonal and impersonal pattern transitional knowers and interindividual and individual pattern independent knowers. He simultaneously invited students to entertain the pattern that was not their usual preference. Mutual construction of meaning took the form of connecting students' evolving understandings of math concepts with the rules mathematicians have constructed (the underlying structure of math).

Chris Snowden's insistence that scientific inquiry involved human judgment about scientific data called both modes of knowing into winter biology. He modeled the scientific inquiry process of identifying questions, determining steps to inform them, implementing those steps, and making judgments about the results. The objective nature of the scientific experiments and their attempts to isolate factors contributing to a particular phenomenon highlighted the rational mode of knowing and probably validated the knowing processes the individual pattern independent knowers used most often. The subjective nature of deciding what questions to pursue, what steps to use in that pursuit, and how to implement them and judging the results emphasized the aesthetic mode and was likely more comfortable for the interindividual pattern independent knowers. Chris effectively used the story of his research agenda to illustrate how one decision leads to another and how a decision can sidetrack a research agenda. As he presented existing knowledge about cryopreservation, Chris asked students to join him in both looking at objective data and making subjective judgments about its meaning. The research project called on students to use all of these processes and thus both modes of knowing. Using both modes welcomed interindividual and individual pattern independent knowers and invited them to use both patterns to strive for more complex ways of knowing.

Although to varying degrees and in different forms, all four courses encouraged what Shirley Pendlebury calls perceptive equilibrium, or a balance of using one's perception from immersion in a situation and general principles, coherent arguments, and standing commitments that exist outside the situation. She advocates wise practice as "a loving dialogue between principles and particulars, responsibility and perception. It is through such dialogue that perceptive equilibrium is accomplished" (1995, 55).

Pendlebury's argument that wise teaching practice involves both modes of knowing resonates with my longitudinal research finding that complex knowing involves integrating both modes of knowing (Baxter Magolda 1995). Contextual knowers among my longitudinal participants (see chap. 2) used both modes more routinely than did participants using earlier ways of knowing. Those persons tended to use one mode of knowing, or pattern as I called them, more so than the other. Extensive evidence also suggests that many women use the aesthetic mode of knowing in their interest in connection with others (e.g., Belenky et al. 1986; Gilligan 1982; Gilligan, Lyons, and Hanmer 1989; Jordan, Kaplan, Miller, Stiver, and Surrey 1991; Lyons 1983). Belenky and her colleagues labeled their participants' use of each mode of knowing as separate and connected knowing. To help students learn to use both modes of knowing, teaching has to connect to and nurture both.

INTEGRATING SEPARATE AND CONNECTED KNOWING

Clinchy (1994) describes separate knowing as a detached, impersonal stance in which knowers use rules or procedures to arrive at unbiased judgment. In contrast, connected knowing involves an attached, personal stance in which knowers try to see an idea from the others' point of view before judging it. Clinchy notes that "the voice of separate knowing is argument; the voice of connected knowing is narration" (1994, 39). These characterizations coincide with the gender-related patterns I described in chapter 2 as impersonal (separate) and relational (connected). My longitudinal study participants found in their postcollege years that using both patterns of knowing was more effective than using one primarily (Baxter Magolda 1995). Similarly, Clinchy advocates that an integration of the two is the ideal. Recent writing about critical thinking (Elbow 1994; Gallo 1994; Walters 1994) supports this view.

Clinchy (1994) notes that students told her and her colleagues that teachers who had helped them grow had "'believed' in them, seen something 'right' in their essays" (40) before judging their work. Clinchy's recommendation for an integrated approach is for teachers to "first believe, then doubt" (40) to establish a connection that places criticism in a collaborative context. The principles of validating students as knowers and situating learning in their experience are ways to establish connection to enable mutual construction of meaning, the latter principle inherently involving judgment. The first two principles also ensure that teaching connects to both voices: separate and connected.

Chris Snowden modeled the "first believe, then doubt" notion. In his interactive lectures he shared the shortcomings of his own research and times that faulty thinking had foiled him. He did the same with the scientific community at large. By the time students offered their own research efforts for public consumption and critique, a connection between Chris and them as collaborative researchers had been established (except in the case of absolute knowers, a topic addressed in chap. 8). Chris also taught in ways that promoted both attachment, particularly through telling stories about his own experiences and using experiential examples, and detachment, particularly through sharing scientific data and the meaning scientists have made of it.

Sam Rivers was an expert at believing before doubting. When students in his class advanced conjectures that he doubted, he acknowledged having some concern about it to avoid an "I gotcha" scenario later. However, he simultaneously responded with a "let's see what we can learn from this" attitude, which implied that the student might be right and in the worst case he and the students would learn from understanding where their thinking went awry. Sam consistently put listening to students to hear what was good about their thinking before sharing what he found problematic about it. In some cases, which he graciously acknowledged, what he initially thought was problematic turned out not to be when he understood the students' point of view. When students discovered some fault in their thinking, Sam introduced ways of stepping back to analyze the situation using math concepts. His welcoming of both intuitive and procedural responses noted earlier connected to both voices among his students.

I appreciate Sam's ability to believe first and listen carefully with judgment suspended. It has taken substantial effort for me to work against my own socialization as a separate knower to hear and value students' stories. The interviews and theme analyses students conduct in the theory course help all of us focus on the story first, attaching ourselves to students' experience and hearing what is "right" about it. Detachment is then valued as we compare experience and theory, critiquing both in the process. Situating learning in students' experience in this instance also brings the separate and the connected voices into the conversation. Some students are far more active as we practice attachment whereas others come to life when we practice detachment. Validating both and encouraging the dialogue of the two in order to mutually construct meaning help students think about integrating both. Our discussions of application of theory resonate with connected knowers as we use case studies to get inside the situation; they resonate with separate knowers as we stand outside the situation to use principles for applying theory in practice. These practices are an attempt to model Pendlebury's perceptive equilibrium.

The narrative approach of EDU 200 might have tipped the scale in favor of connected knowers. The narratives, both oral and written, often invited students into the story. Students' own stories about schooling abounded in the seminars. Analyzing educational discourse and practice from the particulars of the stories seemed more prevalent than analyzing from abstract principles. However, the assignments balanced attachment and detachment in requiring students to access a person, text, or issue before analyzing it. The open atmosphere of the course also allowed voices of either pattern to be expressed.

KNOWLEDGE COMMUNITIES' MULTIPLE WAYS OF KNOWING

Sam, Chris, Jo, Kim, Jan, and I invited students into the ways of knowing of our knowledge communities. We shared current thinking in our knowledge communities and the process by which knowledge is constructed in those communities. In doing so, we presented those ways of knowing as both rational and aesthetic. Introducing the construction of ways of knowing in a knowledge community, or discipline, was probably most important in mathematics and zoology because students (and some teachers) are less prone to view that knowledge as socially constructed. Sam Rivers was the most adamant about sharing with students that math did not come down on the stone tablets. Recall his succinct philosophy from chapter 5: "People need to understand that mathematics is human created." Chris Snowden, too, wanted his science students to understand that facts were tentative and science was subject to change and revision. Both teachers wanted students to understand that members of the discipline negotiate with one another to establish the communities' beliefs and that students could participate in that social construction process, thereby establishing the importance of aesthetic knowing. But as Bruffee (1993) noted, members of these disciplines also adhered to agreed upon systems for knowledge construction, the rational component of their ways of knowing. Sam introduced his students to the underlying structure of math used in his discipline and invited them to practice it in their investigations. Similarly, Chris modeled the practice of scientific inquiry and invited students to practice it in their research projects.

Students in EDU 200 were introduced to the educational discourse and how it was constructed in that knowledge community. In addition to exploring those ways of knowing, students were encouraged to critique the ways of knowing of that discipline and determine their own views for future practice. Central goals of the course were being able to interpret narratives and texts to understand various perspectives and how they were arrived at as well as how to arrive at one's own informed perspective. I also introduced my students to theory construction in my discipline and, through their participation in the process, invited them to practice and critique this way of knowing about students. In both courses the socially constructed nature of knowledge construction was stressed along with the need to use both rational and aesthetic knowing in that process.

Inviting students into the ways of knowing of these knowledge communities meant inviting them to view themselves as capable of self-authorship, a notion that many undergraduates have yet to endorse (see chap. 2). Accomplishing their genuine participation in these knowledge communities, and their integration of both modes of knowing, required a constructive-developmental approach to bridge their ways of knowing to those of the knowledge communities they seek to join.

CONSTRUCTIVE-DEVELOPMENTAL PEDAGOGY: A CONTEXTUAL PERSPECTIVE

Just as educators ask students to become contextual knowers, I invite readers to consider constructive-developmental pedagogy from a contextual perspective. Such a perspective means that multiple systems, or perspectives, of education can be integrated under the umbrella of constructive-developmental pedagogy. The constructivist-developmental system establishes growth of the individual student mind, or meaning-making system, as the central priority to enable participation in complex forms of knowing and knowledge construction communities. It operates in conjunction with other systems, each of which has inherent in it assumptions about the purpose and goals of education and means by which to achieve them. For example, the social-constructivist system advocates socializing students into knowledge communities to participate in the construction of knowledge within those communities. The dialectic system advocates enhancing students' knowing to include both rational and aesthetic modes of knowing. Although these three systems represent different and sometimes discrepant perspectives, they can be integrated in a contextual perspective of constructive-developmental pedagogy.*

---

*For example, Kegan (1994) disagrees with Bruffee's (1993) deemphasis of the structure of thought, advocating instead that it is not necessary to ignore the reality-constituting powers of the mind to recognize the power of social context in constituting reality (288).

A contextual perspective on constructive-developmental pedagogy integrates the goals of growth of individual meaning-making systems (epistemological and self), socialization into knowledge communities, and effective integration of both modes of knowing. It makes possible the integration of educators' and students' worlds shown to be at various distances apart throughout this book. Such a perspective also avoids placing either world in a more prominent position than the other in the educational process, heightening the possibilities for building bridges between the two.

The goals of the four courses under discussion illustrate the value of this contextual approach. For example, Kim and Jan wanted students to simultaneously become socialized into educational discourse and participate in its reconstruction in their professional teaching practice. Similarly, Chris wanted students to learn the discourse of scientific inquiry so that they could participate in improving our understanding of adaptations to cold temperatures. In all four courses, learning the knowledge community's discourse was not an end in and of itself; it was a means to continued participation in that discourse from a self-authored vantage point. Given the preponderance of transitional knowers in these courses, and therefore the likely prevalence of third order meaning-making, students were ripe for socialization into a knowledge community. Their tendency to coconstruct themselves and their beliefs enabled them to join these communities, heightening their interest in learning the ways of knowing that would define them as scientists, mathematicians, or educators. As transitional knowers, they were interested in learning the processes for arriving at knowledge. However, as Kegan (1994) pointed out, third order minds are not only "capable of, but subject to, socialization" (288), meaning that they are unable to critically reflect on the community into which they have been socialized. Without independent knowing they could not judge what they were learning. As a result they cannot contribute to the improvement of knowledge in that community or resist socialization into potentially problematic knowledge communities. The goal of our courses for students to operate from a self-authored vantage point within our knowledge communities required growth of the mind to independent knowing and fourth order. Thus, the social-constructivist framework alone was insufficient. Development of self-authorship was necessary for students to become the knowledgeable peers that make decisions about what the knowledge community believes.

Both the social-constructivist framework and the dialectic framework convey a conceptualization of knowledge as constructed through the interplay of rational and narrative knowing. Both systems offer the opportunity to connect to students who use both relational and impersonal patterns of knowing. Yet at the same time, they convey knowledge as uncertain, constructed using subjectivity, and mutually constructed by agreements among

knowers. This understanding of knowledge hinges on contextual epistemological assumptions and the ability to reflect and act on multiple systems through
which to generate beliefs. If these understandings stem from contextual knowing and fifth order meaning-making, how accessible are they to students who
have or are struggling to reach developmental meaning-making that precedes
these? Unless these frameworks are used in combination with a constructivist-
developmental framework, the chances of bridging the gap between educators'
and students' worlds decline.

Likewise, use of the constructive-developmental system without the contextual perspective is insufficient. The constructive-developmental system
defines the process through which educators can help students reorganize
their meaning-making to participate in complex ways of knowing and social
construction of knowledge. This system helps educators effectively entice
students into dialogue. Participation in the dialogue helps students understand knowledge as a social construction involving both objectivity and subjectivity, and develop self-authorship. The knowledge community, however,
with its emphasis on joint construction among knowers, also provides the
context for moving beyond the individual self-system of authorship characteristic of fourth order to the community-oriented use of multiple systems
of authorship characteristic of fifth order meaning-making. The knowledge
community also promotes development of the interplay of both modes of
knowing by offering students opportunities to construct epistemological assumptions that incorporate both. Finally, constructive-developmental pedagogy occurs within the context of a particular discipline. While the growth
of the mind may be a central goal, that growth is in the service of functioning effectively within the knowledge community.

The contextual perspective of constructive-developmental pedagogy I am
advancing here addresses many of the myths about teaching in ways that
connect to students' experience as well as some of the real problems inherent in practicing constructive-developmental pedagogy. At the same time, it
speaks to the possibilities of constructive-developmental pedagogy. The remainder of the book takes up these issues.

CHAPTER 8

The Challenges of Constructive-Developmental Pedagogy

The challenges of constructive-developmental pedagogy are both real and imagined. Those that are imagined—the myths—are more difficult to deal with than those that are real. One reason it is so difficult to address myths about constructive-developmental pedagogy is their origin in our own socialization as learners and educators. Our socialization in the objectivist-dominated educational system spawns many foundational assumptions that guide our teaching practice despite the fact that they are largely unconscious.[*] Because they do not surface regularly for our reflection, we are generally unaware of their influence on our teaching behavior. An example from my student development theory course illustrates.

Rebuilding my ideas about teaching resulted in my developing final exams mutually with students. One semester, the group had a particularly difficult time agreeing on whether the exam should be take-home or in class. Exasperated from the lengthy discussion, one student said, "Why can't we each decide whether we want to do it as a take-home or in class?" Some of her peers looked incredulous at the suggestion; I masked my surprise relatively well. Working hard at that time on learning to believe before doubting, I asked myself and the students why we were so skeptical of her suggestion. Foundational assumptions emerged from me and the students, primarily centered on whether it was fair for students to do different forms of the exam and whether the grading criteria would be different accordingly. I had never seriously reflected on this issue, assuming that consistency was the best policy. This "problem" turned out to be imaginary; through reflecting on our assumptions, we were able to arrive at a perspective that enabled everyone to use a learning approach that was most effective for him or her. Thus, the first step in overcoming the imaginary challenges of constructive-developmental pedagogy is to surface and explore foundational assumptions. This chapter raises some of the imaginary challenges for your consideration.

Developing assumptions and beliefs that are consistent with constructive-developmental pedagogy alleviates the imaginary problems, leaving us to

---

[*]I use the term *foundational* here in Bruffee's (1993) notion of traditional assumptions about education as well as the common use of foundational as serving as a base for belief and practice.

face the real ones. The courses described in this book suggest at least three very real challenges. One is building transitional cultures for students who use absolute assumptions. The bridges constructed in all four courses were effective for other ways of knowing but did not connect effectively with absolute knowing. Because absolute assumptions are in direct contradiction to viewing knowledge as socially constructed, this challenge is substantial. A second challenge is that constructive-developmental pedagogy surfaces multiple voices that are often in conflict with one another. Facilitating these conflictual discussions effectively is difficult, particularly when some students' perspectives are offensive to others. A third challenge is creating transitional contexts for multiple ways of making meaning in the same course. I use reflections and insights here from Jo, Kim, Jan, Sam, Chris, and their students to frame possible ways to overcome these challenges.

IMAGINARY DILEMMAS

Approaching the real challenges of constructive-developmental pedagogy necessitates getting the imaginary ones out of the way first. This is primarily a process of working through assumptions and beliefs about teaching and learning that are inconsistent with the principles of constructive-developmental pedagogy. Of course, I should point out that the challenges stemming from these beliefs are imaginary from a constructivist point of view; they are perhaps very real from a foundationalist point of view. Prawat (1992) identified four sets of beliefs about teaching and learning that support the traditional transmission approach to teaching. One set of beliefs regards students and content as fixed, dichotomous entities that do not interact, leading to a delivery approach to teaching. A second set focuses on student interest and involvement as a sufficient condition for learning, resulting in what Prawat calls "naive constructivism" (369). From this view teachers assume that students can structure their own learning. A third set of beliefs separates learning and application on the premise that what students learn can be applied elsewhere through transfer and generalization. Finally, Prawat argues that teachers view curriculum as a fixed agenda to be followed. These beliefs underlie what Barr and Tagg (1995) call the instruction paradigm. In the instruction paradigm, the purpose of education is to deliver instruction and transfer knowledge from faculty to students through offering courses and programs. The teaching/learning structures focus on standard teaching formats and schedules and covering the material. Beliefs of this nature—about students, content, learning, and teaching—underlie most of the misunderstandings and hesitations about constructive-developmental pedagogy as an effective alternative to traditional teaching.

BELIEFS ABOUT LEARNERS

If we followed the Doonesbury cartoon teacher back to his office after the teaching episode described in chapter 2, we might hear him telling a colleague something like this: "Students are not as bright as they were when I was in college. They don't want to think. They don't come prepared to discuss the material. All they want is to write down what I say; they don't care if it is accurate or not." Parker Palmer noted that teachers today view students as "essentially brain-dead" (1993, 11). In the absence of another framework to interpret students' seeming lack of interest and investment, teachers begin to see students as incapable, unmotivated, resistant, and untrustworthy. These characterizations lead teachers to conclude that students cannot be trusted to participate in the construction of knowledge. It is not a large leap from there to using traditional pedagogy, either as an attempt to get knowledge across or as what seems like the only viable approach, given the circumstances.

Even teachers who view students more positively than just described—and many do—still have difficulty viewing students as knowledge constructors. Beliefs about students' capability in relation to the content often lead to underestimating their ability to take responsibility as knowledge constructors. My experience offers a good illustration here. Perhaps as a result of my human development background, I entered teaching with a positive attitude about students. In the early years of my student development course I routinely provided a passive lecture on each theory, complete with transparencies and handouts. I did this as we began to study each new theory on the assumption that the theories were too difficult for students to grasp by reading. Although I thought of this as a judgment about the course content, it was a belief about students that restricted their opportunity to try out their understandings. Assuming that my understanding was more sophisticated than theirs was, I felt it was my responsibility to convey to them a sophisticated understanding with which we could work. I remember being frustrated during the activities that followed my overview that students hesitated to go beyond the theory as I had presented it. My lack of trust in their ability to construct (or even understand) knowledge effectively was apparent to them and upon reflection even made them lack trust in their own abilities.

Prawat (1992) cited additional examples of teachers who, despite constructivist perspectives, were unable to abandon traditional teaching behaviors due to their assumptions about students' ability. Our experience as learners has socialized us to think of learners as less sophisticated than teachers and to think of teachers as responsible for making sure that students learn the correct understanding. We have come to believe that failure is inevitable for some students rather than believe that all can succeed—the difference between culturally relevant and assimilationist teaching, according to Gloria Ladson-Billings (1994). And perhaps it is true (or so one would hope) that students' understanding is less sophisticated than that of teachers. Yet this does not automatically lead to providing them with a sophisticated understanding. As Tompkins (1990) pointed out,

> It's true that in some cases the students don't deal with the material as well as I could, but that is exactly why they need to do it. It's not important for me to polish my skills, but they do need to develop theirs and to find a voice. (657)

The stories in this book demonstrate that letting students deal with the material, or participate in knowledge construction, helped them develop more sophisticated understandings of educational practice, mathematics, scientific inquiry, and student development theory. Thus, these hesitations about students appear to be unwarranted.

BELIEFS ABOUT CONTENT

Sophie Haroutunian-Gordon recounts a class discussion of Shakespeare's *Romeo and Juliet* in *Turning the Soul* (1991). She reported that she thought it was obvious that Shakespeare intended for readers to understand that Juliet was a Capulet due to her designation as such twelve times in one segment of the text. Haroutunian-Gordon was surprised when the students called this into question and surmised that their comments were mischievous rather than serious ways of making meaning of the text. Haroutunian-Gordon regarded this aspect of the content as clear, despite the very real possibility that she would say Shakespeare's work is open for interpretation. Likewise, my passive lectures on student development theory reflected the view that content is fixed because I wanted students to understand the theory correctly. I was more concerned with their understanding it the way I understood it than with accessing the meaning they were making of it. This notion that the teacher understands the content correctly (and that students probably do not) leads to the teacher taking responsibility for covering the material. Even though I viewed student development theory as a social construction, I did not judge my students capable of participating in that construction until they had the "correct" understanding. My teaching behavior reflected more of my foundational assumption about content than the assumption I espoused about social construction of knowledge.

Nelson (1989) spoke to the dilemma of balancing content and students' understanding in his teaching as a result of what he called "repeated glaring failures of a content focused approach" (17). He described feeling that he faced a trade-off between teaching content in biology and teaching critical thinking. He worked through this dilemma by reframing his biology content according to students' epistemological assumptions based on Perry's (1970) scheme of intellectual development. What Nelson created in the process was an interaction between learners and content, the kind of interaction Prawat argued is hindered by the fixed view of learners and content. Instead of holding a fixed view of either, Nelson altered the content to connect to students' assumptions, which he further assumed would change due to the interaction with the content. Nelson's success with this approach led him to conclude that the trade-off he was so concerned about was imaginary.

This interaction between content and learner is apparent in the four courses described in this book. Sam Rivers was willing to view the content of mathematical structure as dynamic, something constructed by mathematicians investigating together. His students became more, rather than less, accomplished at thinking about and understanding math structure because he, as Tompkins suggested, let them deal with the material. Despite his veteran status as a mathematician, Sam learned a few new ideas from his students. Similarly, Chris Snowden viewed the content of studying life in the cold as flexible. He selected topics for the first part of the course that he thought students were unlikely to select for their topics, leaving the second half of the content up to them. He shared in an interview that he was not concerned about how much he covered in the course; rather, his goal was for students to understand what was covered. His willingness to explore their ways of making meaning of the content placed their developing understandings as a higher priority than covering the material. His students did not appear to leave the course disadvantaged as a result.

In my theory course I now convey theory as something that is evolving, and I regard students as theory builders. The content of theory depends on the students the class interviews, students' own developmental stories, our interpretations of students' experience, and existing theory. My students leave the course better able to construct theory in the context of their professional practice than they did when I covered the material; in those courses they left with a memorized chart of each theory. Similarly, educational discourse and practice were viewed as dynamic in EDU 200, leaving students to explore their own philosophies and integrate perspectives into their own professional teaching practice. As students reported, many left that course with a clearer sense of the issues they needed to resolve and decisions they needed to make about teaching.

Based on these courses, and others described in the literature on constructivist teaching, the fear that connecting learning to students' experience will lead to less effective learning is unfounded. In all four courses we modeled Ladson-Billings's culturally relevant conception of knowledge—that it is "continually recreated, recycling and shared by teachers and students" (1994, 81). As a result, in all four courses students learned more than content. They also learned how to create math structure, biological questions, educational practice, and human development theory.

BELIEFS ABOUT THE LEARNING PROCESS

Any careful observer of teaching practice in any level of American education would likely conclude that teachers believe students learn from being told what to think. Having visited college classrooms as a part of a study of the undergraduate experience in America, Boyer (1987) reported what he had seen:

> Today, the lecture method is preferred by most professors. With few exceptions, when we visited classes, the teacher stood in front of rows of chairs and talked most of the forty-five or fifty minutes. Information was presented that often students passively received. There was little opportunity for positions to be clarified or ideas challenged. (149-50)

The important part of Boyer's observation is that students were passive observers of the lectures. Some teachers transmit knowledge to passive recipients because they believe that this is how learning takes place; others do it because they think it is the only way to get students to learn knowledge correctly.

Still others transmit knowledge in a passive process without an awareness that they are doing so or in direct contradiction to their espoused beliefs about teaching. Grennon Brooks and Brooks (1993) describe a middle school teacher's lesson taught in a constructivist school. She began with a question to solicit the students' views on life science. Receiving a few one-word answers, she quickly moved on to read a story to the students. At the close of the story she told the students the point of the story. She then gave them copies of an optical illusion, telling them that developing a critical eye in science was important. In asking them to write down what they saw, the teacher asked, "Who can see a vase?" and "Who can see two faces?" (12). Grennon Brooks and Brooks note that the teacher's plan had many elements of constructivist teaching, such as asking students for their views and using the story as an analogy. However, they point out that she did not pursue their views, she drew the analogy for them, and she defined the range of responses to the optical illusion before students could see other possibilities. They conclude, "The lesson was not an invitation to explore the theme. It was a methodical telling of the theme" (13). Some of the EDU 200 instructors struggled with this tension between letting students explore and telling students information.

Some teachers, in response to the evidence that telling students does not constitute effective learning, avoid telling completely. Prawat (1992) calls this stance "naive constructivism" (369). This swing away from telling students leads to a number of assumptions, the primary one being that students should be given complete freedom. Recall Kim Conlin's initial reaction to the pedagogical approach to EDU 200. She felt that she should be "hands off" and let the students do what they wanted to with the discussions. Her initial understanding of constructive-developmental pedagogy was that any intervention on her part would interfere with the students' freedom to learn. Yet she had the sense that class discussions in which she took that stance were not very productive. She and her colleagues' discussions in their instructors' meetings clarified that the course coordinator was after an integration of students' experience and the course content.

Related assumptions that stem from this naive constructivism include the notion that activity equals learning. This assumption focuses on the fact that students are involved in some way rather than what meaning they are making of their involvement. Kim's undirected discussions in early sessions would be perceived by some as effective because the students were involved. Another version of this assumption is that verbal discussion automatically leads to learning and lecture automatically does not. Kim found that only guided verbal discussion leads to learning. Chris Snowden illustrated how a different kind of lecture can also lead to learning. Richard Hake's (1998) distinction between hands-on and heads-on learning is relevant here. Hake notes that while both are helpful, heads-on learning in which students' minds are engaged is essential. The fear that connecting learning to students' experience means they can think anything they want also stems from this set of assumptions, due to its hesitancy to keep existing knowledge in the learning process. Using Shor's (1992) notion that empowering education is not a know-nothing process puts teacher knowledge back into the learning process.

The four courses in this book show that connecting existing knowledge and students' experience can be an effective learning process. Genuine dialogue, in all its forms, helped students develop more sophisticated understandings of their disciplines and make progress on viewing themselves as knowledge constructors. Instructors, myself included, perceived student performance and subject mastery to be of high quality in these courses. Students reported progress on their participation in knowledge construction. The students' and instructors' assessments of these courses suggest that the sacrifice of "telling" students in order to connect to their experience is an imaginary sacrifice.

BELIEFS ABOUT TEACHING

As teachers, we reproduce the teaching practices we experienced as learners. As noted earlier, Shor (1992) argued that what we have experienced as learners results in this belief about teaching: "to be a teacher means talking a lot and being in charge" (26). This short phrase contains an enormous volume of beliefs that interfere with constructive-developmental pedagogy. In addition to covering most of the beliefs in the previous sections, this phrase highlights at least two more foundational beliefs about teaching: (1) that teachers should be omnipotent authorities in their knowledge area, and (2) that they should be omnipotent authorities in shaping the teaching-learning process.

No one would disagree that teachers should be knowledgeable about their subject matter. The responsibility to be knowledgeable for many teachers becomes the responsibility to know everything. Having watched teachers who transmit objective knowledge to students, who do not show their thinking processes, and who do not admit gaps in their knowledge, what else could the next generation of teachers surmise? Clinchy (1990) offered an illustration in recounting a student's story. The student was in a class in which the teacher gave an interpretation of a novel. The students wrote down the interpretation, much to the professor's frustration. He chastised them, saying, "Listen. This is just my interpretation. You should be ripping it apart" (61). The student reported that she agreed with it, so there was nothing to rip apart. Many students are also intimidated to "rip apart" a professor's interpretation, assuming that the professor has worked diligently on making it airtight.

In addition to being "in charge" of the knowledge of the discipline, teachers often believe they are responsible for being "in charge" of every other aspect of the teaching process. When I was a new teacher (and for some years after), I took various roles for granted: teachers determine the curriculum, teachers identify and implement the plans for studying the material, teachers decide how students' work should be evaluated, teachers make evaluation judgments independent of students, and teachers control the classroom environment to ensure that it is conducive to learning. I had seen these roles enacted by teachers, and they were consistent with the hierarchical relationships I had experienced with teachers. I did not view myself as authoritarian because I allowed students some involvement in my plans as I implemented them; yet I never questioned whether these areas were anyone's purview other than mine until the transformation I described in chapter 3.

Holding these beliefs in the face of considering constructive-developmental pedagogy leads to a number of problems. First, if students' experience is to become central, they must have some role in the determination of content—thus the fear of sacrificing content discussed earlier.

Second, promoting self-authorship implies they should have input in how the learning environment is structured. This leads to the fear that teachers will lose control and the classroom will become chaotic. This fear is based in part on assumptions about the lack of capability of learners and in part on the false dichotomy that either the teacher or the students are in complete control. The constructive-developmental pedagogy principle of mutually constructing meaning resolves this imaginary problem and offers another arena, the process of learning, in which students can practice self-authorship.

Third, if teachers and students coconstruct meaning, this suggests that students should have some role in evaluating their work. This idea immediately raises consternation regarding whether students are objective in evaluating their work (assuming, of course, that teachers are), whether they would use this opportunity to manipulate the system for a better grade, whether students' making decisions about evaluation is fair, and the like. We have grown accustomed to thinking that students have nothing valuable to offer in the evaluation process, but the stories in this book show that they have very valuable perspectives about how evaluation affects their learning. Our evaluation practices have been built on the domination of the rational mode of knowing, leading us to be suspicious of introducing the aesthetic into the process. Yet many writers argue for and offer evidence that using both modes of knowing is more effective. We have grown accustomed to the idea that treating all students the same in evaluation is fair when it may be more appropriate to treat them differently. Mutually constructing evaluation promotes self-authorship by requiring the student to evaluate his or her learning in the context of the expert's judgment about it, a dynamic consistent with contextual knowing.

All of the dilemmas stemming from foundational assumptions about students, content, learning, and teaching are dilemmas only if educators believe in these foundational assumptions. Substantial evidence that these beliefs are faulty exists in numerous bodies of literature about education, constructivism, human development, leadership, and organizational change. Letting go of these assumptions is the first step in considering constructive-developmental pedagogy as a viable alternative to traditional pedagogy.

REAL DILEMMAS

Constructive-developmental pedagogy poses some real problems as well. The three major ones evident in the courses I encountered involve creating transitional cultures for students who use absolute assumptions about knowledge, effectively facilitating the conflict that emerges when multiple voices are encouraged, and effectively connecting multiple ways of making meaning in the same course.

CREATING TRANSITIONAL CULTURES FOR ABSOLUTE KNOWERS

Jan, Kim, Sam, Chris, and I encountered a few students who felt less positively than the majority about our courses. Revisiting their concerns indicates that they stem from holding some absolute assumptions about the nature of knowledge. None of the students who completed the Measure of Epistemological Reflection (MER) used absolute assumptions entirely, but viewed knowledge as absolute in some areas. This is not surprising given the evidence that education is predominated by traditional pedagogy that teaches and reinforces such assumptions. I adopt the stance that epistemological assumptions have both a learned and a developmental component. The assumptions are generated to make sense of experience; thus, absolute assumptions are learned in the process of making sense of knowledge presented as fact by omnipotent authorities. There is, however, a developmental component to the evolution of epistemological assumptions. They are altered as they no longer adequately explain one's experience; new and more complex assumptions that more adequately explain experience are constructed, and this evolution represents development of the mind. From this perspective, students can "develop" their epistemic assumptions when learning contexts promote and support more complex epistemic assumptions.

The students who expressed frustration in EDU 200, math, and zoology did express absolute assumptions on their MERs. There are very few absolute knowers among my graduate students, but the anxiety of starting graduate school often surfaces some earlier learned behavior, such as relying on the instructor to determine what knowledge is important. Perhaps these are similar to the foundational assumptions of teachers discussed earlier that lag behind our reconstructed ways of making meaning about the nature of knowledge. An exploration of concerns from these students helps explain their dissatisfaction and provides useful insight into connecting to their meaning-making more effectively.

Supporting the Acquisition of Concrete Information

In chapter 6 I quoted one unidentified student's comment from the EDU 200 written course evaluation form. The comment, which captured the essence of some students' dissatisfaction with the course, bears repeating here:

> I was somewhat disappointed with this entire class—perhaps because I am just not used to this type of class set-up. I prefer more structure and challenge. I blew off most of the assignments and did not give my best effort at all and still made high grades. At this stage, I feel that I should be learning things that I can take with me as I enter the teaching profession and quite honestly I haven't compiled as much information and ideas from this course as I thought I would.

Two absolute assumptions are evident in this comment. The first is that learning is the compilation of information. The second is that the instructor is responsible, through grading procedures, for ensuring that students give their best effort. Despite the course's involving a wide array of readings, performances, and discussions, which one could regard as an extensive amount of information, this student views the quantity of information received as less than expected. Another student's comment clarifies this apparent discrepancy. Melissa (also quoted in chap. 6) noted that she liked concrete information, and while she knew nebulous knowledge was important, she struggled with it throughout this course. Her final assessment was that she "learned nothing." The absolute assumption inherent in Melissa's thinking is that because she did not know how to put it all together in concrete form at the end, she was left with nothing.

Both Jan and Kim had ideas in the postcourse interviews about how to reach these students more effectively, some of which they had already implemented as they started their next semester. Both decided to capitalize on students' interest in concrete, practical information about teaching. Since the students viewed the *Schools that Work* text as concrete and practical, Jan introduced it at the outset of the course to set the stage for exploring educational practice. Kim used parts of the text at the start of the course to explain the pedagogical project more explicitly. Kim also reported that she was being much more explicit about the project in general. Jan shared that she was explaining the purpose of all the assignments and their relationship to the course more specifically to help students understand what they were supposed to accomplish. These responses to students' interest in compiling concrete information and instructor structure would be meaningful to students with absolute assumptions.

Kim shared some students' frustrations that the discussions sometimes "didn't go anywhere." She complained in her interview that "we all said what we thought and have a nice day." By the time we talked, she had begun introducing more structure to support the students in thinking about the readings. She asked them to free-write on each reading before the class discussion so that they would be better prepared and she would be able to move the conversation beyond a reporting of what everyone thought. Jan responded to her students who wanted answers by explaining to them that the issues they were struggling with had not been resolved throughout history, using the readings to support her contention. She reported that "some got it that way." These actions, too, are ones that provide support for students who are struggling with knowledge presented as uncertain. As Kegan (1994) pointed out, many contexts have plenty of challenge, and what students really need is to be supported in facing their curriculum. Jan's and Kim's ideas and plans seem to offer that support by connecting to the absolute assumptions they encountered.

Supporting Acquiring the Instructor's Knowledge

Students using absolute assumptions about knowledge also expected the instructor to know what was important and to tell the students. Recall Ann's comments about Chris Snowden's course (chap. 1). She said, "If he had just said cryoprotectants whatever, just said the point, I would believe him because he is the teacher. I don't need the proof. It's not like I'm going to argue with him about it." She felt the same way about the presentation portion of the course, about which she said, "I would have learned more if he had lectured and [we had] gotten tested over it rather than each person talking about polar bears or whatever." It is clear that Ann assumed Chris knew the scientific facts (which she believed existed in winter biology) and should share them directly with students. Her notion that being tested would help her learn more matches Melissa's belief that the instructor is responsible for student learning through evaluation procedures. Similarly, Maryann expected Chris to know how she should proceed on her grant proposal. Her comments from chapter 4 warrant repeating as well:

> I just wish he would be a little bit more clear. . . . He's being very vague when he talks. He's saying basically, "You have to convince me that this is interesting." What exactly does that mean, "convince you that it is interesting"? I am not exactly sure how or what to do with this. I think he should know. He knows that I have had absolutely no experience with doing this. I wish he could be a little bit more concrete.

Maryann thought Chris should know how to tell her exactly how to convince him that her proposal was interesting. And she preferred that he would do just that.

Chris recognized in reflecting on the course in our postcourse interview that his philosophy of assisting students was discrepant with Maryann's preference. He explained his philosophy:

> I tend to give people a lot of rope doing research. I tell them up front, "I don't want to have to look for you when it is time to get something done." I expect them to come when they need help. Some don't function that way. I tend to err on the side of giving them too much freedom. I think you just get a feel for how they respond. When they come back, I give them ideas, "have you thought about this," etceteras. Any student who shows interest, wants to come in and talk about stuff, takes me up on my offer. I want to meet them more than halfway.

The students who "don't function that way" may be those with absolute assumptions. Maryann went to Chris for help, but hesitated to go back because she thought his response was vague. His comments in chapter 4 reveal that he recognized that the way he had tried to help did not work for her; he subsequently told her specifically what to focus on instead of the extraneous things she had focused on, and her final paper was much better as a result. At the end of the course Chris was contemplating making one conference on the project mandatory to bring in those students who did not come when they needed help. That would be meaningful to those with absolute assumptions because it would provide a structure they perceive as important to calling forth their effort to learn. Given a chance to interact with each student, he could also try to get a sense of what type of response he could offer that would be most helpful. For absolute knowers, he could give them guidance on how to begin and a framework to organize their work.

Challenging Students to Let Go of Absolute Assumptions

The only student to express absolute assumptions in Sam Rivers's course reported a different experience from the students in EDU 200 and winter biology. Melissa reported that her conception of math prior to the course was "there has always been one answer and how you arrive at it." She acquired this conception through teachers talking *at* her and telling her the way each math operation is done. She was aware, however, that Sam was trying to get her and her peers to see that there is more than one answer. Her acceptance of this latter notion enabled her to have a more positive experience than that of her peers with absolute assumptions. Apparently, Sam's teaching connected for Melissa in a way that allowed her to let go of her absolute assumptions. Melissa shared three ideas that show how Sam's teaching was meaningful and therefore offered a transitional context for this shift. First, she was surprised about interacting with professors and liked it a great deal. What she perceived as a personal relationship with Sam, described as him talking *with* her instead of *at* her, increased her trust in trying out his idea that there was more than one answer. Second, he supported her by giving her time to think before class discussion, something that she found interesting and fun to do. Third, Sam convinced Melissa that math was an area in which "you are always improving and adding on ideas" as opposed to history, which she said "is something that happened; it is part of the past—you can't really go back and change it." The transitional context offered through Sam's pedagogy helped move math from the certain category to the uncertain category.

Challenging Students to Surface Foundational Assumptions

I think most graduate students in my theory courses believe that theory is constructed rather than the absolute truth. Most students complete the MER to study assessing intellectual development, and very few express absolute assumptions. However, it is fairly common for them to come from undergraduate experiences in which objective knowing dominated. This domination meant that theory took priority over story, and theories written in texts were largely objective. I think some of these foundational assumptions still existed for the students who wanted me to spell out all the theories more specifically, to move the conversation through the material more quickly, and to decide weights for grading based on my judgment of what was most important for students to learn. Having the benefit of insights from Jan, Kim, Sam, and Chris to assist me, I developed a few plans to create a more effective transitional culture in my theory course.

Borrowing from Jan's idea of showing students that issues are unresolved and Sam's notion of improving math, I am more explicit about the possible ways of knowing in student development theory. Because students have already encountered the rational mode, I can show how the principles and generalizations of theory reflect that mode of knowing. Introducing the aesthetic, or narrative, mode of knowing as equally valuable gives students a concrete explanation of why we need to explore both. Illustrating how theories about student development have evolved from analyzing students' stories makes our narrative explorations more meaningful. I now use the discrepancies that emerge as we integrate insights from both stories and theories to help students understand the importance of our building theory rather than "spelling it out."

Kim's plans to improve the quality of conversation led me to two additional approaches. First, synthesizing the major points of each discussion helps students feel that we are accomplishing something. Engaging the group in a short conversation near the end of each two-and-a-half-hour session brings out the major insights we discovered and pressing questions that remain for future discussion. A second strategy for synthesis is to summarize what we have come to know about that particular theory at the end of each theoretical segment of the course. These efforts are meaningful to students who want to "know" more about the theory and "know" what ideas from the discussion are important without sacrificing the theory-building focus of the course.

Like Chris, I hesitate to "make rules" that dictate what students will do. The request for me to determine weights for assignments seems like such a request. Recognizing, however, that some students do not see themselves as equally knowledgeable about what is important, I adjusted how I present the percentages selection process, including minimum critical specifications to consider for choosing percentages. I did not previously share how I viewed the importance of each assignment; now I do so while trying to communicate that my view is not the only one. Sharing my view is meaningful to those who trust me to decide; sharing it as one view is meaningful to students who want freedom to use their own perspectives. I also convey that it is equally acceptable to consult with me about this decision or to make it without consulting. Encouragement to consult conveys to those who want my input that it is available. This stance conveys to those ready to decide for themselves that they are free to do so. Trying to convey both messages addresses another real issue—creating multiple transitional contexts for multiple ways of making meaning, a topic to be taken up shortly.

Key Aspects of Creating Transitional Cultures for Absolute Knowers

Our four courses reveal some of the characteristics of transitional contexts that are meaningful to those holding absolute assumptions or foundational assumptions that produce preferences similar to those of absolute knowers. First, in inviting students to join us in mutual knowledge construction, we must simultaneously respect and gently challenge their belief that knowledge is certain and objective. Explaining how math, science, or theory can be improved (to help students let go of absolute assumptions) while valuing what is currently known (through concrete information and instructor guidance) can achieve this delicate balance. Openly talking with students about the nature of knowledge, and particularly about the two modes of knowing, may be the bridge needed to connect their view with educators' view of knowledge.

Second, the educator's participation in the mutual construction is crucial, given absolute knowers' interest in acquiring knowledge from authority. Explicit discussion of course purposes, goals, and means of achieving them offers essential structure for students to see how these parts fit together. Structure for assignments, both at the outset and in process, is helpful in keeping the tasks within range of the student's assumptions about teacher and learner roles. Guidance in facilitating synthesis of discussions helps balance the value of constructing knowledge with the value of having something constructed at the close of the conversation. These two characteristics—open discussion about the nature of knowledge and educator participation in the dialogue—may be necessary for students to appreciate learning situated in their own experience and their own validation as knowers.

A third characteristic that could be gleaned from these four courses is the nature of teachers' relationships with students. By talking with his students rather than at them, Sam Rivers created what his student with absolute assumptions saw as a personal relationship. That relationship and the opportunity to talk with Sam and her peers in class gave her a transitional context for moving across the bridge to seeing math as uncertain. Chris Snowden talked with his students, too, and told them that science could be added to and improved. Despite hearing both messages, Ann did not believe him; she kept her absolute assumptions. Ann also shared that Chris intimidated her because he walked around the room and looked students in the eye, practices she was not used to because in most of her classes the instructor was so far away he could not see her. Somehow identifying this reaction and creating an opportunity to overcome it would have been part of an effective transitional context for Ann. Chris's notion of mandatory individual conferences might create that opportunity. Part of the real challenge of constructive-developmental pedagogy is to access and respond to these, as well as other, ways of making meaning.

CONNECTING TO MULTIPLE WAYS OF MAKING MEANING

Despite narrow ranges of class ranks in the four courses here, wide ranges of meaning-making existed. EDU 200, primarily first- and second-year students, included students with absolute, transitional, and independent assumptions about knowledge. Math by Inquiry, mostly seniors, was dominated by transitional and independent knowers. Winter biology, also mostly seniors, included absolute, transitional, independent, and contextual knowers. My graduate course usually includes transitional, independent, and contextual knowers. It is likely that most undergraduate and graduate courses involve students with different ways of making meaning. This complicates the task of creating bridges to each way of meaning-making. What is useful and therefore reaches one way of making meaning may not be useful for another.

However, there is a lot to be hopeful about in turning to constructive-developmental pedagogy to create multiple transitional contexts. The existence of multiple ways of making meaning among students in a course can be advantageous. Situating learning in students' experiences inevitably brings out a variety of experiences. Validating students as knowers, similarly, brings out a variety of perspectives and ways of making meaning. The expression of these multiple voices in classroom discussion offers perspectives that are both meaningful and facilitative for other ways of making meaning. For example, independent knowers' expressions of the uncertainty of knowledge connect with transitional knowers' growing awareness of uncertain areas of knowledge, yet simultaneously challenge their assumptions about certainty in other areas. Recall the dialogue in my student development theory course (chap. 3) in which students were discussing issues in integrating theories. Jo, an independent knower, advanced that any combination of placements on various theories was possible. Craig had initiated this discussion by expressing a frustration that the theories made sense individually but did not fit together nicely as students shared examples from their projects. His thinking could be interpreted as a transitional knower's belief that the theories were certain when applied individually, yet discrepant with the concrete experiences of his peers when used in an integrated way. Jo's reaction challenged the certainty of the individual theories and supported their uncertainty both individually and collectively. A continued dialogue between Jo and Craig might encourage Craig to view the theories from independent assumptions.

Contextual knowers' emphasis on knowledge as constructed points to its uncertainty (meaningful to independent knowers' assumptions) as well as the use of evidence for its construction (facilitative of independent knowers' assumptions). In the same theory discussion, Jo was adamant that theories were just one theorist's perspective or value. Her independent assumptions were challenged by Cara, who offered justification for a possible combination of ways of making meaning, and William, who used an aspect of the theory to disagree with Jo's possibilities. I also tried to acknowledge the uncertainty of theory while simultaneously focusing on evidence for deciding what to believe in my reaction to Jo in that conversation. Transitional knowers' beliefs about the certain areas of knowledge connect to absolute knowers' experience whereas their beliefs about uncertainty challenge absolute knowers' meaning-making. Although there were no absolute knowers in the theory discussion, had there been, Craig's initial comments about the theories would have appealed to their belief in certainty; his questions about integration would have challenged that certainty. Some students' meaning-making naturally creates transitional contexts for others.

Taking advantage of the transitional contexts created by students' participation in the dialogue is possible even when students' ways of making meaning do not connect. For example, contextual or independent knowers' expressions may not be meaningful for absolute knowers. However, teaching students to work collaboratively in discussion can create the needed transitional context. If students grow accustomed to helping one another understand their perspectives, transitional knowers can translate independent knowers' contributions in ways that absolute knowers might find meaningful. Such participation helps transitional knowers participate in the process of learning, something that they find meaningful in light of letting go of acquiring knowledge from authorities. Independent knowers participating in this way would find meaningful opportunities to express their newfound ideas. Contextual knowers, whose growing edge as I noted earlier is in integrating both modes of knowing, might hear from their peers and practice their integration through dialogue with their peers. It would seem that absolute knowers would have the least support in peer interactions; perhaps that explains why we were less successful in creating transitional contexts for them in our four courses. The suggestions for connecting to absolute assumptions in the previous section show that it may be the instructor—the person who is regarded as authority by absolute knowers—who provides the most meaningful support for absolute knowers.

The challenge of capitalizing on the natural diversity of students' meaning-making is first in bringing it out and then in helping students work with it effectively. The instructor must be articulate in multiple ways of making meaning to help students build bridges between their ways of knowing rather than criticizing them. Clinchy's advice to first believe, then doubt would be an effective approach to teach students. Helping students learn to validate one another as knowers would also contribute to positive processing of multiple meaning-making. Mutually constructing meaning helps focus on working through diverse perspectives together. Perhaps one of the most crucial instructor skills, however, is helping students work effectively with the inevitable conflict that arises when multiple ways of making meaning are present. This issue warrants detailed discussion because ineffective response to conflict can undermine both learning and growth of the mind.

MULTIPLE VOICES: DISSONANCE AND HARMONY

The notion of accessing and hearing students' experiences and voices sounds innocuous enough on the surface. However, calling forth multiple voices into the dialogue usually results in conflicting perspectives about which students and educators have strong feelings. This dissonance can be a teachable moment, an opportunity to explore what students really think and feel in an open and trusting environment. Using the dissonance produced by diverse perspectives effectively enhances learning. The challenge here is that many educators and students tend to avoid conflict in favor of harmony. Ineffective use of dissonance can push students' thoughts and feelings underground where they remain inaccessible to the teaching-learning interaction.

An example of a difficult and conflictual dialogue that emerged from constructive-developmental pedagogy illustrates this challenge. One week the EDU 200 course focused on the concepts race, racism, institutional racism, and prejudice. During the two weeks prior to this session, students had independently viewed an interactive video on multicultural awareness in the campus computer lab. The interactive video contained scenarios regarding student life in the classroom, with roommates, at a party, and in interracial dating, all of which raised the central concepts selected for the week. Students could interact with the scenarios via the computer. The creators of the Interactive Video Project* also offered peer facilitators to lead discussions to process the experience of the video. Kim relinquished the facilitation to the peer facilitator, Brad, who was an undergraduate. He introduced his purpose as getting discussion going, saying, "I don't have the answers; our purpose is for you to say what you want—feel free to say anything."** Brad asked

---

*Faculty in Miami's Communication, Psychology, and Educational Psychology Departments created the Interactive Video Project.

** The dialogue that follows was previously published in M. B. Baxter Magolda, "Facilitating Meaningful Dialogues about Race," *About Campus* 2, no.5 (1997): 14–18.

the group to go over the scenarios to describe what happened and subsequently asked the group to identify themes from them. A lively conversation about stereotypes ensued with students expressing surprise at the way African-Americans were treated in the scenarios. This segued into a discussion of low minority enrollment and recruiting difficulties, a conversation that was to open the door for diverse perspectives.

Up to that point, all participants had advocated increasing the diversity of the student body despite their different perspectives on why it was not diverse and what should be done to remedy that. The notion that college was a time of being exposed to many things had just been introduced as a reason for increased diversity when Lauren brought the conversation to a new level. She said,

> This will come off snobby, but it's not racial. I am not a racist; I have black friends; my friends date black people. But I don't want to go to a diverse school. I wanted to be at a school like this. If you want to go to a diverse university, then apply to one. Why ruin it for people here?

Others immediately challenged Lauren's position. She insisted that "it's not a color thing—there are blacks here that have interests same as me and as long as that is the case, I don't care about color." Jane said that because she was an Ohio resident, she needed to come to this state school and wanted to be exposed to diversity. She noted that both she and Lauren would have to function "in the real world." Lauren reiterated that she did not "want to be exposed to it." Jane asked, "Why not? You don't want to learn about others?" Lauren replied, "I just don't want to. I'm just being honest. There are others in this room and around this building tonight that feel this way too and just won't say so. You can think I'm a bitch, but I'm being honest."

At this juncture Walter, the only African-American student in the group, chimed in, saying, "You have 10,000 people, conservative. What is the harm of having 5,000 diverse people? You don't have to be around them—you don't have to change your view. You say go to another school. That is wrong. I should be able to come here."

Another woman asked Lauren what it was she did not want to be exposed to. Lauren said she liked it that there were people who dressed like her, liked the Greek system, and she did not care about race. She added, "I don't think you should recruit people because of the way they are. If you are too intimidated to apply to this school because of the way it is, you probably won't make it here."

Hugh then posed this question: "Isn't the job of the university to prepare us for the world, to educate us about what is out there? There is a diverse atmosphere in the U.S. Shouldn't that be a priority of the school?" Jessica agreed, saying, "I'm preparing for teaching and half of the class will be minority. You should have experienced that by then. If you don't learn to handle it, you can't succeed."

Mandy extended this by noting that in her major, they are supposed to volunteer with different ages of people, and that she felt part of life was getting experience with different people. Mandy continued, "What will happen if a Chinese person needs help and I've never talked to one before?" Theo picked up on Mandy's reference to nationality and asked if his peers ever encountered foreign exchange students. He offered, "They always have different perspectives. It opened my eyes to things I never thought of. Not that I was wrong, but I can think better." Mandy responded, seemingly toward Lauren: "You don't have to be best friends with them but it is neat to learn from them." Time was running out at that point so Brad asked for any final thoughts. There was no response.

Any teacher can imagine the sinking feeling that arises when a comment like Lauren's is put on the table. As a teacher, one is simultaneously concerned with how to deal with the perspective raised, how to deal with others who are offended by it, and how to manage the potentially emotional responses that it may solicit. Because Brad did not intervene, however, Lauren's peers responded and did so relatively effectively. Although it was clear they did not agree with Lauren, they pursued her perspective a bit farther, asking her to explain why she felt the way she did. They also shared their own hopes for their college education, which were different from hers. Both Mandy and Walter seemed to offer Lauren a compromise—don't interact or don't feel the need to be friends with diverse others, but accept their presence. On the one hand, it is remarkable that this conversation was effective at all, given Brad's lack of participation and the group consisting of forty students (two of Kim's seminar sections combined). It could have been a teacher's worst nightmare had the students not already learned that respecting others' views in the dialogue enhanced their learning in the course. On the other hand, the conversation did not really access the depth of the issue Lauren raised because the students "resolved" their differences by offering a compromise.

Using the three principles, one could facilitate this and other conflictual conversations to dig deeper into the issue and mutually construct meaning about it. Diverse experiences surfaced during this interchange that could have been pursued to further situate the issue in students' experience. Lauren would have been validated by a more open invitation (rather than as a defense of her position) to talk about her experience and how it led her to this view. Had that occurred, her peers would have learned (as I did in the end-of-the-semester interview) that she attended a small private school with a graduating class of twenty. This would have put her view in perspective and validated her as a knower without validating her view. Inviting Walter to tell more about his experience would have generated an experience for all the students that would contradict Lauren's view. However, by hearing Walter's perspective and seeing his experience validated, Lauren might have been able to see why his view was appropriate too. This may have had more effect than her peers' arguments about learning from others, something Lauren probably viewed as a politically correct perspective.

Exploring these and other students' experiences more thoroughly could form the foundation for raising the question of how students with these varied backgrounds come together to function interdependently in adult society. By this time, everyone could be working together to explore this issue rather than trying to convince Lauren that her view was wrong. By using students' experiences to set the stage for why this dilemma exists, the conversation could move away from whose experience is "right" to the implications of the reality. Mutually constructing meaning about education's role in preparing students for a diverse world then could give students an opportunity to consider other perspectives openly. As the conversation went, Lauren did not hear her peers' ideas openly, nor they hers. Despite the relatively cordial nature of the interaction, Lauren would probably not be prone to bring the issue up again.

Other kinds of conflicts emerge from inviting students into the dialogue as well. Some of my students expressed frustration with peers who were cynical about the value of student development theory, feeling that the cynical perspective got in the way of our moving through the material. We surfaced this issue in one discussion whereupon a couple of the skeptical students became aware of how their approach was affecting others. The difference of opinion was useful throughout the course because it raised important issues and sparked important discussions. Some of Sam Rivers's students complained that one student dominated the conversation in math class. They never raised the issue with her or Sam, and Sam's awareness of the situation led him to call on the student less. She in turn had an intuitive feeling that Sam and her peers were not supportive of her, and she volunteered less. Raising this issue in the group would have given her a chance to explain her enthusiasm and given her peers a chance to share that they were intimidated by her. Approaching this dissonance would have been more conducive to everyone's learning than avoiding it.

Conflicts, whether about the course content or learning interactions, do not go away if they are ignored. They remain under the surface where they continue to aggravate the situation in ways that are not open for discussion and resolution. Conflicts among students' views may never become public unless the teaching-learning environment welcomes them to emerge from the students' private worlds. Constructive-developmental pedagogy, in connecting learning to students' worlds, is inherently fraught with conflict.

Viewing conflict as creative rather than problematic integrates conflict as a useful component of the learning environment. Parker Palmer, in advancing this view, writes, "*Communal conflict* is a public encounter in which the whole group can win by growing" (1987, 25, italics in original). He argues that the existence of opposing views results in coming to a fuller understanding for community members. Truth, Palmer believes, "comes as we air our differences in public, pay special heed to those who dissent, and seek a deeper insight—whether the subject is a statistical table, a laboratory experiment, an episode in history, or an epic poem" (1990, 15). Bringing students into the process of knowing means bringing them into the conflict that knowing contains and helping them self-author their perspectives more effectively.

THE NEXT STEP

I have attempted in this chapter to raise both tangible and intangible obstacles to implementing constructive-developmental pedagogy. My own experience, the experience of the educators whose teaching is highlighted in the book, and scholarship on constructivist teaching suggest that the imaginary challenges posed by our foundational assumptions can be overcome. I have tried to describe the insights and skills needed to address the real challenges posed by constructive-developmental pedagogy. Assuming we transform our assumptions and develop the needed skills to implement constructive-developmental pedagogy, we are still faced with convincing our constituents (colleagues, promotion and tenure committees, the public, students) that constructive-developmental pedagogy is a viable approach in an increasingly outcomes-oriented world. The final chapter addresses this crucial task by exploring the possibilities of constructive-developmental pedagogy for enhancing education and students' participation in a contemporary society.

CHAPTER 9

The Possibilities of Constructive-Developmental Pedagogy

> He would ask, "What do you think about this?" It is not just blatant memorization that is learning; learning comes into it when you are utilizing the ideas toward something new, going toward something new, something that hasn't been done.
> —JEREMY

Jeremy's comment about Chris Snowden's winter biology course reveals the kind of experience we all hope education will be. Unfortunately, descriptions of the typical educational experience do not sound like Jeremy's experience. In fact, Jeremy compared winter biology to the usual fare he experienced, which he described as "just regurgitating the facts . . . being like a computer and storing this information to really do nothing with." The majority of the evidence about the nature of higher education concurs with Jeremy's report; it reflects an educational experience in which genuine engagement is scarce, including engagement of teachers and students, of students and subject matter, and of learning and life. The absence of these linkages accounts for most of the complaints about higher education today. Students complain that their education is irrelevant to their lives and future careers. Teachers complain that students are not motivated, will not think, and just want the grade and credential, making teaching a boring endeavor at best. Parents and employers complain that graduates are not critical thinkers and are unprepared for adult roles of parent, worker, and citizen. Advocates for equal opportunity in higher education argue that it is lacking. Numerous groups have summarized higher education's problems in scathing national reports (see chap. 1 for examples). These dynamics exist despite many teachers' interest in student learning and serious reform efforts. I believe these conditions persist because we have not created the conditions for students to construct complex ways of making meaning.

Constructive-developmental pedagogy holds the possibility of resolving these issues. The most important aspect of constructive-developmental pedagogy is its potential to promote self-authorship. Constructive-developmental pedagogy offers the opportunity for students to view themselves as capable of constructing knowledge, as in control of their thoughts and beliefs, and as capable of expressing themselves. By developing students' minds, selves, and voices, constructive-developmental pedagogy results in a far more dynamic educational experience than the one captured by most national reports. Students who are moving toward self-authorship participate genuinely in the dialogue and in connecting learning to their lives, offering the possibility for more effective learning. Evidence suggests that constructive-developmental pedagogy could have these effects in elementary, secondary, and higher education. Self-authorship, in turn, helps people function in our contemporary society, something most critics identify as a shortcoming of current education. Meeting the demands of modern society requires making meaning in complex ways that are fostered by constructive-developmental pedagogy. Finally, self-authorship prepares people not only to survive in contemporary society, but also to contribute to its improvement. Complex ways of making meaning are necessary to address the complex problems facing our society today.

This chapter addresses four possibilities offered by constructive-developmental pedagogy for improving education and in turn our society: (1) fostering self-authorship and lifelong learning; (2) enhancing education by linking students' lives—including diverse students' lives—to academic learning in a genuine and substantive way; (3) preparing students to meet the demands inherent in adult roles in contemporary society; and (4) preparing students to take an active role in creating a better society.

FOSTERING SELF-AUTHORSHIP AND LIFE-LONG LEARNING

Constructive-developmental pedagogy, as it is portrayed in this book, aims to help students become knowledge constructors—thinkers capable of gathering, interpreting, and analyzing information in order to form sound judgments about what to believe. This ability to author one's own perspective enables lifelong learning outside the context of formal education. Adults who make meaning from the vantage point of self-authorship view knowledge as continually constructed and view themselves as ongoing participants in that evolving construction. Subsequently, this would seem to be a central aim of education.

Many may agree on self-authorship as a central *aim* of education, but evidence abounds that it is not a central *outcome* of education. In my longitudinal study (Baxter Magolda 1992) of college students' epistemological development (detailed in chap. 2), 80 percent of the seniors still used transitional knowing, relying on authorities for knowledge in certain areas and on their own opinions in uncertain areas. Comparably, King and Kitchener (1994) reported that seniors generally exhibited quasi-reflective thinking, a way of making meaning that assumes "many possible answers to every question and no absolutely certain way to adjudicate between competing answers. Individuals with this assumption will therefore argue that knowledge claims are simply idiosyncratic to the individual" (225). This does not reflect the concept of self-authorship as it is discussed here. Kegan (1994) estimated that half of the adult population has yet to achieve an internally generated sense of self, an important component of self-authorship. One plausible explanation for this state of affairs is that traditional socialization and education inhibit self-authorship.

In our society, children get a lot of experience being told what to do and think. Patricia Williams illustrates this effectively in a story she recounts about a conversation she overheard on the street between a couple and their four- or five-year-old son. Williams reports that the child was apparently afraid of big dogs, and as his parents attempted to understand why, he reiterated "because they're big" (1991, 12). His parents pointed out two dogs to him, one a large wolfhound and another a small Pekingese, and explained that there was really no difference. Williams thought to herself:

> Talk about your iron-clad canon. Talk about a static, unyielding, totally uncompromising point of reference. These people must be lawyers. Where else do people learn so well the idiocies of High Objectivity? How else do people learn to capitulate so uncritically to a norm that refuses to allow for difference? How else do grown-ups sink so deeply into the authoritarianism of their own world view that they can universalize their relative bigness so completely that they obliterate the subject positioning of their child's relative smallness? (1991, 12-13)

Here the parents' intentions of alleviating their son's fears resulted in their ignoring his experience. As Williams pointed out, they ignored his vantage point and his interpretation of his experience, and essentially told him his interpretation was wrong. Such experiences promote absolute epistemic assumptions and thus erode children's ability to construct their own perspectives.

Lyn Mikel Brown and Carol Gilligan (1990) portray the socialization of girls in our society as inhibiting self-authorship. In their study of adolescent girls, those at age eight or nine expressed their thoughts readily; by the age of eleven or twelve, the girls hesitated to say what they thought out of concern for maintaining relationships. Brown and Gilligan's conversation with a girl named Jesse illustrated this dramatic shift. At age eight, Jesse told a story about feeling left out while at a friend's house. Jesse shared her feelings with her friend, who in turn shared hers by telling Jesse to "just go home" (11). At age eleven, Jesse told the interviewers that "if a girl doesn't like another girl, . . . she 'should pretend that [she] likes her'" (16). Jesse's shift in perspective, according to Brown and Gilligan, represents an attempt to become the "perfect girl," one who is cooperative, kind, and good—as young women are supposed to be. Jesse's loss of self-authorship stems from her fear that being herself will jeopardize her relationships with others. Her socialization as a young girl tells her that others will want to be with her only if she is the kind and good person that girls are supposed to be.

These examples show that our society communicates strong messages to children and adolescents about what they should think and how they should be. This socialization is compounded by traditional education. Ira Shor writes, "In traditional classrooms, students develop authority-dependence; they rehearse their futures as passive citizens and workers by learning that education means listening to teachers tell them what to do and what things mean" (1993, 29). Recall the example from chapter 3 of the teachers doing a lesson on irony. Teacher A insisted on soliciting a definition from students, something they could not generate. Teacher A's persistence in having a definition, rather than the examples the students could generate, resulted in his telling them the definition. On the other hand, Teacher A' went along with the students' examples, guiding them to form a definition from the examples. The former approach is the most common and the one that leads students to authority-dependence. It also reduces their interest in working toward a definition because there is no process to do so; they simply wait until the definition is provided.

The good news inherent in the notion that authority-dependence is learned is that it can be unlearned, or even more encouraging, it could never be taught in the first place. Higher education is faced with students who have already learned authority-dependence and come to college expecting teachers to continue to tell them what to do and think. The prevalence of absolute knowing among entering college students (Baxter Magolda 1992; King and Kitchener 1994) reflects the learned dependence on authority for defining and distributing knowledge. The four courses discussed in this book suggest that this dependence can be altered, that students can learn authority-independence if you will, in the context of constructive-developmental pedagogy in college. Students in my longitudinal study reported learning self-authorship when their teachers used the three principles (see chap. 3). The courses recounted in this book are also rich with examples of how students learned independence from authority (see chap. 7). The challenge of shifting from dependence on authority to independence from authority in college is that authority-dependence has become ingrained and reinforced outside of formal education. Brenda spoke to this issue in talking about her experience in Sam Rivers's math course:

Dr. Rivers is probing; he's not satisfied with the smart kid with a good answer. He would say, "Is there another way?" Acting like he is inquiring himself, really pushing. Pursuing is the point. It is believable that he is inquiring too, and he says there are things he hasn't thought of and I believe him. You go into college class thinking the professor is God and knows all. The last step is letting go. . . . If the teacher doesn't know, then what am I worrying about? He is genuinely inquiring. There are times when . . . he really discovers something he hadn't thought of. That is a sign of a good teacher to admit that he is constantly learning and learning from students.

Making the shift from "professor is God" to a "good teacher learns from students" in four years requires letting go of long-held assumptions about knowledge, authority, learning, and self. The stories in this book suggest that effective use of constructive-developmental pedagogy in college could help students accomplish this difficult transition, just as Sam Rivers did with Brenda.

The evidence is also mounting that students can learn self-authorship in elementary and secondary education, creating the potential that entering college students may not be absolute knowers. Jeannie Oakes and Martin Lipton (1990) describe the effect of constructive-developmental pedagogy on children. A relational math lesson involves groups of students using rulers and building materials to construct a class project. During the activity, they add and subtract feet and inches, as the teacher earlier explained, in order to construct the project. Actually using the addition and subtraction for a practical purpose helps the children learn how to do it and see themselves as part of a knowledge construction community. Oakes and Lipton contrast this with a math lesson in which the teacher explains addition and subtraction and assigns twenty practice problems. This creates rote learning and dependence on authority to identify the right answer. Oakes and Lipton share similar examples in other disciplines, noting that those that "allow children to connect what they do with what they learn, [help them] feel in charge of their learning" (64). Wood, Cobb, and Yackel (1994) describe constructivist elementary mathematics lessons in which students and teachers developed norms, such as attempting to explain and justify solutions to problems and trying to make sense of explanations given by others. Their examples illustrate how elementary students can be engaged in exploring mathematical ideas and working together to reach understanding of mathematical concepts. Similarly, Deborah Schifter (1996) shares examples of this approach with first- and second-grade students. This approach fosters children's positive self-concepts—a crucial component of self-authorship.

Examples of constructivist classrooms in junior high reveal that students are capable of learning independence from authority. Jacqueline Grennon Brooks and Martin Brooks (1993) offer numerous examples from the study of photosynthesis and English to social studies and math in which junior high students think, work together, and arrive at understanding with the guidance rather than the authority of their teachers. Similar examples exist at the high school level that show those students can learn independence from authority. Candace Julyan and Eleanor Duckworth (1996) share examples of high school science classrooms in which students explore problems and come to mutually constructed solutions. Sophie Haroutunian-Gordon (1991) reports what she calls interpretive discussion in which students explore their thoughts, offer their ideas, pursue new questions, and construct their own understanding of the subject at hand. She used this pedagogy, which I would argue is constructive-developmental, to study Shakespeare with two high school classes. One class was in a private, racially integrated school in metropolitan Chicago (Chalmers); the other was in an urban public school in Chicago's black ghetto (Belden). Both high school classes learned independence from authority through these interpretive discussions, albeit differently. Haroutunian-Gordon speculated that the Chalmers students started with experience in discussion but tended to overlook their personal experience in analyzing literature. The Belden students, in contrast, started with a wealth of personal experience but were unaccustomed to linking it to the literature. The success of both groups in exploring Shakespeare indicates that constructive-developmental pedagogy can reach students who come to education from different vantage points, an issue taken up further in the next section.

ENHANCING EDUCATION BY LINKING STUDENTS' LIVES AND LEARNING

Just as students learn to be authority-dependent, they become accustomed to not connecting their lives to what they learn in school and to having distance from their teachers. Ann, a senior in Chris Snowden's winter biology course, reported: "This class is weird because I devoted so much energy just sitting in class and being attentive. It was a big thing; it was not like you could just hang out because he would look at you, right in the eye! [I'm] sitting there, thinking, *Stop making eye contact with me.*" Ann was used to large lecture halls in which she could "hang out," or "zone" as she called it, because the teacher could not see her. It is important to put Ann's comments in context. She is a senior, taking a course in her major, at a selective institution where students are predominantly white, from middle- and upper-class economic backgrounds, and academically capable. Ann is the kind of student, at the kind of institution, who we would project would be most likely to find the connection between her life and her educational experience. Her experience, and that of her peers, suggests that traditional pedagogy does not reach even the traditional-age mainstream students in higher education. Recall, too, that Ann had a hard time adjusting to the constructive-developmental pedagogy she experienced in Chris Snowden's course due to her previous educational training.

The lack of connection between students' lives and learning is exacerbated in the case of students from nondominant populations, including those based on race, ethnicity, culture, class, or gender. Christine Sleeter and Carl Grant (1991) discuss the bifurcation students experience "between school knowledge and real-life knowledge" (49) as a result of the distance between classroom knowledge and students' cultural knowledge. As a result of their study of a desegregated junior high school in a working-class neighborhood, Sleeter and Grant reported that "the great majority of the students we interviewed considered most or all of what the school was teaching them to be unrelated to their lives" (62). Because school knowledge was unrelated to their lives, and because they had no ownership or control of it, Sleeter and Grant surmised that "school knowledge was not being absorbed by students as a conceptual system for helping them understand and act on the world— it was compartmentalized within their own conceptual system and thought of as sets of activities done for someone else in a social context" (63). The marginalization of students whose "cultural knowledge" is different from the school knowledge being taught has been well documented, perhaps most extensively in the case of women. Much of the concern about equal opportunity for women in mathematics and science has turned on how the impersonal nature of those fields is distant from the connected approach prevalent among women learners. The marginalization of students from diverse racial, ethnic, and economic class backgrounds has also been documented (Banks 1991; Fordham and Ogbu 1986; hooks 1984; Weiler 1988). Frances Maher and Mary Kay Tetreault summed up the situation:

> Until recently, the content and pedagogy of American education, although projecting the "illusion" that it spoke to everyone, ignored the needs, experiences, and perspectives of the majority of people in this country—women of all backgrounds, people of color, and all women and men who perceive their education as not made for them. (1994, 1)

The outcomes of traditional pedagogy indicate that even the students for whom education was initially made do not perceive it as made for them because it does not connect to their experience. Maher and Tetreault's phrase "until recently" refers to their perception that feminist classrooms are beginning to change this state of affairs. Their description of feminist classrooms contains many of the characteristics of constructive-developmental pedagogy.

Constructive-developmental pedagogy overcomes the dilemma of students perceiving education as "not made for them." It does so precisely because constructive-developmental pedagogy creates education that *is* made for them, "them" being the particular students in a particular educational context. Situating learning in students' experience places their cultural knowledge at the center of the educational experience. Validating them as knowers reinforces the importance of their cultural knowledge and their ability to integrate it with school knowledge. Mutually constructing meaning bridges students' cultural knowledge and school knowledge and gives students the opportunity to decide what to believe based on both. Using these three principles of constructive-developmental pedagogy creates the possibility for reaching students regardless of their cultural knowledge or their epistemological development.

For example, in Sam Rivers's math course Becky reported that she never spoke in math courses because she was too afraid. She (like many of her female peers according to the literature) did not believe she had the knowledge upon which to speak in any math class. Yet she reported,

> Near the end of the class nearly everyone was talking, so I pretty much raised my hand and said things too. It was neat because I thought, *Wow! Somebody sitting next to me said a mathematical thing and it was a hypothesis and it wasn't the teacher's; it was theirs!* And the teacher is showing it to everyone; the teacher wasn't in control. The students were in control. The teacher just helped bring that to order, put some order into what was being said. . . . All of us at one time or another were taught to feel important, like this is so-and-so's conjecture. I remember the first time I had a conjecture. I felt all proud of myself! I was like, "Yeah! All right, I got a conjecture, finally!"

Part of Becky's cultural knowledge included students (perhaps women students) being incapable of generating mathematical ideas. Becky felt free to offer her ideas in this context and was excited that she and her peers could generate mathematical ideas.

Hugh emphasized the value of the EDU 200 course connecting to his cultural knowledge and that of his peers. One of the important aspects of the course for him was the use of student experience:

> There are some days [when] our experience is pertinent—like race or prejudice. Most of us have had some interaction with cultural

minorities and we want to say how we feel. In recent weeks on the topics of gender, race, and sexuality, we all have relevant experience. It is good to get what peers think and why they think it. [This school] is homogeneous. You would think we've had similar experiences, but everybody's got a little different experience and different ways of interpretation. That brings it home. It makes me think about it and remember how I thought about an experience. You can't be totally sure about what you think if you are only coming at it from one direction. This is not just someone telling [us] what to think. I feel equal to the students; I don't feel that my opinion is unwanted.

The fact that Hugh can express his opinion, work out his thoughts, and explore others' interpretations makes learning more meaningful to him. The collaboration inherent in both Becky's and Hugh's reports has been advocated for making education more effective for African-American students because collaboration is consistent with black family culture (Joint Center for Political and Economic Studies 1993), as well as making education more effective for all students.

Forms of teaching that are consistent with constructive-developmental pedagogy are being advocated by numerous writers as promoting an inclusive curriculum. Sue Rosser recommended encouraging the development of scientific theories that are "relational, interdependent, and multicausal rather than hierarchical, reductionistic, and dualistic" (1995, 15) in order to connect to females' interest in relationships and interaction among ideas. Given the research on ways of making meaning of nondominant populations, this approach may be inclusive of many students. She also highlighted the importance of linking science and students' lives. Reginald Wilson also advocated these new ways of teaching and learning as moving toward an inclusive curriculum. Using Peggy McIntosh's five-phase model of transformation to a multicultural curriculum, he identified one of the important aspects of phase four as new ways of teaching and learning that allow students to be "active participants in the creation of their own knowledge" (1996, 30), thus acknowledging that knowledge is contextual. Gloria Ladson-Billings reported that this conception about knowledge (as constructed and dynamic), along with conceptions about students as capable knowers and conceptions about relating to students in connected ways, led to the success of elementary students in a predominantly African-American low-income school district. Ladson-Billings described these conceptions on the part of the teachers she studied as culturally relevant pedagogy. Her words capture the essence of this pedagogy:

Teachers who practice culturally relevant methods can be identified by the way they see themselves and others. They see their teaching as an art rather than as a technical skill. They believe that all of their students can succeed rather than that failure is inevitable for some. They see themselves as a part of the community and they see teaching as giving back to the community. They help students make connections between their local, national, racial, cultural, and global identities. Such teachers can also be identified by the ways in which they structure their social interactions: Their relationships with students are fluid and equitable and extend beyond the classroom. They demonstrate a connectedness with all of their students and encourage that same connectedness between the students. They encourage a community of learners; they encourage their students to learn collaboratively. Finally, such teachers are identified by their notions of knowledge: They believe that knowledge is continuously re-created, recycled, and shared by teachers and students alike. They view the content of the curriculum critically and are passionate about it. Rather than expecting students to demonstrate prior knowledge and skills they help students develop that knowledge by building bridges and scaffolding for learning. (1994, 25)

This pedagogy resulted in students demonstrating "an ability to read, write, speak, compute, pose and solve problems at sophisticated levels—that is, pose their own questions about the nature of teacher- or text-posed problems and engage in peer review of problem solutions" (1995, 475). These reports raise hopes that constructive-developmental pedagogy does offer a possibility for including and promoting self-authorship with all students.

Pedagogy "made" for particular students not only promotes self-authorship but also enhances the teaching-learning process for both students and teachers. As students share their experiences, each gains cultural knowledge from the diverse experiences of others. As they work together to construct knowledge, they learn to actively interpret information, identify perspectives behind information, understand how others come to their beliefs, and understand how they come to their own beliefs. This active rebuilding of one's world—both in content understanding and in epistemic assumptions—is far more interesting than recording the teacher's knowledge in one's notebook. Jill commented on this in relation to Chris Snowden's course, saying,

I think that everyone comes from a different background of knowledge, and when you gather everyone together and ask them all to think about the same thing and come up with ideas, it is great because people come to class and bring up things that you have never learned and maybe never would unless that person offered that. We learn from each other as well as from him. When he says, "Does anyone have anything to say about that?" you get everyone's input about that topic and it rounds it out—completes the facets of it. The different knowledge that each student offers can round it out or encourage further thinking about that topic.

The participation sparked by constructive-developmental pedagogy also makes teaching a dynamic process. The frustrated teacher in the Doonesbury cartoon (chap. 2) would be delighted if his students would participate actively in analyzing his comments and constructing knowledge. I learn far more in my classes now that I use constructive-developmental pedagogy. I learn from students' cultural knowledge and from the mutual construction of meaning in which we continually engage. Classroom dialogue is intellectually stimulating and exciting compared to going over material I already know. Chris Snowden said of his course: "[This is] the best class I have ever had as far as people really getting into it and staying into it. Working hard and having a lot of participation in the class. . . . I was pretty happy with the course and the students I had; that made it a positive experience for me." Jane Tompkins described her foray into constructive-developmental pedagogy like this:

> There were days when I decided I had literally opened Pandora's box and that we would all have been better off conducting business as usual. One day I myself was on the verge of tears as I spoke. But this was also the most exciting class I've ever been in. I never knew what was going to happen. Apart from a series of stunning self-revelations, wonderful readings added to the reading list by the students, and reports whose trajectory came as a total surprise, we were led, as a class, by various reporting groups into role-playing, picture drawing, and even on one occasion into participating in a religious ceremony. (1990, 659)

The dialogue inherent in constructive-developmental pedagogy creates an atmosphere of mutual learning. By linking learning with all of our lives, constructive-developmental pedagogy creates a vibrant teaching-learning experience that builds students' confidence in themselves as knowledge constructors. This self-authorship is crucial in students' ability to function in contemporary society.

PREPARING STUDENTS FOR ADULT ROLES IN CONTEMPORARY SOCIETY

Education in the United States has always had as one of its primary purposes preparing young people for adult roles in society. Although differences of opinion abound about what this means, one of the common criticisms of

higher education is that its graduates are not adequately prepared to function in contemporary society. And given the variety of roles one could adopt
in contemporary society, it is difficult to imagine how higher education
could approach the complex task of preparing students for these roles.
Robert Kegan's (1994) conceptualization of modern society as a school with
its own curriculum is useful here. The complex set of tasks and expectations
placed on us by contemporary society is the curriculum of this school. Kegan
explores adults' ability to work through this curriculum effectively from the
vantage point of their ways of making meaning. (The basic ideas of ways of
making meaning and their evolution are summarized in chap. 2.) He argues
that these expectations amount to a claim on our minds, on the way we
make meaning. Specifically, he writes,

> Policy makers and planners, curriculum designers, higher education
> mission-builders, civic, cultural, and institutional leaders may ben-
> efit from considering, for example, that our current cultural design
> requires of adults a qualitative transformation of mind every bit as
> fundamental as the transformation from magical thinking to con-
> crete thinking required of the school-age child or the transformation
> from concrete to abstract thinking required of the adolescent.
> (1994, 11)

The transformation of mind to which Kegan is referring is the transformation from third order meaning-making to fourth order meaning-making.
Recall from chapter 2 that in third order meaning-making the system by
which meaning is made is external to the self whereas in fourth order meaning-
making that system becomes internal. This same internal system makes self-
authorship possible. Kegan offers compelling evidence that self-authorship is
one of the central demands contemporary society places on adults.

THE DEMANDS OF PUBLIC LIFE

Kegan captures the work world's expectations of adults in one of his chapter
titles: "Working: On Seeking to Hire the Self-Employed" (1994, 137). The
"self-employed" are adults who see their work owned and created by themselves rather than by their employers. They do not depend on external sources
to assess a situation, suggest change, or evaluate their progress. Rather, they are
what Kegan calls "self-initiating, self-correcting, self-evaluating" (153). They
frame problems themselves, determine when adjustments are necessary, and
judge their own work. In addition, these adults have a vision of their work
that guides them, and they take responsibility for their work rather than see
others as responsible for what takes place. Kegan argues that the work world
expects adults to be accomplished masters of their work rather than appren-
tices, and to be able to look at their work organizations as a whole rather

than solely from their own part of the organization. These expectations amount to a demand on the adult mind—a demand that it is capable of self-authorship.

Interviews with my longitudinal study participants in their postcollege years support Kegan's contention that the contemporary work world demands self-authorship. For example, Gavin described starting his job in the insurance industry like this:

> They say, "Here's your desk; here's your office; here's your phone; here's the mailbox. Here's a little bit of clientele to get started. Start your own business. Here's some suggested ways to do it. Here are people who have done it and been successful. But this isn't necessarily the way you have to do it. See if you can build yourself a business." (Baxter Magolda 1994b, 32)

Even though Gavin was a newcomer, Gavin's employer expected him to invent his own work, be self-initiating, and develop his own vision of how to build his business.

Ned described similar expectations in his job selling paper chemicals to paper mills:

> The thing about paper mills is that they're extremely diverse and complex and unique. There's no one paper mill like the next one. So when I go into a mill I've got a basic set of textbook-type learning situations that I draw from and apply in a specific instance to each day, each application, each paper mill. In 65 or 85 percent of the cases, going into it I don't know what the end result is going to be. And I don't know how to get to the end result. So, . . . I get into this quote-unquote insurmountable task, get halfway through it, and figure things out as I go along and adapt, change, redefine, what have you, until [I] get to the final conclusion. And as a result I think one of the indirect things that I've learned is you can be smart about it. I can cut down the amount of rework time by approaching it based on other past histories or other experiences that I've had that lead me or lend me a more accurate picture or more accurate hypothesis of what's going to happen. So that's going to cut down on my reworks; that's going to cut down on asking the basic questions and getting those answers because they're already going to be answered. (Baxter Magolda 1994a, 18)

Ned makes it clear that he has to think as he goes, that although the basics help, he has to apply them to each individual situation. He initiates where to start, adjusts as he goes, and continually evaluates his progress. Because Ned works independently from his boss, he is expected to be able to envision what needs to be done, do it, and take responsibility for the outcome. Because Ned is working for a client (the mill) at the same time, he has to negotiate what he thinks should be done with what the client is willing to accept.

Gavin and Ned offer experiences similar to those of most of their peers entering the workforce after college. Their occupations run the gamut: they are in business, education, mental health, law, medicine, and the ministry, to name a few. To succeed in their work, they have found that the ability to make meaning from their own self-generated system is essential. The literature on organizational development (e.g., Morgan 1986) and leadership (e.g., Bensimon and Neumann 1993; Rogers 1992; Rost 1991) advocates that adults take increasingly independent and responsible roles in improving organizations. Thus, the central outcome of constructive-developmental pedagogy—self-authorship—is essential in preparing adults to work in contemporary society. Students who have experience mutually constructing meaning with their instructors have a foundation for mutually constructing meaning with their coworkers and employers. Seeing themselves as knowledge constructors and as capable of making meaning from an internal system results in the self-authorship necessary to succeed in the work world.

Another arena of public life that poses increasing demands on adults is the diversity of the American population and the increasing interdependence of the world's nations. The intense struggle to deal with diversity effectively (or to deal with it at all, for that matter) is evident in all facets of higher education and society at large. Disagreement abounds regarding what effectively dealing with diversity means, and tensions and conflicts among diverse groups are prevalent on college campuses and beyond. Taking a developmental view on cultural conflict, Kegan asserts that it stems from our own constructions of our cultural rules and the meaning we make of others who appear to violate them. Because we make sense of others' behavior from our own cultural rules, we judge as right only what matches our cultural constructions. Kegan argues that one of the demands of contemporary society is to resist this tendency, to resist judging the familiar as right and true and judging the unfamiliar as wrong and false. To do this, one needs to be capable of looking at and evaluating "the values and beliefs of our psychological and cultural inheritance rather than be captive of those values and beliefs" (1994, 302). This includes recognizing stylistic differences, such as gender-related patterns of knowing or moral meaning-making, as preferences rather than superior ways of being.

To meet these demands to step outside our values and beliefs to reconsider those constructions, Kegan writes that one needs a mind that can stand enough apart from its own opinions, values, rules, and definitions to avoid being completely identified with them. It is able to keep from feeling that the whole self has been violated when its opinions, values, rules, or definitions are challenged. (1994, 231)

This type of mind makes meaning from the fourth order. People making meaning from this vantage point can entertain alternate constructions of cultural rules and difference because they do not construct that they have been violated, only that their beliefs have been challenged. This distinction stems from the fact that their meaning-making system is internal, not buffeted about by external controls.

For example, recall Lauren's disagreement with her classmates in EDU 200 (chap. 8) about increasing the diversity of her college. She felt attacked, as demonstrated by her continual attempts to assure her classmates that she was not racist, that others felt as she did, and her comment that her classmates probably thought she was a "bitch" for saying that she did not want people unlike her to come to the school. Lauren seemed more intent on convincing her classmates to approve of her rather than articulating her point. Both her stance on wanting people like her around, which she could not articulate any more clearly, and her reactions to her peers reflect a third order mind, which is *authored by* values, beliefs, and relationships with others. The students who disagreed with her, arguing that encountering diverse others was a positive experience, reflected the stance that diversity is not threatening. One of those students, Hugh, was an independent knower. It is likely that he and the others who were not threatened had reached some degree of self-authorship that helped them feel secure in the face of difference.

Sheila, a participant in my longitudinal study, confirmed Kegan's contention that gender differences can be dealt with if one can view style as preference. Talking about her relationship with her husband, whose separate pattern of knowing contrasted with her connected one, she offered this perspective on their difference:

> Whereas [he] is leading to a knowledge outside himself, . . . which is important, but he needs to be more in touch with himself, spiritually, emotionally. . . . I need to be a little bit more logical. So I can say I have a basis for my feeling on this situation. I think it's intelligent in both ways, but I've come to see how important it is to have both things. (Baxter Magolda 1995, 212)

Sheila is not threatened by the difference between her and her husband. She thinks she can benefit from adopting aspects of his approach, just as he can benefit from adopting aspects of hers. She is not defined by her preference; she recognizes it as something she constructed and thus can re-construct.

The need to interact successfully with both men and women, people of various races and cultures, people with various sexual orientations, and people from varied economic backgrounds is prevalent in our society. The fear that is apparent among groups who advocate white supremacy, denial of rights to gay, lesbian, and bisexual people, and affirmative action as discrimination against white males indicates a lack of preparation to deal with difference in adult life. This fear could stem from the inability to look beyond our own ethnocentric values, from being captive of those values. Learning to look beyond them and become the author of our beliefs and values is essential to functioning in a diverse society. Constructive-developmental pedagogy contributes to this ability by promoting self-authorship. It also contributes by giving students opportunities to encounter their diversity effectively in classroom dialogue that welcomes their experience regardless of its nature. Whether people choose to self-author beliefs that appreciate difference is another matter, taken up later in the chapter.

Learning constitutes another arena of public life that makes demands of adults. The rapid growth of technology continues to change adult work life; information-sharing technology requires adults to be lifelong learners to participate in the ever-changing modes of communication. Despite the documented lack of modeling self-direction, most educators expect learners to be self-directed, particularly adult learners. We want them to think for themselves; to think critically; to be able to engage in the gathering, interpretation, and analysis of relevant information; and to make appropriate judgments as a result. Kegan interprets these expectations as a demand for fourth order meaning-making. To be self-directed as a learner, the learner has to be free from the third order system, which relies on external sources to make meaning. The self-authorship that comes with fourth order meaning-making, consistent with constructing one's own knowledge in contextual knowing, enables self-directed learning either in formal education or in everyday life.

THE DEMANDS OF PRIVATE LIFE

Kegan also argues that contemporary society makes demands on adults in their private lives. Although higher education is not specifically charged with enhancing adults' ability to function in their private lives, there is substantial evidence that difficulties in private life spill over into public life. Statistics for divorce, child abuse, and domestic violence indicate that adults struggle to function effectively in private life. Exploring the mental demands on private adult life, Kegan suggests that as intimate partners, we are expected to "be psychologically independent from our partners" and "have a well-differentiated and clearly defined sense of self" (302). The importance of this sense of self is in its ability to avoid taking responsibility for others' feelings. Kegan uses a story about a couple, Peter and Lynn, to demonstrate this issue. Lynn confronts Peter with her displeasure over his extending an invitation to his parents to join the couple on what was to be a second honeymoon. He explains that his parents seemed depressed, and he thought it might cheer them to be included. She explains that she is upset because he sacrificed their plans to please others. Peter's difficulty in this situation is that he organizes himself to please others. He wants to please his wife and his parents. In this instance he reports how he felt:

> The Bad Feeling, that impossible feeling of having to "be" in several places all at the same time, the feeling of being ripped apart, or being pulled in different directions, the feeling of wanting everyone you love to be happy, of even feeling you could *make* them all happy—if only they would cooperate and somehow didn't need it all at once. (Kegan 1994, 117)

This feeling of being ripped apart stems from Peter's organizing himself first to please his wife and then reorganizing himself to please his parents, resulting in his present dilemma. Peter takes responsibility for everyone's feelings and is captive to his relationships.

As Kegan explains, Peter cannot avoid taking internal responsibility for what is not his, because from his third order meaning-making, it *is* his. His lack of a well-differentiated sense of self means that he cocreates himself in his relationships with others. If Peter possessed the sense of self characteristic of fourth order meaning-making, he would no longer be made up by his caring for others. He would be able to consider his parents' unhappiness and decide what to do about it without feeling that he was ignoring their feelings. He could consider Lynn's displeasure with him and decide what to do about it without feeling as if he was being ripped apart. If Peter understood that his parents and Lynn are the makers of their own feelings, and he the maker of his, he could maintain relationships with all of them without feeling responsible for and guilty about their feelings.

Advice for healthy relationships usually includes communicating feelings directly and listening empathically and nondefensively. As is evident from Peter's story, making meaning from the third order makes direct communication and empathic, nondefensive listening extremely difficult. Sheila, whose comments about her relationship with her husband appeared earlier in this chapter, was able to listen nondefensively to her husband and communicate directly about their differences because she had an internal sense of self. Preserving relationships also means managing competing relationships, such as children and parents, in ways that do not negatively affect a couple's relationship. Third order meaning-making makes it impossible to manage these competing relationships and results instead in a futile attempt to please everyone.

Relationships become even more complicated when one becomes a parent. Kegan notes that as parents, we are expected to establish rules and roles for the family, induct family members into a vision we have created, support the development of children, and manage the boundaries between generations. Attempting these tasks from the third order is difficult. Rules and roles for the family stemming from third order meaning-making will be rules and roles cocreated with others, probably the family of origin. Any vision for the family will also be cocreated rather than self-authored. Supporting the development of children requires separating one's relationships with them from what is in their best interests. Parents who make decisions based on maintaining relationships with their children or maintaining children's approval often find themselves making choices that are not best for the children. Managing these relationships can be done more effectively from a separate, internal identity that makes meaning through considering relationships but is not captive to them.

Contemporary society requires interaction with others in private and public life. Self-authorship is essential in managing these complex relationships successfully. Perhaps the most important goal of education should be to promote self-authorship and the kind of meaning-making that makes effective participation in private life and public life possible. Mary Catherine Bateson (1994) offers this perspective:

> It is a mistake to try to reform the educational system without revising our sense of ourselves as learning beings, following a path from birth to death that is longer and more unpredictable than before. Only when that is done will we be in a position to reconstruct educational systems where teachers model learning rather than authority, so that schooling will fit in and perform its limited task within the larger framework of learning before and after and alongside. The avalanche of changes taking place around the world, the changes we should be facing at home, all come as reminders that of all the skills learned in school the most important is the skill to learn over a lifetime those things that no one, including the teachers, yet understands. (1994, 212)

Constructive-developmental pedagogy offers the possibility of promoting this kind of meaning-making, this kind of learning to learn, that makes mastery of one's discipline possible in an ongoing fashion.

PREPARING STUDENTS FOR ACTIVE ROLES IN ENHANCING EDUCATION AND SOCIETY

The development of self-authorship has the potential not only to help adults effectively meet the demands of education and contemporary society, but also to contribute actively to their improvement. Many pressing problems in education and contemporary society stem from inequality among people who must increasingly function interdependently to survive. Constructive-developmental pedagogy promotes self-authorship in the context of working collaboratively with others, thus offering students experience in functioning interdependently through democratic dialogue. This experience, and the complex meaning-making that it makes possible, could result in a more complex understanding of inequality in education and society, and the conviction to actively reduce it. Henry Giroux defines *empowerment* as "the ability to think and act critically" (1992, 11). He argues that individual empowerment must be linked to social betterment, saying, "The freedom and human capacities of individuals must be developed to their maximum but individual powers must be linked to democracy in the sense that social betterment must be the necessary consequence of individual flourishing" (1992, 11).

Constructive-developmental pedagogy reduces inequality in education by placing student experience at the center of the teaching-learning process. When students are invited to contribute their experience and interpretations of that experience to the dialogue, space is created for all experience and all voices. Legitimate exploration of these experiences and views in a mutual dialogue no longer marginalizes experiences of students from nondominant populations. Validation of all students as knowers, and inclusion of their experiences in knowledge construction, creates an educational process made for all participants rather than made for only a few. Constructive-developmental pedagogy develops the voices of students who have previously been silenced or marginalized, helping them achieve self-authorship. Their contributions to the dialogue broaden the understanding of their peers, who are also developing self-authorship. All students gain experience participating in the dialogue, working together to analyze various perspectives, working through conflicts, and creating knowledge together.

Mutual construction of meaning is inclusive of different perspectives and ways of knowing. For example, both relational and impersonal knowing are valued in mutually constructing meaning, modeling a partnership rather than domination of one mode over another. Broadened understanding that emerges from this process, the experience with the process itself as a partnership, and the increased openness to difference that comes with an internal system of making meaning could lead students from dominant populations to promote equality in education rather than resist it. The Joint Center for Political and Economic Studies' (1993) call for an inclusive university to offer equal opportunity for African-American students identifies as an essential goal helping students "to internalize the understanding that there are valid perspectives other than one's own" (38). The dynamics of constructive-developmental pedagogy work toward achieving that goal. At the very least, constructive-developmental pedagogy includes students marginalized by traditional pedagogy and helps them participate in education effectively.

Although the causes of inequality in society are extremely complex, they are surely complicated by our own self-evolution and epistemological beliefs. Kegan builds a compelling argument that more complex forms of making meaning lead to a more complex and open perspective on difference. As noted earlier, third order minds are unable to stand outside their own cultural values and beliefs to entertain alternatives and thus see their perspectives as right. Alternatives are wrong and threatening. Fourth order minds have the ability to separate self from values and beliefs and are willing to consider alternatives as possible and acceptable. Similarly, absolute and transitional knowers are unlikely to consider alternative perspectives from those they have acquired from their cultural authorities due to their belief that knowledge is certain and truth exists. Independent and contextual knowers, with their belief that knowledge and truth are constructed, are willing to entertain new possibilities and continually construct new cultural values and beliefs. More complex forms of making meaning enable us to look at society as a whole, to reflect on the meaning of its organization for all of us, rather than look at it only from our own perspective and its meaning for us personally. These forms of making meaning are essential to the kind of education Giroux advocates—education in which students cross borders to understand other perspectives, locate themselves in history, and "shape the present as part of a discourse and practice that allows people to imagine and desire beyond society's existing limitations and practices" (1992, 22). He suggests that effective education offers students opportunities to analyze conditions that disable others, and offers students designated as "other" to reclaim their voices and visions. Constructive-developmental pedagogy has the potential for such opportunities.

Reflecting on society as a whole and self-authoring one's beliefs about it do not necessarily translate into active work toward equality. Frances Maher and Mary Kay Tetreault note, "The exposure of privileged students to a critique of existing social arrangements does not necessarily make them more willing to give up some of their advantages for a more equal and just society" (1994, 231). Becoming part of a partnership does mean giving up one's privilege. As Riane Eisler (1987) pointed out, however, it means only giving up the right to *dominate* other people. In the partnership society Eisler advocated, all people are included equally in the partnership, each group's development advanced along with, rather than at the expense of, another group's development. There is evidence that complex epistemological development is accompanied by complex moral development, the latter having an influence on willingness to consider a just relationship between self and others, a willingness to join a partnership society.

Blythe Clinchy (1993) explored the connections between epistemological and moral development on the basis of extensive research with both college-age and adult women. Clinchy explained that students who believe knowledge is certain tend to deny different moral perspectives they encounter. For example, two roommates who have different beliefs about sexual relations are aware of the difference but survive as roommates by ignoring it; neither lets the other see any indication of the behavior, and it does not disrupt their relationship. Actual engagement with their differences occurs only when the students believe that some knowledge is uncertain, that it is possible for the roommate to have another view. From this perspective, however, students still rely on their own authorities and acquired values without really listening or entertaining the alternate perspective.

Genuine consideration of different ways of being is possible for the first time in what Clinchy and her colleagues call procedural knowing (Belenky, Clinchy, Goldberger, and Tarule 1986). In procedural knowing, students use a process for coming to know. This process may be a separate one in which the knower stands apart to understand, or a connected one in which the knower attempts to get inside the subject at hand. These processes are similar to what I call individual and interindividual patterns within independent knowing (Baxter Magolda 1992). Clinchy suggested that procedural knowing is accompanied by moral breadth or the appreciation of diverse ways of being, or moral perspectives. However, the separate knower's detachment from the creator of the moral perspective makes her judgment detached from that perspective; the connected knower's immersion in the other's experience makes her unable to judge the moral perspective.

Only at constructed knowing (comparable to contextual knowing) does the person acquire moral depth, defined by Clinchy as bringing oneself into active engagement with others' realities so that one is truly alive to other possibilities. Clinchy describes this active engagement as a person meeting another, experiencing the interaction from the other's perspective, yet still experiencing the interaction from one's own perspective. I take this to be the same distinction Kegan makes between third and fourth order meaning-making—the ability to genuinely experience the other without confusing the other with the self. Clinchy argued that the attainment of moral depth makes other moral perspectives genuine possibilities for the self.

Clinchy also portrayed moral development as occurring through a mutual dialogue. She writes, "In real talk, each participant is an active subject; each speaks as well as listens, trying to articulate her own perspective as well as eliciting others' perspectives. Together, the participants construct new perspectives" (1993, 197). This sounds like the dialogue of constructive-developmental pedagogy, in which each party expresses himself or herself, elicits others' perspectives, and works with others to construct meaning. Mark Tappan and Lyn Mikel Brown suggest this same dialogue to promote moral development: "A narrative approach to moral education provides students with the opportunity to tell their own moral stories and thus to express and enhance their own authority and responsibility through the process of authoring" (1991, 184).

Tappan (1991) elaborated on the dynamics of narrative, authorship, moral authority, and moral responsibility. He advanced that in telling stories about our experience, we make meaning of our experience from a moral perspective. Through this process of authorship, which is mediated by the cultural stories that both enable and constrain our thinking, we develop moral authority. Tappan described this authority as "internally persuasive discourse" (17), or a telling in one's own words rather than the authoritative discourse characterized by reciting others' words. This development of authority is similar to self-authorship in epistemological terms or self-authorship in self-evolution terms.

Tappan also bridged moral authority and moral responsibility, suggesting that people take responsibility for the moral perspectives they author. Yet he believes, following Bakhtin, that moral authority and responsibility occur in dialogic relations with others. Specifically, Tappan writes,

> When an individual claims authority and responsibility for his moral actions, that is, when he achieves authorship, he does not do so on his own, "standing alone." Rather, he does so in the context of an ongoing dialogical relation with others—specific others and generalized others—on whose authority he draws to define and author himself and his own thoughts, feelings, and actions. (1991, 13)

This dialogic nature of moral authority and responsibility is consistent with the dialogic nature of contextual knowing and fourth order meaning-making. In contextual knowing, the self constructs knowledge by drawing on the authority of others as well as one's own, determining one's own thoughts in the process. In fourth order meaning-making, one defines self through the internal system that generates meaning, drawing on others but also drawing on the self-authored meaning-making system.

Viewing development holistically, that is, recognizing that epistemological, self-evolution, and moral development are intertwined in the developing person, suggests the possibility that self-authorship in one arena is accompanied by self-authorship in another. And because theorists describe self-authorship in all arenas as stemming from the same dialogic process, the process could promote self-authorship in any arena. Although constructive-developmental pedagogy is explored in this book primarily as a means to promote knowledge construction, it offers the possibility of promoting self-authorship beyond the epistemological realm. And while there is no guarantee that holistic self-authorship will lead to productive contributions to society, the possibility is still greater than it is with traditional pedagogy.

CONCLUSION

I began this project with a belief that constructive-developmental pedagogy did promote complex epistemological development and effective knowledge construction. This belief stemmed in part from stories that my longitudinal participants told and in part from my own attempts to use constructive-developmental pedagogy. I was less certain about whether constructive-developmental pedagogy worked in various contexts, with various epistemological perspectives, and with diverse instructors. Jo Fischer, Jan Nichols, and Kim Conlin convinced me that constructive-developmental pedagogy could be effective in large classes with entering college students. Sam Rivers convinced me that mathematical structure can be explored productively through constructive-developmental pedagogy and that women who did not believe they could do math could leave such an experience viewing themselves as mathematicians. Chris Snowden convinced me that constructive-developmental pedagogy is useful even in the hardest of sciences. Watching, listening to, and talking with these teachers have broadened my perspective of the forms that constructive-developmental pedagogy can take. Talking with their students, as well as with my own, has deepened my conviction that constructive-developmental pedagogy is not only useful, but also essential to our educational system and our society.

Recapturing student experience and meaning-making as the center of the learning enterprise is crucial to educational reform. Support for this notion is widespread in the educational and human development literature. Much of that literature has been interwoven throughout this book, particularly constructivist perspectives on teaching and constructive-developmental perspectives on human development. Writers focusing on student learning also advocate student experience as the centerpiece. Alexander Astin (1984, 1993) has offered extensive research supporting the notion that student involvement is a key ingredient in successful learning. Increasing students' investment and involvement in learning can be accomplished via constructive-developmental pedagogy. Numerous publications sponsored by the

American College Personnel Association (1994, Blimling 1996) advocate a focus on student learning as an integration of personal development and academic knowledge. Patricia Cross's (1990) well-known concept of classroom research advocates teachers accessing how their particular students think and adjusting their teaching accordingly. Initiatives of the American Association of Higher Education (Hutchings 1996) advocate a new culture for teaching and learning. All of these perspectives are consistent with the concept of constructive-developmental pedagogy.

Much of the literature, this book included, is set in the context of the classroom as a space where teacher and students physically come together. With the advent of technology—the Internet, distance learning, interactive video, and the like—some predict that a substantial portion of education in the future will occur without a "live" interaction between instructors and students. How does that affect constructive-developmental pedagogy? Because constructive-developmental pedagogy is not simply rapport between teacher and student, but a perspective on learning and human development, the three principles can be implemented without physical proximity. Chris Snowden's course demonstrated that mental engagement could be created by an interactive lecture that had minimal verbal interaction. The mental engagement created by validating students as knowers, situating learning in their experience and meaning-making, and mutually constructing meaning can also be created in electronic interactions. An electronic response to a student's thought can be validating of the student as a knower and challenge the person to move toward self-authorship. Perhaps the major barrier in teaching environments without physical contact will be accessing students' meaning-making and helping them share it with their peers. However, if the underlying structure of constructive-developmental pedagogy is used as a way of thinking about learning, teaching, and human development, we can develop new processes to translate this structure into new teaching environments. Creating transitional cultures for the development of students' minds has more to do with linking our thinking with theirs than it does sharing physical space in the same room. Research on creating such cultures in distance learning and other new technological forms will be needed to stretch our thinking on how to reconceptualize our "interactions" with students.

Education will be meaningful to students only if it connects to their lives and their ways of making meaning. Meaningful education in which students are validated as knowers and taught to mutually construct meaning with others can help students learn the knowledge of their disciplines and learn how to contribute to those disciplines by participating in knowledge construction. Terence O'Connor (1997) captures this in what he calls the social action approach to higher education's civic role. Two critical values of a university education characterize the social action approach. First, education should enhance students' ability to contribute to their intellectual traditions. Second, it should assist people in creating shared public institutions. He writes, "In essence, the university becomes a special crossroad where people educated to advance their own cultures meet to understand how to construct a public at the epistemological and cultural intersection of their communities" (1997, 11). He advocates using "the skills of democratic relationships—critical listening, border crossing, caring, conflict resolution, to name a few" (11)—to bring together differences in local traditions to form a cosmopolitan public order. Constructive-developmental pedagogy creates the conditions for this process.

At the same time, and I would argue perhaps more important, constructive-developmental pedagogy develops students' minds to achieve the self-authorship that is necessary to construct knowledge, meet the demands of contemporary society, and take one's place as an active contributor in a democratic society. Constructive-developmental pedagogy, therefore, is not a technique to make education more interesting or to add to our current repertoire. It is, instead, a qualitatively different way to make meaning of the teaching-learning enterprise—a substantial shift in our foundational assumptions about knowledge, authority, and learning. Constructive-developmental pedagogy calls on educators to practice the kind of learning and thinking that our society demands of us as adults.

Appendices

Appendix A

OBSERVATIONAL STUDY METHODS

The qualitative approach is appropriate in studying constructive-developmental pedagogy for a number of reasons. I have used qualitative inquiry because both constructive-developmental pedagogy and students' epistemological development are complex phenomena. How constructive-developmental pedagogy affects students' ways of knowing is a complex phenomenon, playing out differently depending on the instructor, the student, and the interaction of the two. What promotes complex knowing for one student may not for another. Gaining insight into these multiple realities necessitates an approach that is open, flexible, and responsive to new perspectives as they emerge. Although I had sketched a perspective on constructive-developmental pedagogy from educators' writings and possible effects on students' ways of knowing from my previous research, it was not my intention to use these course observations to confirm those perspectives; rather, it was my intention to gain further insight to develop a broader and more complex understanding of constructive-developmental pedagogy.

In this context the project fits a number of categories Peshkin (1993) defined as outcomes of qualitative research. He argued that *description* is valuable in its own right; certainly, a rich description of constructive-developmental pedagogy across diverse contexts offers educators insight into teaching possibilities. Further, a description of students' reactions to constructive-developmental pedagogy can aid faculty in choosing pedagogical goals and strategies to promote complex thinking. Peshkin offered *interpretation* as another qualitative outcome. This project is primarily focused on interpretation in the form of elaborating the existing concept of constructive-developmental pedagogy and its effect on students' ways of knowing, as well as remaining open to new conceptualizations of teaching to connect to students' experience. To some degree, the project also matches Peshkin's category of *verification* in that it helps establish the utility of current assumptions about constructive-developmental pedagogy. Although the project is not an *evaluative* one, the fourth of Peshkin's categories, the collective story that emerges might be used by educators to make judgments about educational practice.

Of course, the choice of the qualitative approach makes certain commonly desired claims impossible. The data will not confirm the utility of constructive-developmental pedagogy for students at large, and it will not describe all the possible forms of connecting teaching to students' experience. Because it is assumed that students will react differently to the same pedagogical practices, the data will not result in a definitive generalization about how constructive-developmental pedagogy affects students' ways of knowing. It will, however, help to expand possibilities for how constructive-developmental pedagogy affects students—possibilities that will help educators consider new pathways for effective teaching.

The issue of subjectivity is central to qualitative research. Because I am advocating the use of student subjectivities in teaching, I can hardly discount them from research on teaching. Students' epistemologies, race, class, gender, and numerous other subjectivities will affect their reaction to pedagogical strategies as well as their expression of their thoughts in an interview. My values of constructive-developmental pedagogy must be taken into account as well. On this issue I followed Peshkin's (1988) advice on use of "a formal, systematic monitoring of self" (20) from which Peshkin discovered his own subjectivities. Noting reactions and analyzing their meaning helped him identify biases, and his increased awareness of them made it possible to manage their influence. I followed this process in order to capitalize on subjectivity and simultaneously avoid its disabling potential (Glesne and Peshkin 1992). This took two primary forms. First, I routinely wrote analytical memos to myself to record my reactions. These memos allowed me to surface assumptions I was making as I observed and talked with participants, monitor reactions, and subsequently identify my biases over time. The biases that I was able to surface included assumptions that constructive-developmental pedagogy required verbal exchanges, that an interpersonal approach on the part of the instructor was necessary, and that any form of lecture was inconsistent with connecting to students' experience. As noted in various discussions in the text, these assumptions turned out to be faulty. Second, I routinely discussed my reactions with my research partner, a graduate student who joined me for observing two of the three courses. We regularly shared our reactions and analytical memos, explored the source of our reactions, and challenged each other to maintain an awareness of our subjectivities during our interpretation of data.

I selected three semester-length college courses to observe constructive-developmental pedagogy in various disciplines (education, math, and science), in various educational levels (lower and upper division, graduate), and in various class sizes (small and large). I approached the instructor of each course on the basis of information I had that indicated the course or the instructor's style might constitute constructive-developmental pedagogy. Instructors agreed to participate and invite their students to participate. These courses are described in more detail below. Observations occurred between 1993 and 1995 at Miami University, a midsize midwestern liberal arts institution. The institution values teaching over research, has a 1-to-20 faculty-to-student ratio, and attracts students who have excelled in high school.

I or my research partner attended all class sessions of each course to observe instructors' teaching practices, interaction between teachers and students, and students' behavior in class. We made field notes on a portable computer during each observation and expanded the notes after each class session. Informal, conversational interviews (Patton 1990) with instructors at the start of the term were conducted to (a) understand the instructor's philosophy of teaching and how it developed from previous experience, (b) understand the instructor's thoughts on the conceptualization and implementation of the course to be observed, and (c) understand the instructor's expectations of what would happen in the course. Similar interviews at the end of the term obtained their reflection on their use of connected teaching in the course and their assessment of its effectiveness. In these interviews my research partner and I also shared our observations and the themes we had generated from our field notes and asked the instructor to reflect on and respond to the interpretations. For EDU 200, I also attended the weekly instructors' meetings.

Students in each course, selected via purposeful sampling when the class was too large to interview all students (primarily in EDU 200), completed the Measure of Epistemological Reflection, or MER (Baxter Magolda and Porterfield 1988), at the start of the term to assess their assumptions about the nature, certainty, and limits of knowledge. The MER (see Appendix B) asked for the respondent's perceptions about the roles of learners, experts, instructors, and peers in learning as well as how learning should be evaluated and how decisions about what to believe are made. The questions are open-ended to avoid leading the response, and follow-up questions ask for reasons for the respondents' perspectives. Although the MER is a qualitative approach, its validity and reliability were documented as part of its construction. Validity data include significant differences across levels of education (Baxter Magolda and Porterfield 1988) and a .93 correlation with an epistemological interview (Baxter Magolda 1987). Interrater reliability is supported by a .80 correlation (N=752) and by interrater agreement ranging from 70 to 80 percent (Baxter Magolda and Porterfield 1985).

An informal, conversational interview with each student at the end of the term focused on the student's reaction to the course and the instructor's teaching practices, reflection on intellectual development and learning during the course, and assessment of the effect of the teaching practices on learning. The student was reminded at the outset of the interview that the interview was confidential. The interview began with a general invitation to talk about reactions to the course. The interview flowed from topics the student introduced. We did ask about topics when students did not introduce them, such as particular course objectives, whether learning included students' experience, and reactions to our interpretations. In the Zoology 400/500 interviews we showed students our interpretation of the teaching format (see fig. 4.1) and asked for their assessment of its accuracy.

Document analysis of syllabi, handouts, assignment descriptions, completed assignments, and course evaluations augmented the observations and interviews. Each syllabus is included in these appendices. For EDU 200 I had access to the written assignments completed by students who participated in the interviews; I observed their class presentations for the pedagogical project. I also read course evaluations for EDU 200 at large and for the two sections observed. For Math by Inquiry and winter biology the instructors talked about students' work and evaluations in the end-of-term interview, but we did not read them directly. In winter biology we received outlines of the student research presentations and attended those presentations. We had access to the reading material in all three courses.

Patton's (1990) process for finding patterns and developing category systems was used to analyze field notes. My research partner and I analyzed field notes individually, coding each idea we identified as we read. We then met to compare our coding systems, talked through discrepancies, and made judgments about the most appropriate codes for each idea. We then used Glaser and Strauss's (1967) constant comparative method for processing naturalistic data, dividing the ideas into units. We then sorted the units into categories that fit together and developed a classification system based on the categories (Patton 1990). The quality of the classification system is determined by judging whether the units in a category fit together in a meaningful way and whether the distinctions between categories are clear (Patton 1990). We adjusted the categories until they accounted for the units accurately. The categories that emerged form the interpretations of each course found in chapters 4 through 6. We used this process to analyze student interview data as well, beginning with coding the transcriptions of the taped interviews.

Use of this systematic process heightened the credibility of our interpretations. Although the subjectivity I and my research partner brought to the data analysis was valuable in gaining an in-depth understanding of the participants' thinking, it was equally important to ensure that our interpretations were grounded in the data. The constant comparative method allows for revisiting interpretations to keep them consistent with the data. Because naturalistic data analysis is an inherently subjective process, we also used some of Lincoln and Guba's (1985) recommendations for enhancing credibility. I sent summaries of my interpretations to participants in EDU 200 to solicit their feedback on my interpretation of that course. The EDU 200 course coordinator and two instructors I observed also read drafts of the chapter on EDU 200 and offered their critiques, which were incorporated into the final version. This member-checking technique served as a test of the accuracy of my interpretations because I had no research partner to observe that course. For the math and zoology courses we discussed our evolving interpretations with the instructors and the students in the postcourse interviews and used their feedback to adjust our interpretations. The instructors also read those chapters, and their critiques were incorporated in the final versions to ensure that our interpretations accurately portrayed what they recognized as having occurred in the courses. Prolonged engagement for fifteen weeks of the semester allowed us to build trust and rapport with the participants, increasing the likelihood of our obtaining their genuine perspectives. This enhanced the trustworthiness of the students' responses in the interviews and to our interpretations. The thick description of the participants and the detailed stories offered here are intended to help the reader judge transferability to contexts beyond the ones in which these examples of constructive-developmental pedagogy took place.

Appendix B

The Measure of Epistemological Reflection

> *Instructions:* The questionnaire that follows has to do with your perspective on learning in college. Each of the questions on the following pages asks for your opinion or choice on a given subject, and the *reasons* why you have that particular perspective or opinion. We are interested in understanding your perspective as fully as possible. Please give as much detail as you can to describe how you feel about each question. Feel free to use the backs of pages if you need more space. Thank you!

PLEASE WRITE YOUR RESPONSES IN INK

NAME: _____

AGE: _____

SEX: (circle one)   MALE   FEMALE

COLLEGE MAJOR: _____

FATHER'S JOB: _____

MOTHER'S JOB: _____

TODAY'S DATE: _____

CLASS RANK: (circle one)

Freshman
Sophomore
Junior
Senior
First-year masters
Second-year masters
Doctoral student
Ph.D.
Other _____

Code# _____
(for office use only)

Measure of Epistemological Reflection   Protocol #_____
Page 2

THINK ABOUT THE LAST TIME YOU HAD TO MAKE A MAJOR DECI-
SION ABOUT YOUR EDUCATION IN WHICH YOU HAD A NUMBER
OF ALTERNATIVES (E.G., WHICH COLLEGE TO ATTEND, COLLEGE
MAJOR, CAREER CHOICE, ETC.). WHAT WAS THE NATURE OF THE
DECISION?

_____
_____
_____
_____

WHAT ALTERNATIVES WERE AVAILABLE TO YOU?

_____
_____
_____
_____

HOW DID YOU FEEL ABOUT THESE ALTERNATIVES?

_____
_____
_____
_____

HOW DID YOU GO ABOUT CHOOSING FROM THE ALTERNA-
TIVES?

_____
_____
_____
_____

WHAT THINGS WERE THE MOST IMPORTANT CONSIDERATIONS IN
YOUR CHOICE? PLEASE GIVE DETAILS.

_____
_____
_____
_____

Measure of Epistemological Reflection   Protocol #_____
Page 3

DO YOU LEARN BEST IN CLASSES WHICH FOCUS ON FACTUAL IN-
FORMATION OR CLASSES WHICH FOCUS ON IDEAS AND CONCEPTS?

_____
_____
_____
_____

WHY DO YOU LEARN BEST IN THE TYPE OF CLASS YOU CHOSE
ABOVE?

_____
_____
_____
_____

WHAT DO YOU SEE AS THE ADVANTAGES OF THE CHOICE YOU
MADE ABOVE?

_____
_____
_____
_____

WHAT DO YOU SEE AS THE DISADVANTAGES OF THE CHOICE YOU
MADE ABOVE?

_____
_____
_____
_____

IF YOU COULD GIVE ADVICE TO ANYONE ON HOW BEST TO SUC-
CEED IN COLLEGE COURSEWORK, WHAT KIND OF ADVICE WOULD
YOU GIVE THEM? TALK ABOUT WHAT *YOU* BELIEVE IS THE KEY TO
DOING WELL IN COLLEGE COURSES.

_____
_____
_____
_____

Measure of Epistemological Reflection   Protocol #_____
Page 4

DURING THE COURSE OF YOUR STUDIES, YOU HAVE PROBABLY HAD INSTRUCTORS WITH DIFFERENT TEACHING METHODS. AS YOU THINK BACK TO INSTRUCTORS YOU HAVE HAD, DESCRIBE THE METHOD OF INSTRUCTION WHICH HAD THE MOST BENEFICIAL EFFECT ON YOU.

_____
_____
_____
_____

WHAT MADE THAT TEACHING METHOD BENEFICIAL? PLEASE BE SPECIFIC AND USE EXAMPLES.

_____
_____
_____
_____

WERE THERE ASPECTS OF THAT TEACHING METHOD WHICH WERE NOT BENEFICIAL? IF SO, PLEASE TALK ABOUT SOME OF THE ASPECTS AND WHY THEY WERE NOT BENEFICIAL.

_____
_____
_____
_____

WHAT ARE THE MOST IMPORTANT THINGS YOU LEARNED FROM THE INSTRUCTOR'S METHOD OF TEACHING?

_____
_____
_____
_____

PLEASE DESCRIBE THE TYPE OF RELATIONSHIP WITH AN INSTRUC-TOR THAT WOULD HELP YOU TO LEARN BEST AND EXPLAIN WHY.

_____
_____
_____
_____

<u>Measure of Epistemological Reflection</u>   Protocol #_____
Page 5

DO YOU PREFER CLASSES IN WHICH THE STUDENTS DO A LOT OF
TALKING, OR WHERE STUDENTS DON'T TALK VERY MUCH?

_____
_____
_____
_____

WHY DO YOU PREFER THE DEGREE OF STUDENT INVOLVEMENT/
PARTICIPATION THAT YOU CHOSE ABOVE?

_____
_____
_____
_____

WHAT DO YOU SEE AS THE ADVANTAGES OF YOUR PREFERENCE
ABOVE?

_____
_____
_____
_____

WHAT DO YOU SEE AS THE DISADVANTAGES OF YOUR PREFER-
ENCE?

_____
_____
_____
_____

WHAT TYPE OF INTERACTIONS WOULD YOU LIKE TO SEE AMONG
MEMBERS OF A CLASS IN ORDER TO ENHANCE YOUR OWN LEARN-
ING?

_____
_____
_____
_____
_____
_____

Measure of Epistemological Reflection   Protocol #_____
Page 6

SOME PEOPLE THINK THAT HARD WORK AND EFFORT WILL RESULT
IN HIGH GRADES IN SCHOOL. OTHERS THINK THAT HARD WORK
AND EFFORT ARE NOT A BASIS FOR HIGH GRADES. WHICH OF
THESE STATEMENTS IS MOST LIKE YOUR OWN OPINION?

_____
_____
_____
_____

IDEALLY, WHAT DO YOU THINK SHOULD BE USED AS A BASIS FOR
EVALUATING YOUR WORK IN COLLEGE COURSES?

_____
_____
_____
_____

WHO SHOULD BE INVOLVED IN THE EVALUATION YOU DESCRIBED
ABOVE?

_____
_____
_____
_____
_____

PLEASE EXPLAIN WHY YOU THINK THE RESPONSE YOU SUGGESTED
ABOVE IS THE BEST WAY TO EVALUATE STUDENTS' WORK IN COL-
LEGE COURSES.

_____
_____
_____
_____
_____
_____
_____

Measure of Epistemological Reflection   Protocol #_____
Page 7

SOMETIMES DIFFERENT INSTRUCTORS GIVE DIFFERENT EXPLANA-
TIONS FOR HISTORICAL EVENTS OR SCIENTIFIC PHENOMENA.
WHEN TWO INSTRUCTORS EXPLAIN THE SAME THING DIFFER-
ENTLY, CAN ONE BE MORE CORRECT THAN THE OTHER?

_____

_____

WHEN TWO EXPLANATIONS ARE GIVEN FOR THE SAME SITUATION,
HOW WOULD YOU GO ABOUT DECIDING WHICH EXPLANATION TO
BELIEVE? PLEASE GIVE DETAILS AND EXAMPLES.

_____

_____

_____

_____

CAN ONE EVER BE SURE OF WHICH EXPLANATION TO BELIEVE? IF
SO, HOW?

_____

_____

_____

_____

_____

IF ONE CAN'T BE SURE OF WHICH EXPLANATION TO BELIEVE, WHY
NOT?

_____

_____

_____

_____

_____

Appendix C

OVERVIEW OF LONGITUDINAL STUDY METHODS

I began a longitudinal study of college students' epistemological development, fall semester, 1986. Fifty men and 51 women first-year students were randomly selected to participate during their first semester of college at Miami University, a midwestern, public, four-year institution (described in chap. 1). They came from a variety of majors within all six divisions of the university, which has a liberal arts focus. Admission is competitive, and these students entering class had a mean ACT score of 25.8; 70 percent had ranked in the top 20 percent of their high school class. The campus culture encouraged high involvement in campus activities, with one-third of the student body involved in Greek organizations. Of these 101 students, 80 participated in all four years of the study.

Seventy participants continued in the postcollege phase of the study, 59 graduated within four years, and the remaining 11 in five years. Only 2 were members of ethnic/racial minorities. The group remained fairly balanced by gender, with 37 women and 33 men in the fifth year, 29 women and 22 men in the sixth year, 27 women and 21 men in the seventh year, 24 women and 18 men in the eighth year, 22 women and 19 men in the ninth year, and 20 women and 17 men in the tenth year. The occupational fields of the postcollege participants included insurance, sales, accounting, computing, teaching, mental health, advertising, communications, business, banking, real estate, retail management, airline services, and government services. Twelve were in advanced academic settings full-time, and 13 pursued a formal advanced education while holding full-time jobs. Seventeen were married, 3 had children, and 2 were divorced.

In annual interviews I invited students to talk about their role as learners, the role of instructors and peers, the perception of evaluation of their work, the nature of knowledge, and decision making. These revealed epistemic assumptions, as well as experiences that affected those assumptions. The question in each area introduced the topic but did nothing to frame the response. For example, I introduced the nature of knowledge with, "Have you ever encountered a situation in which you heard two explanations for the same idea?" When students said yes, I invited them to describe the experience, their reaction to it, and the way they decided what to believe. Follow-up questions clarified each student's responses, and I routinely summarized the responses to make sure I understood the perspective. The interviews were tape-recorded and transcribed verbatim. Students also completed the Measure of Epistemological Reflection (Baxter Magolda and Porterfield 1988) as another means to acquire their epistemic assumptions.

I altered the interview process during the postcollege phase of the study. I used qualitative interviews similar to those used in the college phase to keep the focus on learners' stories. The fact that few researchers have explored epistemological development after college increased the importance of allowing insights to emerge from the learners' experiences, prompting the use of an informal conversational interview (Patton 1990). I began the annual interview with a summary of the project focus, reiterating my interest in exploring how participants learned and decided what to believe. The participant was then asked to think about important learning experiences that had taken place since the previous interview one year ago. The participant volunteered those experiences, describing them and their impact on her or his thinking. I asked questions to pursue why these experiences were important, which factors influenced the experiences, and how the learner was affected. The interview addressed learning experiences in work life, everyday life, and academic life, if applicable. Work experiences invariably involved discussion about the worker's role, relationships with coworkers, supervision issues, and daily decisions. Academic experiences involved discussion of the learning environment; the role learners, teachers, and peers played; and how work was evaluated. Discussions about everyday life revolved around insights that participants gained from interpersonal relationships and everyday living. All interviews were by telephone, and they ranged from sixty to ninety minutes. All interviews were tape-recorded and transcribed verbatim.

I analyzed interview responses using Glaser and Strauss's (1967) constant comparative method for processing naturalistic data. I reviewed transcriptions of the interviews, dividing them into units that represented one idea. I then sorted the units into categories that fit together and developed a classification system based on those categories (Patton 1990). The quality of the classification system is determined by judging whether the units in a category fit together in a meaningful way and whether the distinctions between categories are clear (Patton 1990). I adjusted the categories until they accounted for the units accurately. The analysis met Lincoln and Guba's (1985) recommendation that an accurate classification system should contain no more than 5 percent miscellaneous items.

This systematic process heightened credibility of my interpretations. The subjectivity I bring to the analysis is valuable in gaining an understanding of the participants, but it is equally important to ensure that my interpretations are grounded in the data. The constant comparative method allows for revisiting interpretations to keep them consistent with the data. Because naturalistic data analysis is an inherently subjective process, I also used some of Lincoln and Guba's (1985) recommendations for enhancing credibility. I sent summaries of my interpretations to participants and solicited feedback during interviews. This member checking served as a test of accuracy. Prolonged engagement over ten years allowed me to build trust and rapport with the participants, increasing the likelihood of my obtaining their genuine perspectives. This enhanced the trustworthiness of the students' responses to the interviews and to my interpretations.

A full description of the methods and findings of the college study can be found in *Knowing and Reasoning in College* (Baxter Magolda 1992), and findings from the postcollege phase are published as well (Baxter Magolda 1995, 1998).

Appendix D

SYLLABUS FOR STUDENT DEVELOPMENT THEORY

EDL 601 STUDENT DEVELOPMENT THEORY II
Spring, Miami University

"A bridge must be well anchored on both sides, with as much respect for
where it begins as for where it ends." KEGAN 1994, 62

Dr. Marcia B. Baxter Magolda
311B McGuffey Hall
9-6837

Office Hours:
By Appointment: sign-up
sheets are on my door

Course Goals: To engage in dialogue about

1. Central themes of human development—self-evolution, meaning-
   making, separation—connection, and moral meaning-making—as
   they offer possible windows into late adolescent and adult life.
2. Integration of these themes with those addressed in EDL 600 (psychosocial and epistemological) and critical evaluation of the value of
   this theoretical knowledge base.
3. Assessing student (including adult) development and integrating assessment with theory development.
4. Effective application of student (including adult) development theory
   in practice.

NATURE OF THE COURSE

This course explores how college students and other adults construct themselves and the meaning they make of their experience. Because this construction takes place in the context of one's culture and psychological "surround,"
we will explore in an integrated fashion a) the environments created for late
adolescents and adults in colleges and everyday life and b) these environments' interplay with epistemological structures that govern how one makes
meaning of experience. The course begins at adolescence to pursue possibilities regarding why college students make meaning in particular ways when
they arrive at college; it then moves to adult development to pursue possibilities regarding how meaning-making might evolve during college; finally, it

moves to later adulthood for possibilities of future evolution that may be required in our culture. The purpose of this journey into adult meaning-making is to understand and respect both sides of the possible bridges through adult life. Our role as educators is to be bridge builders—helping students to span the distance between our culture's expectations of them and the way they make meaning. In order to effectively play that role, we must understand what anchors each bridge at its beginning, what it takes to get across, and what anchors the other side.

This course will continue the "theory development" approach used in EDL 600. This approach is based on the view that student development theory is constructed by observing and talking with students about their experiences. As such, existing theories describe particular students in particular contexts. Because no theory is able to describe the diversity that exists among students, understanding students requires understanding how to develop theory. As we add to our theoretical base from EDL 600, we will continue to do so from a "theory development" approach. This means we will collect data from students [as part of an application assignment] and interpret it to generate new theoretical possibilities. We will compare these to existing perspectives and combine them to form the basis for application. In addition to developing an advanced knowledge of theory, the course aims to advance ability to develop practice to intentionally promote development.

This course will require integration—of previous knowledge and experience with the readings, of the readings with the data we collect—and synthesis of all of this for how we practice. It is an opportunity for you to develop expertise through reading widely, engaging in spirited discussion, to engage in critical thinking, to develop your perspective on student development theory, and to integrate that into your professional practice. I believe we can best accomplish this through a collaborative work setting. Successful collaboration requires a number of characteristics: preparing prior to class; sharing ideas, insights and questions in class; taking risks to share thoughts that are not fully developed; helping each other express ideas; avoiding domination; building on each other's ideas; disagreeing when it is helpful to do so; and genuinely listening to each other, to name a few. As most of you know, relational pedagogy—or connecting learning to students' lived experience—is a cornerstone of my thinking about teaching and learning. This perspective has evolved from my research on students' intellectual development and teaching processes that promote complex thinking. My commitment to this form of teaching means that I will attempt to convince you that you do possess knowledge about student development, situate our discussions in your experience, and encourage you to engage in mutually constructing meaning with the authors of the readings, me, and your classmates. As Ira Shor notes, this type of learning is not a "know-nothing" process. I take this to mean that it is my responsibility to introduce you to various forms of knowledge about student development and it is your responsibility to work with me to connect that knowledge to your own experience and beliefs. I think this is consistent with our learning community and consistent with the nature of the evolving issue we are studying. The course expectations regarding participation stem from this perspective.

COURSE EXPECTATIONS

1. Active Learning. This involves active reading and participation, described below:

    A) *Active Reading:* Active reading means doing the following for each reading: list points you think are important, questions you have, inconsistencies you find, areas of interest, and connections with other readings both in this course and others. Active learning means that you not only read the readings, but that you develop points of view about what the authors say and do some critical analysis of the ideas in the readings. The nature of the course necessitates completing the assigned reading prior to class sessions. Some are *extensive* and many are difficult reading, so review the reading schedule in order to organize your time effectively. One number on the outline may mean several chapters. I have intentionally reduced the reading load in this course in favor of in-depth processing of the reading selected. We will discuss in the first session how to work with these readings and what you will be expected to bring to class as a result. Our discussions will hinge on the readings and the quality of the discussion will depend on class members' understanding of the readings. You will also need to use this information in your assignments.

    B) *Active Participation:* Active participation means that you bring your insights and contribute them to the class discussion. It also means engaging actively with the thoughts of your colleagues—listening carefully, responding openly to, and making connections among others' contributions. It probably goes without saying that attendance is essential for active participation; however, unsaid expectations do not make for effective communication. Attendance is essential; although I know that circumstances sometimes prevent attendance, it is your responsibility to minimize absences. Missing three sessions will require additional work to complete the course; missing four will result in being automatically dropped from the course.

2. Class members are expected to complete assessment instruments as assigned, as well as administer assessment instruments as assigned, to develop assessment skills.

3. Assignments are explained on attached pages. Details regarding these assignments are attached, and due dates are on the course outline.

4. Deadline policy: All assignments are due at class time. Late papers must be accompanied by a written explanation justifying the delay. Should I judge the explanation to be reasonable you will receive the same credit you would have received had it been on time. If the justification is not reasonable, I reserve the right to alter or eliminate credit for the assignment.

REQUIRED READING

Required Texts:

1. Kegan, R. (1994). *In over our heads: The mental demands of modern life.* Cambridge, MA: Harvard University.

2. Gilligan, C., Ward, J. V., and Taylor, J. M. (1988). *Mapping the moral domain: A contribution of women's thinking to psychological theory and education.* Cambridge, MA: Harvard University Graduate School of Education.

Additional required reading is noted on the attached Required Reading List, which also incorporates use of the above texts. Readings are on reserve in King Library and 311 McGuffey Hall (except texts).

Evaluation (To be negotiated)

Application   _____%
Self-Reflection _____%
Proposal   _____%

Course Outline

Dates	Topics	Readings
1/16	Introduction, Negotiate class plans, Themes of Development, define holding environment	
1/23	Adolescent Themes	1, 2 **SR Part 1 due**
1/30	Adolescent Themes continued: tie in psychosocial and intellectual from 600	3, 4 and review 5 & 6 **AA Part 1 due**
2/6	Implications of Adolescent Themes for college students; campus issues	**SR Part 2 due**
2/13	Adult Themes	7 **AA Part 2 due**
2/20; no meeting; Monday classes meet		Work on your assignments!!
2/27	Assessment (S-O Interview)	8, 9
3/5	Patterns within Adult Themes	10, 11, 12 **SR Part 3 Due**
3/12	Implications for college issues; college environment	13, 14, 15
3/26	Application of Adult Themes: educational & work environments	16, 17 **AA Part 3 Due**
4/2	Application of Adult Themes: diversity issues	18 **SR Part 4 Due**
4/9	Later Adult Themes	19, 20 **SR Part 5 Due** **Proposal Due**
4/16	Later Adult Themes	21
4/23	Integration	22, 23 **SR Due**
4/30	AA dialogue	**AA Due**

EDL 601 Student Development Theory II
Required Reading List
Spring

1. Brown, Lyn Mikel. (1991). A problem of vision: The development of voice and relational knowledge in girls ages seven to sixteen. *Women's Studies Quarterly,* 1&2, 52-71.

2. Kegan, R. (1994). *In over our heads: The mental demands of modern life.* Cambridge, MA: Harvard University. [prologue, Chapters 1 and 2]

3. Gilligan, C., Ward, J. V., and Taylor, J. M. (1988). *Mapping the moral domain: A contribution of women's thinking to psychological theory and education.* Cambridge, MA: Harvard University Graduate School of Education. [prologue, Chapters 1, 7, 8, & 9]

4. Lyons, N. (1987). Ways of knowing, learning and making moral choices. *Journal of Moral Education,* 16 (3), 226-39.

5. Review Baxter Magolda, M. B. (1992). *Knowing and reasoning in college: Gender-related patterns in students' intellectual development.* San Francisco: Jossey-Bass. [Chapter 2; pp. 28-72—you already read this for 600]

6. Review Chickering, A. W., and Reisser, L. (1993). *Education and identity,* second edition. San Francisco: Jossey-Bass. (Chapter One, A Current Theoretical Context for Student Development, pp. 1-41— you already read this for 600) for overview of intellectual and psychosocial development.

7. Kegan, R. (1994). *In over our heads: The mental demands of modern life.* Cambridge, MA: Harvard University. [Chapters 3 and 4]

8. Lahey, L., Souvaine, E., Kegan, R., Goodman, R., & Felix, S. (1988). *A guide to the Subject-Object Interview: Its administration and interpretation.* Cambridge, MA: Subject-Object Research Group. (Available from Subject-Object Research Group, c/o Dr. Robert Kegan, 201 Nichols House, Harvard Graduate School of Education, Cambridge, MA.) [pp. 290-355]

9. Gibbs, J. C., Widaman, K. F., & Colby, A. (1982). Construction and validation of a simplified, group-administerable equivalent to the Moral Judgment Interview. *Child Development,* 53, 895-910.

10. Gilligan, C., Ward, J. V., and Taylor, J. M. (1988). *Mapping the moral domain: A contribution of women's thinking to psychological theory and*

education. Cambridge, MA: Harvard University Graduate School of Education. [Chapters 2, 3, & 4]

11. Kegan, R. (1994). *In over our heads: The mental demands of modern life.* Cambridge, MA: Harvard University. [Chapters 5 and 6]

12. Surrey, Janet L. (1991). The "self-in-relation": A theory of women's development. In Judith Jordan et al. (eds.), *Women's growth in connection: Writings from the Stone Center,* pp. 51-66. New York: Guilford Press.

13. Kegan, R. (1994). *In over our heads: The mental demands of modern life.* Cambridge, MA: Harvard University. [Chapters 7 and 8]

14. Ignelzi, M. (1986). *Developmental Supervision: A constructive-developmental Case Analysis.* Class paper, Harvard University.

15. Ignelzi, M. G. (1990). Ethical education in a college environment: The just community approach. *NASPA Journal,* 27 (3), 192-98.

16. Ireland, L. (ed.). (1995). *Bridging the gap: A student development approach to helping SEAP students meet the demands of understanding and appreciating diversity.* Oxford, OH: Miami University, Department of Educational Leadership.

17. Tappan, M. B., and Brown, L. Mikel. (1991). Stories told and lessons learned. In C. Witherell and N. Noddings (eds.), *Stories lives tell* (pp. 171-92). New York: Teachers College Press.

18. Review Chapter 6 of Kegan.

19. Kegan, R. (1994). *In over our heads: The mental demands of modern life.* Cambridge, MA: Harvard University. [Chapter 9]

20. Daloz, L. A. (1986). *Effective teaching and mentoring.* San Francisco: Jossey-Bass. [Chapter 7, pp. 186-208; Chapter 8, pp. 209-35]

21. Kegan, R. (1994). *In over our heads: The mental demands of modern life.* Cambridge, MA: Harvard University. [Chapter 10]

22. Daloz Parks, Sharon. (1993). Young adults, mentoring communities, and the conditions of moral choice. In A. Garrod, ed., *Approaches to moral development: New research and emerging themes,* pp. 214-27. New York: Teachers College, Columbia University.

23. Clinchy. B. M. (1991). Ways of knowing and ways of being: Epistemological and moral development in undergraduate women. In A. Garrod, ed., *Approaches to moral development: New research and emerging themes,* pp. 180-200. New York: Teachers College, Columbia University.

Supplementary Reading List
EDL 601 Spring

On Moral Development

1. Colby, A., & Kohlberg, L. (1987). *The measurement of moral judgment:* Volume 1. Cambridge, MA: Cambridge University Press. (pp. 1-35)

2. Gilligan, C. (1982). *In a different voice.* Cambridge, MA: Harvard University. (Chapter 3; pp. 64-105)

On Assessing Moral Development

3. Colby, A., & Kohlberg, L. (1987). *The measurement of moral* judgment: Volume 1. Cambridge, MA: Cambridge University Press. (pp. 151-58)

4. Gibbs, J. C., Arnold, K. D., Morgan, R. L., Schwartz, E. S., Gavaghan, M. P., & Tappan, M. B. (1984). Construction and validation of a multiple-choice measure of moral reasoning. *Child Development, 55,* 527-36.

[see also the syllabus for the EDL 661 Inquiry Course, Spring]

On Sex Differences in Moral Development

5. Gibbs, J. C., Arnold, K. D., & Burkhart, J. E. (1984). Sex differences in the expression of moral judgment. *Child Development, 55,* 1040-43.

6. Stiller, N. J., & Forrest, L. (1990). An extension of Gilligan and Lyon's investigation of morality: Gender differences in college students. *Journal of College Student Development, 31,* 54-63.

7. Baumrind, D. (1986). Sex differences in moral reasoning: Response to Walker's (1984) conclusion that there are none. *Child Development, 57,* 511-21.

8. Walker, L. J. (1986). Sex differences in the development of moral reasoning: A rejoinder to Baumrind. *Child Development, 57,* 522-26.

On Using Moral Development Theory in Practice

9. Hotelling, K., & Forrest, L. (1985). Gilligan's theory of sex-role development: A perspective for counseling. *Journal of Counseling and Development, 64,* 183-86.

10. Thomas, R. L. (1987). Systems for guiding college student behavior: Punishment or growth? *NASPA Journal, 25,* 54-61.

11.   Porterfield, W .D., and Pressprich, S. T. (1988). Carol Gilligan's per-
       spectives and staff supervision: Implications for the practitioner.
       NASPA Journal, 25 (4), 244-48.

On Later Adult Development

12.   Merriam, S. B., and Caffarella, R. S. (1991). *Learning in adulthood.*
       San Francisco: Jossey-Bass. (Chapter 6, pp. 96-119)

13.   Merriam, S. B., and Caffarella, R. S. (1991). *Learning in adulthood.*
       San Francisco: Jossey-Bass. (Chapter 10, pp. 181-202)

14.   Heath, D. H. (1991). *Fulfilling lives: Paths to maturity and success.* San
       Francisco: Jossey-Bass. Chapters 28 (pp. 309-14) and 29 (pp. 315-27)

15.   Merriam, S. B., and Clark, M. C. (1991). *Lifelines: Patterns of work,
       love, and learning in adulthood.* San Francisco: Jossey-Bass. (Chapters
       1-2; pp. 1-36)

APPLICATION ASSIGNMENT

This assignment is an opportunity for you to explore using theory in practice in an area that interests you, with an issue you find pressing, with a student group you wish to engage. The process outlined below is a generic one,
usable for all areas of practice. Using it in one specific area will help you gain
an in-depth understanding of translating theory to practice that you can
then use in other areas of your practice. This assignment is similar to—but
more in—depth than—the EDL 600 application assignment. The emphasis
here is on a) learning to conceptualize a practice issue from a developmental
frame, b) gathering the data you need to interpret what is taking place from
a developmental frame and to ground your practice in actual assessment, c)
designing or redesigning practice based on your developmental interpretation, and d) persuading student affairs professionals to implement your practice plan.

Steps in the process:

1.   Describe a Student Affairs goal in educating college students [e.g., treat
      each other with respect (reduce hazing, date rape, cultural discrimina-
      tion); respect self (reduce eating disorders, alcohol abuse, etc.); engage
      in healthy relationships; self-authorship in and out of class . . .]. Next,
      describe a context in which you can pursue this [e.g., a group you work
      with, an office, a residence hall]. Explain why this is a good context for
      your project. Read about this area and talk to professionals and stu-
      dents in order to identify: a] what demands are placed on students, b]

what holding environment exists for them, and c] how they are affect-ed by these holding environments. [*due 1/30*]

2. Figure out what ways of making meaning [Kegan orders of conscious-ness, moral voice orientations, ways of knowing] our Student Affairs culture (at Miami, and in the larger context of what our profession believes) demands from students in the context you selected in #1 above. In other words, what ways of making meaning would be required to function in the ways Student Affairs would like students to function to achieve the goal in question? [*due 2/13*]

3. Assess students' ways of making meaning [Kegan orders of conscious-ness, patterns within those, moral orientations, ways of knowing]. This means giving the appropriate assessment instruments/interviews to the students in the group with whom you choose to work and interpreting the results. [*due 3/26*]

4. Build the bridge for transforming students' ways of making meaning from where they are to where the culture wants them to be. This requires understanding their side of the bridge [ways of making meaning] well enough to know how to build the transition. You want to design practice specifically to transform their orders of conscious-ness to accomplish in the long-term their ability to meet the demands in the area in which you are practicing. Use both knowl-edge from this course and 600 to articulate specifically what this bridge looks like and what it is supposed to accomplish. Write this in a way that helps convince practitioners that they should implement this plan. [*due 4/30*]

This is an individual assignment, but collaboration is encouraged and sharing of your work in class is also expected. We will share progress on these as we go and use the data you collect to update existing theory. I also devoted the last session to sharing the bridges. I established due dates for portions of this assignment to keep your work in sync with the class dis-cussions.

Rather than assigning a grade to each segment, I would prefer to read each one, provide feedback for improvement, and offer my perception of a grade for that portion for that draft. You may then decide whether to maintain that portion as is or enhance it before turning in the final paper. This means that you will be able to receive feedback and potentially revise the first three parts before turning in the final version. *The entire project is due 4/30.*

SELF-REFLECTION ASSIGNMENT

Processing theoretical perspectives is often enhanced by processing them in the context of your own developmental experience. Kegan, among others, argues that we make meaning from our own frame of reference—thus our work with college students is "made sense of" within the context of our own development—how we construct ourselves, how we relate to others, how we interpret the situations in which we work. Understanding ourselves is essential to understanding how we interact with, or in our case, work to guide, students. Self-reflection also provides a critique of theoretical perspectives against one set of empirical data—our own experience. This self-reflection extends the work you did in EDL 600 on your story.

Segments of this self-reflection include:

1. A description of the holding environments you can identify that have surrounded you recently and how they are affecting you; [*due 1/23*]

2. Frustrations, current dilemmas, issues, struggles or major questions you can identify that you are currently experiencing; [*due 2/6*]

3. An assessment of your ways of making meaning (Kegan orders, moral orientations, both integrated with psychosocial and intellectual assessments from 600); this would involve using the Subject-Object interview, a moral orientation assessment tool, and other means you might identify as well as your own self-reflection; [*due 3/5*]

4. Insights about how your ways of making meaning affect the issues you raised in part 2—raise possibilities here; [*due 4/2*]

5. An analysis of how your current holding environment helps or does not help with these issues; [*due 4/9*]

6. Thoughts about this overall interpretation of yourself . . . [*due 4/23*]

I think this self-reflection will be most helpful if it takes place simultaneously with our class explorations. Knowing the demands on your lives, and that those demands with what appear to be faraway deadlines get put off, I have chosen due dates for portions of this assignment. This will also give us an opportunity to exchange thoughts on your self-reflection while it is in progress.

Rather than assigning a grade to each segment, I would prefer to read each one, provide feedback for improvement, and offer my perception of a grade for that portion for that draft. You may then decide whether to maintain that portion as is or enhance it before turning in the final paper. This means that you will be able to receive feedback and potentially revise the first five parts before turning in the final version. *The entire reflection is due 4/23.*

Note: As always, this assignment is confidential. You are free to judge the degree to which you wish to divulge your experience in completing this assignment. If you would be more comfortable with an assignment that does not involve self-reflection, I will be happy to develop one with you.

PROPOSAL FOR DEVELOPMENTALLY BASED PRACTICE

You are nearing graduation from your Masters program in CSP and are in the midst of your job search. In many of your interviews, the issue of creating student affairs practice to promote student development has been a hot topic. Three of the positions you really like require a proposal for developmentally based practice as part of the application process. They are all mid-size schools with comprehensive student affairs divisions. Luckily for you, this proposal is also one of the assignments for your theory two course!

Prepare a proposal that includes the following content:

1. A basic position on the role of student development theory in student affairs practice. Your position should be substantiated with the literature you've studied in your theory courses.

2. A framework for translating theory to practice. This could be a framework you develop, or one that exists in the literature. In either case, you will need to explain the framework clearly and justify its use as a reasonable way to use theory.

3. Two examples of how to use this framework in two different student affairs areas. These examples should include the developmental goal, how practice would be organized to achieve it, and how progress toward the goal would be assessed.

4. A brief statement about the possibilities and dilemmas inherent in your proposal. This should include how you think this approach will improve practice and any constraints you envision with this approach.

The style of your proposal should take into account the following:

1. The reader may not be familiar with student development theory or the related language. You will have to decide how to communicate your ideas in language that maintains the integrity of the ideas, yet is accessible to most professionals with limited knowledge of theory.

2. Because you are doing this for a job application, the length must be reasonable. Five pages would be ideal; seven is the maximum you would dare to submit. This means thinking through your content

carefully and writing concisely. To do so without sacrificing content and clarity is very difficult; I recommend that you have a peer and a practitioner review drafts of your proposal before you submit the final version.

3.   Again, because this is related to a job application, attention to small details is crucial! Make sure you adhere to APA style, avoid errors, and use appropriate grammar and punctuation.

The employers are expecting sound proposals—particularly from those of you who have had two student development theory courses. This is your chance to make a difference in practice by articulating how to use theory effectively in student affairs work.

Appendix E

CSP LEARNING COMMUNITY PHILOSOPHY
Miami University

The Student Affairs profession is founded on promoting the holistic development of students. Our approach to addressing this dimension of preparation is to create within our graduate program what we call a "Community of Scholars." This phrase suggests that members of our learning community—students, faculty, and student affairs practitioners—are all scholars who come together to share their expertise, and to expand and deepen their understanding through the sharing of divergent ideas. Our education starts with learners' experiences and encourages them to develop their understanding of knowledge sources in connection with their own lives and beliefs. This pedagogy draws learners into the process of knowing, exploring, critically analyzing, and making decisions about various forms of knowledge.

A significant dimension of our preparation is preparing students to use others' expertise, share one's own expertise, learn from multiple perspectives, make reasonable judgments about those perspectives, and engage in collaborative decision-making about educational practice that promotes holistic student development. Higher education institutions are lifelong learning communities where students, faculty, and staff continually explore new perspectives, reconstruct knowledge as conditions change, and transform their practice to maintain a successful educational environment. Acquiring the skills to engage in these activities is an essential foundation if student affairs educators are to effectively put their knowledge into practice.

Inherent in this type of learning community are expectations for participation that differ from those assumed in more traditional forms of education. CSP students are expected to actively participate in the process of learning. Class time is spent in discussion involving critical analysis of the material, sharing connections between individual experiences and the material, and working collaboratively to make meaning of the multiple perspectives we study.

Appendix F

SYLLABUS FOR WINTER BIOLOGY
Zoo 400/500 Winter Biology

Spring   Chris Snowden, Instructor

Course Objective: This course provides an introduction to biochemical, physiological and ecological adaptations of plants and animals to not only survive, but remain active during the winter. Emphasis is placed on integrating students' previous knowledge in the physical and biological sciences to understand the cellular, organismal and evolutionary challenges faced by organisms, including humans, living in environments that experience low temperature and related winter stresses. This course requires extensive reading of primary scientific literature, completion of a collaborative small group library assignment, writing a major research paper and grant proposal, and presenting a formal seminar (3 semester credits).

Class: Tuesday and Thursday Lecture 2:00-3:15 P.M., plus 1-2 evenings.

Office hours: Tuesday and Thursday 1:00-2:00 P.M. or freely by appointment at 529-0000 (office) or 523-0000 (home).

Textbook: Marchand, P. J. 1991. *Life in the Cold.* University Press of New England (2nd ed.), Hanover. 239 pp.

Evaluation: Grades will be assigned as follows:

Class participation	10%
Group library assignment and chapter review	5%
Mid-term exam	25%
Research paper	20%
Seminar presentation	20%
Final exam (Research Proposal)	20%
Total	100%

TENTATIVE SCHEDULE FOR ZOO 400/500 WINTER BIOLOGY

Spring   Chris Snowden, Instructor

Jan. 17	Assign chapter review groups (provide 1-2 page handout)
Jan. 24	Library Reference Lecture in Science Library
Jan. 31	Group Library Assignment due
Feb. 7	Research paper/seminar topic due with a typewritten list of at least 10 references from the primary literature. Topics must be approved by the instructor prior to this date.
Feb. 21	Monday/Tuesday Class Exchange Day (Monday classes meet)
March 2	Detailed Outline of Research Paper Due
March 9	Mid-term exam
March 14 & 16	No class (Spring break)
March 28	Research Paper Due (Research papers will be graciously accepted before this date.)
March 28	Begin Student Seminars*
April 13	Symposium at Western Lodge (2:00-6:30 P.M.)
April 24-28	Individual Consultations Regarding Grant Proposals
May 1	Final Exam—Research Proposal Due at 2:45 P.M. (Once again proposals will be gladly accepted before this date.)

*Seminar Handout (no more than 5 pages)

    1. Outline (1-2 pages)

    2. Figures/Tables with indication of the source of each (2-3 pages)

    3. Bibliography (1 page)

Each student will provide collated and stapled copies of the handout for distribution to the class.

COURSE OUTLINE FOR WINTER BIOLOGY

Chris Snowden, Instructor

I.   Introduction
     A.   Historical perspective
     B.   Life at low temperature: cryobiology

II. Water, Ice and Snow
     A.   Physical and chemical properties
     B.   Supercooling and nucleation
     C.   Formation and metamorphosis of ice and snow

III. Winter Environment
     A.   Climatic regions
     B.   Weather
     C.   Thermal environment of terrestrial and aquatic habitats
     D.   Microclimatology: subnivean versus supranivean

IV. Adaptations to Cold in Ectotherms (insects, molluscs, frogs, etc.)
     A.   Cellular mechanisms of chilling/freeze injury and cryopro
          tection
     B.   Biochemical and physiological of cold-hardening
     C.   Ecological and behavioral overwintering strategies

V.   Overwintering in Endotherms (mammals and birds)
     A.   Migration
     B.   Hibernation and lethargy
     C.   Energetics and thermogenesis
     D.   Ecological and behavioral adaptations

VI. Low Temperature Adaptation in Plants
     A.   Annual rhythm of primary production
     B.   Mechanisms of cold acclimation and winter dormancy
     C.   Freeze tolerance and avoidance

VII. Microbes and Low Temperature
     A.   Survival and dormancy
     B.   Ice nucleating bacteria

VIII. Humans in the Cold
     A.   Physiological adaptations
     B.   Hypothermia—cause and prevention

IX. Polar and High Altitude Life: A Comparison

TOPICS FOR WINTER BIOLOGY SEMINARS

Spring   Chris Snowden, Instructor

1. Activity of phytoplankton and zooplankton in ponds under ice. Is there diurnal migration?

2. Growth and photosynthesis of plants under the snow.

3. Fish in winter—physiology, migration, feeding, growth, ecology.

4. Reproduction in subnivean mammals.

5. Overwintering of aquatic and terrestrial invertebrates.

6. Winter-to-summer transition—loss of cold tolerance in plants or animals.

7. Plant-animal (deer, snowshoe hare, caribou, rodents) feeding relations in winter.

8. Activity of terrestrial arthropods beneath the snow.

9. Homeoviscous adaptation in cell membranes.

10. Changes in the cell membrane associated with cold-hardening.

11. Constraints of body size on supercooling capacity—insects versus vertebrates.

12. Limits of freeze tolerance in plants or animals.

13. The supercooling point: A misnomer.

14. Seasonal patterns of blood glucose elevation in amphibians in relation to cold tolerance.

15. Use of vitrification for cryopreservation.

16. Anoxia and cold tolerance in insects, frogs and turtles.

17. Cold shock hemolysis in red blood cells.

18. Role of pH in the regulation of dormancy.

19. Modification of lipid phase behavior by membrane-bound cryoprotectants.

20. Freeze tolerance in plants.

21. Physiology of overwintering in lichens, seeds or trees.

22. Regulation of supercooling and ice nucleation in trees.

23. Winter ecology of beaver, chickadee, moose, etc.

24. Temperature regulation in Arctic insects

Appendix G

SYLLABUS FOR MATH BY INQUIRY
MTH 400/500; Spring 4:00–5:15 MW (room #)

TEXT: There is no text

INSTRUCTOR TEAM: Professor June Roberts (another university)
Professor Sam Rivers, Miami University
Professor Mark Willis (another university)

Mr. Rivers will be the student's primary contact. His office is in 390 Smith Hall, phone 529-0000. His original set of office hours is MWF 10-11, TH 11-12, and T 1:30-3:00. He is in his office often, and you are welcome any time the door is open. If he has a student in already, please make sure you let him know you are there before waiting in the outer room of the office suite.

MTH 400/500 is an outgrowth of Ohio's Project Discovery, a multimillion dollar statewide systemic initiative (SSI) funded by the National Science Foundation and the Ohio Legislature. The purpose of this program is to strengthen the teaching of science and mathematics in Ohio's schools. This course was developed and has been taught in this program for the past two years. **Its two major purposes are to strengthen the mathematical knowledge of teachers and to model the inquiry learning process.**

Those, then, are the forces guiding your instructors. You will be expected to take a major role in this class, both during class time and out-of-class. Yes, that's correct, in class, too. We want you to be actively engaged in the classroom learning environment, proposing solutions, forming hypotheses, asking questions, even arguing. Your own personal construction of mathematical ideas is our goal. When this is all over, if we have done our job well, you will be much more confident about why mathematics works as it does. We are sure that will make you a much more effective teacher.

This is somewhat new for your instructors, too. We were not taught this way, in general, and thus, we are learning along with you. We also are taking part in a research study looking at students' thinking. This study is part of a longitudinal study that has been directed for several-years by Professor Baxter Magolda of the Miami faculty. This should make the course a more enriching experience for students and faculty alike.

PROBLEM SOLVING: We wish, of course, to continue your problem solving experiences, since the concept of "problem" as opposed to exercise and problem solving **strategies** are so central to today's school mathematics. We expect to use problems on a weekly basis. Just to review, here is a partial set of problem solving strategies you probably are able to use: Draw a picture; Look at a simpler problem; Work backwards; Make an organized list; Use a chart or graph; Make a table (function); Look for a pattern; Try a different point of view; Guess, check and revise; . . .

EVALUATION: The principal (needed to leave ourselves an out) means of evaluation will be by attendance/participation, portfolio, projects/assignments, and a journal. The journal is to contain reflective thinking about your mathematical thinking, your growth, your frustrations, etc. Since you are to take an active role in class in this inquiry atmosphere, **it is essential that you be in class.** We will discuss these items later.

PROPOSED SCHEDULE:

Jan 10 Clock arithmetic
Jan 19 Clock arithmetic
Jan 24 Moving into modular arithmetic
Jan 31 Modular systems
Feb 7 Comparing arithmetic in the rationals with modular systems
Feb 14 Groups, transformation groups
Feb 22 Fields, proofs of "arithmetic" theorems
Feb 28 Proofs
Mar 7 Proofs
Mar 21 Number systems and projects
Mar 28 Number systems
Apr 4 Number systems and exponents
Apr 11 Functions
Apr 18 Matrices—structure and applications
Apr 25 Matrices

Final Examination

Appendix H

SYLLABUS FOR SOCIOCULTURAL STUDIES IN EDUCATION
EDU 200   Miami University   Fall

An Introduction to the Course

EDU 200, Sociocultural Studies in Education, is an introduction to the Social Foundations of Education that applies a cultural studies approach to the investigation of selected educational topics. The course serves as the social foundations of education requirement for undergraduate education majors, and as an introductory course in the cultural studies thematic sequence, Cultural Studies and Public Life, and as a humanities course under the Miami Plan foundations requirement.

EDU 200 is a theme-based course, that draws upon different disciplines and fields of study to address certain fundamental questions and issues in the sociocultural study of education. We might consider this a *trans-disciplinary* course (rather than *inter*-disciplinary) because we are less interested in the study of specific disciplines (e.g., the history, sociology, or philosophy of education) and more interested in examining problems and issues in the sociocultural study of education. It might be helpful in understanding the nature of this course to introduce the three major fields upon which the course is drawn: the social foundations of education, cultural studies, and the humanities.

The social foundations of education is a field of study that draws upon the disciplines of history, sociology, philosophy, and anthropology to study and debate the foundation of educational practice and ideas. In a social foundations of education class, students examine, critique, and explain education in light of its origins, major influences, and consequences, by utilizing three perspectives: the analytical, interpretive, and normative perspectives. We will study the nature of these perspectives in more detail as the course proceeds. As an introductory course in the social foundations of education, EDU 200 offers students the opportunity to study those sociocultural conditions, including social institutions, processes, and ideals, which underlie educational ideas and practices.

EDU 200 also introduces students to themes and concepts of *cultural studies,* an area of study where we study culture as something that is actively produced and debated by different people in different social contexts. Culture is viewed as a process which is constructed out of the power relations, debates, and negotiations of the wide range of people who make up a society. Because culture is seen as the result of relations between people (and not merely a fixed, abstract thing), then cultural studies is also intrinsically concerned with the analysis of power relations between people. Who is in more of a position of authority and power to influence what culture is? Who is in less of a position of power, and is, therefore, powerless about defining or controlling culture? The field of cultural studies presents a number of methods of analysis of studying culture, and students will be introduced to those methods in this course, in particular the use of textual analyses of original narratives on American education and culture. Through explorations of written and visual texts, students will study the construction of and the meaning of social texts and culture, and will explore the ways in which educational goals and practices are influenced by those constructed texts and discourses. Students will learn that education and schooling as we know it today has been and continues to be actively constructed, and is not, in and of itself a neutral "fact" or undebatable quality.

The cultural studies emphasis of the course is closely linked to the *humanities* approach of the course, because in both areas of study, we examine the cultural meaning of personal and public narratives and arts. As a humanities course, EDU 200 begins not with a social science approach to understanding impersonal educational institutions, but by inviting students to analyze and reflect upon the way in which people have created ideals, images, and constructs of education as part of American culture. In other words, the readings in the course are representative of the cultural *meaning* that people give to education (as opposed to social science studies of what actually happens in education). As in any humanities class, for example, English Literature or Art, students will be asked to understand how meaning is created within the text. Like any reading of a Charlotte Bronte novel or a Picasso painting, educational texts are cultural constructs that reflect a combination of cultural beliefs, images, common practices, hopes, and dreams.

COURSE OBJECTIVES

1) Students will learn to think critically about education in contemporary America by learning to recognize, evaluate, and defend positions found in educational discourse with an emphasis on cultural issues such as difference and diversity, subordinated and marginalized groups, cultural politics, their own lived experiences, and the lived experiences of other students and teachers.

2) Students will learn to think critically about schooling in contemporary America by learning to interpret, critique, and judge educational practices as they relate to different discourses addressing the purposes of schooling.

3) Students will come to a better understanding of the context of contemporary American education by learning to interpret, critique, and judge educational practices as historical and cultural texts located in sociocultural contexts.

COURSE ORGANIZATION

The readings and presentations for each week will be organized around particular concepts that connect and guide both the reading and discussion. The course is organized around narrative presentations in large group sessions which meet for 50 minutes once a week. These narratives will consist of visiting speakers, panels, films, and other performances, each of which raises the central concepts to be discussed in small group sessions over the week. These narratives will become a focus of student discussions in small groups which will meet for 50 minutes twice a week. The small group meetings will be primarily devoted to a clarification of the key concepts, and discussion of the various readings that students make of the large group narratives and the assigned written texts. Crucial concepts and background information will be presented in the form of short written lectures and in the small group sessions (rather than the large group sessions).

The course is organized around the following core themes:

Theme 1: Schools as Historical/Cultural Texts. Students read material related to the concept that education is and has historically been used for purposes of national and cultural formation, social practices and norms, and economic goals.

Theme 2: Society and Culture in Schools. Students are introduced to key concepts, debates, and positions in education, including essentialism and progressivism in education, social and economic reproduction of schooling, the role of cultural capital, exceptionalism and differentiation of students by race, class, gender, sexuality, and physical and mental ability.

Theme 3: Education in the Contemporary World. Students are introduced to current issues and debates in education and to alternative reforms. Through the completion of a group project students will learn ways in which they can participate in the public dialogue around these issues.

ASSIGNMENTS AND EVALUATION

(See the Assignment Due Date and Description sections for further explanation.)

(1) Attendance. Attendance is required at *every* class meeting and large group session. Unexcused absences will result in a lowered grade. Instructors need written and official explanatory notes for any absence due to doctors' appointments, illness, or family circumstances.

(2) Group Pedagogical Project (field experience assignment). In the field experience assignment students participate and observe in the world outside of the classroom, applying concepts and skills learned in the course to a specific project. In the Group Pedagogical Project, students work in small cooperative groups to identify and study the way in which educational text is constructed in a local community, group, or organization. Each group will be required to give a presentation of their project. [This will serve as a minimum of four hours' field experience for professional education majors.] Five class meetings will be available for group meetings, but students must also arrange to meet and work on this project on their own time outside of class.

(3) Cultural Interview (clinical experience assignment). Students interview a peer from a different cultural, ethnic, class, or racial background about their experience of schooling. In this assignment, students investigate through personal interaction the linkages between culture and educational experiences. [This serves as clinical experience for professional education majors.]

(4) Two Text Analyses. In these two assignments, students conduct textual analyses of cultural texts. Text Analysis #1 is a textual analysis of a children's book, to be completed with a partner. Text Analysis #2 is a textual analysis of a popular film.

(5) Discussion and Participation in Small Group Sessions. The heart of learning in this course occurs in the small group sessions, where students will explore together the major themes, concepts, and debates raised in the week's readings and large group sessions. Instructors may ask that students contribute occasional free-writes and in-class response papers to the readings, or to contribute discussion questions for the group.

(6) Final Exam. Students will be able to pull together and address the major concepts, themes, and issues raised in the course.

EDU 200 CLASS SCHEDULE

FALL SEMESTER

WEEK 1: INTRODUCTION: AUGUST 23–27
At least one meeting with small groups during this week.
Introduction and explanation of syllabus, readings, assignments,
and the organization of the course.

WEEK 2: AUGUST 30–SEPTEMBER 3
INTRODUCTION TO THE SOCIOCULTURAL FOUNDATIONS OF EDUCATION

Concepts:
        education
        schooling
Large Group Narrative:
        film: *All American High School*
Written Lecture:
Class 1:
        A Nation at Risk
        Kahil Gibran, "On Teaching" from *The Prophet*
Class 2:
Dennis Littkey, "Caring and Respect: Key Factors in Restructuring a School"

Theme 1: School as Historical/Cultural Texts

WEEK 3: SEPTEMBER 6–10
READING THE WORD, READING THE WORLD

Concepts:
        text
        reading
        discourse
Large Group Narrative: (meets on Tuesday, September 7-Labor Day exchange day)
        film: Bill Moyers's *The Public Mind: (Part I) Consuming Images*
Written Lecture: The Reading of Texts
Class 1:
        Paulo Freire, "The Importance of the Act of Reading"
Class 2:
        John Berger, *Ways of Seeing,* pp. 7-34

WEEK 4: SEPTEMBER 13–17

PURPOSE OF EDUCATION: EDUCATION AND THE CREATION OF A DEMOCRATIC NATION
ASSIGNMENT DUE: CULTURAL INTERVIEW

Concepts:
> educational construction of a democratic nation

Large Group Narrative:
> film: 1950s or '60s school film on the founding of the nation

Written Lecture: History of Education and American Culture

Class 1:
> Puritan Children Reminded of Their Duties (1682)
> Massachusetts School Law of 1647
> Mississippi Law Forbidding Education of Slaves or Free Negroes
> Thomas Jefferson, "Bill for the More General Diffusion of Knowledge"
> "Female Influence" (1795)

Class 2:
> James Clavell, "The Children's Story"
> James Baldwin, "A Talk to Teachers"

WEEK 5: SEPTEMBER 20–24

PURPOSES OF EDUCATION: SOCIAL EDUCATION

Concepts:
> social solidarity
> ritual
> symbol
> socialization
> hidden curriculum

Large Group Narrative:
> film: *Millennium, A Poor Man Shames Us All,* OR the other one

Written Lecture: Social Education

Class 1:
> Senator Daniel Webster on the Schools as a Wise and Liberal System of Police (1820)
> James G. Carter on Public Education as a Way of Securing Social Unity (1824)
> Louisa May Alcott, "Training the Girl to Patience"
> Merrill Harmin and Sidney Simon, "The Year the Schools Began Teaching the Telephone Directory"

Class 2: Project Meeting #1

WEEK 6: SEPTEMBER 27–OCTOBER 1

PURPOSES OF EDUCATION: ECONOMIC
ASSIGNMENT DUE: TEXT ANALYSIS #1

Concepts:
   human capital
Large Group Narrative:
   Guest Presenter: Robert Wehling
Written Lecture:
Class 1:
   Horace Mann, 1848 Report, "Intellectual Education as Means of
   Removing Poverty and Securing Abundance"
   The Superintendent of the Choctaw Academy Recommends
   Vocational Education for Indian Youth (1832)
   "The Little Philosopher," from McGuffey's *Third Eclectic Reader*
   (1848)
   "The Saber-Tooth Curriculum"
Class 2:
   discussion of text analysis project

Theme 2: Society and Culture in Schools: Inside Schools

WEEK 7: OCTOBER 4–8

WHOSE KNOWLEDGE?

Concepts:
   progressivism
   essentialism
   perennialism
   reconstructionism
   canon
Large Group Narrative:
   Two alternative schools: Hughes High School (Paidea) and Garfield
   School, Hamilton
Written Lecture: Whose Knowledge?
Class 1:
   John Dewey, "The Child and the Curriculum"
Class 2:
   William C. Bagley, "An Essentialist's Platform for the Advancement
   of American Education"

WEEK 8: OCTOBER 11-14 (NO CLASS ON FRIDAY OCTOBER 15)

SOCIAL CLASS AND SCHOOLS

<u>Central Concepts:</u>
>social class
>social reproduction
>cultural capital
>tracking

<u>Large Group Narrative:</u>
>film clips: social class in films

<u>Written Lecture:</u> Social Class and Schools

<u>Class 1:</u>
>Jonathan Swift, "A Modest Proposal"
>Michael T. Kaufman, "Of My Friend Hector and My Achilles Heel"
>Mike Rose, "I Just Wanna Be Average"

<u>Class 2:</u> Project Meeting #2

WEEK 9: OCTOBER 18–22

ETHNICITY, CULTURE, AND SCHOOLING

<u>Central Concepts:</u>
>culture
>ethnicity
>cultural politics
>youth culture

<u>Large Group Narrative:</u>
>film: *Skinheads*

<u>Written Lecture:</u> Ethnicity, Culture, and Schooling

<u>Class 1:</u>
>Michele Wallace, "Tim Rollins and KOS: The Amerika Series"
>Forest Carter, "The Dog Star"
>Alice Kessler-Harris, "Multiculturalism Can Strengthen, Not Undermine, a Common Culture"

<u>Class 2:</u> Project Meeting #3

WEEK 10: OCTOBER 25-29

RACE AND SCHOOLS

<u>Concepts:</u>
>race
>racism

institutional racism
prejudice

Large Group Narrative:
Prime Time Live: different daily experiences of black and white
Miami student: what it's like to be black at Miami

Written Lecture: Race and Schools

Class 1:
Linda Howard, "Unless You're Mixed, You Don't Know What It's Like to Be Mixed"
Imani Perry, "A Black Student's Reflection on Public and Private Schools"
Peggy McIntosh, "White Privilege: Unpacking the Invisible Knapsack"
Brent Staples, "Just Walk on By: A Black Man Ponders His Ability to Alter Public Spaces"

Class 2: Project Meeting #4

WEEK 11: NOVEMBER 1–5

GENDER AND SCHOOLS

Concepts:
sex
the cultural construction of gender
gender roles
feminism

Large Group Narrative:
CSP Student role-play on gender roles in college

Written Lecture:

Class 1:
Marcia B. Baxter Magolda, "Gender-Related Patterns in Knowing"

Class 2:
Carol Gilligan, "Images of Relationships"
Dorothy Holland and Margaret Eisenhart, "Strategic Moves: Postponing, Feigning, and Dropping Out of Romance"

WEEK 12: NOVEMBER 8–12

EXCEPTIONALISM AND DIFFERENTIATION

Concepts:
deviance
normalcy
exceptionality

<u>Large Group Narrative:</u>
>   film: *From Warehouse to White House* OR *Tell Them I'm a Mermaid*

<u>Written Lecture:</u> Exceptionality and Education

<u>Class 1:</u>
>   Robert Bogdan and Steven Taylor, "The Judged, Not the Judges: An Insider's View of Mental Retardation"
>   Sucheng Chan, "You're Short, Besides"
>   Colene Ann Flynn, "Young Authors: The Life of a Handicapped Person"

<u>Class 2:</u> Project Meeting #5

WEEK 13: NOVEMBER 15–19

YOUTH, SEXUALITY, HEALTH, AND SCHOOL POLICY

<u>Concepts:</u>
>   sexuality
>   sexual identity
>   sexual preference

<u>Large Group Narrative:</u>
>   Rick Jones on gay stereotypes

<u>Written Lecture:</u>

<u>Class 1:</u>
>   Leslea Newman, "A Letter to Harvey Milk"

<u>Class 2:</u>
>   Eve Sedgwick, "Axiom 1: People Are Different from Each Other"
>   "For Better or Worse" comic, series on gay teenager
>   Michael Moffatt, "The New Sexual Orthodoxy," in *Coming of Age in New Jersey,* pp. 194-202

Theme 3: Education in the Contemporary World

WEEK 14: NOVEMBER 22–23 (THANKSGIVING WEEK)

ALTERNATIVE EDUCATION: MAKING SCHOOLS WORK

<u>Concepts:</u>
>   democratic education
>   Large Group Narrative:
>   Foxfire Group

<u>Written Lecture:</u>
<u>Class 1:</u>
> George Wood, *Schools that Work*

<u>Class 2:</u>
> George Wood, *Schools that Work*

WEEK 15: NOVEMBER 29–DECEMBER 3
DEMOCRATIC SCHOOLS

<u>Large Group Narrative:</u> to be announced
<u>Class 1:</u> group project presentations
<u>Class 2:</u> group project presentations

WEEK 16: DECEMBER 6–10
CONCLUSION

Large Group: group project presentations

EDU 200

Assignment: Interview a person from a different cultural, religious, ethnic, racial or class background than you. Base your interview questions on that person's schooling experiences. Then write a 3–5-page typed, double-spaced report responding to the following question: How did the background and/or identity of my interview subject play a part in his/her schooling experience?

When choosing your subject, remember that the object of this assignment is to discuss difference between *individuals,* and not differences between school structures. The point here is not to compare school systems (for example, the difference between attending a private school and a public school, or between attending a school in France and a school in China), but rather to understand how a person's cultural identity played a part in his or her schooling experience. For this reason, it is not always a good idea to interview an international student for this assignment because your interview may focus on the differences between schools and cultures as you learn about different ways that schooling happens in the world—a very interesting project, but not the objective of this assignment.

As you consider who to interview, think about what "cultural difference" might mean to you, and talk with your friends and classmates, look around your living or work place, and think about people who you know or know about who are from a different cultural background than you. Some students have called organizations in the community for recommendations, including the Hillel Foundation, Christian organizations, Appalachian groups, the Center for Black Culture and Learning, the Women's Center, the Student Activities Office, Community Service Office, or Affirmative Action in Hanna House.

Interview: Individuals experience schooling differently and to some degree receive different educations due (in part) to different cultural backgrounds and/or identities. Issues of culture, religion, ethnicity, race, and class contribute to the multiple experiences that individuals encounter while engaging in school. During your interview, try to identify the ways in which your interview subject has had schooling experiences that differed from your own because of his/her background or identity. For example, you may interview a student who identifies herself or himself as coming from the working class, and who was tracked into lower tracked classes. Or you may interview a person who identifies as a member of a certain religion or denomination, or who comes from a different racial or ethnic background than you. Questions which focus on how this student experienced school should be the key element of this interview. You may also need to gather information that helps support why you consider this person to be different than you. Remember that the central objective of this exercise is to identify *difference* and to understand how that difference affects one's schooling.

Procedure and Format: You should spend *at least* three hours speaking with your interview subject. The paper cannot include everything that you learned from the interview, so you must select the ideas, information, and quotations from the interview to make an interesting and coherent paper. Like any paper, you should have an introductory thesis, a descriptive narrative, and a conclusion. You must include in the paper the following: (1) a thesis that presents your reasoned position on the findings of the project (i.e., how did your subject's difference make a difference in his/her schooling?); (2) some reflection on how your subject's experience differed from your own schooling experience; (3) a brief analysis of the educational implications of your findings. What has this interview taught you about the way schools work?

PLEASE KEEP THE NAME OF YOUR INTERVIEW SUBJECT CONFIDENTIAL. DO NOT MENTION YOUR SUBJECT'S NAME IN CLASS OR IN THE PAPER!

CLINICAL TEXT ANALYSIS ASSIGNMENTS

Two assignments for the course are text analyses. These assignments draw on our understanding of the reading of texts that we are studying in the course. This assignment sheet outlines the expectations for each assignment and provides guidelines for your analyses.

Text Analysis #1 is a text analysis of a children's book, to be completed with a partner.

This assignment draws upon the concepts and discussions raised in the first theme of the course ("Schools as Historical/Cultural Texts") and, in particular, upon the notion of hidden curriculum and the economic, national, and social purposes of education.

Find a children's book (for early and young readers) and identify the ways in which cultural lessons about the American economy and democracy are embedded in the text. What are these lessons, or cultural values? How are they translated to children through the literature?

The final paper should be about three to five pages long. Within each paper make sure that you have:

1) Described the text. (What is the story? How is it told or conveyed through words and images?)

2) Identified what you believe are the key messages about American cultural ideas (especially those related to democracy and the economy).

3) Explained *how* the text conveys these messages, i.e., through the story line? Through the mood of the story? Through the moral or lesson of the story?

4) If you and your partner disagree or have differing ideas about the text, include that in the paper as well.

5) How well do you utilize the analytical, interpretive, and normative perspectives within your analysis?

6) How clearly written is your essay? Have you made a clear and consistent point about the text under study?

Text Analysis #2 is an analysis of a form of popular culture (film, TV show, art exhibit, music, etc.). After examining a piece of popular culture, develop an argument about the way in which the piece educates. What is the message that is presented by this piece of popular culture and how is that message presented? How does this piece educate the world?

The final paper should be about three to five pages long. You should write it with your peers in EDU 200 as your audience. Within each paper make sure that you have:

1) Developed an *analytic* reading: Have you briefly described the piece? What is the underlying narrative? Have you described the imagery?

2) Developed an *interpretive* reading: Can you place the piece within a particular discourse? Why is this a piece of popular culture? How does it relate to the broader popular culture?

3) Developed a *normative* reading: Have you identified the underlying moral assumptions and ideologies of the piece? Do you bring your own clear moral and ideological positions to your analysis?

4) Clearly written your essay: Have you developed a clear and convincing argument about a particular point of the piece?

PEDAGOGICAL PROJECT

PROJECT DESCRIPTION

This project constitutes a "field experience." In other words, it gets you out of the classroom where you are studying the world from texts and into what educators refer to as "the field." How can we apply our learnings from the isolated environment of the university classroom to the world? Do the concepts, suggestions, methods, and proposals raised in our large and small group classes and in our readings apply to what actually happens in the very messy and complicated world?

In the Pedagogical Project, students work in cooperative groups to identify some form of educational dialogue or public conversation in the community. Once that educational dialogue has been identified and understood, students contribute to that educational process by literally inserting themselves into the dialogue. You might think of this project as having two parts: first, the identification, analysis, and understanding of a public educational dialogue, and second, your own active participation in that dialogue.

How does education "happen" in the world? We suspect that it happens in a lot more places than the classroom, and that in fact education occurs everywhere from TV advertisements, to daily conversations with friends, to our interactions with doctors, car mechanics, and sales clerks. These are relatively individualistic educational encounters. How does a more public educational conversation take place?

For this project, you should look around your community and identify a public educational dialogue or conversation. What is the nature of the public discussion on this campus about student housing, sex education, or some particular aspect of student social life? In the broader public community, what is the discussion about public policy issues, schooling, or social events? As you think about the range of educational conversations that occur in the public world, consider *how* the conversation takes place. What methods of communication are used? What agencies or groups participate in the conversation, and how do they participate? You might also want to consider where a conversation is *not* going on.

Your group should brainstorm, and come to a consensus on a project topic and a proposal for approaching the project by the third week of the semester.

The second important part of this assignment is your group's active participation in the educational dialogue that you have identified. What is your response to what you are studying? How might you contribute to or change the nature of that dialogue? What kind of action can your group take to make a difference in public education? The nature of this action will depend on the educational dialogue in which your group is participating. It may be a presentation to a relevant community, the writing of articles for a newspaper, or the designing of a flyer for distribution. It could be a video production for a dormitory or student group, or for public access TV or WMUB. You might design an informational campaign through public posters, letters to the editor, or street theater. You are limited only by your imagination, the law, and the discretion of your instructor.

To help organize and focus your work, you should create the following reports, following the recommended time-line and your instructor's expectations:

Project Proposal (due around Week 3)

This proposal should be the result of your group's discussion of the project and your proposed ideas. It should identify what you are planning to look at and how you are considering going about the work.

Project Strategy (due around Week 6)

The Project Strategy should be a more formalized version of your proposal that is based on some preliminary involvement with your subject of study. The Strategy should include two parts:

1) What is the nature of the educational text that you are observing, and how do you plan to analyze your text?

2) What social action are you considering? How are you thinking about participating in the educational dialogue?

Action Plan (due around Week 8)

This is a clarification of the social action that you are proposing to take. Explain the action that you are planning to undertake, and justify its significance.

Project Presentation (due in the last weeks of the semester)

Project completion and presentation—to be arranged with your instructor.

References

American Association of Higher Education, American College Personnel Association, National Association of Student Personnel Adminstrators. 1998. *Powerful partnerships: A shared responsibility for learning.* Washington D.C.: American Association of Higher Education, American College Personnel Association, National Association of Student Personnel Administrators.

American College Personnel Association. 1994. *The student learning imperative.* Washington D.C.: American College Personnel Association.

Arons, A. B. 1997. *Teaching introductory physics.* New York: Wiley.

Arons, Arnold B. 1989. *What science should we teach?* Biological Science Curriculum Study. Colorado Springs. Curriculum development for the year 2000.

Association of American Colleges. 1990a. *Liberal learning and the arts and sciences major.* Vol. 1, *The challenge of connecting learning.* Washington, D.C.: American Association of Colleges.

Association of American Colleges. 1990b. *Liberal learning and the arts and sciences major.* Vol. 2, *Reports from the fields.* Washington, D.C.: American Association of Colleges.

Astin, Alexander W. 1984. Student involvement: A developmental theory for higher education. *Journal of College Student Personnel* 25:297–308.

———. 1993. *What matters in college: Four critical years revisited.* San Francisco: Jossey-Bass.

Bakan, D. 1966. *The duality of human existence.* Boston: Beacon Press.

Banks, James A. 1991. A curriculum for empowerment, action, and change. In *Empowerment through multicultural education,* ed. Christine E. Sleeter, 125–41. Albany, N.Y.: State University of New York Press.

Barr, Robert B., and John Tagg. 1995. From teaching to learning—A new paradigm for undergraduate education. *Change,* November/December, 13–25.

Bateson, Mary Catherine. 1994. *Peripheral visions: Learning along the way.* New York: HarperCollins.

Baxter Magolda, Marcia B. 1987. A comparison of open-ended interview and standardized instrument measures of intellectual development on the Perry scheme. *Journal of College Student Personnel* 28:443–48.

———. 1992. *Knowing and reasoning in college: Gender-related patterns in students' intellectual development.* San Francisco: Jossey-Bass.

———. 1994a. Integrating self into epistemology: Young adults' experiences as contextual knowers. Paper presented at the American Educational Research Association meeting, April, New Orleans.

————. 1994b. Post-college experiences and epistemology. *Review of Higher Education* 18, no. 1:25–44.

————. 1995. The integration of relational and impersonal knowing in young adults' epistemological development. *Journal of College Student Development* 36, no. 3:205–16.

————. 1998. Developing self-authorship in young adult life. *Journal of College Student Development* 39, no. 2.

Baxter Magolda, Marcia B., and William D. Porterfield. 1985. A new approach to assess intellectual development on the Perry scheme. *Journal of College Student Personnel* 26:343–51.

————. 1988. *Assessing intellectual development: The link between theory and practice*. Alexandria, Va.: American College Personnel Association.

Belenky, Mary, Blythe Clinchy, Nancy Goldberger, and Jill Tarule. 1986. *Women's ways of knowing: The development of self, voice, and mind*. New York: Basic Books.

Bensimon, Estella Mara. 1994. Culture, knowledge, and pedagogy: Rethinking higher education programs: Division J Vice Presidential Address. Paper presented at the annual meeting of the American Educational Research Association, April, New Orleans.

————, and Anna Neumann. 1993. *Redesigning collegiate leadership*. Baltimore, Md.: Johns Hopkins University Press.

Bereiter, Carl. 1994. Constructivism, socioculturalism, and Popper's World 3. *Educational Researcher* 23, no. 7:21–23.

Blimling, Gregory S. 1996. Special issue: The Student Learning Imperative. *Journal of College Student Development* 37, no. 2.

Boyer, Ernest L. 1987. *College: The undergraduate experience in America*. New York: HarperCollins.

Branch-Simpson, G. E. 1984. A study of the patterns in the development of black students at the Ohio State University. Ph.D. diss., Department of Educational Policy and Leadership, Ohio State University.

Brightman, Harvey J. 1993. Improving critical thinking in class sizes up to 120 students. Presentation at the 13th Annual Lilly Teaching Conference, November, Oxford, Ohio.

Brown, Lyn Mikel, and Carol Gilligan. 1990. The psychology of women and the development of girls. Paper presented at the annual meeting of the American Educational Research Association, April, Boston, Massachusetts.

————. 1992. *Meeting at the crossroads: Women's psychology and girls' development*. Cambridge, Mass.: Harvard University Press.

Bruffee, Kenneth A. 1993. *Collaborative learning: Higher education, interdependence, and the authority of knowledge*. Baltimore, Md.: Johns Hopkins University Press.

Bruner, Jerome. 1986. *Actual minds, possible worlds.* Cambridge, Mass.: Harvard University Press.

———. 1990. *Acts of meaning.* Cambridge, Mass.: Harvard University Press.

Buerk, Dorothy. 1985. The voices of women making meaning in mathematics. *Journal of Education* 167, no. 3:59–70.

Carlson, Dennis, and Michael W. Apple. 1998. *Power, knowledge, pedagogy: The meaning of democratic education in unsettling times.* Boulder, Colo.: Westview Press.

Chickering, Arthur W. 1969. *Education and identity.* San Francisco: Jossey-Bass.

Chickering, Arthur W., and Linda Reisser. 1993. *Education and identity.* 2d ed. San Francisco: Jossey-Bass.

Clinchy, Blythe McVicker. 1990. Issues of gender in teaching and learning. *Journal on Excellence in College Teaching* 1:52–67.

———. 1993. Ways of knowing and ways of being: Epistemological and moral development in undergraduate women. In *Approaches to moral development: New research and emerging themes,* ed. Andrew Garrod, 180–200. New York: Teachers College Press.

———. 1994. On critical thinking and connected knowing. In *Re-thinking reason: New perspectives in critical thinking,* ed. Kerry S. Walters, 33–42. Albany, N.Y.: SUNY Press.

———. 1996. Connected and separate knowing: Toward a marriage of two minds. In *Knowledge, difference, and power: Essays inspired by* Women's Ways of Knowing, ed. N. R. Goldberger, J. M. Tarule, B. M. Clinchy, and M. F. Belenky, 205–47. New York: Basic Books.

Cobb, Paul, Erna Yackel, and Terry Wood. 1992. A constructivist alternative to the representational view of mind in mathematics education. *Journal for Research in Mathematics Education* 23, no. 1:2–33.

Cooper, Joanne E. 1991. Telling our own stories: The reading and writing of journals or diaries. In *Stories lives tell: Narrative and dialogue in education,* ed. Carol Witherell and Nel Noddings, 96–112. New York: Teachers College Press.

Cross, K. Patricia. 1990. Teaching to improve learning. *Journal on Excellence in College Teaching* 1:9–22.

Daloz, Laurent A. 1986. *Effective teaching and mentoring: Realizing the transformational power of adult learning experiences.* San Francisco: Jossey-Bass.

Dewey, John. 1916. *Democracy and education.* New York: Free Press.

Driver, Rosalind, Hilary Asoko, John Leach, Eduardo Mortimer, and Philip Scott. 1994. Constructing scientific knowledge in the classroom. *Educational Researcher* 23, no. 7:5–12.

Dykstra, Dewey I., Jr. 1996. Teaching introductory physics to college students. In *Constructivism: Theory, perspectives, and practice,* ed. Catherine Twomey Fosnot, 182–204. New York: Teachers College Press.

Eisler, Riane. 1987. *The chalice and the blade: Our history, our future.* San Francisco: HarperCollins.

Eisner, Elliot. 1985. Aesthetic modes of knowing. In *Learning and teaching the ways of knowing,* ed. Elliot Eisner, 23–36. Chicago: National Society for the Study of Education.

Elbow, Peter. 1994. Teaching two kinds of thinking by teaching writing. In *Re-thinking reason: New perspectives in critical thinking,* ed. Kerry S. Walters, 25–31. Albany, N.Y.: SUNY Press.

Ernest, Paul. 1997. *Social constructivism as a philosophy of mathematics.* Albany, N.Y.: SUNY Press.

Fordham, Signithia, and John U. Ogbu. 1986. Black students' school success: Coping with the "burden of acting white." *Urban Review* 18, no. 3:176–206.

Freire, P. 1988. *Pedagogy of the oppressed.* New York: Continuum. First published in 1970.

Frye, Marilyn. 1990. The possibility of feminist theory. In *Theoretical perspectives on sexual difference,* ed. Deborah L. Rhode, 174–84. New Haven, Conn.: Yale University Press.

Gallo, Delores. 1994. Educating for empathy, reason, and imagination. In *Re-thinking reason: New perspectives in critical thinking,* ed. Kerry S. Walters, 43–60. Albany, N.Y.: SUNY Press.

George, Melvin D. 1996. Fourth working plenary session: Review of undergraduate education. Presentation at the NSF Working Conference, Dynamic Partnerships, June, Washington, D.C.

Gilligan, Carol. 1982. *In a different voice.* Cambridge, Mass.: Harvard University Press.

Gilligan, Carol, Nona Plessner Lyons, and Trudy Hanmer, eds. 1989. *Making connections: The relational worlds of adolescent girls at Emma Willard School.* Troy, N.Y.: Emma Willard School.

Giroux, Henry A. 1988a. *Schooling and the struggle for public life: Critical pedagogy in the modern age.* Minneapolis: University of Minnesota Press.

———. 1988b. *Teachers as intellectuals: Toward a critical pedagogy of learning.* Granby, Mass.: Bergin and Garvey.

———. 1992. *Border crossings: Cultural workers and the politics of education.* New York: Routledge.

Gitlin, Andrew. 1990. Understanding teaching dialogically. *Teachers College Record* 91, no. 4:537–63.

Glaser, Barney, and A. Strauss. 1967. *The discovery of grounded theory: Strategies for qualitative research.* Chicago: Aldine.

Glesne, Corrine, and Alan Peshkin. 1992. *Becoming qualitative researchers: An introduction.* White Plains, N.Y.: Longman.

Goldberger, Nancy R. 1996. Cultural imperatives and diversity in ways of knowing. In *Knowledge, difference, and power: Essays inspired by* Women's Ways of Knowing, ed. N. R. Goldberger, J. M. Tarule, B. M. Clinchy, and M. F. Belenky, 335–71. New York: Basic Books.

Grennon Brooks, Jacqueline, and Martin G. Brooks. 1993. *In search of understanding: The case for constructivist classrooms.* Alexandria, Va.: Association for Supervision and Curriculum Development.

Grudin, Robert. 1990. *The grace of great things: Creativity and innovation.* New York: Ticknor and Fields.

Hake, Richard R. 1998. Interactive-engagement versus traditional methods: A six-thousand-student survey of mechanics test data for introductory physics courses. *American Journal of Physics* 66, no. 1:64–74.

Haroutunian-Gordon, Sophie. 1991. *Turning the soul: Teaching through conversation in high school.* Chicago: University of Chicago Press.

Hofer, Barbara K., and Paul R. Pintrich. 1997. The development of epistemological theories: Beliefs about knowledge and knowing and their relation to learning. *Review of Educational Research* 67, no. 1:88–140.

Holland, Dorothy C., and Margaret A. Eisenhart. 1990. *Educated in romance: Women, achievement and college culture.* Chicago: University of Chicago Press.

hooks, bell. 1984. *Feminist theory: From margin to center.* Boston: South End Press.

———. 1994. *Teaching to transgress: Education as the practice of freedom.* New York: Routledge.

Hopkins, Richard L. 1994. *Narrative schooling: Experiential learning and the transformation of American education.* New York: Teachers College Press.

Hutchings, Patricia. 1996. Building a new culture of teaching and learning. *About Campus: Enriching the Student Learning Experience* 1, no. 5:4–8.

Joint Center for Political and Economic Studies, Inc. 1993. *The inclusive university: A new environment for higher education.* Washington, D.C.: Joint Center for Political and Economic Studies, Inc..

Jordan, Judith V., Alexandria G. Kaplan, Jean Baker Miller, Irene P. Stiver, and Janet L. Surrey. 1991. *Women's growth in connection: Writings from the Stone Center.* New York: Guilford Press.

Josselson, Ruthellen. 1987. *Finding herself: Pathways to identity development in women.* San Francisco: Jossey-Bass.

Julyan, Candace, and Eleanor Duckworth. 1996. A constructivist perspective on teaching and learning science. In *Constructivism: Theory, per-*

spectives, and practice, ed. Catherine Twomey Fosnot, 55–72. New York: Teachers College Press.

Kegan, Robert. 1982. *The evolving self: Problem and process in human development.* Cambridge, Mass.: Harvard University Press.

———. 1993. Minding the curriculum: Of student epistemology and faculty conspiracy. In *Approaches to moral development: New research and emerging themes,* ed. Andrew Garrod, 72–88. New York: Teachers College Press.

———. 1994. *In over our heads: The mental demands of modern life.* Cambridge, Mass.: Harvard University Press.

Kerby, Anthony Paul. 1991. *Narrative and the self.* Bloomington: Indiana University Press.

King, Patricia M., and Karen S. Kitchener. 1994. *Developing reflective judgment: Understanding and promoting intellectual growth and critical thinking in adolescents and adults.* San Francisco: Jossey-Bass.

King, Patricia M., Paul K. Wood, and Robert A. Mines. 1990. Critical thinking among college and graduate students. *Review of Higher Education* 13, no. 2:167–86.

Kitchener, Karen S. 1983. Cognition, metacognition, and epistemic cognition. *Human Development* 26:222–32.

Kitchener, Karen S., and Patricia M. King. 1990. The reflective judgment model: Ten years of research. In *Adult development.* Vol. 2, *Models and methods in the study of adolescent and adult thought,* ed. Michael L. Commons, Cheryl Armon, Lawrence Kohlberg, Francis Richards, Tina A. Grotzer, and Jan Sinnott, 63–78. New York: Praeger.

Labouvie-Vief, G. 1990. Modes of knowledge and the organization of development. In *Adult development.* Vol. 2, *Models and methods in the study of adolescent and adult thought,* ed. Michael L. Commons, Cheryl Armon, Lawrence Kohlberg, Francis Richards, Tina A. Grotzer, and Jan Sinnott, 43–62. New York: Praeger.

Ladson-Billings, Gloria. 1994. *The dreamkeepers: Successful teachers of African American children.* 1st ed. San Francisco: Jossey-Bass.

———. 1995. Toward a theory of culturally relevant pedagogy. *American Educational Research Journal* 32, no. 3:465–91.

———. 1998. Who will survive America? Pedagogy as cultural preservation. In *Power, knowledge, pedagogy: The meaning of democratic education in unsettling times,* ed. Dennis Carlson and Michael W. Apple, 289–304. Boulder, Colo.: Westview Press.

Lambert, Linda, D. Walker, D. P. Zimmerman, J. E. Cooper, M. D. Lambert, M. E. Gardner, P. J. Ford Slack. 1996. *The constructivist leader.* New York: Teachers College Press.

Lincoln, Y. S., and E. Guba. 1985. *Naturalistic inquiry.* Beverly Hills, Calif.: Sage.

Lyons, Nona Plessner. 1983. Two perspectives: On self, relationships, and morality. *Harvard Educational Review* 53:125–45.

Lyons, Nona P. 1993. Luck, ethics, and ways of knowing: Observations on adolescents' deliberations in making moral choices. In *Approaches to moral development: New research and emerging themes,* ed. Andrew Garrod, 133–54. New York: Teachers College Press.

Maher, Frances A., and Mary Kay Thompson Tetreault. 1994. *The feminist classroom: An inside look at how professors and students are transforming higher education for a diverse society.* New York: Basic Books.

McEwan, Hunter, and Kieran Egan, eds. 1995. *Narrative in teaching, learning, and research.* New York: Teachers College Press.

McLaren, Peter. 1989. *Life in schools: An introduction to critical pedagogy in the foundations of education.* New York: Longman.

Miami University. 1994. Miami Bulletin, general ed. Oxford, Ohio: Miami University.

Miller, Theodore K., and Roger B. Winston Jr. 1990. Assessing development from a psychosocial perspective. In *College student development: Theory and practice for the 1990s,* ed. Don G. Creamer, 99–126. Alexandria, Va.: American College Personnel Association.

Morgan, Gareth. 1986. *Images of organization.* Beverly Hills, Calif.: Sage.

National Research Council. 1991. *Moving beyond myths: Revitalizing undergraduate mathematics.* Washington, D.C.: National Research Council.

National Science Foundation. 1996. *Shaping the future: New expectations for undergraduate education in science, mathematics, engineering, and technology.* Washington, D.C.: National Science Foundation.

Nelson, Craig E. 1989. Skewered on the unicorn's horn: The illusion of tragic tradeoff between content and critical thinking in the teaching of science. In *Enhancing critical thinking in the sciences,* ed. L. W. Crow. Washington, D.C.: Society for College Science Teachers.

Noddings, Nel. 1984. *Caring: A feminine approach to ethics and moral education.* Berkeley: University of California Press.

————. 1991. Stories in dialogue: Caring and interpersonal reasoning. In *Stories lives tell: Narrative and dialogue in education,* ed. Carol Witherell and Nel Noddings, 157–70. New York: Teachers College Press.

Oakes, Jeannie, and Martin Lipton. 1990. *Making the best of schools: A handbook for parents, teachers, and policymakers.* New Haven, Conn.: Yale University Press.

O'Connor, Terrence. 1997. Higher education and the promise of democracy: Can colleges and universities prepare citizens? Presentation at the 17th Annual Lilly Conference on College Teaching, November, Oxford, Ohio.

Palmer, Parker J. 1987. Community, conflict, and ways of knowing: Ways to deepen our educational agenda. *Change,* September/October, 20–25.

———. 1990. Good teaching: A matter of living the mystery. *Change* 22 (January/February): 11–16.

———. 1993. Good talk about good teaching: Improving teaching through conversation and community. *Change,* November/December, 10–13.

———. 1998. *The courage to teach: Exploring the inner landscape of a teacher's life.* 1st ed. San Francisco: Jossey-Bass.

Parham, Thomas A. 1989. Cycles of psychological nigrescence. *Counseling Psychologist* 17, no. 2:187–226.

Patton, Michael Quinn. 1990. *Qualitative evaluation and research methods.* Newbury Park, Calif.: Sage.

Pendlebury, Shirley. 1995. Reason and story in wise practice. In *Narrative in teaching, learning, and research,* ed. Hunter McEwan and Kieran Egan, 50–65. New York: Teachers College Press.

Perry, William G. 1970. *Forms of intellectual and ethical development in the college years: A scheme.* Troy, Mo.: Holt, Rinehart, & Winston.

Peshkin, Alan. 1988. In search of subjectivity-one's own. *Educational Researcher* 17, no. 7:17–21.

———. 1993. The goodness of qualitative research. *Educational Researcher* 22, no. 2:24–30.

Piaget, Jean. 1932. *The moral judgment of the child.* Translated by M. Gabian. New York: Routledge & Kegan Paul.

———. 1950. *The psychology of intelligence.* Translated by M. Piercy and D. Berlyne. London: Routledge & Kegan Paul.

———. 1970. *Structuralism.* New York: Basic Books.

———. 1977. *Equilibration of cognitive structures.* New York: Viking.

Polkinghorne, Donald E. 1988. *Narrative knowing and the human sciences.* Albany: State University of New York Press.

Prawat, Richard S. 1992. Teachers' beliefs about teaching and learning. *American Journal of Education* (May):354–95.

Project Discovery. 1993. Miami University, Oxford, Ohio.

Rogers, Judith L. 1992. Leadership development for the 90s: Incorporating emergent paradigm perspectives. *NASPA Journal* 29, no. 4:243–52.

Ropers-Huilman, Becky. 1998. *Feminist teaching in theory and practice: Situating power and knowledge in poststructural classrooms.* New York: Teachers College Press.

Rosser, Sue V., ed. 1995. *Teaching the majority: Breaking the gender barrier in science, mathematics, and engineering.* New York: Teachers College Press.

Rost, J. C. 1991. *Leadership for the twenty-first century*. New York: Praeger.

Ryan, M. P. 1984. Conceptions of prose coherence: Individual differences in epistemological standards. *Journal of Educational Psychology,* 76, no. 6:1226–1238.

Schifter, Deborah. 1996. A constructivist perspective on teaching and learning mathematics. In *Constructivism: Theory, perspectives, and practice,* ed. Catherine Twomey Fosnot, 73–91. New York: Teachers College Press.

Schniedewind, Nancy. 1987. Feminist values: Guidelines for teaching methodology in women's studies. In *Freire for the classroom: A sourcebook for liberatory teaching,* ed. Ira Shor, 170–79. Portsmouth, N.H.: Boynton/Cook.

Schommer, M. 1994. An emerging conceptualization of epistemological beliefs and their role in learning. In *Beliefs about text and instruction with text,* eds. R. Garner and P. A. Alexander, 25–40, Hillsdale, N.J.: Erlbaum.

Schroeder, Charles C., ed. 1996. *Journal of College Student Development Special Issue: The Student Learning Imperative*. Vol. 37, no. 2. Washington, D.C.: American College Personnel Association.

Shor, Ira. 1992. *Empowering education: Critical teaching for social change*. Chicago: University of Chicago Press.

———. 1993. Education is politics: Paulo Freire's critical pedagogy. In *Paulo Freire: A critical encounter,* ed. Peter McLaren and Peter Leonard, 25–35. New York: Routledge.

———. 1996. *When students have power: Negotiating authority in a critical pedagogy*. Chicago: University of Chicago Press.

Shor, Ira, and Paulo Freire. 1987. *A pedagogy for liberation: Dialogues on transforming education*. South Hadley, Mass.: Bergin & Garvey.

Shrewsbury, C. M. 1987. What is feminist pedagogy? *Women's Studies Quarterly* 3 and 4:6–13.

Simon, Martin A. 1993. Reconstructing mathematics pedagogy from a constructivist perspective. Paper presented at the American Educational Research Association, April, Atlanta, Georgia.

Sleeter, Christine E., and Carl A. Grant. 1991. Mapping terrains of power: Student cultural knowledge versus classroom knowledge. In *Empowerment through multicultural education,* ed. Christine E. Sleeter, 49–67. Albany, N.Y.: State University of New York Press.

Straub, Cynthia. 1987. Women's development of autonomy and Chickering's theory. *Journal of College Student Personnel* 28:198–204.

Stunkel, Kenneth R. 1998. The lecture: A powerful tool for intellectual liberation. *Chronicle of Higher Education,* June 26, A52.

Tappan, Mark B. 1991. Narrative, authorship, and the development of moral authority. In *Narrative and storytelling: Implications for understanding moral development,* ed. Mark B. Tappan and Martin J. Packer. New Directions for Child Development, 5–25, 54. San Francisco: Jossey-Bass.

————, and L. M. Brown. 1991. Stories told and lessons learned: Toward a narrative approach to moral development and moral education. In *Stories lives tell: Narrative and dialogue in education,* eds. C. Witherell & N. Noddings, 171–192. New York: Teachers College Press.

Taub, Deborah J., and Marylou K. McEwen. 1991. Patterns of development of autonomy and mature interpersonal relationships in black and white undergraduate women. *Journal of College Student Development* 32:502–8.

Taylor, Peter C. S., and Mark Campbell-Williams. 1993. Critical constructivism: Towards a communicative rationality in the high school mathematics classroom. Paper presented at the annual meeting of the American Educational Research Association, April, Atlanta, Georgia.

Terenzini, Patrick T., and Ernest T. Pascarella. 1994. Living with myths: Undergraduate education in America. *Change* (January/February): 28–32.

Thorne, Barrie. 1990. Children and gender: Constructions of differences. In *Theoretical perspectives on sexual difference,* ed. Denise L. Rhode, 100–113. New Haven, Conn.: Yale University Press.

Tompkins, Jane. 1990. Pedagogy of the distressed. *College English* 52, no. 6:653–60.

Twomey Fosnot, Catherine, ed. 1996. *Constructivism: Theory, perspectives, and practice.* New York: Teachers College Press.

von Glasersfeld, Ernst. 1995. A constructivist approach to teaching. In *Constructivism in education,* ed. Leslie P. Steffe and Jerry Gale, 3–15. Hillsdale, N.J.: Lawrence Erlbaum.

Walters, Kerry S. 1994. Critical thinking, rationality, and the vulcanization of students. In *Re-thinking reason: New perspectives in critical thinking,* ed. Kerry S. Walters, 61–80. Albany, N.Y.: SUNY Press.

Ward, Jane Victoria. 1989. Racial identity formation and transformation. In *Making connections: The relational worlds of adolescent girls at Emma Willard School,* ed. Carol Gilligan, Nona P. Lyons, and Trudy J. Hanmer. Troy, N.Y.: Emma Willard School.

Weiler, Kathleen. 1988. *Women teaching for change: Gender, class and power.* South Hadley, Mass.: Bergin and Garvey.

————. 1998. Freire and a feminist pedagogy of difference. In *Minding women: Reshaping the educational realm,* ed. Christine A. Woyshner and Holly S. Gelfond, 117–45. Cambridge, Mass.: Harvard Educational Review.

Williams, Patricia J. 1991. *The alchemy of race and rights.* Cambridge, Mass.: Harvard University Press.

Wilson, Reginald. 1996. Educating for diversity. *About Campus: Enriching the Student Learning Experience,* May/June, 4–9, 30.

Witherell, Carol S. 1995. Narrative landscapes and the moral imagination: Taking the story to heart. In *Narrative in teaching, learning, and research,* ed. Hunter McEwan and Kieran Egan, 39–49. New York: Teachers College Press.

Witherell, Carol, and Nel Noddings, eds. 1991. *Stories lives tell: Narrative and dialogue in education.* New York: Teachers College Press.

Wood, George H. 1992. *Schools that work: America's most innovative public education programs.* New York: Penguin.

Wood, Terry, Paul Cobb, and Erna Yackel. 1994. Reflection on learning and teaching mathematics in elementary school. In *Constructivism in education,* ed. Leslie P. Steffe and Jerry Gale, 401–22. Hillsdale, N.J.: Lawrence Erlbaum.

Index

MARCIA B. BAXTER MAGOLDA is professor of educational leadership at Miami University. She is also the author of *Knowing and Reasoning in College* (1992) and *Assessing Intellectual Development* (1988).